Comparative Politics in a Globalizing World

Comparative Politics in a Globalizing World

Jeffrey Haynes

Polity

First published in 2005 by Polity Press

Polity Press
65 Bridge Street
Cambridge CB2 1UR, UK

Polity Press
350 Main Street
Malden, MA 02148, USA

ISBN 0 7456 3092 8
ISBN 0 7456 3093 6(pb)

A catalogue record for this book is available from the British Library.

Typeset in 10 on 12 pt Times
by SNP Best-set Typesetter Ltd, Hong Kong
Printed and bound in Great Britain by T. J. International Ltd, Padstow, Cornwall

For further information on Polity, visit our website: www.polity.co.uk

Contents

Contents

List of Tables

List of Abbreviations

AI	Amnesty International
AU	African Union
BCSD	Business Council for Sustainable Development
CEC	Commission for Environmental Cooperation
CEE	Central and Eastern Europe
CEO	Corporate Europe Observatory
CIA	Central Intelligence Agency (USA)
CL	civil liberties
CP	Comparative Politics
CUSFTA	Canada–US Free Trade Agreement
EC	European Community
ECHR	European Convention of Human Rights
ECIS	European Centre for Infrastructure Studies
EFGP	European Federation of Green Parties
ENGO	environmental non-governmental organization
ERT	European Roundtable of Industrialists
EU	European Union
FAO	Food and Agriculture Organization (of the UN)
FBI	Federal Bureau of Investigation (USA)
FDI	foreign direct investment
FH	Freedom House
FTA	Freight Transport Association
FTAA	Free Trade Area of the Americas
GAO	General Accounting Office
GDP	gross domestic product
GEN	Genetic Engineering Network
GGC	Global Green Charter
GM	genetic modification
GPEW	Green Party of England and Wales
HSA	Hemispheric Social Alliance
IBA	internationally based actor
ICC	International Chamber of Commerce
IFI	International Financial Institution
IGO	international governmental organization
IMF	International Monetary Fund
INGO	international non-governmental organization
IOSP	international opportunity structure for participation

IR	International Relations
IWTC	International Women's Tribune Center
LID	Low Intensity Democracy
MAC	Manufacturing Alliance of Connecticut
MAI	Multilateral Agreement on Investment
MEA	multilateral environmental agreement
MERCOSUR	El Mercado Común del Sur
NAAEC	North American Agreement on Environmental Cooperation
NAFTA	North American Free Trade Agreement
NATO	North Atlantic Treaty Organization
NGO	non-governmental organization
NHRI	National Human Rights Institution
NRA	new regionalism approach
OECD	Organization for Economic Cooperation and Development
OIC	Organization of Islamic Conference
OSCE	Organization for Security and Cooperation in Europe
OSP	opportunity structure for participation
POS	political opportunity structure
PR	political rights
PR	proportional representation
RCC	Roman Catholic Church
SAP	structural adjustment programme
SEA	Single European Act
SEM	Single European Market
TAN	transnational advocacy network
TCG	transnational citizen group
TCS	transnational civil society
TE	transitional economy
TNC	transnational corporation
UDHR	Universal Declaration of Human Rights
UN	United Nations
UNEP	United Nations Environmental Program
WHO	World Health Organization
WTO	World Trade Organization

Introduction

While it is now difficult to pick up a serious newspaper or watch a current affairs programme on television without coming across the term 'globalization', scholars only began seriously to be interested in the concept relatively recently. The catalyst was a series of developments, including both the end of the cold war in 1989 and the recent emergence of a global economy. These developments led Webber and Smith (2002: 15) to claim that 'one of the most common descriptive labels of world politics in recent years has been that of transformation'. They also pointed to 'far-reaching processes of change that have been identified in global affairs'. What were they?

It is plausible to suggest that five recent developments have profoundly affected how we think about and analyse politics, both domestically and internationally. First, not only are there now more countries than ever but there also growing numbers of 'failed' or 'collapsed' states.[1] While in 1945 there were just over 50 members of the United Nations, there are now more than 190, nearly four times as many. In the three decades after World War II, most new countries emerged as a result of decolonization, but recently it was the collapse of existing states that led to new ones. From the early 1990s many new countries emerged from (1) dismemberment of federal entities, notably the Soviet Union and the Federal Republic of Yugoslavia, and (2) divisions of African (Ethiopia/Eritrea, Somalia/Somaliland) and Middle Eastern countries (incipiently, Israel/Palestine). In addition, some states have effectively collapsed – but without leading to new countries being created. As Migdal (1997: 210) notes, 'flimsy reeds' – such as Liberia, Afghanistan and now Iraq – have imploded, becoming new sources of both domestic and international political instability.[2]

Second, from the mid-1970s, democracy spread from Southern Europe to Latin America and East Asia, by way of Eastern Europe, sub-Saharan Africa and South Asia, thus ending numerous dictatorships and other forms of non-democratic rule. This was Huntington's (1991) famous 'third wave' of democratization. Often, however, such countries – suddenly released from the grip of non-democratic rule – found themselves confronted not with a smooth passage to democracy and democratic consolidation but instead to often serious outbursts of religious, ethnic and/or nationalist conflict.

[1] The term, 'state', is used in the political science and international relations literature in two, more or less, discrete ways. The state is both (1) 'a community of people who interact in the same political system and who have some common values', as well as an entity (2) enjoying exclusive recognition under international law (Willetts 2001: 358). In this book I shall use the term in both senses.
[2] See Rotberg 2003 for a comprehensive survey of 'failing', 'failed' and 'collapsed' states.

Third, there was the apparently universal triumph of capitalism. This encouraged a renewed focus on the economic and political power of forceful cross-border actors, including transnational corporations, such as Microsoft, McDonald's, Shell and Nestlé, and international financial institutions, including the International Monetary Fund (IMF) and the World Bank. This focus was especially important for the 'anti-globalization movement' that emerged in the 1990s, the fourth political development of note. The anti-globalization movement is an important example of what is known as 'transnational civil society' (TCS). It is widely accepted that the burgeoning of TCS is closely linked to globalization, as it was much facilitated by the rapid evolution of cross-border networks in the 1990s that were able to exploit the technological revolution of the internet and email.

Fifth, there was enhanced regional integration, involving dozens of countries, not only well-established entities like the European Union (EU), but also the North American Free Trade Agreement (NAFTA) and Latin America's MERCOSUR (El Mercado Común del Sur). In the EU and NAFTA, and to a lesser degree in MERCOSUR, burgeoning cross-border interactions are seen as increasingly consequential for both domestic political and economic outcomes. However, the EU provides the best current example of the importance of cross-border actors for regional political and economic outcomes. All EU member states must have democratic systems, characterized by (near) universal suffrage, and regular 'free and fair' elections. But beyond this, as Hay et al. (2002: 1) note, there is a collective ethos among member states characterized by 'dynamic relationships between transnational, international and domestic processes and practices'. In short, they aver, the EU is the globe's 'most regionally integrated political and economic space'. Among member states, political and economic outcomes are informed by regular inputs not only from a supranational institution – the Commission – but also from various transnational and international actors.

The importance of cross-border actors for EU member states is exemplified in the accession processes of the new members – Cyprus, the Czech Republic, Estonia, Hungary, Latvia, Lithuania, Malta, Poland, Slovakia and Slovenia – that joined the Union in May 2004. These countries had both to be democracies and to have market economies in order to join the EU. To explain the provenance of the necessary political and economic reforms, especially in the former communist countries that now belong to the EU, analysts often refer to the necessity of conforming to the regional body's norms (Pridham 2000); and in this regard, cross-border actors of various kinds were significant.

Analytically, these five developments – numerous new and failed states; widespread, yet often problematic, attempts at democratization; global entrenchment of capitalism; emergence of transnational civil society; and enhanced regional integration – combined to challenge long-held assumptions about the separateness of domestic and international political analysis. This is because, as Migdal (1997: 211) puts it, all countries are now 'battered' not only 'by global economic and information systems'; in many cases, they are also beset by various political and/or cultural challenges, including 'virulent ethnic and tribal forces'. As a result, the key challenge for states, Poggi (1990: 117) suggests, is located in a 'complex of economic, technological, ecological, and cultural structures', which, he suggests, collectively 'ignore or deny the relevance of any state's territory'.

In sum, these observations point to the analytical importance of various aspects of globalization in order to explain political and economic outcomes within countries.

Comparative Politics and Globalization

The main purpose of this book is to survey how globalization affects comparative political analysis, and this introductory chapter sets out how I intend to do it. Traditionally, comparative political analysis has been concerned almost exclusively with domestic political structures and processes. As Sodaro (2001: 50) explains, 'comparative politics examines political realities in countries all over the world. It looks at the many ways governments operate and the ways people behave in political life.' States are judged to be analytically crucial for four main reasons. First, they are widely regarded as 'natural' units of analysis; second, they are confined political territories, administered by national and sovereign entities; third, they have distinct national economies; and, fourth, theoretically – although never in practice – they encompass discrete *nation*-states.[3]

Comparativists normally start, sensibly enough, from the assumption that to acquire information it is necessary to compare the things that, demonstrably, have clear similarities. From there, attention shifts to investigate reasons for any discovered differences. But if the focus is restricted to domestic structures and processes, then it is likely that we would miss other, external sources of influence. What we need to do is to incorporate the impact of globalization on and in domestic political outcomes.

How might we include in comparative political analysis factors associated with globalization? Little sustained work has so far been done in this regard, but we can note the endeavours of Douglas Chalmers (1993). Chalmers offers a relatively comprehensive, albeit regionally delimited, attempt to bridge the gap between comparative politics and international relations. He wants to explain and account for the 'internationalization of domestic politics' in Latin America. He argues that certain 'internationally based actors' (IBAs) – notably, transnational corporations and foreign governments – are a significant, long-term presence in domestic political and economic environments in Latin American countries and, as a result, are now 'normal parts of the system'. He suggests that this signifies a de facto 'internationalization' of their political and economic systems, as IBAs have been involved in Latin American countries' 'domestic politics over a period of time', are 'built into the political institutions' and are 'identified with international sources of power'.

Chalmers also contends that in the 1980s and 1990s, the 'numbers, types, scope and resources' of IBAs in Latin America grew, a development that reflected 'the post-Cold War trend of globalization', notably democratization and economic liberalization. Similarly, Yilmaz (2002: 82) suggests that, in relation to Turkey, a transitional democracy, 'the net result of the process of globalization has been the internationalization of domestic politics'. The inference is that, as in Latin America, Turkey is now open to the influence of IBAs. There seems no obvious reason to assume that the involvement of IBAs in Latin America and Turkey is an aberration. Instead, I hypothesize that a key effect of globalization is to increase the porousness of state borders and to enhance the significance of external actors for many domestic outcomes.

[3] Willetts (2001: 358) points out that *nation*-states do not exist. This is because the notion of nation-state is predicated on the existence of a single state within which are organized almost all members of a single nation without members of others being present. In the real world, such conditions are never found.

The Book's Concerns and Structure

The main goal of this book is to examine comparatively the influence of external actors on domestic political outcomes. Smith (2000: 4–5) notes that comparative political analysis typically uses a certain conceptual framework that 'downplays . . . necessary and logical transnational connections between domestic political and economic structures and international politics'. This implies a lack of sustained analytical concern with external agents, other than when, intermittently or on an ad hoc basis, 'intervention, dependency, subversion and foreign aid' become important to domestic outcomes (Yilmaz 2002: 68). Lane and Ersson (1994: 165) observe that 'in comparative politics the existence and impact of international regimes are hardly ever included in model building'. For example, the difficult problem of how to enter state membership in international organizations into models of state stability and state performance is often overlooked. As Risse-Kappen (1994: 209) suggests, such concerns underline the contention that attention might usefully be paid, on the one hand, to interactions between structures and processes of globalization and, on the other, domestic 'political system[s], society, and the policy networks linking the two'.

There is no consensus about how globalization affects domestic political outcomes; instead, the debate often seems polarized. On the one hand, there is the view that the concept of the 'national state' is now a hopelessly outdated construct. While Max Weber argued long ago that states possess ultimate coercive power within defined internal borders, organized in and through 'the apparatus of government . . . covering the executive, the legislature, the administration, the judiciary, the armed forces, and the police' (cited in Willetts 2001: 358), much modern theory of the state assumes that its 'controlling power has dwindled, or' even, as Karl Marx believed, 'is destined entirely to disappear' (Bealey 1999: 309). Opello and Rosow (1999: 225) aver that 'present developments not only seem to be challenging the current forms of the state, but are also questioning the *possibilities of territorialized, sovereign power*' (emphasis in original).

A second view contends, however, that the state is actually holding its own, with external forces having only intermittent and erratic impacts on domestic outcomes. To those adhering to the first view, globalization conjures up metaphors like 'the hollowed out state' and 'a borderless world'. Use of these terms suggests the probability of the eventual extinction of the state as presently understood. This is because globalization is thought to affect states by significantly reducing their sovereignty and corresponding ability to make definitive and binding political (and, by extension, economic) decisions. Opello and Rosow (1999: 225) aver that now 'most people live in states whose sovereignty is regulated and disciplined by norms of the international system and by the organizations of the global capitalist economy'.

Before examining what I suggest are the key issues of globalization that impact on comparative political analysis, I summarize the concerns of this book. The key aim is to try to bridge what is increasingly recognized as an artificial disciplinary gap, particularly as political science is practised in the United States, between Comparative Politics (CP) and International Relations (IR). Whereas CP is concerned with the 'comparative method [as] a . . . way of learning and teaching political science', IR is 'an academic discipline that studies the international system. It is sometimes seen as a branch of political science, but generally claims autonomy as a subject' (Bealey 1999: 76, 169). As we have already noted, the traditional focus of comparative political analysis is to

compare and contrast *domestic* political characteristics of various governments and political systems, 'drawing on specialist knowledge so as to produce new and more general
observations' (Hague and Harrop 2001: 69). However, most comparative political analysis overlooks – or, at best, inconsistently acknowledges – the impact of external actors on
domestic politics. I suggest that various external actors should be taken into analytical
account, not least because all states now have to try to 'deal with a new and more complex
reality, the product of many years of evolution, which appears in important respects to
be irreversible' (Webber and Smith 2002: 18). Recent 'radical, widespread and in many
senses irreversible changes in world politics and the world economy' – we noted five such
changes above – mean that international issues now affect important segments of domestic populations, including a range of 'private' and non-governmental organizations
(Webber and Smith 2002: 15–16, 22). The result, Risse-Kappen (1994) contends, is that
analysis needs to be informed 'by approaches that integrate domestic politics, transnational relations, and the role of ideas if we want to understand the [impact of] recent sea
changes in world politics' on domestic political outcomes.

While both are subdisciplines of political science, CP and IR have developed dichoto-
mously over time. They differ in three respects: their analytical realms; their core
assumptions about the importance of domestic and international spheres; and their perceptions of which actors are analytically important. Unlike CP, IR is interested in a very
broad range of international and transnational conduct, focused on multiple levels of
analysis. This is because 'no one image, explanation, or model, in any composite sense,
could be expected to explain *all* of international behavior' (Sullivan 2002: 2). As a result,
compared to CP, 'international relations . . . is somewhat more complex and contested.
It is partly, as a consequence, rather more difficult to specify' (Hay 2002b: 13). In short,
this book is concerned with a key, contemporary concern of IR: globalization, and what
it means for CP.

However, while the concept of globalization may be relatively new, this is not to
suggest that IR has not been interested in it. Two competing theories of IR, neo-realism
and the 'cobweb model', differ significantly on the issue of the autonomy of the state.
On the one hand, the neo-realist, state-centric ('billiard ball') model of the international
system sees the state, characterized by its autonomy, as the key international actor. On
the other hand, the cobweb model sees the state as 'in retreat' or, even, 'obsolete',
increasingly constricted by countless transnational connections and non-state actors.
Over the years, the influence of the cobweb model has fluctuated: it was prominent in
the 1970s when the importance of transnational actors for IR was widely declared, but
it lost ground in the 1980s – principally as a result of a cooling of the cold war. It
reasserted itself in the 1990s, following the fall of the Berlin Wall, the consequential
demise of the Soviet bloc and the emergence of the global economy.

But it is one thing to state that an issue area appears, potentially, to be analytically
important. It is quite another to develop tools that would enable us to assess the influence of globalization on comparative political analysis. A complicating issue is that it is
most unlikely that the domestic impact of globalization would be uniform for *all* countries. Instead, it is plausible to suggest that globalization would be both modulated and
moderated by the particular characteristics of different kinds of political system. How
might we conveniently divide the world's nearly 200 states for purposes of comparative
analysis? Sodaro (2001) divides them into two categories: 'democracy' and 'authoritarian regimes'. Hague and Harrop (2001) prefer a three-way split: 'established democracy', 'new democracy' and 'authoritarian rule', a formulation also used by Kesselman

et al. (2000) who prefer: 'established democracy', 'transitional democracy' and 'non-democracy'. In this book, I divide the world's states into the same categories.

I employ this three-way division because I believe that while it may simplify things, it also manages to capture important differences between regime types.[4] Each has different political structures and processes, facilitating to greater or lesser extents the political involvement of various kinds of actors.[5] To begin to answer the following question, 'What does globalization imply for comparative political analysis?', we start from the assumption that states have differing political similarities and dissimilarities and that these are important for political outcomes. I expand on this claim in chapters 1, 2 and 3. In chapter 1, I examine the nature and characteristics of political structure and processes in established democracies. In chapters 2 and 3, I do the same thing, respectively, for transitional democracies and non-democracies. Following this survey of the differing political structures and processes in our three kinds of state, we turn in chapter 4 to a survey of how CP and IR have developed their analyses over time. In chapter 5, I present an analytical model to inform the concerns of Part II of the book.

In Part II, we examine a range of issues associated with three aspects of globalization: political globalization, economic globalization and cultural globalization. They are: regionalization; economic globalization and development; the natural environment; political culture; regime change; political violence; religion; human rights; and gender issues.[6] Together, these issue areas comprise what is sometimes known as the 'new international agenda' (Webber and Smith 2002: 120). Table I.1 sets out in tabular form the issues with which we shall be concerned in Part II.

In sum, this book focuses comparatively on how states with different kinds of political regime attempt to adjust and adapt to various aspects of globalization. The book has two main objectives: (1) to examine how globalization affects domestic political structures and processes in various kinds of states, and (2) how this might modify the traditional focus of comparative political analysis. The central argument is that various aspects of globalization affect political outcomes in all states – but that the effects differ from country to country. The book neither randomly discusses a large number of

[4] You will often encounter the term 'regime' in the pages of this book. I use it because it is a useful – not too narrow, not too broad – term that helps us to understand and elucidate certain characteristics of both domestic and international political systems. In a domestic context, a regime refers to rules of behaviour that impact upon political decision-making and the values that underlie relationships between state and citizen. In the book I refer to 'established democracies', 'transitional democracies' and 'non-democracies'. What differentiates each category is the nature of the extant political regime.

The term 'regime' also has a meaning in the context of international relations, where 'international' or 'global' regimes are said to be common. According to Krasner (1983: 2), such regimes are 'sets of implicit or explicit principles, norms, rules, and decision making procedures around which actors' expectations converge in a given area of international relations', such as human rights, development outcomes and democracy.

[5] It is important to note that the three-way categorization that I employ is bound to be controversial. It is neither intended to be definitive nor more than a hopefully useful heuristic device to make analysis more plausible than it otherwise might be. Most significantly, things can change politically – sometimes very quickly! In other words, it is best to use the categorizations as representing a snapshot of various kinds of political regimes at a certain point in time: late 2004.

[6] It is impossible to be precise about such categories as they are not discrete. For example, many of the issues we discuss – for example, 'religion', 'human rights' and 'gender issues' – can be seen as having political, cultural and economic connotations and ramifications.

Table I.1 Issues examined in Part II

Political system	Political characteristics	Domestic issues potentially affected by various aspects of globalization	Impact of globalization on domestic issues
Established democracy	• High level of political and social institutionalization • Democratic 'rules of the game' widely accepted • Thickly integrated into regional and international communities • Military issues of low political significance	*Political* • Quality of democracy • Political culture • Political conflict, including ethnic/religious issues • Environment *Economic* • Regionalization • Development *Cultural* • Human rights • Gender issues	Differential outcomes linked to nature and type of interaction between domestic and external (state and non-state) actors
Transitional democracy	• National identity contested • Intermediate level of political institutionalization • Unevenly integrated into regional and international communities • Political institutions incomplete and/or function poorly • Democratic 'rules of the game' not widely accepted • Military issues of variable political significance	*Political* • Democratization • Political culture • Political conflict, including ethnic/religious issues • Environment *Economic* • Regionalization • Development *Cultural* • Human rights • Gender issues	Differential outcomes linked to nature and type of interaction between domestic and external (state and non-state) actors
Non-democracy	• Low level of political institutionalization • Little or no integration into the international community • One leader, faction or party rules, with little or no participation from extra-state groups • Military issues of high, political significance	*Political* • Democratization and regime change • Political culture • Political conflict, including ethnic/religious issues • Environment *Economic* • Regionalization • Development *Cultural* • Human rights • Gender issues	Differential outcomes linked to nature and type of interaction between domestic and external (state and non-state) actors

countries nor restrains itself to an exceedingly small group. Throughout the following chapters, and especially in the second half of the book where we employ case studies, the following countries receive most attention:

- *Established democracies*: Britain, France, Germany, India, Norway, South Africa, the USA
- *Transitional democracies*: Hungary, Mexico, Poland, Russia, Spain,[7] Turkey
- *Non-democracies*: Arab countries, China, Indonesia,[8] Malaysia, Singapore, Vietnam

Analytically Important Aspects of Globalization

The various definitions of globalization in social science all converge on the notion that, as a result of technological and social change, human activities across regions and continents are increasingly being linked together. Globalism as a state of affairs has been defined as 'a state of the world involving networks of interdependence at multicontinental distances, linked through flows of capital and goods, information and ideas, people and force, as well as environmentally and biologically relevant substances'. (Keohane 2002: 31)

It is undeniable both that globalization is one of the most debated terms in politics, international relations and political economy, as well as often being a rather fuzzy concept. Globalization often seems to be an abstraction, frequently employed, yet rarely satisfactorily defined. To be analytically useful, we must be clear what globalization is and what it is not. Unfortunately, this is by no means self-evident and, consequently, the notion of globalization remains contested terrain. To have analytical utility, the concept of globalization must involve more than the geographical extension of a range of phenomena and issues for which a pre-existing term – 'worldwide' – would suffice. Moreover, as the history of imperialism and colonization and long-term growth of the world economic system over time indicate, geographical extensiveness itself is not a new phenomenon.

Historically, globalization encompasses three distinct, yet interlinked processes. First, moulded by European imperialism and colonialism, a global states system developed from the sixteenth century. This produced forms of government and state around the world based on Western models, whether presidential, monarchical or Marxist. Second, a global capitalist economy began to develop at the same time. This arguably served to divide the world economically into 'core', 'intermediate' and 'peripheral' areas (with each characterized by a certain level of industrialization). Recently, there have been not only major increases in international economic interactions involving, inter alia, states and transnational corporations ('economic globalization'), but also absorption of the former Eastern European communist bloc to produce a truly global capitalist economy. Third, from the eighteenth century, both political and economic globalization were

---

[7] Spain is now generally recognized as an established democracy. In chapter 13, concerned with religion, we examine, from the early 1970s, the role of the Roman Catholic Church in Spain's process of democratization.

[8] Indonesia is now often categorized as a transitional democracy. In chapter 9 we focus upon environmental issues in the period before the current process of democratization commenced in 1998.

underpinned by technological and industrial revolutions that collectively influenced global patterns of both industrialization and communications.

The first problem we face is how to operationalize the concept of globalization to make it appropriate for analysis. As Hay and Rosamond (2002: 147) note: 'While studies of globalization proliferate, we remain relatively under-informed about discourses of globalization and associated issues of power and knowledge.' Because globalization is often presented as both a subjective and abstract notion, attempts to isolate its particular effects are problematic. The issue is complicated by the difficulty of separating out, on the one hand, *objective* effects stemming from globalization and, on the other, political decision-makers' *subjective* perceptions of it (Marsh and Furlong 2002: 35). To try to overcome the problem of abstraction, we start from a simple premise: in various and variable ways, globalization helps shape the nature of relationships between political actors and thus political outcomes within countries.

Do contemporary globalization processes and relationships collectively amount to something qualitatively different compared to what existed before? And, if so, to what extent are they significant for comparative politics? To answer these questions, I start by identifying important processes of globalization, before turning to an examination of how globalization is theorized.

It is common in the literature to see references to various kinds of globalization, including economic, political, technological and cultural globalization. For Mittelman (1994: 429), globalization links domestic, international and transnational levels of analysis:

> Spatial reorganization of production, the interpenetration of industries across borders, the spread of financial markets, the diffusion of identical consumer goods to distant countries, massive transfers of population within the South as well as from the South and the East to the West, resultant conflicts between immigrant and established communities in formerly tight-knit neighbourhoods, an emerging worldwide preference for democracy. A rubric for varied phenomena, the concept of globalization interrelates multiple levels of analysis.

This suggests that globalization can usefully be thought of as a multidimensional process, informed by significant intensification of global interconnectedness between both state and non-state actors. Potentially, globalization implies a diminution of the significance of territorial boundaries and, theoretically, of state-directed political and economic structures and processes. Debate about the phenomenon often seems to be polarized: is globalization 'good' or 'bad'? One group, the 'globalists', express a generally 'positive' perception of globalization. This is in line with the belief, briefly prevalent in the post-cold war early 1990s, that a benign 'new world order' would develop after the cold war. It would be characterized, inter alia, by enhanced international co-operation and progress on a range of peace and development goals, an initiative directed by but not restricted to the United Nations. The aim would be to address a range of perennial – political, economic, social, developmental, environmental, gender and human rights – concerns and injustices. Globalists believe that to address such concerns it is necessary to develop a range of dedicated – state and non-state – global institutions and organizations. For some, the key for success in this regard is to be found in the coming together of local groups and grassroots organizations from various parts to form an important component of transnational civil society.

'Anti-globalists', on the other hand, declare a pessimistic view of globalization, regarding it as 'a force for oppression, exploitation and injustice' (Cook 2001). They point to what they see as unwelcome consequences of globalization, including: restructuring of global trade, production and finance to disadvantage the poor; migratory and refugee movements in the developing world and the former Eastern European communist bloc; international terrorism; cultural clashes exemplified both by 'conflicts between immigrant and established communities in formerly tight-knit neighbourhoods' (Mittelman 1994: 429) and recent resurgence of right-wing populists in various Western European countries (for example, Austria, France, Germany and the Netherlands). In sum, globalists see globalization as a source of increased international stability and security, while anti-globalists see the opposite. Table I.2 sets out their polarized views.

Globalists and anti-globalists agree that four aspects of globalization can influence domestic outcomes: technological, political, economic and cultural globalization.

Table I.2 Globalist and anti-globalist perceptions of globalization

	'Positive' consequences of globalization (globalist view)	'Negative' consequences of globalization (anti-globalist view)
Political Globalization	*Established democracies:* Consolidated democratic systems, although some civil society groups may demand 'more' democracy *Transitional democracies:* Democratization is the result of pressure from both domestic and external actors *Non-democracies:* No democratization, despite domestic and external pressure	*Established democracies:* Ultra-nationalist, xenophobic political leaders and parties *Transitional democracies:* Ultra-nationalist, xenophobic, ethnic and/or religious fundamentalist parties and groups *Non-democracies:* Ultra-nationalist, xenophobic, ethnic and/or religious fundamentalist groups
Economic Globalization	*Established democracies:* Economic opportunities and constraints *Transitional democracies:* Economic opportunities and constraints *Non-democracies:* Economic opportunities and constraints	*Established democracies:* Economic constraints and opportunities *Transitional democracies:* Economic constraints and opportunities *Non-democracies:* Economic constraints and opportunities
Cultural Globalization	*Established democracies:* Little effect in most cases, as nearly all established democracies are already Western or 'Westernized' *Transitional democracies:* Variable effects *Non-democracies:* Variable effects	*Established democracies:* More 'Americanization' *Transitional democracies:* Increased Westernization or 'Americanization' leading to counter-forces, including Islamic fundamentalism and 'Asian values' *Non-democracies:* Increased Westernization or 'Americanization' leading to counter-forces, including Islamic fundamentalism and 'Asian values'

Technological globalization

> The technological revolution is a [key] aspect of globalization, describing the effect of new electronic communication which permits firms and other actors to operate globally with much less regard for location, distance, and border. (Woods 2001: 290)

The impact of this technological revolution is apparent in key areas of political globalization, especially democratization and terrorism. However, we should note that the third wave of democracy (1974–*c*.1995) had clear limits: various non-democracies, including China, as well as most Middle Eastern and North African countries, did not democratize. This suggests that, on their own, pro-democracy global trends are not sufficient, but must be augmented by propitious domestic circumstances that are conducive to democratization. Certain non-democratic governments – for example, those of China, Iran and Saudi Arabia – were able to use their ability to control communications technology to limit the impact of external democratization pressures. Their intention was to maintain 'the autarchic isolation of people from wider international currents' (Clark 1997: 21). Often, however, democratization was facilitated by the ability of various state and non-state actors to communicate, principally via electronic media, enabling ideas, programmes and capital to be speedily transmitted from place to place. In sum, communications technology was often an important factor in recent democratization, with various media employed to transmit ideas, programmes, policy and capital from place to place. In addition, it is widely agreed that the ability of important transnational terrorist groups, such as al-Qaeda, to proselytize and organize was linked to the global communications network.

Political globalization

The sudden, spectacular collapse of the Soviet Union and its regional communist allies in the mid-1980s no doubt encouraged many people living under authoritarian regimes around the world to demand democracy. Whereas during the cold war (late 1940s–late 1980s), Western governments tended, in the name of fighting communism, to turn a blind eye to their allies' often poor democratic records, once state communism in Europe collapsed, both democracy and 'good governance' became key focuses of concern.

Political globalization centres on what Mittelman (1994: 429) identified a decade ago as the 'emerging worldwide preference for democracy'. As already noted, during the 1980s and 1990s, authoritarian regimes collapsed in numerous developing and former communist countries, to be followed in some cases by democratically elected governments. However, it is clear that democratization did not often occur solely as the result of spontaneous, fragmented efforts by individual civil societies and opposition political parties. In many cases, it was also the result of the interaction of domestic and external factors.

However, as Gillespie and Youngs (2002b: 1) note, 'the complexities of the international dimension to political change ha[ve] been inadequately factored into studies of democratization'. During the 1960s and 1970s comparative analyses of democratization and democracy were primarily concerned with the domestic circumstances of the first and second wave democracies clustered in North America and Western Europe. A key focus was the manner in which – primarily economic – modernization and its outcome, associated restructuring of social and class alliances, was believed to have led to certain identifiable changes in domestic political structures, including democracy. Later, in the 1980s and 1990s, multiple democratizations occurred during the third wave of democracy. Attempting to analyse what appeared to be a new global trend towards democracy, comparative political analysis sought to comprehend the multiple transitions from authoritarian rule not only by a focus on causation but also on likely outcomes: theoretically, consolidation of democracy would follow transitions from authoritarian rule. Most comparativists sought to explain democratization by a primarily domestic focus. Of interest here were (1) authoritarian states and (2) pro-democracy civil society and political parties. The latter were the agencies whose tactical strategies, when successful, helped lead to the demise of authoritarian regimes and democratic transitions. Often, however, the role of external actors – states, intergovernmental organizations and international non-governmental organizations – were either ignored or viewed as marginal.

More recently, some comparative analyses of democratization outcomes were more interested in the impact of external actors in both country-specific and regional contexts. This reflected the fact that both Western governments and various international organizations, such as the EU, not only proclaimed a general and theoretical commitment to encourage democracy around the world but also, in some cases, were able to back up their rhetoric with hard cash. That is, they developed strategies of political and economic conditionality (Yilmaz 2002; Gillespie and Youngs 2002a). For example, recent accounts of comparative democratization in Central and European Europe highlight this as an important influence on democratic outcomes among the region's countries. It is also well documented that such external agents – both governments and non-state actors – were important in recent democratization moves in, for example, Africa and Latin America (Haynes 2001a). In sum, to understand recent democratization processes in various countries we need to take into account external actors and their interaction with domestic agents. However, as we shall see below, to factor in the influence of such actors presents a comprehensive challenge to conventional comparative political analysis, traditionally interested in domestic political agents and structures.

For example, three electoral outcomes in 2002 – the victories of the leftist presidential candidate Luiz Inácio 'Lula' da Silva in Brazil and of the Justice and Development Party (AKP) in Turkey, as well as the entry into government in Pakistan of the Islamist alliance, the Muttahida Majlis-e-Amal (MMA) – exemplified the importance of both domestic and external factors in political outcomes in these countries. The electoral victories of Lula and the AKP, in Brazil and Turkey respectively, highlight domestic opposition to what is widely perceived as 'Western-dominated globalization'. In both countries electoral battles were fought to a considerable degree on a common issue: the divisive social impact of economic liberalization under the auspices of the IMF. Pakistan's MMA was concerned with what the party portrayed as another example of 'Western-dominated globalization': the hunting down and elimination of 'Islamist terrorists'. The point is that to explain outcomes of recent elections in Brazil, Turkey and Pakistan, we need to examine how and in what ways domestic and external issues interact. In sum, both democratization outcomes and cross-border terrorism – key manifestations of political globalization – were affected by external factors.

Economic globalization

How geographically extensive is economic globalization? Hirst and Thompson (1999) argue that economic globalization is not global but a triangular phenomenon, of most importance to North America, Western Europe and Japan and several of its regional neighbours. In their view, as a consequence, economically more marginal regions, such as sub-Saharan Africa and Central Asia, are comparatively little affected by economic globalization. However, others suggest that the effects of economic globalization, around the world, include generally negative attitudes towards neo-liberal economic development programmes in many countries (Schulz et al. 2001).

The concept of economic globalization has three main components: (1) 'the spatial reorganization of production'; (2) 'the interpenetration of industries across borders'; (3) the worldwide 'spread of financial markets' (Mittleman 1994: 429). This, in turn, has various – political and social, as well as economic – connotations for people in numerous countries, such as recurrent fears over the stability of the multilateral trading order and the impact on jobs of the sales of national assets to foreigners consequent to privatizations of formerly state-owned assets.

Like political globalization, economic globalization was facilitated by the demise of the Soviet bloc. Whereas the USSR had developed, since the late 1940s, a parallel non-capitalist economic system, its demise favoured the movement of capital, labour and goods across national boundaries while increasing international economic competition. Economic changes were also reflected in the transformation of production systems and labour markets, and a general weakening of the power of organized labour to pressurize governments to enforce labour standards, such as minimum wage legislation. There is much agreement, however, that the already weak economic position of many poor people worsened as a result of economic globalization (Held and McGrew 2002).

Chief among the presumed culprits in this regard were the ubiquitous structural adjustment programmes (SAPs) adopted in numerous countries from the 1980s at the behest of the IMF. A common outcome of SAPs was reduced welfare programmes that disadvantaged the poor even further (Haynes 2002). As a result of their involvement in SAPs, both the IMF and its partner organization, the World Bank, acquired increased economic and developmental influence in numerous countries. Critics of SAPs allege that the reform programmes typically failed to kick start economic development, and recent research – from the World Bank, the United Nations Development Project and various academic sources – backs this up. Research shows that: (1) poverty has actually grown in recent years; (2) most economic 'progress' has occurred in a small number of countries (some of them with large populations and unusual appeal for foreign investors); and (3) even in successful cases many people are actually no better off, and may actually be poorer, than they were previously (Haynes 2005). Finally, SAPs were often judged to be seriously flawed development strategies. This in turn often led to political dissent and demands for governmental change (the examples of Brazil and Turkey were noted above). In sum, a vast and growing literature points to what many see as declining state control of national economies – and subsequent effects on national political arrangements – in many such countries.

Cultural globalization

For some, the idea of cultural globalization is strongly associated with 'Americanization' or more generally 'Westernization'. A key issue here is the pressures experienced by numerous countries in recent years to install liberal democracy, regarded by some as a Western phenomenon of little relevance to non-Western societies. Others perceive cultural globalization in the global dissemination of identical consumer goods and associated dissemination of American-style consumer culture. This American-style consumerism is said to erode particularistic cultures and values and replace them with a uniform culture of Disney, McDonald's, Coca-Cola, Microsoft and Starbucks. Spread by predominantly US-based transnational corporations, such 'Americanization' is believed to subvert many non-Western, local cultures by encouraging people not only to buy American goods and services but also to adopt what are sometimes perceived as 'American' political and social norms, including liberal democracy and individualistic conceptions of human rights. Some East Asian and Muslim countries have sought to meet the perceived onslaught of 'Americanization' by articulating defiantly anti-individualistic worldviews: popularized, respectively, via a focus on 'Asian values' and Islamism or 'Islamic fundamentalism'. Taken together – as they sometimes are (Huntington 1996) – 'Asian values' and Islamism are believed to represent a significant challenge to Western-style globalization. Influential constituencies in both East Asian and Muslim countries dislike the presumption that their own collective-orientated societies should supinely accept an individualistic, 'Americanized' global culture that would likely undermine deep-rooted communal values.

Conclusion

We began this Introduction with a key presumption: the world has significantly changed since the 1980s, characterized by the fall of the Berlin Wall in November 1989, the consequential demise of the Soviet bloc, and contemporaneous global emphasis on economic liberalization, democratization and the spread of 'Americanization' or 'Western' values. Various aspects of globalization, driven by a technologically sophisticated communications revolution, have collectively impacted upon domestic political outcomes in countries around the world. This is because, as Webber and Smith (2002: 6) put it: 'all states [have] in some way ... been touched by the consequences of the growth of post-war interdependence and by the end of the Cold War'. In the remainder of the book we examine these issues more closely. In the first half of the book, chapters 1–5, we focus upon theoretical and conceptual issues, and in the second half, chapters 6–14, we examine the following topics – regionalization; economic globalization and development; the natural environment; political culture; regime change; political violence; religion; human rights; and gender issues – in relation to our three categories of states.

Part I
Comparative Politics and Globalization: Theory and Practice

1

Established Democracies

In the Introduction, I suggested that various kinds of external actors – in shorthand, 'globalization' – can influence political outcomes within countries. Before we turn to a closer examination of this issue in chapters 4 and 5, we start by examining, in chapters 1, 2 and 3 respectively, the political characteristics of our three categories of states: established democracies, transitional democracies and non-democracies. I suggest that each generic category of political system has characteristic domestic political structures and processes that can help moderate and modulate the impact of globalization. This suggests that policy-makers must, in various ways, attempt to cope simultaneously both with demands from their own domestic political systems as well as those emanating from external sources.

What are the characteristics of an established democracy? Freedom House (FH), a US-based non-governmental organization, annually rates all countries' democratic position in terms of 'political rights' (PR) and 'civil liberties' (CL) (<http://www.freedom-house.org/index.htm>). FH rates both PR and CL on a sliding scale: the highest level of performance in both regards is indicated by '1', the lowest by '7'. Consequently, the best score that a country can conceivably achieve under the FH system is 2 (PR = 1; CL = 1). Diamond (1996) suggests that the FH rating of 'free' – that is, between 2 and 5 – is a 'rough' indicator that democracy is established within a country, while Zakaria (1997) proposes a slightly more restrictive total of 2–4 to denote the same thing. Both Diamond and Zakaria propose a score of 5–10 to denote what FH calls a 'partly free' state. The idea of a 'partly free' state is synonymous with our category of 'transitional democracy', examined in chapter 2. This is a situation where *some* aspects of a democratic political system are present, but not 'all'. Finally, both Diamond and Zakaria propose a combined PR/CL total of 11–14 to signify a state ruled by a non-democratic regime, a category of polity analysed in chapter 4.[1]

---

[1] Go to <http://www.freedomhouse.org/research/freeworld/2003/methodology.htm> to see the methodology and the criteria that FH uses to award its ratings. Bear in mind my earlier expressed warning about not seeing such ratings as overly objective in all cases. Note also that FH categories – and by implication mine – have 'grey areas': if a country gets a '5' in FH ratings there is likely to be endless discussion about whether it is 'really' a democracy or not! Similarly, if a country gets a '10', is it a (slowly) emerging democracy or merely an authoritarian state that has brushed up on its PR in order to present itself in a better light for the purposes of, for example, attracting foreign aid?

Critics have expressed misgivings about the possible use of a rather crude subjective analysis employed by FH (see, for example, Chiriyankandath 2005). Partly funded by several US government departments (US Agency for International Development and the US Information Agency – for a full list of funding bodies, see <http://www.freedomhouse.org/aboutfh/funders.htm>), FH

Characteristics

For most scholars, the bloc of established democracies comprises two discrete groups. On the one hand, there are the 24 countries of Western Europe, plus Australia, Canada, Israel, Japan, New Zealand and the United States. These 30 countries are all highly industrialized and economically developed. What they also have in common is their long-established democratic systems (Diamond 2001: 359). This well-established group of democracies is augmented by a number of other established democracies, that are characterized for the most part by the fact that their democratic credentials are less well established (for example, various Central and Eastern European countries) and/or they are not as economically developed as members of the first group (for example, India and Benin). Overall, FH identified 87 'free states' at the end of 2003, 45.3 per cent of the total number of 192 countries. The regional breakdown of 'free states' ('established democracies') at that time is shown in table 1.1. While such a large number of countries are certain to have many political differences, what they have in common according to FH is both *democratic institutions*, including popularly elected legislatures, and extant *democratic principles*, including popular control of the government and political equality among citizens (Beetham 1999). Overall, most established democracies have the following political characteristics:

- high level of political and social institutionalization, that is, a range of embedded institutional linkages linking state and society;
- democratic 'rules of the game', accepted by all significant political players;
- armed forces with very little or no political significance; and
- 'thick' integration with regional and/or international communities. This reflects considerable interdependence among such states, based primarily on economic goals but also in some cases, as among EU members, reflecting shared political concerns.

Table 1.1 Regional breakdown and total number of established democracies, 2003

Region	Number of established democracies
Western Europe	24
Americas/Caribbean	22
Asia Pacific	18
Central and Eastern Europe/Former Soviet Union	11
Sub-Saharan Africa	11
Middle East/North Africa	1
Total	87

Source: Adapted from 'Freedom in the World 2004. Table of Independent Countries Comparative Measures of Freedom', at <http://www.freedomhouse.org/research/freeworld/2004/table2004.pdf>.

came into being at the onset of the cold war as 'an outspoken advocate of the Marshall Plan and NATO' (<http://www.freedomhouse.org/aboutfh/index.htm>). In 2003, James Woolsey, a former director of the US Central Intelligence Agency chaired its Board of Trustees.

Politically, established democracies are formally organized so as to encourage a high level of citizen participation, diversity of opinion and government accountability. They have political systems characterized both by separation of powers among institutions of government and toleration of mechanisms of political opposition. It is often suggested that Robert Dahl's (1989: 221) seven-part concept of 'polyarchy' captures their main political characteristics: (1) 'free and fair' elections; (2) elected officials; (3) inclusive suffrage; (4) the right of individuals to run for office; (5) freedom of expression; (6) alternative sources of information to those disseminated by the state; and (7) associational autonomy.

In short, established democracies are polities where democracy is said to be stable or 'consolidated'. However, there is disagreement about how to recognize a polity where democracy is established. For Huntington (1991), democracy is established when a polity passes the 'two-turnover test': that is, an incumbent government loses a national election, the opposition wins it and then, next time, loses it, so that a new government from the opposition is formed. This test of democratic establishment has the virtue of being empirically easy to verify but the vice of not being nuanced enough. For example, Japan did not fulfil the criteria of the test until 1993: was it not a democracy until then?

Mainwaring et al. (1992: 3) suggest that democracy can be said to be established when 'all major political actors take for granted the fact that democratic processes dictate governmental renewal'. Linz and Stepan (1996) argue that the establishment of democracy does not depend only on electoral results. For them, it is a concept amounting to a particular, *institutionalized* form of democracy. It is a procedural system with open political competition, freely competing multiparties and an impressive array of civil and political rights – guaranteed by law. Political accountability is crucial, and operates primarily via the electoral relationship between voters and their representatives. For Linz and Stepan (1996: 6) democratic consolidation comprises *behavioural*, *attitudinal* and *constitutional* aspects. First, *behaviourally*, democracy is consolidated when 'no significant national, social, economic, political, or institutional actors spend significant resources attempting to achieve their objectives by creating a nondemocratic regime or turning to violence or foreign intervention to secede from the state'. Second, *attitudinally*, democracy is ensconced when most citizens believe that democratic procedures and institutions are the best means 'to govern [their] collective life'; and where support for 'antisystem alternatives is quite small or more or less isolated from the prodemocratic forces'. Third, *constitutionally*, democracy is habituated when 'governmental and nongovernmental forces . . . become subjected to, and habituated to, the resolution of conflict within the specific laws, procedures, and institutions sanctioned by the new democratic process'. In sum, according to Linz and Stepan, democratic consolidation amounts to the institutionalization of democratic practices and processes. It is in place when the great majority of political actors and citizens concur that such a democratic arrangement is the *only* acceptable way to resolve societal conflicts.

Some observers have argued that a combination of a penetrating state and an elite-dominated party system constitutes the most realistic institutional arrangement to facilitate democratic consolidation, albeit at a relatively 'modest' level. This is a way of saying that a recognizably democratic system – one with a stable democratic order and a good range of secure civil liberties and political rights – will develop only when popular sovereignty is *somewhat* circumscribed, although not excessively so. This is because democratic consolidation is said to be dependent on the protection of elite interests, not their demolition. Political stability is a vital aspect of democratic consolidation – and its embedding will depend on whether political elites and their allies in the military are willing to follow constitutional rules and, more generally, accept the legitimacy of a democratic system. If they do not, democracy will be seriously endangered as authoritarian attempts to grab power would be likely, for example, via military coups d'état. When their position is not threatened, elites gradually become accustomed to a democratic regime, realizing that it does not hurt as much as they initially feared, and move from grudging acceptance to full endorsement of democracy. If this happens, democracy becomes not an expedient alternative to authoritarian rule ('negative' consolidation) but the preferred political order ('positive' consolidation).

In sum, established democracies are characterized by patterns of embedded democratically oriented political behaviour. This initially develops on an ad hoc basis and over time develops into the only acceptable way – both for political elites and the mass of ordinary people – of 'doing' politics. Over time, anti-democrats are politically neutralized and democratically legitimate political actors are admitted into the system according to previously established, legitimately coded procedures. Established democracies are also underpinned by legal guarantees and extensive protections for individual and group freedoms, secured by and through the workings of an independent, impartial judiciary. A third factor – unequivocal civilian control of the military and a competent state bureaucracy necessary to carry out state policies – is also vital. In short, an established democracy has three key characteristics: (1) generally accepted, democratically oriented political rules; (2) stable, durable, democratic institutions; and (3) a wide range, and relatively high level, of state-guaranteed civil and political rights, upheld by the rule of law (Haynes 2001a: 36–8).

Political Institutions Linking Governments and Voters

Policy-making in established democracies is influenced by the preferences of a multiplicity of domestic actors. Among these, the most important is the political executive, especially the office of the president or prime minister. These offices have authority rooted both in the efficiency gained from centralization as well as inherent constitutional and organizational advantages. However, in recent years, and in particular since the end of the cold war, the dividing line between external and internal issues has become less clear than it once was, while at the same time the motivation for, and political dividends of, close executive involvement have grown. Consequently, in many established democracies, the chief executive – whether president or prime minister – is now often personally involved in putting together important policy decisions, or at least is influential in helping establish 'the overall policy context in which lower-level policy making is carried out' (Webber and Smith 2002: 70). However, in established democracies executive direction and dominance is never total, with three potential sources of countervailing influence. First, there is society. As the office of chief executive is an elective one, public opinion – including elections and referenda – is always an important aspect. Second, there is the influence of other state agencies. In particular, the chief executive is subject to the influence of other state agencies, notably the national legislature(s). Third, there are various sectional interests, such as business groups and religious bodies. In sum, all established democracies have representative and participative political institutions of various kinds that proactively link society and government.

In this section of the chapter, we look at political institutions that link governments and voters: (i) elections and electoral systems, (ii) civil society and interest groups, (iii) political parties and party systems and (iv) constitutions and the legal framework. After that, in the final section of the chapter, we examine key structures of government: (i) levels of government, (ii) legislatures, (iii) political executives and (iv) the bureaucracy. Having examined these structures and processes we will later focus (in chapter 5) on an assessment of the political influence of different kinds of external actor.

Elections and electoral systems

Elections

An election is 'an act of choosing someone as a representative. It is therefore an essential part of representative democracy' (Bealey 1999: 113). Elections in established democracies must be both genuinely competitive, as well as 'free and fair'. Through such competitions, rulers are called to account by the voters who can replace them via the ballot box if they see fit. One of the principles of an established democracy is that elections periodically lead to rotation of power through the victory of an opposition party. However, as Hague and Harrop (2001: 129) note, 'choosing rulers is [not] the only function of elections in [established] democracies. [They] can [also] perform a range of other functions, including informing the people about national problems and even showing them the limits of their own political authority.' Further, competitive elections have the virtue of rendering those elected to power accountable to those they govern. While the outcome of an election is to determine *who* governs, the arrival of the next one influences *how* they do so. This points to the fact that competition among political parties between elections forces the former to respond to public opinion, thus reasserting the link between state and society. This highlights an important function of competitive elections: to act as a communication conduit from the electorate upwards to parties and government. On the other hand, as Schedler (2002: 38) notes:

> Democratic norms are not *perfectly* realized anywhere, even in advanced democracies. Access to the electoral arena always has a cost and is never perfectly equal; the scopes and jurisdictions of elective offices are everywhere limited; electoral institutions invariably discriminate against somebody inside or outside the party system; and democratic politics is never quite sovereign but always subject to societal as well as constitutional constraints.

Ginsberg (1982) contends that, even in established democracies, so-called 'competitive elections' are in reality merely procedures for augmenting the power of elites. In his view, elections are the chief means by which elites mould and sustain popular perceptions towards acceptance of the hegemony of the dominant social stratum, facilitated by a perpetuation of ideals serving to consolidate ruling-class hegemony.

Overall, it is perhaps best to conceive of elections in established democracies as fulfilling two objectives. On the one hand, they allow elites to influence voters and vice versa. On the other hand, as Hague and Harrop (2001: 130) suggest, 'democratic elections expand the authority of government while reducing the likelihood of that authority being misused. In that sense, they benefit both rulers and ruled.'

Electoral systems

Elections require a set of rules and the electoral system is the totality of rules that oversee them. Electoral systems are often controversial, with debate often focusing on the nature of the rules that govern the conversion of ballots into seats. While such rules are important, they are also technical, and most ordinary voters may struggle to understand the precise workings of the electoral system under which they cast their votes. Electoral systems in established democracies are either non-proportional representation or proportional representation.

Non-proportional systems are the simplest form of electoral system, based on the well-established notion of selecting a person or persons via the ballot box to represent voters in specific territories. In this system, political parties are not rewarded in proportion to the share of the vote they obtain. Instead, within the contested territory, 'the winner tales all'. Non-proportional systems take one of two forms: plurality or majority.

In plurality systems, also known as 'first-past-the-post', the individual who wins the ballot gains most votes in the contested area. The winner does not have to obtain a majority of all votes cast, only more than any other candidate. This system, which has the virtue of simplicity, is, however, uncommon and becoming more so. It is to be found not only in Britain but also in British-influenced countries that are established democracies, including Canada, various Caribbean islands, India and the United States. The other form of non-proportional system, the majoritarian method is different, as it requires an overall majority of votes for the winning candidate, if necessary obtained via a second ballot.

Proportional representation (PR) is the normal form of representation in democracies elsewhere, commonly employed, inter alia, in Central and Eastern Europe and Latin America. PR is a more recent innovation than non-proportional systems, not widely adopted until the twentieth century. The basic idea of PR, in contrast to non-proportional systems, is that parties are granted seats in the legislature in direct proportion to the overall share of the vote they receive in the election. To some, the system often has a considerable drawback: coalition governments, which may be unstable. This is because a single party only infrequently achieves a majority of seats under PR. Consequently, it often necessarily leads to post-election dialogue in the legislature to ascertain which parties will form the next administration. Because of these factors, PR is often interpreted as a means to choose legislatures rather than governments.

Civil society and interest groups

Civil society

The term 'civil society' crept quietly and largely unexamined into the political science literature in the 1980s. It also seeped into the discourse of leaders of movements for political reform in many countries. However, the idea of civil society has been of importance in much of the literature of Western political philosophy since the emergence of the modern nation-state in the eighteenth century. It reappeared at a point in history when the capabilities of existing states even minimally to satisfy the political and economic aspirations of nationalities and ethnic communities were increasingly called into question.

There are many extant conceptions of civil society and its relationship with the state. A useful one is to understand civil society as encompassing the group of non-state organizations, interest groups and associations – including trade unions, professional associations, further and higher education students, religious bodies and the media – which collectively help maintain a check on the state's power and totalizing tendency. Stepan (1988) defines civil society as that arena where numerous social movements (such as community associations, women's groups, religious bodies and intellectual currents) and civic organizations (such as lawyers, journalists, trade unions and business people) strive to constitute themselves into an ensemble of arrangements both to express themselves and advance their interests.[2]

Civil society is linked to, but separate from, political society (see below). Civil society comprises civil institutions not directly involved in the business of government or in overt political management. Yet this does not prevent some civil society organizations from seeking to exercise profound political influence, on matters ranging from single issues – such as religious influence in society – to the content of a country's national constitution. Civil society can even destroy authoritarian regimes, as in some Central and Eastern European countries – for example, Poland – in the 1980s. However, the shift from a non-democracy, through a transitional democracy, to an established democracy can only take place with the full involvement of political society. This is because the make-up and consolidation of a democratic polity always entails much serious thought and action about key political institutions, such as political parties, elections, electoral rules, political leadership, intra-party alliances and legislatures. It is through these establishments that civil society can constitute itself politically to select and monitor governments.

Civil society is embedded in the conception of free associations of individuals, independent of the state, self-organizing in an array of autonomous and politically significant activities. Sturdy civil societies nearly always stem from 'strong societies'. Such strong societies are typically found in established democracies, characterized by: (1) a comparative lack of ideological and class cleavages, (2) rather ' "politicized" civil societies which can be easily mobilized for political causes, and (3) centralized social organizations, including business, labor and religious bodies' (Risse-Kappen 1995a: 22). Ideally, civil society and the state should form mutually effective counterweights, with the former comprising organizations both limiting *and* legitimating state power, a stalwart defender of society's interests against state dominance. In other words, the institutions and supporting bodies that make up civil society will ideally be strong enough to keep the state within substantive and procedural confinement.

---

[2] Some analysts distinguish conceptually between interest groups and 'social movements'. The latter are identified as being more diffuse, with less well-established membership and leaders, and often with little standing organization. In such a view, social movements are nevertheless a manifestation of civil society. See Haynes 1997 for expansion on this topic.

Interest groups

Interest groups – sometimes called pressure groups – are 'organizations which have some autonomy from government or political parties and . . . try to influence public policy' (Hague and Harrop 2001: 148); as such, they may be regarded as civil society organizations. In this regard, Sodaro (2001: 256) notes the following categories: non-associational, institutional, associational and anomic. They are not found only in established democracies. As Calvert (2002: 153) notes, 'it is now recognised that interest groups – people sharing a common interest – exist in all societies'. Interest groups – typically fulfilling the significant role of assisting communication between government and governed – are regarded as 'intermediate organizations', situated midway between those in power and the ordinary citizen. Consequently, interest groups offer a further mechanism of mass participation in established democracies, promoting the objectives of certain groups. They aim to apply pressure on various actors in political society, including political parties, candidates and government officials. In the terminology of Almond and Powell (1996), interest groups carry out the task of interest articulation, with a key aim of enabling citizens to influence state actions. Thus, interest groups are 'vehicles for both elite *and* mass interest articulation' (Sodaro 2001: 31, 255).

We can note here in passing, before examining the issue in greater length later, that interest groups no longer always confine themselves to national contexts. This is because in some cases, for example among Western European countries, the 'transnationalization of world trade and stronger competition leads world-market-oriented domestic groups to pressure their governments for economic policies that would enhance their success to and competitiveness on world markets' (Schirm 2002: 18). Moreover, the advance of the EU has also encouraged interest groups to adopt a Europe-wide perspective. According to Hague and Harrop (2001: 156), more than '500 European-wide interest groups exist, mainly federations of national groups. . . . Increasingly . . . national interest groups lobby directly in the EU.'

Despite growing concern with regional lobbying in Europe, precisely *how* interest groups function can differ markedly between established democracies. One distinction that students of interest groups frequently make is that between *pluralism* and *corporatism*. Pluralism is a key idea of democracy. It avers that political power in established democracies is not dominated either by one identified group in society (such as big business) or by a small unified power elite. Instead, 'political power is diffused among a *plurality* of groups and interests'. Applied to interest groups, pluralism gives emphasis to: (1) *freedom of association*, that is, citizens may arrange themselves in interest groups as they see fit, and (2) *competition for influence*. This means that, for example in the United States, interest groups representing differing viewpoints compete freely 'for the attention of legislators and other authoritative decision makers and seek to influence their actions' (Sodaro 2001: 258).

The corporatist mode – found, inter alia, in Scandinavia and Germany – contrasts with the US model of pluralism, and is a quite different way of including interest groups in the policy process. The identifying characteristic of corporatism – a system of demand management – is a cooperative relationship between the state, employers' associations and trade unions that enables relevant interest groups to participate in certain decision-making processes. 'One of the most widely shared commonalities of corporatist thinking is the notion that leading representatives of the key groups in society – especially business and labor – should negotiate directly with government officials to work out the country's principal economic and social welfare policies' (Sodaro 2001: 260). Finally, corporatism is not a new phenomenon, but has been associated with various kinds of political regime, both democratic and non-democratic, for a century.

In conclusion, interest groups are significant only if they can be related to the political process through fulfilling the role of intermediary between government and governed. This is a way of saying that there must be some kind of linkage between the two sets of actors. That relationship must to some degree be a reciprocal one: support is offered in return for demands. Theoretically, interest groups can choose both where they try and exert influence and how they do it. Domestically, interest groups have a variety of possible targets, including the chief executive, the cabinet, the bureaucracy, legislators, political parties and the general public (Calvert 2002: 159). We also noted in passing, before a fuller examination later, the possibility of a regional focus of interest groups' concerns.

Political society and party systems

Political society

Political society is 'that arena in which the polity specifically arranges itself for political contestation to gain control over public power and the state apparatus' (Stepan 1988: 3). The key actor is the political party. Political parties are defined by Hague and Harrop (2001: 167) as 'permanent organizations which contest elections, usually because they seek to occupy the decisive positions of authority within the state. Unlike interest groups, which seek merely to influence the government, serious parties aim to secure the levers of power.' Put another way, interest groups are assumed to articulate sectoral demands and political parties to aggregate and weigh these demands.

The literature highlights three different roles for parties: organizational, parliamentary and governmental, and six different functions. They are: recruitment and selection of political leaders; expression of interests and demands; aggregation or weighing of interests and demands; voter mobilization; citizen assimilation and socialization; and interaction with electorate and constituency (Katz and Mair 1994). While their functions in some of these regards are thought to be declining, political parties in established democracies remain fundamental interlocutors between state and citizens. They are thought essential to politics in four main ways:

1   Parties in power suggest to government the direction it might pursue.
2   Parties serve as conduits for elite recruitment, functioning as the major device to recruit and groom aspirants for public office.
3   Parties function as a means of interest aggregation, converting numerous demands into sets of manageable proposals. They filter demands – by choosing, diminishing and joining interests – between society and state, deciding which demands to put forward.
4   To a significant, albeit apparently declining extent, political parties in established democracies serve as a 'point of reference for their supporters and voters, giving people a key to interpreting a complicated political world' (Hague and Harrop 2001: 167).

In most Western established democracies, political parties developed from social divisions stemming from national and industrial revolutions in the eighteenth and nineteenth centuries. This led to four main cleavages that until recently structured party competition: centre versus periphery, church versus state, urban versus rural, and workers versus employers (Lipset and Rokkan 1967).

From the late 1960s, a new cleavage emerged in many Western countries: the 'new politics' or post-materialist cleavage (Dalton 2002). 'New politics' is a multidimensional phenomenon, referring, on the one hand, to 'new', 'post-materialist' issues (such as gender concerns, nuclear disarmament and environmental protection) and, on the other, to different forms of political organization (such as bottom-up, grassroots-orientated concerns, rather than bureaucratic), participation modes (that is, unconventional not orthodox), and attitudes to the political system centring on critical rather than supportive notions. Institutionally, the 'new politics' has manifested itself in two main forms: new social movements and Green parties. For many, the 'new politics' reflects an assumption that citizens in established democracies around the world are turning against established political parties, to the extent that they are widely judged to be in decline. Partly in response, academic observers of politics have attempted to explain, and to some extent qualify, what they see as a growing, anti-party, popular mood. However, as Bale and Roberts (2002: 1) note, it is actually very difficult to be sure that such a decline is in fact the case.

From the mid-nineteenth century, four different phases have been noted in the development of political parties in Western democracies: elite party, mass party, catch-all party and cartel party phases (Katz and Mair 1994). The four phases can be differentiated by differing conceptualizations of the relationship between political parties, civil society and the state. During the first period (c.1850–80), parties amounted to little more than elite committees, organizations of those who jointly made up both the state and civil society. In the second phase (c.1880–1960), mass parties emerged, open to all members of a particular societal group, explicitly claiming to represent its particularistic interests. State and civil society became relatively distinct, with parties filling the role as interlocutors between the two. Because each party sought to represent only one segment of society, the degree of electoral competition was relatively low. After World War II until the 1970s, catch-all parties developed, functioning as competing agents between civil society and the state. By this time, major struggles for political and social rights – such as the right of women to vote – were over. In addition, the uniqueness of experience of earlier social constituencies was further diminished as a result of the development of the mass media.

The fourth phase – the 1970s onwards – is known as the cartel party period. This is a period characterized by the diminishing of ideological division, whereby political goals became increasingly self-referential, that is, there was much emphasis on politics as a profession in itself. Consequently, among Western established democracies there is very limited inter-party competition. What there is is rarely anything deeper than competing claims to be regarded as the most competent and effective national manager. For many observers, this means that parties – no longer significant agents between civil society and the state – are now absorbed by the latter, becoming semi-state agencies. Such parties do not really compete with each other for survival in a determined bid to decide policy. Instead, conditions are ideal for the formation of a cartel, whereby all the parties share in resources and all survive.

Cartel parties are thought to emerge as a consequence of certain conditions, found in certain countries – including the Scandinavian countries, Austria and Germany – where there is state aid and support for parties. It is also suggested that their emergence and development is facilitated by certain kinds of political culture, characterized by traditions of inter-party cooperation and accommodation (Van der Heijden 2002: 191). According to Biorcio and Mannheimer (1995), the development of cartel parties in Western Europe has affected the position and development of democracy. This is because, since the early 1980s, they have found it difficult to deal with citizens' social demands; increasingly, many voters do not identify with them, leading to a growing gulf between citizens and parties. This is explained by the fact that mainstream party programmes look more and more the same and, as a result, popular perceptions grow that electoral outcomes do not really matter as they will not fundamentally mould governmental actions. As a consequence, in such circumstances democracy becomes little more than a way to attain social stability rather than social change. In sum, for Katz and Mair (1995: 22) this implies that elections become 'dignified' parts of the constitution, while Van der Heijden (2002: 191) asserts that cartel parties can be thought of as an 'institutional expression of [the] "end of politics" thesis', a concept associated with the ideas of Francis Fukuyama (1992).

What does the phenomenon of the cartel party imply for the roles and functions traditionally ascribed to political parties? Van der Heijden (2002: 192) suggests that cartel parties, like earlier forms of parties in the past, still carry out the three traditional roles (organizational, parliamentary and governmental). Turning to the six functions noted above, however, it seems that not all parties any longer carry them out or at least they do not perform them in the same way. The mass party is the best example of a party carrying out all six functions, but since the emergence of the catch-all party, some at least have altered, diminished or are now undertaken by other political and social actors, notably social movements and interest groups.

Party systems

Scholarly research on parties has led to a large number of hypotheses and empirical findings focusing on political consequences of various institutional arrangements. Parties are said to have both 'control' and 'representation' functions. Bartlett and Hunter (1997: 104) suggest that their 'control' functions are enhanced under certain kinds of parliamentary government, and 'representation' is improved under some kinds of presidential regime. Presidential systems are normally linked to weak parties directing their appeals to short-term constituent interests. In addition, because the executive and legislature have discrete power bases and electoral mandates, it encourages leaders of parties to pursue individualistic strategies to convey particular benefits to local constituencies. However, this strategy is at the expense of both party unity and national level governance: it serves to reduce chances of cooperation between the two branches and makes it unlikely that coalitions will be successfully constructed. It is also likely to lead to political deadlock, and invite increases in executive power through rule by decree.

Reflecting different weights of representation and control, various combinations of these institutional features result in four general types of party system. First, there are *effective party systems*, characterized by high levels of both control and representation. Second, at the other end of the spectrum, is the *minimal party system*, with low representation and control. Third, *mass-dominated party systems* feature a combination of low control and high representation, with most voters regarding parties as responsive to their interests. However, because party leaders are unable to restrain the demands of the rank-and-file, it stops them from making deals likely to be viewed as credible and binding by the state and other parties. Fourth, there are *elite-dominated party systems*. Here, while representation is low, control is nevertheless high. This allows party leaders to negotiate effectively with other political agents. This encourages elite participation in electoral politics, for example in India, because it reassures those who own large amounts of capital and land that their support of the party system will not threaten their privileged positions. The downside is that, because the ensuing agreements are not bolstered by broad societal support, then ordinary party members do not feel accord with party organizations. This threatens both governance and long-term stability as many ordinary citizens believe that the party system is not inclusive. Instead, it is regarded as an exclusive arena for elites and, as a result, it may be difficult to gain popular acceptance of policies, with individuals and groups seeking their objectives via non-party mechanisms of interest representation.

Political parties of all kinds compete for power within the context of party systems, a distinguishing feature among different democracies. What is clearly significant in this regard is the arrangement of parties – how many there are, what they seek to achieve, their relationship to each other and their disposition to govern or share in government. According to Mainwaring and Scully (1995: 4):

> the political party system is the set of rules that governs the externalization of political parties to the mass public. The defining feature of any party system is its configuration of competition and, like political parties, party competition endures over time, with its structures comprising an important aspect of a country's political operating procedures.

Three different party systems are commonly in operation in established democracies.

First, there is the dominant-party system. This is an arrangement where one party serves in government over an unbroken period of time, although evidence suggests that in established democracies dominant party rule does not last interminably. For example, the Liberal Democratic Party (LDP) governed Japan uninterruptedly for nearly 40 years, from 1955 to 1993. Eventually, however, voters ejected the LDP from power, following widespread dissatisfaction with its performance in government. Other examples noted in the literature in established democracies include: South Africa (African National Congress, 1994–) and India (Congress Party, 1952–77).

Second, the two-party system, where power is fought for by two major parties of broadly comparable size. Their electoral battles provide the definitive framework for political competition, and other third parties have little or no electoral influence, especially on the formation and policies of governments. The core of the two-party system is that neither major party dominates, but together they comprise a strong party system. Few countries have a predominantly two-party system, although the USA and Britain are important examples. But as with dominant party systems, two-party systems now appear to be in decline; where they still endure it is largely because of the nature of the first-past-the-post electoral system. This is captured by Duverger's 'Law' (1954): 'the simple majority single ballot system favours the two-party system' (Sodaro 2001: 253). Recent shifts away from the plurality method in several established democracies, including New Zealand and South Africa, is said to have more generally damaged the prospects of two-party systems. However, even in Canada 'where a favourable electoral regime continues, the two-party system has lost ground' (Hague and Harrop 2001: 177).

Third, there are multiparty systems, characterized by proportional representation. Under this system, as a rule, no single party wins the greater part of seats following an election. Instead, the normal outcome is government by coalition, a form that predominates in Western Europe – apart from Britain. As dominant and two-party systems decline, multiparty systems increasingly become the norm in established democracies. To what extent do multiparty systems result in reliable, stable government?

It was once thought that multiparty governments would typically be weak and unstable, with voters unsure which party or parties were responsible for certain policies, such as good or bad economic performance. However, over time it has become clear that such governments often do produce sound rule. Reflecting this, judgements about multiparty governments in Western Europe since the 1960s became generally more upbeat, an outcome coinciding with post-war economic recovery. It also transpired that coalition rule did not normally produce incoherent, irresolute government – as long as coalitions were made up of parties with broadly similar ideological beliefs. This was especially the case in Scandinavia, where policy was formed in a climate of compromise and pragmatism. However, some observers have traced a decline in consensus, for example, in Denmark where Qvortup (2002) reports it has been undermined over major disagreements about immigration policy. In conclusion, multiparty systems seem to produce policy continuity that is especially helpful when the economic situation is improving, although the essential compromises that necessarily inform coalition rule can be undermined when there are contentious ideological issues to resolve.

Constitutions and the legal framework

'Constitutions are sets of formal written rules governing states and organizations. The term was first used in relation to the Revolution of 1688 in Britain' (Bealey 1999: 85) The term 'British constitution' is in a sense a misnomer, as it is unwritten; the first written constitution was the famous document of 1787 in the USA. The latter has provided a model for many other countries' constitutions, including that of France produced after the 1789 revolution.

In general, the issue of constitutions can be looked at in one of two ways. On the one hand, there is their historic role: formally to legalize the extent of the state's power over its people. On the other hand, constitutions not only specify the structures of government but also stipulate, within the state, the proper distribution of authority. In other words, constitutions delineate how power is exercised and set out necessary procedures to make laws and reach decisions within the state.

Constitutions can differ widely – there are both written and 'unwritten' constitutions, while some are amended more easily than others – but what they all reflect is a coming together of law and politics. The main factor underpinning the development of liberal democracy has been the ability to produce legal restraints on the uncontrolled wielding of power by those who rule. As Hague and Harrop (2001: 185) note: 'A constitutional order, affording both protection for individual rights against arbitrary power and a means of resolving disputes between citizens and state, is the major accomplishment of liberal politics.' Renewed academic interest in constitutions and law in both established and transitional democracies in recent years reflects four developments. First, over the last two decades dozens of new democracies have appeared, for example, in Central and Eastern Europe and Latin America, replacing a variety of non-democratic regimes. Typically, they put in place new constitutions reflecting the changed political circumstances. Second, several established democracies – including, Belgium, Canada, the Netherlands and Sweden – have recently adopted new constitutions.

Third, not only in the United States but also in numerous other established democracies, judges often now seem prepared to engage with political issues. Fourth, there is a growing 'internationalization' of various legal and political issues, an issue of particular significance for the globalization concerns of this book, which reflects the central role that judiciaries have in both stabilizing and limiting democracy. For example, the European Court of Justice is an international judicial body whose decisions amount, cumulatively, to 'a quiet revolution . . . in converting the Treaty of Rome into a constitution for Europe' (Hague and Harrop 2001: 192). The European Convention of Human Rights (ECHR; 1950) supplies judges in EU countries with a quasi-judicial foundation upon which to construct norms of behaviour in a highly political context: a country's human rights realm. For example, in order to bring Britain into line with the EU's extant human rights regime, the 'New' Labour government elected in 1997 incorporated the ECHR into Britain's domestic law. This development is but one example of a phenomenom of increasingly global importance: the 'legalization' of international politics. It increasingly encroaches on domestic politics, and judges are now often requested to adjudicate between 'conflicting claims of supranational and national law' (Hague and Harrop 2001: 185). It is a development that affects not only EU member states; in addition, incorporation of various legal requirements now affects domestic political and legal issues in the member states of NAFTA: Canada, Mexico and the United States (Sodaro 2001: 777–9; Macdonald and Schwartz 2002). Moreover, various international conventions – for example, the United Nations Universal Declaration of Human Rights (1948) – also provide judges around the world with the means to impose their views on sometimes unwilling governments.

Structures of Government

In this section we examine levels of government, legislatures, the political executive and the bureaucracy.

Levels of government

The question of the organization of power within states is basically resolved through one of two solutions: unitary or federal government. Both formats necessarily involve the projection of power from national to local government, the lowest level of authority within the state. In some cases, as we have already noted, there is also a further expression of power at the supranational, that is, above the state, level.

Unitary

Most contemporary states have unitary governments. The term means that both sovereignty and power are held solely by the central government. The most obvious reason why such a power arrangement emerges is due to a country's political history. Unitary states have often developed in societies traditionally ruled by autonomous emperors and monarchs. Examples among established democracies include Japan, Britain, France and Sweden, while others, including China and Indonesia, are also unitary states (Lane and Ersson 1994: 163–4).

The exercise of power in unitary states involves continuous negotiations between levels of government. There are three broad ways by which unitary states diffuse power from the national to local level: deconcentration, decentralization and devolution. The first involves the execution of central government functions by staff located in different parts of the country; decentralization is where 'central government functions are carried out by subnational authorities'; and devolution is when lower-level authorities have some decision-making autonomy (Hague and Harrop 2001: 210). In the EU, such exercise of power also involves interactions between national and supranational levels. It is worth noting that the EU itself has contributed to this trend. Within its member states, the EU has encouraged constituent regions to bid for financial aid via the European Regional Development Fund. As a consequence the EU and these regions enjoy an increasingly interactive relationship, becoming leading policy-makers and, as a result, marginalizing central governments that are left with decreasing tasks.

Federal and confederal

'Federation' and 'federal political system' are two key terms used when discussing modes of government; yet, neither has a standard definition. Opinions differ as to what are their chief characteristics. One school of thought cites devolution of power as the most typical attribute of federalism, contrasting with the centralization of power found in all unitary states. An alternative way of looking at the issue is to focus on the way federal states are typically created: by means of some kind of agreement between states to become sub-states in a new federation. However, this does not necessarily get us very far in determining what this implies for the wielding of power. This is because, as Lane and Ersson (1994: 162) point out, 'it is not easy to pin down what federalism stands for except in a formal constitutional sense'. Among established democracies, there are a number of federal states, including Australia, Austria, Canada, Germany, India, Switzerland and the United States (Calvert 2002: 46).

Less integrated than federal states, confederal polities are groups of states allied by treaty, with some common purposes, usually defensive or economic in orientation. Among established democracies, Switzerland is a prominent example of a confederation. Over time, confederations may transform themselves into 'federations': that is, one state with a federal government. At present the European Union is also a confederation; but there is much discussion about whether it should become a federation. The North Atlantic Treaty Organization (NATO) is also a confederation, but there is little likelihood that it will ever develop into a federation. In general, 'the increase in the visibility and power of international organizations that has taken place during the postwar period may be interpreted as a real form of confederalism, particularly with regard to the EU' (Lane and Ersson 1994: 165).

In sum, the key concern dividing the two concepts – federal and confederal – involves the underlying idea of the state. If it derives primarily from confederalist notions, it implies that the national state consists of member states – for example, former Czechoslovakia, comprising Czech lands and Slovakia – that wish fundamentally to retain separation from each other. Federal states, on the other hand, are engaged in a kind of union implying that the constituent states have certain rights that need to be protected within a constitutional structure; this frequently involves a special court of appeal.

Local

Local government, found within all kinds of polities, is the lowest level of elected territorial organization. It is the system of administering the rule of the state at the grassroots. However, the position and standing of local government is not uniform in established democracies. In some – for example, Australia, Canada, New Zealand and the United States – 'it has a pragmatic, utilitarian character'. Contrast this with the situation in Europe, where local government tends to have a 'higher status and a more coherent character'. This is because the unitary nature of most European states facilitates direct links between local administrations and national government (Hague and Harrop 2001: 211).

Supranational

We have already noted an important example of supranational government in relation to the EU. This is not to imply, however, that supranational government is of similar importance in other parts of the world. As Sodaro (2001: 159) points out, 'the state remains the central form of political organization in today's world'. On the other hand, we cannot overlook the significance of various aspects of globalization in encouraging states to work with each other to the extent that no country can now realistically claim to be completely isolated from others. This situation of cooperation has led in some cases to structured attempts, as in the EU, to promote and develop cross-border state collaboration.

Supranational government is 'rule by the authority of an association of states ... much looser than a federation because all members retain considerable sovereignty' (Bealey 1999: 314). Under the arrangement, member states agree to limit their individual autonomy via the creation of structures with decision-making powers that transcend those of the separate governments. It also entails that the supranational entity has some financial independence to underpin its ability to enforce its decisions. We shall examine the issue of supranational government in a later chapter in the context of an examination of the impact of regionalization on domestic political structures and processes.

Legislatures

It is perhaps easiest to state what legislatures are not: 'They are not governing bodies, they do not take major decisions and usually they do not even initiate proposals for

laws' (Hague and Harrop 2001: 218). Instead, they are major symbols of popular representation, important foundations of the politics of all established democracies, which
claim to reflect citizens' attitudes and outlooks, although to what degree legislatures are
actually ruled by the opinions of their constituents is a matter of opinion. Nevertheless,
legislatures are primarily significant because of what they stand for – linking 'society to
the legal structure of authority in the state' (Olson 1994: 1) – rather than necessarily
what they do.

Significant functions of legislatures include the following: representation, deliberation, legislation, authorizing expenditure, making governments, scrutiny and recruitment. In sum, they enable issues to be ventilated, play a vital role in the structure of
party rule and consent to the levying of taxes and legislation. A contrast can be drawn
between legislatures in European countries and in the United States. In the former, they
'were representative bodies long before they became legislatures with the sovereign
right to pass laws'. On the other hand, in the United States, Congress was given the right
to legislate from the founding of the American state in the late eighteenth century. Its
power was stated in the first section of the first article of the US Constitution: 'All legislative powers herein granted shall be vested in a Congress of the United States . . .'
To this day, many observers believe that Congress is the most important legislature
in the world (Hague and Harrop 2001: 218). More generally, legislatures are crucial
vehicles for the mobilization of consent for democratic systems of rule. In recent years,
reflecting the spread of representative democracy during the third wave of democracy,
legislatures are said to have gained increasing political weight because of their assumed
reflection of the popular will. Overall, legislatures 'remain the centre of political life' in
democratic countries (Bealey 1999: 188–9).

Legislatures represent people in two different ways. First, representatives claim
to convey the sentiments of the territory they represent both to fellow members of
the legislature as well as to the executive. Second, they assert that they exercise control
over the executive. In reality, however, very few actually control, although many might
claim to exercise some sort of supervision. This is not to imply that the executive should
ignore them. This is not least because democratically elected governments typically both
require and depend on majority support. A series of legislative defeats normally results
in a government's removal from power. A further function of legislatures is to provide
a national forum wherein debates take place on issues of national importance. Following the televising of legislative discussions, it is now possible for all citizens to keep
abreast of the debates. In sum, legislatures in established democracies are significant not
least because decisions are legitimized there, often the result of much political bargaining and compromise.

At the beginning of the twenty-first century, around two-thirds of the world's 178 legislatures had one chamber, that is, they were unicameral. The remainder – some 30 per
cent – had two chambers, that is, they were bicameral. Bicameral legislatures have a
lower chamber and an upper chamber. In established democracies, the trend has been
to get rid of second chambers, a course of action taken in New Zealand (1950), Denmark
(1954) and Sweden (1971). The choice of one or two chambers is not simply a technical matter of institutional design but also reflects differing views and visions of democracy. Unicameral legislatures reflect the perceived importance of majoritarian notions
of popular control, with two key assumptions. The first is that an assembly should be
based on direct popular election. It should be an indication of citizens' will and, consequently, should not be foiled by a second chamber. The second criterion is that a single

chamber is believed, because of its singularity, to exclude 'the petty politicking and point-scoring which becomes possible as soon as two houses exist'. Defenders of the bicameral legislatures point to its following claimed advantages. First, a second chamber can provide necessary checks and balances on the workings of a lower chamber. It can also offer 'a restraining and revising' role, as well as a forum to make useful revisions to bills. Finally, a second chamber can provide 'a voice in parliament for distinct territories within the state' (Hague and Harrop 2001: 220).

Political executive

In established democracies, political executives fall into one of three groups: presidential, parliamentary and semi-presidential. Under *presidential government*, the chief executive is elected independently of the assembly for a fixed period of time. Presidents are elected by, and remain responsible to, the electorate. The USA is an example of this kind of system. In *parliamentary systems*, found in most of Europe as well as many other established democracies, the head of government leads a council of ministers. It materializes from the legislature, enduring in office for as long as it retains its support. An elected president or a hereditary monarch serves as a ceremonial head of state in parliamentary systems. Britain is an example of this kind of system. The third category, *semi-presidential government* (sometimes known as the 'dual executive'), is a hybrid, mixing the two types already stated. In this model, a powerful elected president must constitutionally coexist with a prime minister who is accountable to the legislature. Contemporary France is an example of this kind of system.

The relative effectiveness of presidential and parliamentary forms of government is central to the debate about democratization and, beyond that, the achievement and establishment of democracies. Some commentators, such as Mainwaring (1999), suggest that presidentialism can offer certain advantages for the establishment and perpetuation of democracy, while others, for example Przeworski et al. (1996) aver that representative institutions of the parliamentary type may be better for democratic consolidation.

Presidential

Presidential systems are political systems with executive presidents. A key distinguishing feature is the separation of legislature and executive. Consequently, the executive cannot participate in legislation and cannot be responsible to the legislature. The classic example is the USA. In the American system, Rose (2000) contends, the president has three options: 'going Washington', 'going public', 'going international'. The latter reflects the considerable US participation in regional and world affairs. As a consequence of America's global role, every modern president spends large amounts of his time on foreign relations and national security issues; this is especially the case since 11 September 2001, reflecting the significance of the terrorist attacks.

In multiparty governments, a president typically relies on an interparty coalition for support; yet, under presidentialism such coalitions are very often fragile and transitory. This makes it important that appropriate, necessarily robust political institutions, are in place (Swank 2002). Presidentialism can lead to legislative paralysis when a legislature is controlled by a majority hostile to the president, but not numerically dominant to the point of being able systematically to overcome presidential vetoes. The problem is compounded if the party system is fragmented, exacerbating the executive–legislative deadlock. Stepan and Skach (1993: 22), drawing on a wide variety of comparative data, suggest that, *ceteris paribus*, parliamentarianism provides an institutional framework more conducive to democratic consolidation than presidentialism. This is because the former embodies a greater propensity for governments to have parliamentary majorities to implement their programmes and a 'greater tendency to provide long party-government careers, which add loyalty and experience to political society'.

Parliamentary

Parliamentary systems are the opposite of presidential systems. Bealey (1999: 235) asserts that in the former, 'there is responsible government which is not present in presidential systems'. His reason for this remark is that in a parliamentary system, a government, whose members also sit in parliament, necessarily quits or disbands if it is overcome on a confidence motion. This implies that there is no separation, as there is in presidential systems, of executive and legislative powers. In its place, there is a partial fusing of executive and legislative powers, often making for stable and effective government – although this is largely dependent on party and electoral systems. Britain, with its first-past-the-post electoral system, normally has a one-party majority government with a strong executive. This highlights a further contrast with the presidential system: whereas the presidential executive is separate from the assembly and independently elected, the parliamentary executive is closely linked to the legislature.

Semi-presidential

France under the Fifth Republic has a hybrid system often known as a 'semi-presidential system'. Semi-presidential systems are characterized by a dual executive, 'consisting of an elected president with defined political role and a prime minister and cabinet responsible to the assembly' (Calvert 2002: 61). In effect the executive is two-headed: a popularly elected, powerful president and a prime minister, complete with a cabinet, which sits in the legislature and is responsible to parliament. Apart from France, other established democracies that have operated this system include Chile and Peru.

A key weakness of the system becomes apparent when the president and prime minister do not see eye to eye. Under such conditions, there is a strong possibility of conflict between the former and the latter, supported by his or her parliamentary majority. This is especially the case in France when they are elected separately. In France, a second criticism is that the direct election of the president, which began in 1962, makes the institution of the presidency overly responsive to public opinion. Third, such a system is often believed to be 'too "leveraged" – a relatively slight move by the president has a considerable effect on the rest of the system so there is a tendency for every matter to be referred right to the top' (Calvert 2002: 62).

The bureaucracy

The term 'bureaucracy' is a hybrid word that joins the French word, *bureau*, office, and the Greek *kratein*, to rule. Coined in the mid-eighteenth century, it was used to designate an apparently 'previously unknown type of state, one in which power itself had passed into the hands of salaried officials'. Calvert defines a bureaucracy as 'a system of administration by paid, appointed officials arranged in a disciplined career hierarchy'. Analysing the characteristics of bureaucracy, Weber found ten aspects that he considered of particular importance, 'in defining the position of the bureaucratic staff in its purest form'. This can be summarized as follows: 'bureaucracy is a system of administration by paid officials chosen by merit and arranged in a hierarchy by which the higher officials supervise the work of the lower ones' (Calvert 2001: 220–2).

It is almost unanimously believed that a bureaucracy is absolutely necessary for government to function. A bureaucracy is essential because, without one, governments would not be able to administer their responsibilities. A bureaucracy is – or should be – a well-developed system of state organs fulfilling two key tasks: (1) to advise political decision-makers about different policy options, and (2) to put into action policies following decisions to implement them. All modern states – whether established or transitional democracies, or non-democracies – have bureaucratic structures, including ministries, departments, agencies and bureaus. Their spheres of activity range across a wide variety of domestic and external policy areas, including domestic economic and social affairs, such as education, health and the natural environment, as well as external issues, such as international trade and foreign relations (Sodaro 2001: 132).

Conclusion

Established democracies have certain democratic institutions, including popularly elected legislatures, and principles, notably popular control of the government and political equality among citizens. Overall, established democracies have the following political characteristics:

- a high level of political and social institutionalization, that is, a range of embedded institutional linkages linking state and society;
- embedded democratic 'rules of the game', accepted by all significant political players;
- very little or no political significance for the armed forces; and
- often 'thick' integration with regional and/or international communities.

The last point reflects considerable interdependence among most such states, based primarily on economic goals, such as in NAFTA, but also in some cases reflecting shared political concerns, as in the EU.

I suggested in the Introduction that globalization is changing, in various ways, political arrangements and configurations within countries. It is often suggested that this amounts to an erosion of the nation-state's formerly 'hard' boundaries and a consequent – albeit a variable – diminution of states' ability to control their domestic environments and hence policy decisions. How does this affect established democracies?

While leaving this issue to a more detailed examination in chapter 5, we can note for now that, theoretically, established democracies facilitate the political influence of cross-border actors because of the relative openness of their political systems. In other words, while the impact of external actors on domestic political structures and processes is not uniform, as it depends on the nature and characteristics of their political and institutional arrangements, the ability of external actors to influence political outcome should be feasible. We examine this issue further in chapter 5, when we look at opportunity structures for participation in various kinds of political regime, including established democracies.

2
Transitional Democracies

Characteristics

More than 50 countries, about 25 per cent of the global total, are described variously as 'democratizing regimes', 'semi-democracies', 'partly free states' or, the term I use in this book, 'transitional democracies'. Such countries are clustered in four regions: Asia, Central and Eastern Europe (CEE), Latin America and sub-Saharan Africa. Politically, a transitional democracy is a country falling roughly midway between an established democracy and a non-democracy. Compared to the latter, a transitional democracy is *relatively* democratic; compared to the former it clearly shows incomplete signs of *democratic consolidation*. Freedom House (FH) data indicate that in the three decades from the early 1970s to the early 2000s, the number of transitional democracies increased from 38 to 55 (see table 2.1).[1] However, during the same period the *overall* number of countries grew from 150 to 192. This implies that the overall proportion of transitional democracies remained quite steady, moving from 25.3 per cent to 28.6 per cent.

It is important to be aware that transitional democracies do not necessarily develop into established democracies. Arblaster (1999: 33) explains that during the third wave of democracy (mid-1970s until mid-1990s) 'transitions from dictatorship to democracy were very often neither smooth, automatic or complete'. Schedler (2002: 37–8) notes that many such regimes can remain for long periods, 'neither clearly democratic nor fully authoritarian. They inhabit the wide and foggy zone between liberal democracy and closed authoritarianism.' Zakaria (1997: 24) observes that:

> far from being a temporary or transitional stage, it appears that many countries are settling into a form of government that mixes a substantial degree of democracy with a substantial degree of illiberalism. Just as nations across the world have become comfortable with many variations of capitalism, they could well adopt and sustain varied forms of democracy. Western liberal democracy might prove to be not the final destination on the democratic road, but just one of many possible exits.

The key point to note is that after an initial transition from non-democratic rule, the momentum of political reform may not be maintained. Post-authoritarian countries can follow a variety of political paths. There may be major impediments to the wholesale adoption of the institutions that characterize established democracies. Often, such regimes have hybrid characteristics, mixing relatively 'free and fair' elections with forms

---

[1] FH uses the term 'partly free states' to denote transitional democracies. Note the discussion in note 1, chapter 1, on the topic of FH objectivity and methodology.

Table 2.1 Number and regional breakdown of transitional democracies, 2003

Region	Number of countries
Western Europe	1
Americas/Caribbean	10
Asia Pacific	11
Central and Eastern Europe/Former Soviet Union	7
Sub-Saharan Africa	20
Middle East/North Africa	6
Total	55

Source: Adapted from 'Freedom in the World 2004. Table of Independent Countries Comparative Measures of Freedom', at <http://www.freedomhouse.org/research/freeworld/2004/table2004.pdf>.

of strong, centralized government. In short, the category 'transitional democracy' can imply not a clear-cut, emphatic shift from authoritarianism, but a regime with both democratic and non-democratic attributes.

Such regimes are not necessarily politically unstable. However, political stability may be rooted less in a general respect for democratic values than in the ability of a personalistic leader, supported by loyal security services, to embed himself or herself in power. In such circumstances, there will be only limited institutional constraints on executive power, which is effectively personalized and constrained only by the 'hard facts of existing power relations and by constitutionally limited terms of office' (Zakaria 1997: 22). A second factor is that there may not be unequivocal civilian control over the military, perhaps because the armed forces are too strong institutionally to be controlled by the elected civilian regime. Military leaders may well publicly profess support for the elected government, yet strongly resist its efforts to control the armed forces' internal affairs, dictate security policy and make officers subject to the judgement of civil courts. Or it may be that the government recognizes and accepts the crucial importance of having a supportive military and, as a result, proactively forges an alliance with senior military figures. Overall, the crucial analytical point is that while many dictatorial regimes exited from power during the third wave of democracy and were replaced by elected alternatives, this was not necessarily sufficient to oust from positions of power and influence long-entrenched, narrowly based elites and their supporters. In other words, while non-democratic regimes may officially have been followed by new democratic procedures, long-established power monopolies – a key characteristic of non-democracies – may remain politically powerful. In addition, transitional democracies, as a result of an authoritarian past, often have their roots in political competition or collaboration among numerically small elite groups, sometimes exclusive oligarchies dominated by 'informal, permanent, and pervasive particularism (or clientelism, broadly defined)' (O'Donnell 1996: 42). Such countries shift from authoritarian rule but are stuck in a kind of democratic limbo, remaining transitional in nature, exhibiting some democratic features yet strongly influenced by a recent authoritarian past.

Having in most cases emerged from authoritarian rule since the mid-1970s, transitional democracies are officially attempting to develop and embed clearly democratic ways of doing politics. However, such countries may have political systems character-ized by a lack of institutionalization, inhibiting the development of democratic struc-tures. This may be for several reasons. First, there may be survival of both personnel and practices from the *ancien régime*. This involves the adaptation of authoritarian elites into newly democratic arrangements, a process that takes both time and much effort. To democratize implies the removal from public policy-making of certain characteris-tics of authoritarian rule, including a high degree of secretiveness, exaggerated distrust of public involvement and a tendency for the political executive to protect itself from constitutional constraints. Second, there is the impact of political disruption – that may well be long-lasting – that attends all transitions from authoritarian rule, including the necessary reordering of institutions from one political culture to another.

In summary, countries that emerged from authoritarian rule during the third wave of democracy have had to contend with a number of often competing political and social issues. While not every transitional democracy has to deal with them all, the following list summarizes common objectives:

- adopt new principles of both governance and economic management;
- develop robust national identity – especially among the former Soviet-dominated countries of CEE – while addressing demands for greater local autonomy;
- restructure organs of national and local government and develop institutional linkages;
- seek to develop and embed society-wide democratic 'rules of the game';
- decrease the political significance of the armed forces;
- deal with opportunities and constraints resulting from enhanced regional and global interdependence.

In the literature, the ability of transitional democracies to deal with these issues is often linked to two main factors. The first is that, while not necessarily claiming that a transitional country's political future is wholly determined by its past, previous domes-tic political experiments have a bearing on the point of departure for reform pro-grammes. For example, contributors to Dryzek and Holmes' (2002) edited volume on post-communist democratization in thirteen CEE countries all reject the notion that history is the sole determinant of a state's political future. On the other hand, they all agree that history undoubtedly has a bearing on current and future political develop-ments. Second, external sources of influence can be of significance to the advance or retreat of democracy. For transitional countries in CEE, following the demise of the Soviet Union, there was a common desire to 'return to Europe', characterized especially by a wish to join the EU. Turkey, another transitional democracy, also wishes to join the EU and, as a result, has found its political arrangements influenced by external actors. In Latin America, various countries, notably Mexico, share the goal of developing closer relations with the United States, usually for reasons of enhanced trade. In addition, in seeking foreign aid, Africa's impoverished countries find themselves under pressure from external actors demanding political reforms. The overall point is that, in order to gain a variety of perceived benefits, transitional countries may find it important to demonstrate to an array of external actors that they are seriously pursuing political reforms. As we shall see, this can act as a significant catalyst for domestic political changes on a number of different levels.

Political Institutions Linking State and Society

In the next section of the chapter, we look at political institutions that link governments and voters in transitional democracies: (i) elections and electoral systems, (ii) civil society and interest groups, (iii) political society and party systems and (iv) constitutions and the legal framework. After that, in the final section of the chapter, we examine key structures of government: (i) subnational government, (ii) legislatures, (iii) political executive and (iv) the bureaucracy. Having examined these structures and processes we will be in a position later, in chapter 5, to assess the political influence of different kinds of external actors in such regimes.

Elections and electoral systems

An essential part of representative democracy, elections are an act of choosing someone as a representative. We normally think of the act of voting as an important aspect of expressing support for a policy, a person or a party, as it usually involves choice. However, as Bealey (1999: 335) notes, among the communist states of CEE 'one could only vote for or against the party's candidate and it was dangerous to vote against'. The general point is that the introduction of free, fair and competitive elections is characteristic of all new democracies. Typically, the first competitive election following the withdrawal of the non-democratic rulers is marked by a high turnout. This is because for many voters the first democratic elections mark the launch of a new, post-authoritarian regime. They both symbolize and legitimize the demise of the old order and the founding of the new democratic one. They are both a referendum on and an observance of democracy (Haynes 2001a; Mair and Zielonka 2002).

However, 'free and fair' elections are not the whole story. As Schedler (2002: 37–8) explains, one of the key distinctions between established and transitional democracies 'derives from the common idea that elections are a *necessary but not a sufficient condition* for modern democracy' (emphasis added). While all democratic regimes are characterized by their competitiveness, on their own elections are not sufficient. Established democracies feature elections that go beyond the electoral minimum, but transitional democracies may not. That is, they may manage, more or less, to 'get elections right' yet fail adequately to institutionalize other, equally important, aspects of democratic constitutionalism, including the rule of law, political accountability, bureaucratic integrity and public deliberation.

Studies of electoral systems are typically concerned with effects in terms of outcomes, such as the configuration of party systems, levels of representation and democratic stability. Interest in electoral systems was renewed as a result of the demise of numerous non-democratic regimes during the third wave of democracy and the consequent establishment of transitional democracies in several parts of the world. Two questions in particular are asked: (1) how are such systems designed? and (2) why are particular mechanisms chosen? Focusing on eight countries in CEE,[2] a recent book by Birch

---

[2] Bulgaria, the Czech Republic, Hungary, Poland, Romania, Russia, Slovak Republic and Ukraine.

et al. (2002) aims both to provide a descriptive account of the modalities of electoral system change and to explain them by identifying the factors that have determined these choices. The first point is that electoral design is not necessarily a one-off process. After communist rule, new electoral systems, initially introduced to denote the end of authoritarian rule and enable free elections to be held, were invariably changed and substantially altered later, in the light of its initial results.

Different factors may, of course, predominate during the different stages of electoral design or system development. It is clear that some highly specific features mark the post-communist developments. Significantly, recent Eastern European experiences in this regard in no way replicate the experience of established Western European democracies, in terms both of historical sequence and the relationship between the extension of citizen participation and franchise changes and the reform of contestation procedures. Throughout CEE, the latter only began to take a form recognizable in established democracies after 1989.

Why did some regional electoral systems become locked in at an early stage while others remained in flux? There seem to be two main components to the answer. On the one hand, there was diversity in the situations in which the initial electoral laws were formed and, on the other, we need to note the heterogeneity of the decision-makers involved. This is a way of saying that superficial similarities between the post-communist countries were less important than their political differences when it came to design and application of electoral systems. At the same time, the arrangements arrived at soon took on a fair amount of relative autonomy and the electoral systems to some extent became 'part of a set of self-reinforcing institutional structures'. The process of electoral design was therefore 'an iterative, recursive process that both formed political actors and was formed by them' (Birch et al. 2002: 178). In addition, the systems formed were shaped by three embedded sets of factors derived from existing models reflecting the range of alternatives available, contextual factors shaping actors' perceptions and the strategic bargaining that determined actual outcomes (Birch et al. 2002: 187). In other words, there seems to be no simple or unequivocal answer as to why post-communist electoral systems have developed in quite the way they have.

This also helps explain why it is difficult, if not impossible, to construct a simple model or parsimonious theory of electoral design to explain the myriad examples extant in transitional countries of CEE. In some cases, the preferences of individuals and groups were of great importance. For example, at a key stage of developments in Poland the main decision taken was 'almost accidental', while the complexity of Hungary's electoral machinery meant that its consequences would be uncertain because 'neither its architects nor its voters could anticipate' the electoral outcome in terms of seat distribution. In Russia, the leading designer of the model adopted 'appears not to have grasped its essential dynamic', while in Ukraine at least part of the problematic outcome was 'poor drafting' (Birch et al. 2002: 46–8, 132, 151).

In many cases key features of early electoral arrangements seemed to stick for no clear reasons. This may well be explained in part by the fact that throughout CEE both the political class and many ordinary people were very keen to make new democratic procedures work. Put another way, despite apparent imperfections of electoral system design, there was such desire to get away from communist rule that there was near universal effort to make new electoral arrangements work.

Civil society and interest groups

As Pridham (2000: 233–4) notes, 'civil society is often weak at the outset of democratization, depending on the length and brutality of non-democratic rule'. On the other hand, accounts of shifts from non-democratic rule typically emphasize the significance of groups acting independently of the state as integral to the weakening of authoritarian rule. However, the issue of the role to be played by civil society groups in post-authoritarian regimes is an open question, closely linked to the extent to which democracy itself becomes consolidated. In some cases, for example Poland, groups that were identified as important levers of regime change – such as environmental, women's and church groups – have generally declined in influence. This emphasizes how their influence was pivotal but essentially short-term. The point is that such groups, including the well-known trade union Solidarity, were not interest groups in the Western sense. Instead, they began life as de facto opposition groups, later becoming broad-based social movements or popular fronts. Their aim was to replace rather than to influence communist rule. This points to the fact that, once democratic transitions are under way, the chief actors become the political parties. Prior to that, however, interest organizations and civil society associations, as in Poland, can provide the catalyst for political changes. Later, however, once political change is under way, in many transitional democracies civil society groups have found it difficult to maintain their influence. Typically, interest groups in transitional democracies are not consistently developing along the lines of those in many established democracies, any more than political parties in these political regimes are growing into the mass membership organizations once found in Western Europe. Padgett (2000) notes that in CEE it is impossible to find even the beginning of a stable, fully functioning interest groups system. Pridham (2000: 239) suggests several reasons why. First, he argues that associational development has been seriously held back in CEE by both domestic and external factors. On the one hand, there is the impact of the communist legacy that led to widespread mistrust of associational groups, including trade unions. On the other hand, there were the serious consequences of externally encouraged economic reform programmes that centred on marketization. These economic upheavals served to debilitate trade unions through 'structural change in the economy and the reduction in the active employed'. Put another way, the structures necessary to develop socio-economic pluralism remain weak. A second factor is that education is likely to be a long-term influence on civil society. This is for the obvious reason that education has an important role in promoting critical and independent-minded approaches. Third, 'problems of cleavages and ethnic factors, as well as the local dimension of political life, reflect in different ways on the possible depth of change' (Pridham 2000: 239–40).

   A similar story emerges from the post-military democracies of Latin America, where the rise of markets has meant that the corporate negotiating channels once open between unions and the state are being rendered obsolete. Examples from Africa emphasize a further result of democratic transitions. Many new regional democracies witnessed a release of traditional social groups – animated by ethnicity or religion rather than shared political or economic interests. Such groups, in many cases long suppressed under authoritarian rule, proved to be a potent force for (and response to) instability, bringing about the disintegration or division of various African states, including

Ethiopia, Somalia, Liberia and Sierra Leone. It seems clear that democratic or not, many poor African countries have pronounced national differences as well as lacking the complex economies needed to develop the interest group patterns found in affluent established democracies. In conclusion, it would be unwise to assume that civil society in transitional democracies will soon replicate the group patterns of established democracies. If they are to do so, it would be necessary for them to experience both economic development and democratic deepening.

Political society and party systems

Linz and Stepan (1996) regard a strong and independent political society as crucial for democratic consolidation. It is characterized by certain types of interaction among political actors, competing legitimately to exercise the right to control power and the state apparatus. To consolidate democracy, it is necessary to construct – or reconstruct if there has been a previous democratic experience – core political institutions: elections, electoral rules, political parties, political leadership, intraparty alliances and legislatures. Some recent democratic transitions took place after previous democracy institutions had been demolished, while in other cases some institutions were maintained during authoritarian rule – although their functions may have been distorted. Karl (1991) argues that the second scenario should offer a better outlook for the establishment of democracy than the first. She emphasizes the advantages for a country that has retained some democratic mechanisms against one that introduces them *de novo*. Some observers suggest that *only* countries – for example, most Latin American nations had democratic regimes at some time in the past – that previously experienced democratic rule would be capable of democratizing now. This is because democratically relevant intermediate structures and democratic routines can crucially aid the re-emergence of previous alliances among parties and groups, as well as the return to the political scene of interest groups, unions and other important pro-democracy organizations. In addition, a prior democratic experience may encourage the mass of ordinary people to believe that, once democracy is reinstituted, then future political decisions would broadly be in accord with democratic norms. However, such a view would appear to condemn polities that have not experienced democracy to an unremitting undemocratic future.

It is often emphasized that one of the key differences between established and transitional democracies is the varying significance of political parties. While many observers would concur that parties remain of basic importance to the politics and government of established democracies, most would also agree that parties in transitional democracies are typically characterized by a shared insignificance. This is because such parties are normally incoherent, lacking cohesion, mass memberships and ideology, often functioning as little more than personal vehicles for ambitious politicians. Conaghan's (1995) description of the party system in one of Latin America's transitional democracies, Ecuador, 'populated by floating politicians and floating voters', is not atypical of opinions about parties in transitional democracies more generally. In CEE, post-communist parties are typically of the elite caucus type, lacking a mass membership and strong extra-parliamentary structures, and without developed civil society organizations. In other words, parties are underdeveloped, with none showing clear signs of developing into the kinds of mass organization that, for long periods in the twentieth century, following democratization, were typical of most Western European political systems. Often, however, new parties in transitional democracies do not possess the same incentives to build a mass organization as confronted West European mass parties a century ago. Crucially, parties in various CEE countries, including the Czech Republic, Poland, Hungary and Slovakia, 'receive generous state subsidies, eliminating the financial need to build a dues-paying membership' (Hague and Harrop 2001: 181). A further contrast between the two periods and regions can seen in the recent importance of the mass media, which provides a highly significant channel of communication with voters. As a result of these factors, it is sometimes argued that in transitional democracies neither a mass membership nor associated organizational structures are necessary.

This outcome has confounded the optimistic expectations expressed at the beginning of the 1990s: post-communist party systems would speedily develop into a small number of Western-style mass membership parties, linked to social cleavages. Pridham (2000) explains the common failure of post-communist parties in the region to penetrate society as reflective of suspicious political cultures in many regional countries. That is, it is clearly very difficult to whip up support for parties among electors who were denied a political voice under, and sometimes before, communism. In Russia, Light (2000: 224) contends 'the development of strong political parties is exceptionally retarded, Russia will not easily reach a stage where the alternation of parties in power is regular and accepted'.

Turning to party systems, most transitional democracies have decided on multiparty systems based on proportional representation (PR), rather than a two-party system based on the plurality method. A main reason for this choice is that in CEE, Africa, Asia and Latin America, where most transitional democracies are located, PR offers legislative representation to more parties and minority interests than the two-party model. This is especially valued in such countries typically characterized as low-trust societies. More generally, a main reason why much attention is devoted to parties and the party system in transitional democracies is that many observers believe that the chances of democracy becoming established are intrinsically linked to the number and ideological polarization of extant parties.

Chances of democracy becoming established are said to be improved when there are relatively few, not ideologically polarized, political parties competing for power (Sartori 1991). One reason for this is that relatively autonomous, democratically organized political parties can help to keep the personal power aspirations of political leaders in check. Morlino (1998) argues that such political parties are a crucial key to democratic consolidation, especially when there is no pervasive legitimacy during democratic transition. He also contends that the more rapidly the party spectrum forms during transition, then the more likely eventual democratic consolidation will be. When party systems become institutionalized in this way, parties typically orient themselves towards the goal of winning elections through focused appeals to voters. But when the party structure is only slowly or indeterminately established, then citizens may respond better to personalistic appeals from populist leaders rather than to those of parties. This scenario tends to favour the former, who may attempt to govern without bothering to establish and develop solid institutions underpinning their rule.

The point is that institutionalizing party systems matters a great deal, as they are much more likely to help sustain democracy and to promote effective governance than the alternative: an amorphous party system dominated by populist leaders. An institutionalized party system can help engender confidence in the democratic process in four main ways. First, it can help moderate and channel societal demands into an institutionalized environment of conflict resolution. For example, in both India and Costa Rica – initially transitional democracies after World War II that have now developed into established democracies – the party helped over time to prevent 'landed upper class[es] from using the state to repress protests' (Rueschemeyer et al. 1992: 281). Second, it can serve to lengthen the time-horizons of actors because it provides electoral losers with the means periodically to mobilize resources for later rounds of political competition. Third, an effective party system can help prevent disenchanted groups' grievances from spilling over into mass street protests, likely to antagonize elites and their military allies and perhaps help facilitate a return to authoritarian rule ('the need for strong government'). Finally, an effective party system, linked to a capable state, can be important in helping imbue the mass of ordinary people with the idea that the political system is democratically accountable.

Examination of parties and party systems is an indispensable component of analysis of political systems. However, clear understanding of political institutions is enhanced when parties are looked at in relation to state organizations. It is often noted that the establishment and embedding of democracy is dependent on state institutions that are both responsive to the needs of individual agents as well as able to supply society with collective goods, including 'universal law, national defense, fiscal and monetary control, and social welfare'. State ability to supply these goods is heavily dependent on its internal coherence. If this is not present or if there is inadequate concern with social welfare, then many citizens may fall below the poverty line and, as a result, be encouraged to look to non-democratic methods to defend their interests. 'In the absence of robust economic growth, equity-enhancing reforms will require heavy redistribution of resources, which is likely to provoke the ire of economic elites and ignite inter-class and inter-ethnic conflicts' (Bartlett and Hunter 1997: 106–7).

Nagle and Mahr (1999) use the idea of 'embeddedness' to refer to sets of connections – involving both informal and institutionalized associations – that link state agencies and non-state actors. While this concept has been used to explain the economic success of various 'developmental states' in East Asia, we can also note its significance in relation to chances of democratic consolidation in post-authoritarian countries. The general theme linking the two sets of examples is that supplying necessary social welfare and other collective goods that are fundamental to stable democracy necessitates that state actors build well-developed links to private agents. The cooperation of the latter is essential if economic stabilization policies are to be successfully implemented, and if economic growth is to be established or re-established. The latter, if reasonably equally shared out, is crucial, many observers contend, in encouraging citizens to perceive democratic politics as a positive-sum game. However, the experience of many transitional democracies is that high levels of embeddedness enable small groups of elites to gain an unequal share of national income, underpinning many ordinary citizens' perceptions that the state functions for the benefit of rich and powerful elites. In conclusion, the consolidation of democracy in transitional countries is premised on two factors. It calls for *a delicate balance* between, on the one hand, state coherence that underpins social equity and, on the other, the embeddedness that gives elites advantaged access to the state and its institutions. The balance is crucial because if coherence takes precedence over embeddedness, then democracy may deteriorate into authoritarianism. If the opposite is the case, that is, when embeddedness overrides coherence, then 'rent-seeking alliances between state agencies and private actors may compromise the provision of essential collective goods' (Bartlett and Hunter 1997: 106–7).

Among Latin America's transitional democracies, Bartlett and Hunter (1997: 111–12) identify four kinds of state: effective, minimal, penetrated and penetrating. When an effective state is joined by an effective party system, the result will be consolidated democracy. 'This configuration favours stable democracy by providing both the mass citizenry and elite groups with well-institutionalised mechanisms of interest representation', and examples include Chile and Uruguay. A second arrangement – minimal party system, minimal state – results in what Huntington (1968) has called 'praetorianism'. This institutional arrangement is thought to be least propitious for democratic consolidation, as it represents a condition of extreme polarization. Peru is the best example of such a regime among Latin American countries.

The third configuration is the 'mass-dominated party system, penetrated state' arrangement that leads to what is known as 'fragmented' democracy. The supply of the collective goods necessary for democratic consolidation assumes a state that is not overly subject to unchecked demands from society. The idea of fragmented democracy describes a system where 'party leaders cannot mediate claims of their followers and the state itself is heavily embedded in society but internally divided' (Bartlett and Hunter 1997: 113). In several Latin American countries, including Brazil and Argentina, such conditions have facilitated the emergence of neo-populist leaders with authoritarian tendencies. Such rulers promise to deliver beneficial outcomes for the mass of ordinary people via rule by decree. However, when interest group infiltration stops the state from supplying universal coverage of social welfare, many ordinary people can fall below the poverty line. This leads to widespread disillusion among many poor people.

Another scenario is the 'elite-dominated party system, penetrated state', which results in rule by oligarchy. This is when the state is taken over by a small group of political elites who express their domination via highly controlled parties. This results, as in Paraguay, in a lack of meaningful separation between party and state, as state institutions aim to achieve 'the valorization of individual party politicos rather than broad collective goals'. Finally, there is the 'elite-dominated party system, penetrating state', which results in limited democracy (Bartlett and Hunter 1997: 113). Under this arrangement, as in the previous example, the political system is characterized by very centralized party organizations. The difference between them is that the dominant parties' political power is partially balanced by a state bureaucracy that has a strong corporate identity, as in Mexico. Here, 'ideology and overarching vision of party elites animate the penetrative activities of the state, [but] the internal cohesion of the bureaucracy shields the state from complete capture' (Bartlett and Hunter 1997: 113–14).

Constitutions and the legal framework

To break with the authoritarian past and to remove the source of power associated with it – for example, ruling one-party state or unelected military junta – nearly always requires a new constitutional settlement. According to Merkel, to achieve democratic consolidation post-authoritarian states must go through four stages in the following order: 'constitutional, intermediary, behavioural and attitudinal levels of consolidation

... a sequence, according to which the entire socio-political system completes its democratic consolidation'.[3] The first stage consists of the constitutional foundations of democracy. Because fixed constitutional norms represent the first step in the process of democratic consolidation, getting the constitution in place is often judged to be even more significant than the post-authoritarian founding elections. This is because it provides standardized, formal patterns of behaviour for social and political contestation, initially developed or negotiated during the transition process (Merkel 1998: 42–3). The overall point is that to embed and then sustain democracy requires that initially ad hoc patterns of democratically orientated behaviour must eventually develop into an accepted way of 'doing' politics, both for political elites and the mass of ordinary people. Under such circumstances, 'democratically legitimate' political actors are admitted into the system according to previously established, legitimately coded procedures, while anti-democrats are politically neutralized. A democratic constitution underpins and formalizes this process.

Merkel argues that the constitution has a crucially important position in the process of democratization, as 'it leads to the first drastic reduction of contingency concerning political action in the transformation of political systems'. Political actors' necessarily ad hoc actions during the transition are formalized through the constitution, facilitating the achievement of a basic consensus that aims to reduce mutual distrust. This is because the constitution *guarantees* the fixed procedures of political decision-making. But whether and how transforming the written constitution into constitutional reality takes place depends on the 'drafting process itself, the character of the constitution, and the historical development of "social capital" in the socio-cultural environment embedding the constitution' (Merkel 1998: 43).[4] It is also crucial for eventual democratic consolidation that core political institutions complement the electoral and party systems, the interest groups, the state administration and the recruitment of elites. However, under certain circumstances there are very few checks and balances that can defend a transitional democracy from deteriorating into what O'Donnell (1994) calls a 'delegative democracy'. This is where the power of an elected president is hardly checked at all by the constitution and he or she governs by way of personal authority. According to O'Donnell (1994: 55), delegative democracies 'are not consolidated democracies, but they may be enduring. In many cases, there is no sign either of any imminent threat of an authoritarian regression or of advances toward representative democracy.' In contrast to representative (or institutionalized) democracies, delegative democracies are marked by an extremely personalistic style of leadership. Horizontal accountability (that is, accountability to other autonomous institutions such as the legislature or political parties) may be seen as a 'nuisance' by political executives. Those who are already in power, and especially if their power rests on personal popularity, tend to find rules, procedures and a robust second tier of leaders unnecessarily constraining; they often view other political institutions, such as legislatures, more as obstacles than facilitators of effective rule, tedious impediments seeking to prevent the popularly elected president from fulfilling his or her mission.

---

[3] Merkel (1998: 43) remarks that 'this is of course purely an analytical sequence because the 2nd to 4th phases of consolidation may begin even when the core constitutional institutions have not been completely stabilized'.

[4] 'Social capital' is the degree of extant trust between political actors.

Two contrasting models highlight differing outcomes in this regard. The first is relatively clear-cut. It is when the reshaping of the balance of power occurs among new or newly refreshed, constitutionally acceptable institutions and leads to a swift, apparently unproblematic consolidation of democracy, as in Spain in the mid-1970s and Ghana and South Africa two decades later. Such a development is characterized by robustly democratic political systems and is linked to the following: the process has been well prepared, enjoys popular support and is executed by a strong, ruling party. The constitutionally determined democratic system is underpinned by legal guarantees and extensive protections for individual and group freedoms, secured by and through the workings of an independent, impartial judiciary that guarantees citizens' civil and political rights, upheld by the rule of law. In addition, 'particular legal devices may be used to enhance the prospects of nation-building in multi-ethnic societies. Constitutional amendments provide, as a rule, strong constraints and therefore a form of institutional guarantee' (Pridham 2000: 263). Unequivocal civilian control of the military and a competent state bureaucracy – necessary efficiently to carry out state policies – are also vital.

A second model is when instituting a new constitution does not lead to democratic consolidation. That is, where a 'state of law' is sought but not achieved – a state of affairs characterizing many post-military democracies in Latin America and post-communist countries in CEE. Hague and Harrop (2001: 197) suggest that Latin America's post-authoritarian 'experience suggests that the rule of law should be a long-term aspiration for, rather than an immediate achievement of, new democracies'. In many cases, failure to embed the rule of law reflects the fact that constitutional reforms are ad hoc, the result of political confrontation, or not executed by a powerful ruling party. The consequence is that any constitutional settlement is likely to be poorly formulated and enjoy only patchy popular support. For example, in several post-communist states – such as Albania, Ukraine, Russia and the post-Soviet Central Asian countries – the initial shift from non-democratic rule was not followed by the establishment of strongly democratic structures and processes, but was instead characterized by continuing political fragmentation and fierce political competition. However, as one might expect from a large and complex region of more than 20 countries, as with other aspects of democratic consolidation, the post-communist countries of CEE vary considerably in the degree to which they have succeeded in instituting constitutional authority and the rule of law. For example, in the more European and parliamentary systems, such as Hungary, the Czech Republic and Poland (said by Pridham to be the first CEE consolidated democracy), the new constitutional order, underpinned by constitutional courts, is now substantially embedded (Pridham 2000).

Structures of Government

Subnational government

Among the post-communist countries of CEE we can note a contrast between those that have managed to establish layers of viable subnational government and those that have not. Those with pluralist traditions and with political cultures informed by pre-communist heritages, such as Hungary, Poland and the Czech Republic, have all managed to introduce and apparently embed viable structures of subnational government. For example, in Poland there are two lower levels: districts, comprising around 80,000 people, and, below them, local community councils, suggesting that Poland has now moved to the three-level subnational structure familiar in Western Europe. Another influential factor in the regional development of local government is the pull of international institutions, notably NATO and the EU, both organizations that demand that their members are fully democratic. Hague and Harrop (2001: 216) claim that Poland's emphasis on subnational government was partly 'stimulated by the desire to join, and extract resources from, the EU'. Several other regional countries, including Estonia, Hungary, Poland, Romania, Slovakia and Ukraine, are also said to want to 'return to Europe', a desire manifested by pursuit of EU and/or NATO membership. Pursuit of this goal is said to stimulate the restructuring of local self-government as well as the rebirth of regional identities (Batt and Wolczuk 2002). However, the development of viable subnational governing structures in transitional democracies is dependent upon the existence of appropriate legal and economic frameworks, and these are not necessarily present in all former communist countries in CEE.

In some of the region's countries, a dozen years after communism collapsed, the relationship between 'the centre' and subnational government is still often inherently conflictual, while the notion of the neutral state seems not yet credible. Examples include several regional geographically areas remote from the EU, including Russia and the countries of Central Asia. They still have highly centralized and authoritarian models of government without coherent local-level governing structures, while there are common problems of nation-building still unresolved. Various solutions to this problem have been suggested, including decentralization or federalism. Here, the aspiration is that 'institutional structuring may provide for managing, though not necessarily resolving, possible difficulties arising from nation-building, where the sequence and timing of such decisions can well matter'. The purpose of decentralization or federalism is to devolve power from the centre and to make regional and local autonomy stronger. This theoretically makes it possible to deal with the coexistence of multiple nationalities within one country. However, 'the inauguration of federalism cannot as such be regarded as the solution to the problem, for it is the operation of the decentralized framework that matters, particularly if this occurs in a manner conducive to political confidence-building' (Pridham 2000: 261–2). This statement would prove equally valid if applied to a study of African, Asian or Latin American transitional democracies.

Some of the same kinds of difficulties experienced trying to develop subnational governmental structures in the post-communist states of CEE are also found among Latin America's post-military regimes. In the latter region there is a deeply rooted tradition of centralized personal power that, still politically influential despite democratization, can undermine attempts to increase both the standing of elected local officials as well as the development of decentralized political institutions. For example, Mexico is a federal and substantially democratic state at the national level. However at the subnational level the political legacy of centralized control by the former ruling party, the Institutional Revolutionary Party (PRI), coupled with traditional dominance of large-scale rural landowners, combine to thwart the development of a truly federal system. In Brazil, where federal structures have more plausibility, some states have overspent so considerably that it has posed serious problems for the national government in trying to maintain its credibility with the international financial community. In sum,

Dominguez and Giraldo (1996: 27) suggest that there are difficult political and economic questions to resolve about the desirability of decentralization in contemporary Latin America. While they accept that decentralization of political power can theoretically increase the political involvement of ordinary citizens and make their rulers more accountable, they contend that this position has not yet been reached in the region. Instead, they suggest, 'decentralization can . . . undermine democratization by reinforcing the power of local élites, their practices of clientelism and the power of their military or paramilitary allies'. Economically, 'subnational governments can undermine the efforts of national governments to carry out economic reforms'.

Legislatures

It is clear that democratic transitions offer opportunities for legislatures to assert themselves. Because parliaments encapsulate the notion of citizen representation, it is plausible to expect that new democracies will have legislatures with more prominence than those under the former authoritarian regime. There is generally agreement in the literature that this is indeed the case. On the other hand, there is also much agreement that legislatures in transitional democracies are still in most cases both weaker and less institutionalized than counterparts in most established democracies. This is for several reasons. First, rulers in transitional democracies are generally not convinced that legislatures should enjoy full investigative rights. This implies that the issue of executive scrutiny is a strongly contested function which most assemblies are still struggling to develop. Second, most members of post-authoritarian national legislatures are relative novices without much in the way of relevant political experience. In some cases, in addition, term limits apply, as in many Latin American countries. In sum, limited powers, inadequate resources and lack of experience combine to restrict the authority of parliament in nearly all transitional democracies. As a result, the post-authoritarian revitalization of legislatures in transitional democracies is a task that is likely to take a considerable time.

It is not necessarily the case, however, that legislatures had to wait for the demise of authoritarian rule before asserting themselves. In some cases, the experience gained unquestionably helped legislatures to be more authoritative following democratic transition. For example, prior to the disintegration of communist rule, parliaments in both Poland and Hungary were already raising grievances and modestly influencing policy-making. In addition, for another common reason, post-communist legislatures may be in a favourable position following the demise of authoritarian rule modestly to influence both legislation and policy. The reason for this is linked to a point made earlier. That is, in many transitional democracies, both political parties and interest groups remain weak and underdeveloped. This allows legislators much autonomy in carrying out their work. On the other hand, the potential to take on often assertive and confident executives is often only partly realized, due to a combination of high turnover of legislators, their often limited calibre, a lack of societal or state support and weak internal procedures. The weaknesses that many post-communist parliaments manifest has led to a sharp drop in many cases in popular regard, once the immediate crisis of the transition came to an end. In Russia, for example, parliament's standing remains inherently uncertain (Light 2000: 94–7). Lack of popular regard is matched in some cases by presidential disdain. For example, during his time in power President Boris Yeltsin often disregarded Russia's parliament (the Duma), to the point of not allowing it 'the funds needed to buy paper on which to print its own laws' (Hague and Harrop 2001: 235).

Turning to Latin America and Africa, the position of many legislatures has become somewhat strengthened following the demise of authoritarian rule. However, parliaments in both regions have typically failed to attain more than marginal status, while institutionalization often remains limited. This outcome reflects the normal tradition of 'strong', individual political leadership, where the ruler ensures that the legislature is in a peripheral position in order to enhance his or her own power. To ensure that this is the case, some rulers go so far as to deny legislators even the most basic of facilities. The ability of legislatures to assert themselves is not aided by the fact that legislators may well be of low calibre, a factor underlined by extant political cultures and in many cases rapid turnover of representatives. In addition, many parliamentarians seem to be less concerned with shaping policy than with acquiring patronage for themselves and/or the territory they represent. As Hague and Harrop (2001: 234) note, despite the shift from authoritarian to democratically elected governments, a realistic short-term goal for legislatures in many transitional democracies is not to increase their own power but instead to find effective means to restrain leaders who, in many cases, seek to exercise power without being undermined by elected representatives.

Political executive

Post-authoritarian democracies established since the mid-1970s are anything but uniform when it comes to choice of executive structure. However, more than 20 transitional democracies in Latin America have adopted presidential systems following the end of military rule in the 1980s, in spite of some serious academic reservations about their desirability. We can account for the region's continuing preference for presidential government by pointing to the propensity of many Latin American countries for social instability and political violence. Under such circumstances, where there is both lack of strong political authority and widespread tradition of 'strong', individualistic rule, the presidential option is considered a safer choice than the parliamentary alternative. This is despite the fact that some presidents make policy by decree without consulting the legislature, relevant interest groups or political parties.

What might be done to control excesses of presidential power? Observers have noted the difficulties in trying fundamentally to reform one of the region's most enduring political institutions: the 'strong' president. Nohlen (1992) argues that the presidential tradition in most Latin American countries is simply too strongly anchored to be abandoned and, as a consequence, the only realistic course of reform is to stick with the existing system, attempting to reform it via pressure from political and civil society. But not all regional countries have the requisite structural characteristics to support democratic political mechanisms. Consequently, it may be unrealistic to put too much emphasis on the independent role of political institutions – as there is no clear indication that newly democratized institutions would be able to overcome traditionally undemocratic ways of 'doing' politics. Regional political systems still generally lack what many would see as the essence of democratic politics: adaptability, complexity, autonomy and coherence; in short, the competitive pluralism capable of constraining government power through peaceful means. It is doubtful to what extent the latest batch of elected Latin American presidents accepts the political wisdom of democratizing their polities – if for no other reason than that it might well result in an unacceptable loss of personal power. In a comment about Peru, but which could be applied to most contemporary Latin American countries, de Soto and Orsini (quoted in Wiarda and Kline 1996: 59) aver that 'the only element of democracy in Peru today is the electoral process, which gives Peruvians the privilege of choosing a dictator every five years'. In sum, Latin America's *nouveau présidentialisme*, while ostensibly utilizing democratic structures and processes, often in practice leads to concentration of power in the figure of the chief executive. On the other hand, we should note recent regional challenges to what was perceived as inappropriate or excessive use of presidential power. Brazil's Congress and courts removed an elected president, Fernando Collor de Mello, from office for corruption in the early 1990s. But the fact that Brazilians then voted to continue a strongly presidential form of government – over other suggested models – suggests that it was primarily Collor himself, not the institution of the 'strong' president per se, which many Brazilians saw as the problem.

The post-communist states of CEE have done things differently, adopting either parliamentary or in some cases semi-presidential systems, as in Poland, Russia and Slovakia, in attempts to contain and not to concentrate political power (Calvert 2002: 62). Constitution makers were often anxious to try to reflect extant social and political divisions within the national legislature, and to create a balance within the executive between president and prime minister. The region's political history and tradition of communism was also an important factor: the primary task was to seek to control government, to prevent rulers from acquiring excessive power. Consequently, many regional countries adopted forms of government combining a president with a prime minister accountable to parliament. Over time, in cases where the post-communist government has stabilized, then the parliamentary dimension has often gained ground – while the power of the president has declined. Examples include the Czech Republic, Hungary and Slovakia (Hague and Harrop 2001: 251–3).

It will be apparent by now that the relative effectiveness of presidential and parliamentary forms of government is central to the debate about democratic consolidation and how to achieve it. While Mainwaring (1999) argues that presidentialism may offer advantages for democratic consolidation, Przeworski et al. (1996) aver that representative institutions of the parliamentary type are often better for democratic continuity. In a multiparty regime, presidents very often find it helpful to have the support of an interparty coalition; however, many presidents find that such coalitions are usually neither durable nor long lasting. Under such circumstances, it is very important that a polity has strong political institutions. When a legislature is controlled by forces hostile to the president, the result is often an impasse, a situation made worse if the legislature is filled with numerous parties. The result is executive-legislative deadlock. According to Stepan and Skach (1993: 22), a parliamentary system is more likely to lead to an institutional framework conducive to democratic consolidation. Why should this be the case? The answer is because in parliamentary systems, the government is more likely to have a legislative majority to facilitate the enactment of their programme.

A country with representative, parliamentary-type institutions is often thought to have a better chance of democratic consolidation than those with unrepresentative pre-

sidential systems. This is partly because presidentialism is often associated with legislative paralyses, for example, when a legislature, controlled by a majority hostile to the
president, is, however, too divided among many parties to overcome presidential vetoes.
A second problem with presidentialism is that underused state institutions can become
both atrophied and corrupt. Third, the independence of courts is crucial – especially in
the absence of strong, stable party systems and legislatures willing and able to take on
the president and form a counterweight to his power. Lievesley (1999) notes that the
trend has been towards the growing marginalization of the courts in some Latin American countries. Some presidents, such as Alberto Fujimori in Peru and Hugo Chavez in
Venezuela, brazenly sought to override elected legislatures, courts, judges and other
institutions in their attempts to reform their polities (Philip 1999). Finally, Nagle and
Mahr (1999: 248) point out that support from the armed forces can help bolster the position of an elected president to the extent that he or she can be 'dependent on the good
will of the military to back even more concentration of power', encouraging them to act
as autocrats, 'via "state of siege" or "state of emergency" declarations'. For example, the
'anti-system', former military man Hugo Chavez won power via the ballot box in
Venezuela in the December 1998 election and, supported by the military, proceeded to
build his own personal power.

The bureaucracy

While there are many forms of non-democratic rule, what they tend to have in common
are over-powerful, unaccountable and corrupt bureaucracies. To overcome this legacy
is a difficult but essential task to undertake during the process of democratic consolidation. In effect, what needs to be accomplished is the pre-eminence of elected over
unelected bureaucratic authority. But how this might be accomplished is a difficult issue.
The main task is clear enough: to shift the bureaucracy from a customary highly political mode of operation towards a new professionalized model, where appointments are
based on merit and corruption is contained.

In transitional countries, there are always great difficulties in establishing efficient
public administrations. In post-communist countries, the problems are especially pronounced. This is because communism's demise was more than just the end of a particular political system; it was also the collapse of a hegemonic, highly extensive and
inherently politicized bureaucracy. Under such circumstances it was hardly surprising
that the end of the old regimes led throughout CEE to administrative disarray. Under
the circumstances of a sudden political vacuum, many bureaucrats found that they were
in a position either to influence the privatization of state assets and/or to make use of
the monopoly position of newly privatized companies for personal benefit. The consequence of this was that in many cases post-communist bureaucracies did not develop
the necessary ability to operate according to the constant application of formal regulations. Over time, however, some post-communist states, including the Czech Republic,
Hungary, Poland and Slovenia, have now made considerable progress in overcoming
these problems. Some others, for example, Bulgaria, have made much less progress
(Pridham 2000).

Conclusion

Transitional democracies are countries that undergo a transition from non-democratic rule yet fail emphatically to develop and embed consistently democratic successor regimes. This implies that there will be major impediments to the wholesale adoption of the institutions that characterize established democracies. Transitional democracies may have ruling regimes with hybrid characteristics, for example, mixing relatively 'free and fair' elections with forms of strong, centralized government. In short, the category 'transitional democracy' implies not a clear-cut, emphatic shift from authoritarianism, but a regime with both democratic and non-democratic attributes.

There are several explanations as to why this might be the case. On the one hand, leading political figures from the authoritarian regime may retain their hold on power; it is often difficult for such people to become bona fide democrats. On the other hand, a transition to democracy involves ending the modus operandi of authoritarianism, such as excessive governmental secrecy, suspicion of public political involvement, and a desire by the executive to be unconstrained by constitutional 'niceties'.

We saw in the Introduction that globalization is changing, in various ways, political arrangements and configurations within countries. It is often suggested that this amounts to an erosion of the nation-state's formerly 'hard' boundaries and a consequent – albeit a variable – diminution of states' ability to control their domestic environments and hence policy decisions. What does this imply for transitional democracies?

Transitional democracies have to contend with a range of cross-border actors in the circumstances dictated by globalization. In particular, many transitional democracies are seeking to join regional organizations, for example, post-communist European countries and Turkey want EU membership. In addition, many Latin American countries are interested in becoming members of a currently embryonic regional economic grouping, the Free Trade Area of the Americas. Further, Mexico has recently joined NAFTA. But if transitional democracies wish to join a regional grouping whose members are established democracies, then they will be required to adopt their political and economic characteristics. Other transitional democracies may be more interested in foreign aid than belonging to regional organizations. However, the result is likely to be the same: there is a requirement to mould their domestic political and economic arrangements to those preferred by external donors.

Finally, the impact of external actors on domestic political structures and processes in transitional democracies is likely to be variable. This is because transitional democracies have political systems characterized by variable political and institutional arrangements that may serve to reduce the potential of what I shall describe in chapter 5 as 'opportunity structures for participation'. This means that both domestic and external actors may have difficulty in influencing political outcomes unless the regime is in agreement with their aims.

3
Non-Democracies

Characteristics

According to Freedom House (FH), there were 47 'not free' countries (in our terminology, 'non-democracies') at the end of 2003, thirty years after the start of the third
wave of the democracy. This is just under a quarter of the total number of countries
(192). As table 3.1 indicates, non-democracies are particularly common in the Arab
countries of the Middle East and North Africa. Other regions – including, Asia Pacific,
Central and Eastern Europe, and Sub-Saharan Africa – also have significant percentages of such regimes.

To some extent, the category of non-democracy is a residual term, as it is primarily
what such countries *lack*, in terms of representative political institutions, that sets them
apart from both established and transitional democracies. Non-democracies are, by
definition, devoid of most conventional democratic credentials. This does not necessarily imply that non-democracies are politically unstable. Often, indeed, the main
achievement of their ruling regimes is to develop forms of political and social stability
that are intimately connected to their non-democratic systems of rule and control.

Two generic kinds of non-democratic government can be noted: authoritarian and
totalitarian rule. According to Bealey, the term 'authoritarian' relates to 'any form of
organization or attitude which claims to have the right to impose its values and
decisions on recipients who do not have the right or means of responding or reacting
freely'. Totalitarian rule, on the other hand, implies a situation where 'the state through
its instruments dominates society' (Bealey 1999: 21, 322). Thus, totalitarian government
implies strongly state-controlled political and social systems. Examples include communist governments, for example in China, the Soviet Union and Cuba. Authoritarian
rule implies that ruling regimes are, or aim to be, the unchallenged rulers, albeit without
the totality of control that signifies totalitarian states. Examples of authoritarian
governments include pre-2001 Mexico, Indonesia until 1998, and numerous African
countries, including Cameroon, Democratic Republic of Congo and Togo.

Governments and policy-making in non-democracies are sometimes characterized by
personalist, rather than institutional, forms of decision-making and control. Some non-
democracies – such as one-party states and some military governments – profess forms
of corporate rule, but even here power is typically in the hands of a single powerful
individual or a small group, who make all key policy decisions. This state of affairs is
underlined when a controlling leader – for example, in Zimbabwe, Libya or, until the
overthrow of Saddam Hussein in 2003, Iraq – may appear to be rather insensitive to
advice, as well as holding strong personal normative beliefs about the nature and direction of state policy. However, even in such personalistic regimes, there is rarely an

Table 3.1 Non-democracies by region, 2003

Region	Number of countries	Percentage of regional countries
Western Europe	0	0
Americas/Caribbean	2	6
Asia Pacific	10	26
Central and Eastern Europe/Former Soviet Union	7	26
Sub-Saharan Africa	17	35
Middle East and North Africa	11	61
Total	47	

Sources: Adapted from: 'Freedom in the World 2004. Table of Independent Countries Comparative Measures of Freedom' (available at <http://www.freedomhouse.org/research/freeworld/2004/table2004.pdf>), and 'Freedom in the World 2002. Liberty's Expansion in a Turbulent World' (available at <http//www.freedomhouse.org/research/survey2002.htm>).

absolute concentration of power, as such individualistic leaders will often seek the counsel of a tight-knit coterie of senior advisers. Competition among those seeking the ear of the leader can lead to intra-regime political factionalism. Sometimes this leads to various forms of political conflict, including attempts to neutralize political opposition, pressures for democratization, coups d'état and, in extreme cases, civil war.

In short, various forms of policy-making and power-wielding characterize non-democracies. First, the political executive – often dominated by a small, elite group – is typically the most important component of policy-making. Second, policy-making is subject to processes of bargaining and competition – so that the executive operates to some degree within constraints imposed by political actors outside the key circle. Third, non-democratic political system differences can seem less significant when we consider them in the light of other criteria of comparison.

In sum, non-democracies are characterized by some or all of the following factors:

- Power is in the hands of a powerful individual and/or a small elite group. One leader, faction or party rules, typically without institutionalized participation of groups from outside the elite group.
- Political systems deny a political voice to ordinary citizens and at least some sectional interests, other than perhaps via an infrequently expressed symbolic vote.
- The armed forces have significant political voice.
- Regime legitimacy is primarily measured in terms of economic success rather than democratic accountability or representativeness.

Categories of Non-Democratic Regime and their Chief Political Characteristics

In this section, I identify and briefly discuss the political characteristics of four generic types of 'non-democratic' regimes: communist governments, non-communist single-party states, 'personalist' governments (including autocratic monarchies), and military administrations.

Communist governments

Following the swift and wholesale demise of socialist totalitarian regimes in Central and Eastern Europe after 1989, five communist governments remain. They are found in China, Cuba, Laos, North Korea and Vietnam. Collectively, these countries are home to more than 1.3 billion people. All are characterized both by their lack of conventionally democratic structures and processes as well as by the pervasive power and presence of their various communist parties.

The main theoretical justification for this kind of totalitarian rule is that only the Communist Party ('The Party') has the capacity to organize the defence of the revolution against counter-revolutionary forces, plan and oversee expansion of the forces of production and supervise the reconstruction of society. The Party, as a result of its total control of the state, is the main vehicle used to build the framework for communism. Following the collapse of Eastern Europe's communist regimes, the remaining communist governments were to some degree affected by external factors. This was most clearly manifested by the influence of economic globalization, although in a few of the communist countries, including Cuba and, to a lesser extent, China, there were also often timorous calls for more and better human rights and environmental protection. The impact of economic globalization encouraged the governments of both China and Vietnam to allow capitalism to grow to previously unexpected heights, to the extent that many observers would agree that it is hard to argue that the classless society is still a primary goal of ruling regimes. It is clear, however, that this is not a form of capitalism over which the Party will easily relinquish control. Instead, in both countries the influence of capitalism is strongly regulated by their communist governments.

Non-communist single-party regimes

Examples of this kind of non-democratic regime were to be found, until 2001, in Mexico and, until 1998, in Indonesia. Numerous African countries also fell into this category until the early 1990s, including Cameroon, Zaire (now Democratic Republic of Congo) and Togo. While communist governments typically achieved power as a result of revolutionary change, non-communist single-party regimes normally came to power either by the ballot box or following a military coup d'état. The establishment of such regimes in numerous countries in Africa and Asia in the 1950s and 1960s followed a sustained period of decolonization. At that time, many observers expected that indigenous political parties would increasingly come to resemble those of the West, as part of a wider process of political modernization. Featuring the same forms and functions, parties were expected to become integral parts of multiparty systems that would offer an increasingly educated and discerning public both organized electoral choice and channels of accountability. What actually happened in many cases, however, was something quite different and unexpected: soon after independence, numerous multiparty systems throughout Africa and Asia gave way to single-party regimes. Between 1958 and 1973, twelve African countries abandoned multipartyism, mostly for single-party rule (Doig 1999: 23). Some observers saw this as a broadly progressive development, because such single-party governments were often judged to be the only 'modern' political organizations to be found among Africa's predominantly traditional societies, often characterized by religious and ethnic rivalry and competition. In this context, single-party regimes were seen as 'agents of national integration in states whose new and often arbitrarily imposed boundaries commanded less loyalty than "primordial" ties of language, religion or locality' (Randall 1988: 2).

Single-party regimes are not democratic in the sense of allowing citizens the periodic right to select their government via the ballot box. Instead, their legitimacy is strongly rooted in their claimed ability to preside over satisfactory rates of economic development, while building national integrity to weld together often disparate peoples into a nation-state. In the 1960s and in some cases the 1970s, both tasks seemed within the grasp of some single-party regimes. However, over time it became clear that the integrative and developmental abilities of most such regimes were actually, at best, modest. Consequently, popular demands for democracy and economic reforms surfaced in many regimes in the 1980s and 1990s. Observers saw regime failure to preside over acceptable levels of economic development or to engineer national integrity as the key reasons why.

Personalistic regimes and autocratic monarchies

Many examples of personalistic regimes and autocratic monarchies are found in the Middle East and North Africa. Focusing on the former category, Kamrava (1998) identifies a genus of government that he calls 'sultanistic' states, which he divides further into 'oil monarchies' and 'civil myth' regimes. Examples of oil monarchies include Bahrain, Kuwait, Oman, Qatar, Saudi Arabia and the United Arab Emirates. Typically unchallenged by other substantive political institutions, such regimes are led by rulers who enjoy large amounts of personal power. Such countries also characteristically have substantial oil wealth and relatively small populations, while their governments have often been little challenged by popular demands for greater political participation and accountability in recent years. Only one such country, Kuwait, experienced recent political liberalization, in part a result of events associated with the first Gulf War of 1990–1.

Civil myth regimes have rulers whose power is derived from their personal religious and/or secular attributes. Examples include the governments of Jordan and Morocco. Both countries lack large oil reserves and the associated wealth it can bring and, partly as a result, each has recently experienced economic problems. Politically, they were also affected by the global trend towards democracy associated with the third wave of democracy and the demise of the Soviet Union. Both countries, especially Jordan, have recently seen tentative trends towards political liberalization.

In both kinds of regime, powerful political leaders wield a great deal of personal power, sometimes unchallenged by other political institutions. The main justification for such rule is that it ensures political stability, while enhancing chances of economic development. However, under such regimes, the 'luxury' of plural political parties and free and fair elections are rarely allowed. Such governments argue that this is because necessary resources and energy needed to contest elections and to fight associated political battles detract fundamentally from the state development efforts. In sum, under such regimes, many political rights and civil liberties are routinely denied, including in most cases, freedom of expression, assembly and organization.

Military regimes

Military government is rule by the armed forces, usually following a successful coup d'état. Until recent shifts to democracy, such regimes were commonly found in various regions, notably Latin America, Asia and Africa. However, there are various forms of military government. Some are dominated by a charismatic figure, usually a middle-ranking or senior military officer, and described as 'military dictatorships'. Others are led by small groups of military personnel and labelled 'juntas'. However, while the make-up of military regimes can vary considerably, they all have a dislike or distrust of representative democracy, while many are adept at suppressing political rights and civil liberties. While military personnel nearly always claim to be temporarily in power – in order to rid the country of the corruption generated by civilian rule and to put 'the ship of state back on an even keel' – they often prove reluctant to leave office and, in some cases, can stay for years. In recent years, as a consequence of democratization in Latin America, Africa and Asia, the number of military-led regimes has declined. However, this does not necessarily imply that the political power of the military has necessarily fallen away. In fact, in many countries it remains great, to the extent that military support is often seen as fundamental to a regime's survival, even if it is elected.

Political Institutions Linking State and Society

In this section of the chapter, we look at political institutions that link governments and voters in non-democracies: (i) elections and electoral systems, (ii) civil society and inter-est groups, (iii) political society and party systems and (iv) constitutions and the legal framework. After that, in the final section of the chapter, we examine key structures of government: (i) subnational government, (ii) legislatures, (iii) political executive and (iv) the bureaucracy. Having examined these structures and processes we will be in a position later, in chapter 5, to assess the political influence of different kinds of external actor in such regimes.

Elections and electoral systems

The idea of democracy has become so closely identified with elections that we are in danger of forgetting that the modern history of representative elections is a tale of authoritarian manipulations as much as it is a saga of democratic triumphs. Historically, in other words, elections have been an instrument of authoritarian control as well as a means of democratic governance: Arab countries, sub-Saharan Africa, the Caucasus and Central Asia are all homes to electoral authoritarianism (EA). The percentage of countries hosting EA regimes runs as high as 87.5 per cent in Central Asia, 54.2 per cent in sub-Saharan Africa, and 52.2 per cent in North Africa and the Middle East. Sub-Saharan

Africa alone accounts for nearly half (44.8 per cent) of all EA regimes (Schedler 2002: 48).

In democratic systems, 'an election is an act of choosing someone as a representative. It is therefore an essential part of representative democracy' (Bealey 1999: 113). Elections in such democracies are often characterized as being both 'genuinely competitive' and 'free and fair'. That is, as Bealey (1999: 335) notes, 'to vote is to express support for a policy or person. Usually it involves choice.' However, under communist and single-party non-communist regimes it was usual for choices of candidate to be limited to those approved by the ruling party. Consequently, citizens were able to vote for or against the party candidate. Usually, it was dangerous to pursue the latter course of action. This implies that such elections are not competitive, a point underlined by Schedler in the quotation above. Put another way, 'in authoritarian systems, elections are often corrupt affairs, with the winner known in advance and electoral malpractice playing its part in delivering the desired result' (Hague and Harrop 2001: 144). On the other hand, even the most extreme autocrat is usually loath to abolish elections completely. This is partly due to the influence of important external agents. Often under pressure from a variety of foreign state and non-state actors, many authoritarian governments like to give at least the illusion of choice of those in power to their citizens. It should be noted, however, that voters are denied real freedom via the ballot box to select their rulers. This enables such governments to give the illusion of choice – while at the same time enabling them to control electoral outcomes.

What are the mechanisms of these kinds of election? How do they enable non-democratic regimes to retain themselves in power? We can note three distinct forms. First, there are elections controlled by a dominant party or leader. Second, there are 'acclamatory' elections and, third, 'candidate choice' elections. Let us look at each type briefly. Mexico provides a good example of the first kind. The Institutional Revolutionary Party (PRI) first achieved power in 1929, following a civil war, and did not lose it until 2000, more than 70 years later. The party's hold on power was facilitated by Mexico's modernization, which, based on strong economic growth rooted in expanding oil exports, allowed the party to preside over increases in living standards for most ordinary people. While for years this served to mute political challenges, the PRI's ability to deliver relatively broad-based development gradually waned, resulting in the election of an opposition candidate, Vicente Fox, as president in 2000. For seven decades prior to this, however, the PRI-dominated government had moulded the country's political arrangements, including its electoral system. Mexico's single-party system was traditionally less repressive than many of the region's military dictatorships, as it was characterized by a more inclusionary and pragmatic political system than found in many other contemporary single-party regimes, such as that of the Soviet Union (Ortíz 2000). While there was certainly widespread electoral fraud, the PRI also enjoyed a substantial level of popular support. Over time, however, the PRI's hold on power weakened, and poorly restrained paramilitary groups and unprosecuted human rights abuses by the army and the police became common. We can see that the ability of the PRI to dominate elections in Mexico for a long period of time was due both to its hegemony over society, as well as an entrenched belief among many ordinary people that the PRI deserved to retain its dominance.

According to Hague and Harrop (2001: 1454), acclamatory elections, as practised in various communist countries, including Cuba and the Soviet Union, are the 'purest form

of non-competitive elections'. Under this electoral regime there is no choice of candidates. Instead, the state-sanctioned candidates are simply presented to the voters for
their ritualistic approval. Those citizens who want to approve the official candidate –
understandably a huge majority – deposit their voting slip into the ballot box in front
of state officials; those who do not want to do so must proceed to another, separate area
where they can cross out the name of the official candidate. While such elections came
to an end in the Soviet Union following the demise of the communist government in
the early 1990s, the same form continues in contemporary Cuba.

Candidate-choice elections are the third kind of non-competitive election. They were
characteristic both of communist Eastern Europe in the 1970s and 1980s, as well as
contemporary China at local level. In contrast to acclamatory elections, this kind of
election allows a choice of candidates. However, as all candidates necessarily have to
be supported by the communist party, the degree of ideological choice is very limited.
During the 1980s, as communist rule in Eastern Europe began to crumble, such elections became a focal point for opposition. This was the case in Poland, where in 1989
Solidarity was able to field candidates in the elections in one-third of the seats, and proceeded to win every one. As a result, it was clear that the writing was on the wall for
the communist government. In China, the government has allowed candidate-choice
elections at the local level since 1979. It is a useful device for the communist party to
ensure that local candidates retain the confidence of their neighbourhoods, while in no
way threatening the overall dominance of the Party.

Civil society and interest groups

We can note three generic categories of civil society that broadly correspond to the
nature of the political system. There are:

- *weak civil societies* (typically found in non-democratic countries);
- *maturing civil societies* (often found in transitional democracies);
- *strong civil societies* (typically found in established democracies).

The power and influence of interest groups in non-democracies can be contrasted to
the comparatively influential position of civil society in most established democracies
and some transitional democracies. Typically, non-democratic countries have weak
and/or fragmented civil societies, ineffective counterweights to state power. Rulers of
non-democracies nearly always regard strong civil society organizations as a potential
threat to their positions. Consequently, they aim to deal with them in one of two ways:
repress them or co-opt them into the state power structure.

The position of non-party interest groups under communist states is at best marginal.
Indeed, in some, such as North Korea, it is doubtful whether they exist at all. However,
in some of the communist countries of Eastern Europe, notably Poland and Hungary,
they grew from marginality to be influential during the 1980s, contributing significantly
in some cases to the fall from power of regional communist regimes at the start of the
1990s. The lack of influence of independent civil society organizations was a deliberate
result of communist ideological norms, as the Party was often unable to countenance
alternative sources of interest articulation beyond itself. However, some sectional

groups, such as the military and heavy industry, did carry political and/or economic weight, with the latter significant as economies matured and decisions became more technical.

During the 1980s, independent sectional interests began to be openly expressed, particularly in Poland, Hungary and Yugoslavia, in part due to the encouragement of external actors (Pridham 2000: 222). The best example comes from Poland, where the Solidarity trade union became a focal point at this time for the organization of civil society and ultimately became a significant factor in the demise of the country's communist government a few years later. More generally, use of coercion and terror also declined at this time in many Eastern European communist states, while conflicts over policy issues became more visible. Note however that the increased significance of civil society organizations in former communist countries of Eastern Europe contrasts with the contemporary situation in China where, despite recent economic reforms, the 'Western notion of an "interest group" still carries little meaning' (Hague and Harrop 2001: 164).

We turn now to the characteristics of civil societies in the context of other forms of non-democratic government – non-communist single-party, personalistic and military regimes. Such governments have been common in Africa and the Middle East. A former president of the World Bank, Robert McNamara, argues that despite democratization in many African countries, there is a common problem of civil society that adds to the general problems of governance. These 'are . . . far more severe than those of other regions', and include a lack of transparency and accountability in government operations (quoted in Harsch 1996: 24). This is a reference to the fact that in many regional countries civil society is underdeveloped, with inadequate popular participation. As Villalón (1995: 24) notes, social groups in Africa typically fail 'to organize in such a way as to defend and promote their interests'. As a result, civil society lacks the capacity to 'counter the state's hegemonic drives'.

Like African governments, many Middle Eastern states have also long been adept at buying off, co-opting or, if necessary, crushing expressions of discontent funnelled through civil society. Bromley (1994: 166) not only links this power to the region's mostly weak and divided civil societies, but also posits that this situation is very likely to be an important problem in the 'future process of democratization'. Said (1996) asks rhetorically why 'real' – that is, effective – civil societies are absent in the Arab societies of the Middle East. His answer is that civil societies are frail for reasons similar to those found in Africa: ruling regimes are often, or at least give the appearance of being, strong; societies are typically fragmented by various – ethnic, tribal and/or religious – divisions.

The lesson seems to be in relation to civil society that, in some cases, even entrenched authoritarian or totalitarian governments can be ousted as a result of sustained societal pressures. However, there is only likely to be *democratic* progress when there is consistent pressure from 'below', focused in and through a strong civil society, perhaps aided by external encouragement (Rueschemyer et al. 1992; Haynes 1997, 2001a; Törnquist 1999). Under such circumstances, civil society organizations do not only help push the limits of newly created political space. When capable of linking up with representative political parties at home and with allies abroad they can be pivotal in helping to deliver democratic reforms. In such cases, pressure could be instrumental in encouraging authoritarian governments in various parts of the world to announce and implement programmes of democratic reform. They would be encouraged to articulate political reform agendas and ultimately to allow relatively free and fair multiparty elections. In sum, in recent years, nearly all non-democratic regimes have faced pressures to introduce substantive political reforms, often due to a combination of internal and external pressures. Not least, international pressures for democratization have increased, manifested in part by the presence of foreign election observers on hand. Their purpose is to give expert opinions about the democratic quality of elections. Pressure by external economic actors, such as the World Bank and the International Monetary Fund, has also been applied to reduce the public sector in many countries. This has served to reduce 'the crucial supply of patronage by which dominant parties have bought support' (Hague and Harrop 2001: 179).

We have already seen in earlier chapters that both to establish and to embed democracy require a shift from a situation where power is exercised by and for a numerically small elite to one where it is exercised for the good of the many. We have also noted that the attainment of a democratic political environment can be facilitated by *sustained* pressure on incumbent non-democratic regimes from both civil and political society, perhaps augmented by external encouragement. But when both civil and political society are fragmented, this situation plays into the hands of non-democratic governments. Under such regimes, elitist power monopolies typically cluster at the apex to form the political superstructure. Organski (1965) long ago identified such power monopolies, what he called the 'syncratic alliance'. This is a non-democratic concord that unites traditional agrarian interests with urban-based elites, with the effect of focusing power in their hands. The two sets of interests strike a bargain: powerful urban-based actors agree not to disturb significantly the often semi-feudal conditions of the countryside, in exchange for obtaining the political support of agrarian interests.

Prior to democratization, in both Latin America and parts of Asia, large landowners traditionally represented the rural side of the power coalition. In India, successive post-colonial governments, despite being legitimated through the ballot box for over half a century (apart from the State of Emergency, 1975–7), have failed to break with powerful rural allies. Although rural-based powerful families were often formally shorn of traditional powers after independence in 1947, many still managed to maintain their long-standing powerful position via a very successful alternative: the elected route to power. Although Organski's description may be less relevant to Africa, it seems clear that support from those with wealth and power was, and is, more crucial to political decision-makers than support from other classes. Clapham (1988: 49) notes that personalist dictatorships have been in power for long periods in many African countries. This is a type of authority that 'corresponds to the normal forms of social organization in [Africa's] pre-colonial societies'. In short, while precise bases of power differ, elite control in non-democracies meant that civil society remained both underdeveloped and politically insignificant, characterized by a lack of independent articulation of group interests.

Much of the relevant literature contends that civil societies that struggled against one-party and military dictatorships had the potential to weaken the cultural foundations of authoritarianism – that is, to serve as a genuine base for democracy. What was needed, it was suggested, was the creation and embedding of a new democratic consensus that, while reducing political instability, must also erect and sustain robust electoral and institutional forms that enable democratic governments to work. If this were to happen, democratically elected regimes would not be at the mercy of self-interested elite politicians. But for this to come to pass, there has be a learning process, a development explicit to Linz and Stepan's (1996) conception of democratic consolidation: the destructive confrontations of the past must not be repeated by the new generation of politicians seeking power. Instead, they must seek to deepen and extend democracy to previously excluded classes and groups.

Political society and party systems

Like civil societies, political parties – other than ruling parties – are generally less significant under authoritarian and totalitarian regimes, compared to democracies. In some cases – for example, certain military governments – political parties may be dispensed with completely. The claim is that parties are not needed in a country singularly united behind its leader. In another arrangement, the personalistic ruler develops a system of individual rule behind the façade of a one-party state. Under communist regimes, the Party is a pivotal political instrument through which government seeks to achieve total control over society. In this section, we briefly examine parties in, first, one-party state arrangements and, second, military regimes and communist rule.

Prior to 2001, when it was ousted from power, Mexico's Revolutionary Party (PRI) had enjoyed decades of virtually unchallenged power. Its rule came to an end as a result of sustained pressure to democratize from both domestic and external sources, respectively civil society and hitherto weak opposition political parties and foreign actors, especially the government of the United States. For years before then, however, the structural characteristics of Mexico's authoritarian political culture were highly conducive to single-party rule. The PRI managed to instal itself as a dominant societal actor to such an extent that it is hard to overestimate its political influence. It was a cradle-to-the-grave party, with control over everything from schools to health care, and broadcasting to real estate. But this came with a political price: under PRI rule, Mexico's post-revolutionary political culture was moulded by the characteristics of the powerful, centralized state and party system, with correspondingly underdeveloped civil and political rights for the mass of ordinary people. Latinobarometer surveys from the 1990s and early 2000s (<http://www.latinobarometro.org/index.htm>) have consistently shown that only around 5 per cent of Mexicans have 'much confidence' in several key state institutions, such as the police and judiciary, the lowest figures in the eight regional countries surveyed (Turner and Martz 1997).[1] For many poor Mexicans the rule of law in relation to basic individual rights deteriorated even further towards the end of PRI rule – to the point that even minimal socio-economic rights did not exist for millions of people. Under such circumstances, support for the PRI ebbed away until its candidate heavily lost the presidential election of December 2000 to the main challenger, Vicente Fox.

[1] 'Latinobarímetro is an annual public opinion survey of approximately 19,000 interviews in 18 countries in Latin America representing more than 400 million inhabitants. The study is produced by Latinobarímetro Corporation, a non profit NGO based in Santiago Chile, the only organization responsible for data production and publication. It surveys development of democracies, economies and societies applying attitudinal, opinion, and behavioral indicators. Data is used by social and political actors, international organizations, governments and mass media. The executive director is Marta Lagos' (<http://www.latinobarometro.org/index.htm>).

Single-party rule has long been common in many Middle Eastern and North African countries, including Algeria, Egypt, Iraq, Sudan, Syria and Tunisia. Its claimed justification is that it is the best, most efficient system available both to direct a planned economy and to supervise and preside over countrywide systems of mobilization and control. Single-party regimes were created after colonial rule either by the national liberation organization that led the struggle for independence or later following a coup d'état – often called a 'revolution' – led by military personnel. Single-party regimes were established in about a third of Middle Eastern countries. Such parties tended to call themselves 'socialist', yet what often seemed most important was the altogether more prosaic goal of grabbing as much political and economic power as possible. Some Middle Eastern governments, however, have banned political parties altogether, preferring to rule through the auspices of an individual. In Kuwait, for example, political parties were banned in the 1960s and are still officially illegal. However, bowing to pressure from a variety of sources, the country's ruler, the emir, now allows five distinct political 'tendencies' to operate, with ideological orientations ranging from the secular left to radical Islam.

The position of parties under military governments is very often one of institutional and political subservience. For example, Pakistan, a country that has experienced several long periods of military rule since it was founded in 1947, has failed to develop a viable party system. Political parties were banned in the late 1950s and, in the often brief periods that followed when they were allowed to function, were heavily controlled by the state. Following a brief period of freedom for parties in the 1970s and first half of 1980s, the military dictator, General Zia, banned them again, claiming that the very concept of pluralistic parties was 'non-Islamic'. When they were allowed to operate, parties were essentially sectional in character, largely ineffectual at mobilizing citizens and prone to enter – and quickly leave – unstable multiparty alignments.

Under communist rule, only one party is allowed to function: the Communist Party. The reasoning behind this rule is simple: it is justified by Lenin's idea of the 'vanguard party', whereby only the Communist Party could represent the interests of the working class. Underpinned by this understanding, after the revolution of 1917 the Party sought to put into practice its vision of a fundamental transformation of society. According to the communist model, the Party's control, significantly underpinned by the assistance of the secret police, was exerted through a variety of means. It acted as a watchdog over society, vetted appointments to all positions of responsibility, controlled the media and carried out agitation and propaganda activities (Hague and Harrop 2001: 179). Communist parties were strongly top-down organizations that facilitated dominance of the centre. In contemporary China, the small group of senior communists who make up the Standing Committee of the Chinese Communist Party are enormously powerful figures who significantly control the country's political direction, while allowing China's economy to be influenced increasingly by 'market forces'.

Constitutions and the legal framework

While constitutions may well exist under non-democratic regimes, they tend to be weak documents, often flouted or ignored by those in power. This is because of the authoritarian characteristics of such states, where the kinds of restraints on rule that constitutions set out to identify are seldom recognized. This point can be illustrated by turning to legal frameworks under authoritarian regimes. We have already noted that the viability of democratic systems can be judged to a considerable degree by the independence of the courts. Under authoritarian regimes, however, rulers typically keep the judiciary on a tight leash, particularly when there are important cases with political overtones to judge. This underlines how under authoritarian regimes political rule is not demonstrably underpinned by the legal guarantees and extensive protections for individual and group freedoms, secured by and through the workings of an independent, impartial judiciary, which characterize democratic rule. Instead, authoritarian rulers may seek to marginalize judges and courts – if they are not compliant to their wishes – by sometimes brazenly seeking to override their decisions. This general pattern of judicial subordination to authoritarian executives is often particularly marked under military rule, for example during the 1970s and 1980s in Argentina and Chile (Hague and Harrop 2001: 195).

Communist states have a very different perspective on the role of constitutions and the judiciary compared to Western-style democracies. This is explained by the fact that communist ideology unambiguously rejects the Western model of constitutional rule, underpinned by a stress on limited government, individual rights and private property. In contrast, under communist rule, ruling regimes are party-led not legally constrained. This point is emphasized in communist constitutions, where the vanguard role of the Party is highlighted. In China, after the triumph of the 1949 communist revolution, 'legal perspectives were initially dismissed as reflecting "bourgeois thinking" ' (Hague and Harrop 2001: 196). Now, however, the country's constitution explicitly grants rights to all, although this is tempered by the declaration that freedoms are conditional upon supporting socialist principles, including the dictatorship of the proletariat.

Under communist rule, judicial independence is also regarded differently from how it is in Western democratic models. Judges must contribute to building socialism, principally by protecting the Party's position. However, in Eastern Europe, things were beginning to change in this regard prior to the revolutions of 1989, as some judges, encouraged by the gradual relinquishing of communist hold on power, began to act more independently. In China, there has been a renewed focus on the status of laws following the Cultural Revolution of the 1960s and early 1970s. The country passed its first criminal laws in 1979. Since then, especially in the context of what might be described as a form of capitalist development in the country, the rights of individuals are protected – as long as the dominance of the Party is not threatened.

Structures of Government

Subnational government

Under both authoritarian and totalitarian rule there is a fundamental difference between local government and local power. Local government exists but its authority is typically weak and inconsequential. This is because power under such rule emphatically comes from the top down and, consequently, bottom-up bodies of local representation are intrinsically inferior. The result is that local government often functions merely as a local administration, a local expression of the power of the centre, and does not manage to have a role as a manifestation of local autonomy. When national power is exercised through the military or by a ruling single party, it is often the case that their institutions normally create a parallel presence away from the capital city. The intention is that the authority of such institutions will supersede that of local government officials. A good example comes from Ghana, a country under military rule in the 1980s and 1990s. Claimed attempts to decentralize political power were actually little more than a cosmetic attempt to give the illusion of 'passing power to the people' with none of the expected substance that such a policy would imply (Haynes 2003b).

However, it would be erroneous to conclude that authoritarian regimes are highly centralized in a conventional institutional sense. Instead, state leaders typically seek comprehensive penetration of society whereby control is sought over lesser political actors and groups. To achieve this aim, central rulers often depend upon networks of allies to help them sustain themselves in power. Both central and local power-holders are linked together by patronage. In effect, the national ruler procures the support of local big men by financial means. These local notables sequentially maintain their positions by encouraging the same kind of clientelistic relationships with their own supporters. Thus it is patronage, rather than representative institutions, that connect the centre to the periphery. The implication is that central–local relations are often both more personal and less structured than the institutional relationships that characterize established democracies. Local 'big men' rule by virtue of their personal relationship with the national leader and his close allies.

The nature and characteristics of subnational rule under communist regimes reflect the top-down arrangement of political power. As a result, lower-level authorities are weak, and local government is merely a subordinate subdivision of the centre. Some communist regimes, notably that of the Soviet Union, managed to achieve an impressive degree of political centralization. While the country was supposedly a 'Union of Soviet Socialist Republics', the idea of federation that this idea represented was underdeveloped. Moscow retained its position as the centre of power and the constituent parts of the federation were unable to act independently. However, there was a degree of centralization introduced from the 1960s, a policy linked to the regime's concern with encouraging national cultural diversity. After communist rule, the legacy of this policy is that many of the USSR's independent republics became new countries, while those that did not manage it – such as Chechnya – have continued aggressively to try to achieve self-government.

Legislatures

We have already noted that under democratic regimes legislatures are representations of popular political involvement. Under authoritarian regimes, their significance is limited precisely because their representative purpose is diminished. However, few non-democratic rulers do away with assemblies completely. Around 90 per cent of all independent states have them in one form or another, and only five countries – all 'traditional dynastic states in the Arabian Gulf' (Hague and Harrop 2001: 233) – have never had assemblies. Typically, under authoritarian regimes parliaments lack autonomous substance, often functioning instead as mere 'shadow institutions'. Their sessions are typically characterized by short duration and a lack of incisive debate. This is because some or all of their members are appointed by the ruling regime and, as a result, are certainly not expected to ask the government awkward questions or seek contentious information. Moreover, the policy-making role of such parliaments is usually marginal. But this does not necessarily imply that those who sit in such legislatures simply do nothing. Instead, what they might do is to bring forward complaints, pursue 'constituency interests and sometimes [line] their own pockets – all of which are regarded as non-threatening activities by the real rulers. The real issues of national politics are left untouched' (Hague and Harrop 2001: 233).

In sum, there are three main reasons why assemblies exist under authoritarian rule. First, even the most subservient of assemblies can offer at least a cosmetic legitimacy to an authoritarian regime. This suggests that even non-democratic rulers prize the show of apparent public consent – however bogus it really is – that even the most compliant legislature can impart. Second, we should not underestimate the importance of bringing to the fore citizens' grievances and the ability to petition for local interests. This supplies at least a measure of interaction between the political centre and the rest of the country, helping to link state and society. Third, assemblies under authoritarian regimes can deliver possible new recruits to the government.

In communist systems, legislatures were often fairly representative assemblies, with certain groups – for example, women and industrial workers – enjoying favoured status. On the other hand, this arrangement still reflected the control of the communist party, with the result that those who managed to occupy the seats reserved for such groups were unlikely to play an independent role in the assembly. In addition, such assemblies often played an overall political role that might be described as little more than ritualistic. This is because the assembly would meet for only a short period each year, around ten days, and its sessions would be used by the Party primarily to proclaim both its past successes as well as its future targets. In contemporary China, on the other hand, the national legislature has acquired some autonomy in recent years. Since the introduction of significant economic reforms in the 1980s, the national assembly – the National People's Congress (NPC) – has flourished in the context of a growing focus on the rule of law. Nevertheless, the NPC has remained strongly hierarchical, with authority focused strongly on a small number of senior figures, rather than the assembly as a whole. In short, as Hague and Harrop (2001: 234) explain, 'the NPC has become a part of the Chinese power network but even today its position cannot be understood through Western notions of the separation of power and the representative function of parliaments'.

Political executive

Important institutions – including the legislature and the judiciary – are less autonomous under authoritarian rule compared to those in democratic states. The same cannot necessarily be said for the office of the political executive. The objective here is to achieve as much power as possible for the national leader, not to share it among competing institutions, as the democratic model would suggest. This is the case whether the top office comprises a presidency – often the case in non-military regimes – or a ruling council (typical of military governments). In both cases, a relative lack of institutionalization is a common characteristic. For example, prior to democratization in the 1980s and 1990s, long periods of non-democratic rule in Africa and Latin America had resulted in many such countries having few, if any, democratically accountable institutions. This legacy has often made building democratic institutions problematic because there are so few democratically congruent foundations to build on. Bratton and van de Walle (1997: 278) suggest that trying to build a stable democracy in countries with little or no heritage of political competition is likely to result in experiments that are 'fragile, possibly transitory and constantly threatened by reversal'. The implication is that rulers will be tempted to continue to depend heavily on the state's controlling and repressive apparatuses: the bureaucracy, the police and the security services, just as many of their unelected counterparts did during non-democratic rule. As Hague and Harrop (2001: 247) note, 'weak institutionalization creates characteristic difficulties: struggles over succession, insufficient emphasis on policy, poor governance and even the danger of regime collapse'.

The Middle East and North Africa offer many examples of countries with non-democratic political systems that are presided over either by powerful individual leaders or by small elite groups. Kamrava (1998) notes three categories of these kinds of regime: (1) 'exclusionary'; (2) 'inclusionary'; (3) 'sultanistic'. The first type, exclusionary governments, are found in Algeria, Syria, Sudan and Tunisia, and can be subdivided into two kinds: 'military' and '*mukhaberat*' (that is, non-military, non-monarchical). What they have in common is that power is heavily focused in the hands of a supreme leader or those of a few people, while the mass of ordinary people is denied any substantive voice in how they are governed. Such regimes rely heavily on the intelligence services and/or the armed forces to enforce a depoliticization of society, principally through repression and fear. Among states in this category, only Algeria has allowed relatively free elections in recent years, and this followed the trauma of a civil war in the 1990s that led to the deaths of an estimated 100,000 people (Haynes 2001a: 168–79).

Second, there are inclusionary regimes. Despite their name, they are not conventionally democratic. They are based either on single-party or 'no-party' systems and are found in Iran, Libya and, until 2003 following the American and British invasion, Iraq. These are polities, Sadiki (1997: 133) observes, where governments seek to deflect any demands for change that surface by turning 'streets and neighbourhoods into political theatres . . . successfully divert[ing] popular political energies into projects that actually sustain the very basis of the regime'.

Third, there are the 'sultanistic' states, subdivided into 'oil monarchies' and 'civil myth' regimes. Among the former are Kuwait, Bahrain, Qatar, Oman, Saudi Arabia and the United Arab Emirates. Characteristically, they are regimes dominated by personalistic rulers, substantial oil wealth and relatively small populations. Governments of the oil monarchies have often been little concerned to accommodate the intermittent demands for greater political participation and accountability that have surfaced in recent years. Only one country in this category, Kuwait, has a recent history of tentative democratization, stimulated by the events surrounding the Gulf War of 1990–1. In contrast, civil myth regimes have rulers whose power is derived from their personal religious or secular attributes. They are found in Jordan and Morocco. Neither country has large oil reserves and associated wealth and both have experienced economic problems in recent years. However, they were also affected by the global trend towards democracy associated with the third wave and the demise of the Soviet Union.

Both Jordan and Morocco have seen recent, albeit tentative, moves towards political liberalization, although it is not clear to what extent this is leading to democratic political systems in either country. However, Jordan's moves towards political liberalization that began under the late ruler King Hussein, who died in 1999, seem to have been curtailed under his successor, his son King Abdullah. This suggests that Abdullah is not prepared to countenance a democratization that would necessarily reduce his own power. In Morocco, there is a long tradition of sultanistic rule, bolstered by the claims of successive monarchs to both religious and political legitimacy. However, what has been a problem is the monarchy's inability to count on the absolute loyalty of some of the key institutions of the state. This reflects the fact that the Moroccan royal family is too small numerically to place princes in control of the armed forces and all other important state institutions. Instead, the late king, Hassan (d. 1999), as well as his successor King Mohammed VI, have used both favouritism and patronage to ensure the loyalty of both high-ranking military officers and senior civilian figures. This policy was instituted partly as a result of a state of emergency (1965–71), which led to the armed forces emerging as the bulwark of the regime, as the military was pivotal in repressing and controlling opposition political parties that were seeking political changes. Since then, the power of the regime has focused upon the considerable personal power of the monarch, underpinned by military support. Some observers expected King Hassan's death in 1999 to lead to a process of democratization, although so far these expectations have not been realized.

Under communist governments the key political institution is the Party, but this does not imply that there is no clear governmental structure. An executive body fills the top position in the power structure. This comprises a presidium (council) headed by an individual. In effect, he or she is the prime minister, leading a body that is really a communist version of a Western-style cabinet. The latter is the steering body of a larger group of ministers, who are formally 'elected' by parliament. Consequently, the formal structure is to some extent reminiscent of the Western model of parliamentary government. However, the Party controls the state's formal institutions and the key person in the power structure is the General Secretary of the Communist Party. In China, things are done slightly differently from how they were in the USSR. This reflects the fact that politics is a more personalized business – to the extent that senior leaders have no formal positions at all.

The bureaucracy

As with the armed forces, bureaucracies under authoritarian governments are often more powerful compared to their political role under democratically elected governments. As we have already noted, representative institutions – elections, competitive parties and freely organized interest groups, focused in civil society – are all weak under authoritarian rule. This enables state-controlled bodies to fill the gap and to acquire large amounts of power and influence. The underlying principle is that authoritarian rulers may do away with competitive elections and representative legislatures but it is implausible that he or she might direct affairs without the supportive assistance of civil servants. As a result, the latter can play an unexpectedly significant role, especially in some economically underdeveloped countries. Sometimes working hand in hand with the armed forces, the bureaucracy can become a leading political and economic force. This is because it can claim both technical expertise and the ability to resist popular pressures and, as a result, assert that it is the best agency to deliver developmental goals.

Latin America under military rule provides a good example of the ability of the bureaucracy to develop considerable autonomous influence and power. The region was much affected by the global economic depression of the 1930s and the world war that ended in 1945. Whereas in Africa, Asia and the Middle East the main result was to stimulate nationalist challenges to imperial rule, in Latin America, mostly independent since the early nineteenth century, there were different outcomes. Increasing industrialization and urbanization, coupled with strong population growth, combined to generate strong popular pressures for increased social spending and greater mass political participation. First, there was widespread, albeit tentative, democratization, then a period of sustained authoritarian rule. This lasted from the 1960s to the 1980s, following a series of military coups. Between 1964 and 1976 democratic regimes fell in a number of countries, including Brazil, Peru, Uruguay, Chile and Argentina.

O'Donnell (1973) labelled the resulting governments 'bureaucratic authoritarian' (BA) regimes. BA regimes, O'Donnell argues, both guarantee and organize the political and economic domination of a small, exclusivist group, whose chief loyalty is to itself rather than to the nation. This oligarchy seeks to exclude the mass of people from political decision-making through a ban on competitive elections, while directing state spending to particular areas that will increase the likelihood of greater investment of foreign capital. The developmental strategy is to be delivered by the state bureaucracy, supported by the armed forces. This arrangement implies a distinct separation between state and civil society, enabling the bureaucracy to pursue developmental goals unhindered by popular pressures.

The BA model was also adopted in two of Asia's most dynamic and economically successful countries: Taiwan and South Korea. During the 1960s and 1970s both countries' governments transformed themselves into BA regimes. As in Latin America, the chief characteristics of these regimes were that political competition was restricted to a small elite, competitive elections were not allowed, while the bureaucracy was given a virtual free hand to pursue development goals unhindered by popular pressures.

Communist bureaucracies are both large in scale and strongly politicized. Such bureaucracies had the former characteristic because they were charged with the role of building a new society, controlling all aspects of political and economic development. In the Soviet Union, such was the control of the Party that private business was entirely abolished, with all economic aspects of life coming under its control. Because the numbers of state employees ran into the tens of millions, the USSR became the most bureaucratized state in the world, necessary to execute both administrative and coordinating functions.

Communist bureaucracies were also highly politicized, as the Party's control was exercised throughout its structure. Because the Party regarded the bureaucracy as both crucial and potentially untrustworthy, then the former sought to dominate the latter by controlling all senior appointments. In the USSR this was accomplished through the *nomenklatura*, a Russian expression meaning 'a list of names'. According to the Party, those on the list were sufficiently reliable, politically speaking, to be worthy of bureaucratic appointment. The *nomenklatura* system continues in present-day China, where the approved list is said to amount to more than eight million names (Manion 2000: 434).

Conclusion

The major conclusion of this chapter is that non-democracy is a residual term, encompassing political characteristics that democracies necessarily have. Non-democracies can differ quite substantially, but what they have in common is a deficiency: their political institutions are not representative. This does not necessarily imply that such regimes are unstable; on the contrary, many authoritarian governments remain in power for years, even decades.

What of the influence of external actors on politics in non-democracies? In the Introduction, I suggested that globalization is changing, in various ways, political arrangements and configurations within countries. What this amounts to is a variable erosion of the nation-state's formerly 'hard' boundaries and a consequent – albeit a variable – diminution of states' ability to control their domestic environments and hence policy decisions. However, given the characteristics we have noted of non-democratic political systems, it is highly likely that the impact of external actors on domestic political structures and processes will be, under most circumstances, limited. This is because non-democracies have political systems characterized by political and institutional arrangements that reduce the potential of what I shall describe in chapter 5 as 'opportunity structures for participation'. This means that both domestic and external actors have great difficulty in influencing political outcomes unless the regime is in agreement with their aims.

4

Methodologies and Globalization

In the Introduction, we briefly surveyed theories and practices of globalization. In chapters 1–3, we focused on three categories of states: established and transitional democracies, and non-democracies, noting their differing political characteristics in relation to political institutions linking states and citizens and structures of government through which these relationships are manifested. In passing, we also saw that various – state and non-state – external actors can affect political outcomes within countries. It is necessary to be concerned with this category of actors because while there is disagreement about precisely how things have changed politically since the 1980s, there is much agreement that a new analytical agenda exists, affecting how we understand political outcomes within countries (Sullivan 2002: 4). It is now necessary, Macdonald and Schwartz (2002: 154) suggest, to examine 'ways in which . . . national and international politics *can be viewed as synergistically linked, rather than as diametrically opposed realities*' (my emphasis). This implies not only that we need to do away with what is increasingly seen as a rather arbitrary and increasingly problematic division of labour within political analysis. It also suggests a need for disciplinary and subdisciplinary integration between two spheres of endeavour: comparative politics and international relations. This is because 'conventional approaches to the social sciences, based on rigid disciplinary and sub-disciplinary fault lines and demarcations, do not prepare us well for a world of interdependence' (Hay 2002b: 5), an environment captured in the concept of globalization. Consequently, we now need to extend the analytical focus, refuse to accept a clear-cut division of labour between comparative politics and international relations, and examine a range of influential state and non-state external actors that can influence political outcomes within countries.

With such concerns in mind, this chapter seeks to accomplish two main tasks. First, we trace the development of comparative politics since its inception in the 1950s, succinctly surveying key themes, assumptions and contributions. In the second half of the chapter, we examine how we might systematically integrate external actors into comparative political analysis.

Comparative Political Analysis: Approaches

When we think of 'comparative politics' – sometimes the expression used is 'comparative government' or 'comparative political systems' – the underlying principle is that comparative methods are important means by which to learn and teach political science. The starting point is to seek to compare things that appear to have similarities or differences and then to examine reasons for them. To make things doable, comparative political analysis starts with a primary assumption: human behaviour, regardless of when or where it takes place, is predictably constant in the same kinds of circumstance. This may risk the danger of over-generalization. But the problem is that if we did not start from this core premise, then the practical and theoretical problems that we would come across in trying to study politics comparatively would be so complicated as to risk making the task impossible. As a result, to get the job done, comparativists accept the need for unavoidable analytical compromises. But political scientists are like everybody else. They like to be as objective as possible, but they too have prejudices that inform their worldviews. This extends to how they view and comparatively understand political structures, processes and outcomes. This implies that decisions they make about what is the most appropriate emphasis and level to conduct comparative political analysis is not just a technical issue. Instead it reflects both individual preferences and, to some extent, the dictates of fashion over time.

When we seek to undertake comparative political analysis, what are we actually trying to compare? Often the aim is to compare and contrast some aspects of a discrete group of countries' domestic political characteristics. Awareness of diversity and/or commonality of a group of countries' political arrangements offers a convenient starting point for comparative enquiry. Typically, such an enquiry has two main aims. First, to attempt to comprehend over time constants, differences and changes in relation to national governments and politics within various countries. Sometimes the aim is to establish general social scientific generalizations that lead to nomothetic – that is, 'law-like' – theoretical claims that would enlighten and inform studies of social and political phenomena. However, nomothetic generalizations have proved very hard to establish. As a result, most comparative political analysis has a more modest goal: to explain and account for countries' political similarities and differences. The task is to develop some perspective on the mixture of stable factors and changeability that inform different kinds of political system and the political contexts in which political actors function.

But we need to note a further complicating factor. That is, there is no general agreement as to what comprises the content and boundaries of the comparative politics sub-discipline. As Harrop and Hague (2001: 62) point out, the area of knowledge called 'comparative politics' is actually 'an ambiguous compound of method, subject areas and its own intellectual history'. In one view, 'comparative politics' is simply a synonym for 'the politics of foreign countries'. This is the 'meaning used in the book reviews section of the *American Political Science Review* and in the organization of many political science departments, notably in the USA' (Hopkin 2002: 249). This might imply that research carried out under the rubric of 'comparative politics' is actually not comparative at all. Instead, it comprises studies of *individual* countries that are both narrow and 'idiographic' – that is, limited to particular cases or events.

Approaches to understanding political outcomes under the collective heading of the 'comparative approach' employ a variety of methods to collect information about characteristics of and differences between individual political systems. In this perception, the 'comparative approach' is the sum total of approaches and methods utilized in pursuit of a common goal: to advance our comparative understanding of different political structures and processes. Three comparative techniques are commonly used in pursuit of this objective: case studies, focused comparisons and statistical analysis. Let us look briefly at each.

According to Hague and Harrop (2001: 71), a 'case is an instance of a more general category. To conduct a case study is therefore to investigate something that has significance beyond its boundaries.' The case study is a widely used tool of comparative politics, even though only one example is studied. The purpose of examining an individual case is to come up with relevant findings that serve to provide a focused example of a topic with wider interest and application. Put another way, the purpose of focusing upon an individual case is to come up with findings that appear to have wider ramifications. Thus a case will not be chosen at random but once selected it appears to be significant as an example of a broader phenomenon, for example a military government or a transitional democracy.

Because comparative politics lacks a commonly agreed theory for explaining and accounting for the characteristics of individual political systems, case studies are very often used as the basis for seeking to make sense of the political world, by 'drawing analogies between the cases themselves'. For example, how did the process of democratization differ between Western industrial countries a century ago and that of post-communist states in Eastern Europe in the early 1990s? Such a concern suggests that 'much political reasoning, especially in foreign policy, is by analogy. Decision-makers and analysts look for earlier crises which resemble the current one, so that lessons can be learned and errors avoided' (Hague and Harrop 2001: 71–2).

Two conclusions can be drawn from this brief focus on case studies as a means of acquiring knowledge for comparative analysis. First, case studies are an approach that enables us to choose a topic rather than a procedure for conducting research. Thus case studies usually feature a variety of methods to gain the knowledge we seek. The overall purpose, however, is the same whatever techniques are employed: to supply a picture that is both rounded and as comprehensive as possible. This is an objective that the anthropologist Clifford Geertz (1973) labelled as 'thick description'. Second, individual cases can engender wider significance in two main ways. An individual case can be of use because it seems to be representative of a category of similar kinds of case. Or it can be chosen because it appears to be non-standard, unusual in some way. If so, it can help us comprehend exceptions to the rule.

The second technique in common use is the focused comparison, falling midway between the case study and statistical analysis. Focused comparisons are ' "small N" studies which concentrate on the intensive comparison of an aspect of politics' usually in two or three countries (Hague and Harrop 2001: 73). The aim of focused comparisons is to be aware of the particulars of individual countries and courses of action while at the same time adhering to the intellectual discipline necessary to pursue a successful comparative enquiry. This suggests that key dimensions of comparison must be looked at, and similarities and differences addressed so as to try to account for observed contrasts. Focused comparisons often work well when a small handful of countries are compared in historical context, and examination made as to how they vary in their response to common problems, such as the post-1989 transition to democracy in Eastern Europe.

The third approach is statistical analysis. This technique involves variable-orientated research aiming to explore 'covariation between variables, at least some of which are usually measured quantitatively. One variable is dependent – that which we seek to explain. The others are independent or explanatory – those factors which we believe may influence the dependent variable' (Hague and Harrop 2001: 74). Examples of statistical work in comparative politics include tests of various hypotheses, such as (1) the richer the country the more likely it is to be an established democracy, or (2) the more educated a Muslim is the more likely he is to be a supporter of an Islamist group.

Use of the methodology of statistical analysis can be useful, while having two main dangers. First, there may appear to be a strong connection between two variables, but this may because there is a third, unmeasured variable that has not been factored into the comparison. While, in principle, this is a problem that can be dealt with by includ-ing all relevant variables in the analysis, what actually happens is that we simply cannot know what all the relevant variables are. The result is that what is called 'spurious cor-relation' continues to be a problem despite all efforts to deal with it. Second, even if a relationship is genuine, we still need to determine the direction of causation. On the other hand, there is widespread agreement that statistical analysis has a key benefit: it provides us with an important means to predict. For example, counting the number of various kinds of regime – for example, established democracies, transitional democra-cies, non-democracies – will enable us commence our examination with an indispensa-ble means of grasping how the political universe is variable. While statistics necessarily simplify, they nevertheless provide us with an important means to help with the funda-mental job of comparatively accounting for political outcomes.

Schools of Interpretation

The study of comparative politics emerged as a subdiscipline within the discipline of political science after World War II. From the 1950s, interpretations of comparative political analysis can usefully be viewed as a series of shifts in analytical focus. Initially, the chief focus was the state and its institutions. In the 1960s and 1970s, the emphasis shifted to the individuals running those institutions. In the 1980s there was a renewed emphasis on the state. During these decades most comparative political analysis was primarily concerned with domestic political structures and processes. Things changed to some degree from the 1990s, as a result both of discrete political developments – notably the end of the cold war and the demise of communism in Eastern Europe at the end of the 1980s – and a more amorphous one: globalization. A result was growing awareness that political outcomes within countries can be influenced by what external actors do. To put this development into perspective and, more generally, to examine how the subdiscipline has developed over time, we trace differing foci of comparative political enquiry since the 1950s.

The 1950s

Because governments are such key political actors, comparative political analysis fre-quently compares and contrasts governing institutions. This emphasis on institutions implicitly connects with the origins of comparative politics in constitutional studies (Hague and Harrop 2001: 63). The underlying presumption is that institutional roles matter more than the individuals who inhabit them. Thus an institutional approach involves a certain perspective on political analysis: institutions define interests. Institu-tions in this context can usefully be thought of as 'sets of rules which shape expectations, prescribe roles, and constrain activities' (Risse-Kappen 1995a: 10). For the purposes of comparative political analysis, this usually means the *major organizations of national government*, especially the legislature, the executive and the judiciary. Analysts often use the term 'institution' also to refer to other kinds of state or state-connected bodies, such as the bureaucracy and subnational government bodies. Normally, however, the term, 'institution' is reserved for constitutionally mandated structures. Moving away from this core area, the term 'organization' is often substituted. Such organizations – including political parties and civil society associations – may well be institutionalized, yet also enjoy little or no constitutional basis. The implication is that they are not formally part of the state, while having important institutional positions (Delsodato 2002).

During the 1950s, when there was much analytical concern on such institutions, there was little or no interest beyond domestic examples. Things have changed in recent years, however, partly as a result of enhanced regional integration in various parts of the world, notably Europe and North America.

The 1960s/1970s

In the 1960s and 1970s the earlier institutional focus of comparative politics shifted to a new concern with comparing societies more generally. This change occurred for two main reasons. First, the process of widespread decolonization, resulting in dozens of new states in Africa, Asia, the Caribbean and the Middle East, occurred in the 1950s and 1960s. This served to underline that in many postcolonial countries state institutions were of a different calibre compared to their Western counterparts. In particular, many postcolonial countries had states with weak institutions, often more reflective of leaders' personal preferences than of wider societal interests.

A second, more technical, factor also contributed to a diminishing analytical concern with institutions in the 1960s. This was because how they functioned did not readily lend itself to statistical treatments, which at this time was reflected in the rise to prominence of sample surveys of societal attitudes towards political attitudes and behaviour. The overall result of these two contemporaneous developments – the emergence of many postcolonial states and growth of interest in statistically based analysis – led to a fall from favour of the comparative study of institutions. Consequently, many analysts and researchers used comparative method to search for generalizations about the political attitudes and behaviour of individuals and the societies where they lived. Many of these more society-centred approaches were influenced by David Easton's system model of the political system (Calvert 2002: 14).

Society-centred analyses were an important aspect of what became known as the behavioural revolution in politics, an approach that clearly contrasted with institutional analysis. Behaviouralists share a belief in the idea that people, not institutions, should be the key focus of analysis (Hay 2002b: 10). Deriving their focus from the natural sciences, behavouralists employ an emphasis on clinical study of behaviour in relation to what both individuals and very small groups of people do. The behaviouralist approach 'had an important effect on the way we look at politics. Its belief that individual behaviour is invariably rational in some sense has been queried, though it has provided the basis for rational choice theory' (Calvert 2002: 11–12). Inspired by microeconomics and/or game theory, rational choice theory employs both deductive logic and modelling to seek to make nomothetic ('law-like') claims. Chief among these are that social and political actors are rational utility maximizers. In this way, the behaviouralists claim to be able to reveal coherence in political behaviour that underlies what may appear on the surface to be the chief characteristic of political life: chaos. However, critics charge rational choice theory with unwarrantedly oversimplifying a highly complex world, by paying insufficient attention to a shifting hierarchy of issues in politics that in turn can make policy-making increasingly complicated.

The question is sometimes asked: to what extent are notions of rationality analytically useful in the post-cold war, increasingly globalized world? Some scholars contend that apparently significant alterations to the international system – such as the growth of interdependence, the end of bipolarity and the rise of regionalism – have important ramifications for comparative and foreign political analysis that undermines the nomothetic claims of rational choice theory. Neo-realists, such as Kenneth Waltz, discount this assumption, perceiving that what they see as the core attribute of the international system – its anarchic structure – remains. For Waltz (1993), the policy-making calculus of foreign policy is unaltered; state survival is still uppermost in policy-makers' minds, along with other objectives, including promotion of gain and the minimization of loss. This is said to demonstrate the continuing salience of the rational imperative to (foreign) policy-making. Moreover, this is not just abstract reasoning. Using the notion of the state as rational and preoccupied with self-help strategies, neo-realists pointed to what they consider the shaky progress of European integration, the dim prospects for political and military stability in Europe and the emergence of new forms of competition between the great powers after the cold war.

In sum, behaviouralism's main distinctive feature is 'a focus on power as decision-making and a tendency to assume that an analysis of the inputs into the political system, such as the pressure exerted by interest groups upon the state, is sufficient to account for political outcomes' (Hay 2002b: 10). Its key assumption – that political analysis should begin with individuals rather than organizations – has been particularly influential in the USA. This partly reflects the fact that the USA is a country whose governing institutions were consciously created from scratch more than 200 years ago by a group of individuals, known as the 'Founding Fathers'. More generally, to seek to explain legislative outcomes, behaviouralists typically focus on representatives' social backgrounds, individual voting records and the extent to which such factors appear to define their roles. To some contemporary analysts, the 'disregard of institutions by much society-centred analysis of the 1960s now seems extreme . . . [yet] its effect in broadening horizons represents a permanent and positive legacy for comparative politics' (Hague and Harrop 2001: 66).

The 1980s

In the 1980s, the pendulum shifted again and analytical attention returned to the state and its constituent institutions and organizations. This amounted to a 'conscious response both to the "behavioural revolution" of the 1960s and to the growing ascendancy of rational theory in subsequent decades' (Hay 2002b: 10–11). It also marked a deliberately theorized widespread return to an older tradition of institutional analysis, except in the United States where the inheritance of the old institutionalism was relatively unimportant.

Renewed analytical concern with the state in the 1980s was located under the rubric, 'the new institutionalism'. It departed from the political science mainstream of the 1970s in two key respects. On the one hand, it rejected the simplifying assumptions underlying the modelling of political behaviour that informed rational choice theory. On the other hand, it questioned behavouralism's reliance on the twin logic of 'extrapolation and generalization (or induction) rooted in assumptions of regularity in human behaviour' (Hay 2002b: 11). New institutionalism-informed analysis claimed that to explain political outcomes comparatively, we need understanding informed by complex, yet plausible, assumptions. In sum, the overall aim of new institutionalism in the 1980s was both to capture and reflect key issues and processes of social and political change, developments judged to be complex and often open-ended.

This reflected both a belated recognition that states and other political institutions continued to be a central concern of political study, as well as an understanding that statistical and behavioural studies could tell us only so much. Often becoming increasingly technical, to critics such studies appeared to fail fully to come to terms with key changes, notably the third wave of democracy and an accompanying development in many countries: significant economic liberalization. Unlike the earlier state focus in the 1950s – when attention focused on institutional details – the key emphasis in the 1980s was on the role of the state as active agent. This worked from the premise that various kinds of state have different capacities to form and reform society and the latter itself is part of a configuration that the state largely defines. The state is believed to act relatively autonomously and, consequently, it should not be regarded as imprisoned by certain social forces. Thus states might use both general administrative capacities as well as a monopoly on legitimate force to bring about fundamental social changes. Two events, separated by more than half a century, the Russian and Iranian revolutions of 1917 and 1979 respectively, illustrate this point: revolutionaries acquire state control and then use their power to try to engineer fundamental societal and political transformations (Skocpol 1985). Another example comes from Western Europe after 1945: social democratic governments sought to use state power that, building on the gains provided by industrialization, aimed to develop both mass education and modern welfare systems, as a conscious route to fundamental social transformation (Swank 2002).

In sum, new institutionalism emphasized the importance of the mediating role of the *institutional* contexts in which political events occur. It rejected what it saw as the input-weighted political analysis of behaviouralism and rational choice theory and instead focused on the significance of history, timing and sequence to explain political dynamics and outcomes. The approach also pointed to what it saw as the 'path-dependent' qualities of institutional, and hence political, development, an idea rooted in the notion that major, apparently irreversible, consequences may follow from what initially seem relatively minor or contingent factors. In recent years, such events have included the fall of the Berlin Wall, the end of the cold war and the variegated impacts of globalization.

The 1990s and early 2000s

Three developments – the end of the cold war in the late 1980s, the fall of the Berlin Wall in November 1989 and the much-discussed impact of globalization (late 1980s onwards) – formed an important backdrop to a new phase of comparative political analysis. The underlying issue was that these three events were symptomatic of a new era, one that demanded novel ways of explaining both domestic and international political developments and outcomes. Reflecting this concern, a major international symposium was held in 1995, entitled: 'The role of theory in comparative politics'. The distinguished Indian political scientist Atul Kohli (1996) reported on its findings in a special issue of *World Politics*. Kohli reported that participants at the symposium shared the view that, in the mid-1990s, comparative politics was polarized by theoretical controversy, while identifying three competing analytical foci. First, there was the familiar rational actor model, whose assumptions we noted earlier. Second, there is what might be called a 'postmodernist' perspective. Third, there is 'the eclectic messy centre'.

Postmodernism is an enigmatic concept. Its very ambiguity, however, is sometimes seen as reflective of the contemporary confusion and uncertainty that informs much comparative politics analysis after the cold war. Postmodernism can be defined as incredulity towards meta-narratives – that is, rejection of absolute ways of speaking the truth. It has been applied in and to many diverse spheres of human life and activity – including art, literature, architecture and religion, as well as political analysis. In relation to the latter, postmodernism refers to changes in practices and experiences of people and groups, who develop new means of orientation and identity structures, for example, in relation to transnational interactions.

The postmodernist approach to political analysis stands in total opposition to the proclaimed value of 'scientific' causal explanations. It doubts the value of overarching causal explanations altogether and thus of conventional social science theorizing in comparative politics. It also emphasizes contemporary disaffection with the kind of alleged scientific rationalism exemplified in particular by the rational actor model, and heralds a significant departure from earlier conceptualizations about the autonomy of domestic political structures in relation to the external environment. In addition, it posits that to explain reality we need to examine a variety of factors that are not captured by 'scientific' forms of analysis. Finally, the approach suggests that contemporary circumstances serve to encourage rejection of centres and systems of power, especially those of the state, while engendering growth in new sources of identity.

'The eclectic messy centre' view has a different set of assumptions. It considers of central importance theoretically informed empirical political analysis, employing 'diverse conceptual lenses and . . . a variety of – contemporary or historical, qualitative or quantitative – data' (Kohli 1996: 1–2). In the post-cold war era, this form of analysis understands two significant changes that impact upon comparative political analysis: (a) increased global complexity, and (b) closer interaction and integration between domestic and foreign policy. In relation to the first point, there is increased complexity of international events coupled with the perceived porousness of state borders that together necessitate a continuing process of adaptation on the part of policy-making and executing institutions.

Second, globalization-linked complexity increases the interaction between domestic and foreign policy, a concept captured by Robert Putnam's (1988) notion of the 'two-level game'. Policy-makers attempt to cope with the demands of their own political systems while simultaneously dealing with external developments that influence outcomes domestically. The two levels can interact. In some circumstances the attempt to satisfy domestic pressures may constrain the policy-maker, while in others it may embolden him or her.

In conclusion, since the 1990s comparative political analysis has sought to take into account the changed nature of the international political environment as it impacts upon political outcomes within countries. As a result, we now need to explain variations in political responses to pressures, constraints and opportunities that are linked to globalization. A key question is: how precisely does globalization impact upon individual countries' political systems, societies and the policy networks that link them? Domestic political structures and processes encompass the organizational apparatus of various institutions, their routines and the decision-making rules and procedures as incorporated in law and custom, as well as the values and norms prescribing appropriate behaviour that are embedded in political culture. However, it is also clear that one of the significant results of globalization is that what states do with the power at their disposal cannot be fully comprehended simply by routine analysis of specific institutions.

The Impact of Globalization

There is widespread agreement that various kinds of external actor – collectively captured in the term 'globalization' – can influence domestic political outcomes. The consequence for comparative political analysis is that it 'simply cannot afford, if ever [it] could, to get by without a rather more thorough grasp of the cognate disciplines' – such as international relations – 'on whose assumptions we have increasingly come to reply' (Hay 2002b: 5). However, a word of caution is appropriate: I am not claiming that comparative politics and international relations are one and the same. Rather, I am suggesting that what we need is a form of comparative political analysis that is not content to restrict itself analytically to the political variables and processes that occur within countries.

This approach contrasts with many traditional comparative politics approaches that restrict themselves to political environments within countries. I suggest that the impact of the end of the cold war and of globalization means that comparative political analysis now needs to be informed by taking into account how various external actors can affect domestic political outcomes. The analytical aim is to bridge the by now artificial division between comparative politics and international relations. For a fair analysis, we need to adopt a relatively sophisticated balance between the two approaches. On the one hand, there are those who reject the national state as a hopelessly outdated construct. Sometimes such analysts, having 'seen the light' about transnational influences, neglect the complex mix of influences and fail to incorporate domestic factors at all (for example, America-centric explanations for reforms introduced in the 1980s by the then national leader Mikhail Gorbachev in the Soviet Union are one instance of this). On the other hand, there are those who have 'returned to the state' following discovery that external actors can have intermittent, sometimes erratic impacts.

Since the 1980s, this issue has had two key dimensions. First, there are responses to globalization in relation to state *formation* in the case of newly independent governments, for example in Central and Eastern Europe (CEE), a region where many new states have emerged following the demise of the USSR. Second, state *alteration* can be important, for example, in many post-authoritarian states in Latin America, Asia and Africa, which have undergone – and in many cases continue to experience – major political transformations, most obviously from non-democratic rule to democratically elected government. In other words, we need to gauge what might be called the relative vulnerability of states to various aspects of globalization. To take analysis forward, it is insufficient to refer vaguely to the nature of the polity, highlighting factors such as the size and strength of the state. Instead, a more rigorous formulation is needed, as well as a limit to the many variables that may be involved in linking the domestic and international levels. Not to do this runs the risk of making each case study *sui generis* – and this would be of no use for comparative analysis.

A useful starting point is explicitly to recognize that two recent changes in particular can influence our understanding of comparative political analysis. The first is the situation of *increased global complexity, with some states experiencing a general 'porousness' of their national borders*. This requires, on the part of policy-makers, the ability to deal with external inputs when making and executing policy. In this regard, several distinct forms of influence can be seen. Keohane and Nye's (1977) typology of world politics as 'complex interdependence' is analytically useful as a starting point. This perspective is informed by a 'multiple issues' agenda that encourages government departments – hitherto primarily concerned with 'domestic' issues, including energy, telecommunications, food, agriculture and environmental concerns – to take into account external actors that affect outcomes. This not only presents organizational difficulties in coordinating the work of different branches of government, but also 'generates political problems as a proliferation of newly created policy coalitions seek to influence policy' (Webber and Smith 2002: 63–4). In short, there are now multiple channels of contact linking states and societies, both within and between countries, and they can impact upon domestic policy-making and execution.

Second, there is now both *interaction* and *integration* between many states' domestic and foreign policies. One result of this is that attempts to satisfy domestic pressures may act either to constrain or to embolden the foreign policy-maker. Cohen (2001: 48–9) cites data suggesting that a 'strongly dominant trend in opinion (80 per cent or more) . . . will almost automatically impose its choices on decision-makers'. But *how* precisely can public opinion shape policy outputs? For example, Prime Minister Tony Blair (in office at the time of writing, late 2004) operates within Britain's highly centralized political system, and dominates his political party because of Britain's electoral system and party rules. In early 2003, Blair was very aggressive in relation to the desire of the US government to invade Iraq – even though most members of his party and a majority of the British public (prior to the invasion, 80–90 per cent) did not unequivocally support his position. On the other hand, Germany's Chancellor Schröder, facing a different electoral and party system, took a much less aggressive position on this issue than his personal politics might have predicted. The overall point is that domestic political structures and processes can interact with external actors to influence national political leaders in various ways and this can be reflected in an intertwining of domestic and foreign politics. This is particularly important, as policy-makers must now attempt to cope simultaneously both with demands from their own domestic political systems as well as those emanating from external sources. As the two levels now regularly interact, it implies that the traditional subject matter of comparative politics – three primarily *domestic* levels: the institutions of government, the social context of politics and the state as a whole (Hague and Harrop 2001: 63) – must now engage with the cluster of actors and issues captured by the term 'globalization'.

Structured Contingency and
Comparative Political Outcomes

We have seen that state boundaries are now penetrated by various kinds of (economic, political and cultural) external actors, conveniently linked together under the rubric of globalization. Since the 1980s, and especially since the end of the cold war at the end of that decade, there was increasing agreement that 'domestic and international politics [are] only aspects of one interrelated whole' (Calvert 2002: 14). But this statement, while not obviously erroneous, suffers from excessive generality. In this section of the chapter, I offer a model that breaks globalization down into its constituent parts and thus makes it possible to use the term comparatively. In the next chapter, I apply the model.

Waylen (2003: 157) notes 'four streams of the comparative politics research cycle'. The first stream features single-country case studies. The second examines a cluster of case studies, typically in an identified region, for example sub-Saharan Africa or Eastern Europe. The third stream of the research cycle is hypothesis-testing. Typically, two or three case studies are examined, using various comparative methods. The approach adopted here is cognizant with what Waylen (2003: 158) calls the fourth cycle of the research cycle. At this point, the intention is to 'draw evidence from [a] range of different studies and suggest some tentative conclusions. . . . This kind of comparative analysis [allows] us to discern any broad patterns that might contribute to . . . theory building.'

In his study of the policy process in Britain, Marsh (2002) claimed that most work on British politics deals in 'intentionalist explanations because it is based on an explicit or implicit pluralist theory of power'. He argues that in order adequately to study politics in Britain, what is needed is an acknowledgement that certain structures constrain or facilitate what governments can hope to achieve. Marsh argues that 'pluralism is inadequate as a model of the power distribution in Britain because it fails to acknowledge the importance of the structural constraints'. Instead, he suggests, we need a model that recognizes that power is not a zero-sum game, but a relational concept. As a result, the relationships involved are exchange relationships. 'Most of these relationships are asymmetrical and . . . there are consistent and continuing patterns in that asymmetry. White men with money, knowledge and power do have a privileged position in the British polity' (Marsh 2002: 34).

More generally, the relative importance of political structures reflects the overall balance between social forces, the resources available to political agents and the institutions and processes of governance. It is important to bear in mind that these are constraints on, rather than determinants of, outcomes. This highlights, first, that there are various structural constraints impacting on all governments, affecting what they can achieve; and, second, individual political actors also operate within structural constraints. However, the knowledge that political actors have of structural constraints is actually contingent. That is, they may have knowledge of a number of different constraints that apply to them, and these constraints may have contradictory effects. This is because their knowledge is mediated by frames of meaning or discourses. And, because such actors are reflexive, then the relationship between them is not mechanical. Instead, they strategically calculate their interests given their knowledge of the constraints. Finally, actors can affect structures.

In an earlier book, I examined the interrelationship of agents and structures and called this variable relationship, 'structured contingency'. I focused upon the remarkably widespread shift to democracy – the 'third wave of democracy' – that occurred between the mid-1970s and the mid-1990s (Haynes 2001a). I noted that around the world numerous non-democratic governments agreed to democratize their polities during this discrete two-decade period. I argued that this global development could not realistically have been the result of dozens of separate, simultaneous or nearly concurrent decisions by dozens of non-democratic governments. Instead, I suggested, there must have been other significant factors at work. Among these were international and transnational, state and non-state, political actors that, interacting with domestic agents, affected democratization outcomes.

Seeking to extend this model in the current book, I intend to take a step further: to identify *what* aspects of globalization in *which* countries under *what* circumstances can regularly influence domestic political outcomes. To do so, I need to trace the impact of globalization on political outcomes in various countries through 'a mode of analysis . . . capable of reconciling *structural* and *agential* factors within a single explanation . . . an account which is neither structuralist nor intentionalist yet an account which does not simply vacillate between these two poles' (emphasis added; Hay 2002b: 113). In other words, I do not seek to apply an approach only concerned with significant political structures, as it runs the risk of being analytically inadequate. This is because it would overlook the role of contingency, including that of human agency, in explaining political outcomes. In short, my starting point is that, in order to explain adequately political outcomes, we must include in the analysis both structural and agential factors, emanating from both domestic and external sources.

Structures

To understand political outcomes within countries requires taking into account the characteristics of both formal and informal political structures (or, more commonly, institutions) within countries. In referring to *formal* political institutions, what I have in mind are the permanent edifices of public life found in virtually all states: laws, public offices, political society and elections. *Informal* institutions, on the other hand, are also theoretically important, and comprise 'dynamics of interests and identities, domination and resistance, compromise and accommodation' (Bratton and van de Walle 1997: 276). We can note various informal political structures of analytical importance: civil society, historically produced societal behaviour (political culture) and interactions between various interest and societal groups, including class divisions and state power.

During the third wave of democracy, various informal institutions were often judged significant for political outcomes in democratizing countries. Attempts to establish democratic political structures and processes in transitional democracies marked a phase when a range of political and newly politicized actors searched for new, binding, democratically legitimate rules of political competition and engagement (Haynes 2001a). Rueschemeyer et al. (1992) argue that these kinds of relationship were pivotal in explaining political outcomes in non-democracies and transitional democracies. This is because the nature and characteristics of relationships between various groups – for example, large-scale capitalists, the bourgeoisie, the middle classes, industrial workers, landlords and peasants – can profoundly affect domestic political outcomes. Put another way, a country's political trajectory – for example, towards or away from democracy – is typically influenced by various historically determined structures, often driven by particularistic chronicles of capitalist development (Cammack 1997).

Thinking further of influential informal structures, we can also note the economic position and the degree of social polarization in a country. Returning again to the key example of third-wave democratization, it is widely accepted that in order to institute, develop and then sustain democracy, what is needed is a rough balance of power between, on the one hand, the state and, on the other, the array of significant societal interests that organize variously under the rubrics of political and civil society. Note that democracy will almost certainly not be the outcome if the state is either excessively powerful in relation to traditionally subservient social classes, as in many Middle Eastern countries, or is over-dependent on powerful landed classes, as in many Latin American nations. This is because large-scale landowners singularly benefit from control of labour repressive agriculture. In sum, while the precise mix differs from country to country, influential informal political structures may include:

- the legacy of personalistic rule; few if any democratically accountable political institutions;
- national political cultures that do not value democracy higher than other forms of political engagement;
- weak or declining economies, heavily dependent on international financial assistance;
- religious, ethnic and/or ideological conflicts;
- weak, fragmented civil societies;
- a highly politicized military that wants to maintain existing structures of power;
- a government that many citizens regard as lacking legitimacy and accountability;
- unrepresentative, undemocratic political parties, often dominated by powerful individual leaders;
- a small, yet politically powerful, land-owning elite that aims to deny poor, landless people access to land for agricultural purposes;
- monopolistic electoral and economic hold on power at subnational levels by powerful individuals linked to the ruling regime;
- religious traditions; some, such as Confucianism and Islam, have been identified as inherently anti-democracy.

Externally derived factors and actors – they may be informal structures or one-off events – are less often noted. They include background conditions, autonomous and decisive events, and a range of influential state and non-state actors that can be important in helping shape domestic political trajectories and outcomes. For example, in the 1970s and 1980s an influential external actor – the European Union – developed an influential, yet informal, structure of sustained pressure and encouragement on Greece, Portugal and Spain. This had the effect of bolstering those countries' determination to make the decisive shift from non-democratic to democratic government (Pridham 1991; Haynes 2001a: 27–30). As we shall see later, this type of pressure from the EU was also highly influential in the context of post-communist Eastern Europe in helping explain many regional countries' shift to democratically elected form of government.

Actors

But structures are only ever one side of the equation. Structural explanations alone are deficient without also taking into account contingent factors, especially what individuals and groups of actors do. Such actors 'are situated within a structured context which presents an uneven distribution of opportunities and constraints to them. Actors influence the development of that context over time through the consequences of their actions. Yet, at any given time, the ability of actors to realize their intentions is set by the context itself' (Hay 2002b: 115).

To note the importance of this, regard the following, the closing paragraph of an influential book on Africa's democratic transitions in the 1990s:

> A consolidated democracy requires that democratic institutions are not only built but also valued. Democracy can be installed without democrats, but it cannot be consolidated without them. Political actors may initially see a founding election as the 'least worst' alternative to solve an intractable political standoff or to induce political movement in an ossified regime. Democracy may even survive in the short run under the force of these kinds of strategic calculations, but democracy will truly last only when political actors learn to love it. Until elites and citizens alike come to cherish rule by the people and exhibit a willingness to stand up for it, in Africa as elsewhere, there will be no permanent defence against tyranny. (Bratton and van de Walle 1997: 279)

This quotation highlights the importance to democratization of contingent factors, especially the influence of human agency in political outcomes. Implicitly, however, Bratton and van de Walle are suggesting that it is impossible to construct a handy checklist of contingency factors that we can readily turn to when seeking to assess chances of democratic consolidation in an individual country or region. This is because the events that can send things in a democratic direction, or reduce that possibility, are simply too varied to list. More generally, the interrelationship between structural and agential factors is captured in the concept of *structured contingency*.

Structured contingency

We can see the importance of contingent events when we turn to an examination of political outcomes in a number of transitional democracies. For example, there was the pivotal impact of Mikhail Gorbachev's actions in the USSR in the mid-1980s, as well as those of Nelson Mandela in South Africa a few years later. Mandela's decision to enter into political negotiations with the apartheid government following his release from prison in 1990 is widely judged a pivotal event in the shift to democracy in South Africa. In Gorbachev's case, his personal decision to seek to reform the USSR's political sclerotic institutions in the mid-1980s is widely regarded as a key event in relation both to the end of the cold war and the resulting turn to democracy in Russia and Eastern Europe (Sodaro 2001: 633–96). A third, less well-known, example comes from the East African country of Uganda. In 1986, the government introduced an unconventional form of democracy, a 'no-party' variant known as the 'movement system' (Hansen and Twaddle 1995). The interesting question is why the regime did not decree a multiparty route in common with many others in Africa at the time. The issue gains piquancy when we note that there was little doubt that the ruling regime would have won elections if it had chosen to allow a multiparty system. One interpretation is that the country's powerful leader, Yoweri Museveni, sincerely believed that multipartyism was the root cause of the evils of tribalism and religious prejudice that had bedevilled Uganda for two decades from the mid-1960s. The point however is that Museveni's apparently personal decision to pursue an unconventional form of democracy highlights the importance of both structure and contingency to Uganda's political outcomes in the mid-1980s.

A fourth example that highlights the importance of contingency for political outcomes also comes from Africa, this time from Nigeria. The election to power in 1999 of a former military leader, Olusegun Obasanjo, led to optimism that the country would finally put behind it a four-decade period of mostly military rule. President Obasanjo was seen as fervently pro-democracy and, as a result, the government of the United States focused much development assistance on the country. However, it soon became clear that Obasanjo could not easily or quickly overcome anti-democratic structural legacies, such as serious ethnic, religious and regional frictions, as well as the entrenched anti-democracy political role of the military (McGreal 2000a). The overall point is that President Obasanjo's personal desire for democracy, bolstered by US financial assistance, was not on its own sufficient to set the country in a political direction where democracy would be privileged over non-democratic ways of doing politics. It illustrates that, sometimes, structures are more powerfully determinant than the wishes of individuals in shaping political outcomes.

African political heritages are different from those of other countries and regions. For example, not only in most Latin American, but also in some Asian countries, notably South Korea and Taiwan, the authoritarian legacy took on a particular bureaucratic form, known as 'bureaucratic authoritarianism'. Consequently, attempts at democratic consolidation commenced from a different starting point from those in Africa. At the same time, political outcomes were also linked to human agency. For example, a long period of democratic rule in Venezuela – beginning in 1958 – did not lead to democratic consolidation. This was because two leading political parties which shared power dominated the political scene for decades. Eventually, in the late 1990s, Hugo Chavez, a charismatic politician and former coup leader, was popularly elected president via the ballot box. Chavez could have simply continued with the old regime, retained the existing power equation, and drawn on existing political structures and institutions. Instead, he proclaimed that he wanted to construct a new form of popular democracy, remove power from the entrenched political class and 'pass it to the people'. While critics claim that this was simply a form of charismatic authoritarianism, Venezuela under Chavez nevertheless offers a good example of a political environment where both contingency and structures were important for political outcomes. In summary, the concept of structured contingency is characterized by the following:

● all polities have historically established, informal and formal, structures of power;
● political outcomes are not entirely random but to an often considerable degree reflect institutionalized patterns;
● structures of power are reflected in established rules and institutions that limit the available – that is, realistic – alternatives open to political actors;

- political actors select certain courses of action over others; those they choose depend on their perception of what seems most likely to succeed, an awareness linked to the nature of embedded structures of power.

The examples of Uganda's Museveni, South Africa's Mandela, Hugo Chavez in Venezuela and Mikhail Gorbachev in the USSR demonstrate how important it is that individuals can take and seek to implement *personal* decisions which carry potential or actual political weight. Taken together, these cases highlight the essence of structured contingency. The concept can be summarized as 'the interaction of the uncertainties of politics with persistent institutional structures' (Bratton and van de Walle 1997: 278). Our brief case studies above suggest the following hypothesis:

Various kinds of formal and informal structures form the context within which political agents act, but the latter are not slavishly bound by the former.

This implies that what political actors do cannot be overlooked when we seek to explain political outcomes. In sum, the concept of structured contingency highlights (1) that all polities have structures – that is, inherited rules and institutions and recurrent patterns of behaviour – to which political actors are attuned; and (2) that political outcomes may be linked to what individual political actors do.

We are concerned in this book with the comparative impact of certain kinds of external actor on political outcomes in three generic categories of countries: established democracies, transitional democracies and non-democracies. We have already noted that, under the conditions of a 'globalized world', domestic political outcomes may well be linked to the influence of external actors. How else could we explain recent outcomes, such as that linked to the Asian financial crisis of 1997–8? This led not only to a 'global economic slump [and] international financial crisis' (Burnell 1998: 12), but was also linked to regime change in several Latin American countries, including Brazil and Venezuela (Philip 2003). We can also point to external pressures on heavily indebted countries in the 1990s to adopt the then hegemonic neo-liberal economic agenda. This may have also helped persuade economically privileged elites that democratic transition would not seriously harm their interests, and thus helped to limit their opposition. But 'by further entrenching such groups in the economy, these same international forces are possibly dimming the longer term prospects for greater social and political equality' (Burnell 1998: 23).

Structured Contingency:
Where Does Globalization Come In?

Having sought to establish the importance of structures and agents, and outlined the importance of the concept of structured contingency to account for various political outcomes, we are now in a position to examine how 'globalization' – conceptualized here as a range of external (state and non-state) actors – can comparatively influence political outcomes within our three generic categories of countries. I suggested earlier that interaction of structural and agential factors is important in explaining domestic political outcomes, for example, in relation to democratization and chances of achieving democratic consolidation in transitional polities. However, the relative weight of structural and agential factors, as well as the factors themselves, will differ from country to country. What role does globalization play in these processes? While globalization is sometimes regarded as a series of structures, Marsh and Furlong (2002: 34) note that, in fact, 'it is agents who construct globalization'. Note that I am *not* suggesting that external actors can dictate political outcomes over an extended period, even in the 'weakest' of countries. In recent years, even the most powerful government, that of the USA, has not been able unequivocally to achieve its political objectives in various countries, including Cuba, Haiti, Iraq and Somalia.

To explain and account for various ways that external actors can influence domestic outcomes we must start by identifying the relevant domestic agents and how they comprehend and construct globalizing tendencies. Hay (2002b: 114) poses six key questions in this respect:

1   Have we identified an agent or agents?
2   Is our agent individual or collective?
3   If collective, can we account for how this collective agency has been accomplished?
4   Have we contextualized our agent(s) within the broader concerns?
5   How relevant is the context we have chosen?
6   Are there other relevant contexts we have omitted?

Returning to the issue of third-wave democratization, we noted earlier that a country's structural characteristics can significantly influence democratic outcomes. The chances of democratic consolidation in transitional democracies is often linked to: (1) the character of a polity's social and economic system; (2) the constellations of power at both subnational and national levels; (3) the overall clout of civil and political societies in influencing the direction of political change; and (4), in some accounts, the influence of a range of external state and non-state actors (Pinkney 2003; Haynes 2001a). Putting things like this has the benefit of highlighting what structures might be influential, although it tells us nothing about contingent factors, especially what individual actors or groups of agents do.

Turning our attention to the issue of the domestic impact of globalization, a primary question is: what is the significance of external (state and non-state) actors for what happens within countries? Is the impact uniform across a range of countries? It is plausible to suggest that the impact will differ from country to country, but will it be entirely random? I hypothesize that outcomes in our three categories of countries – established democracies, transitional democracies and non-democracies – are influenced in differing ways by external actors.

I seek to illustrate what I am getting at by the use of three examples:

1   *For the established democracies of Western Europe, 'globalization places pressure to roll back their welfare provision'.* This statement implies 'a loosely articulated explanation for welfare retrenchment along the lines, "globalization causes (or necessitates) welfare retrenchment"' Hay (2002b: 114).
2   *For North American countries (Canada, Mexico, USA) globalization places pressure to develop a regional economic grouping: the North American Free Trade Agreement.*

This is a means by which to attempt to increase intra-regional trade and, more gener-ally, to control better the overall economic environment within which these countries find themselves. This statement implies a loosely expressed explanation for North American regional economic development along the lines, 'globalization causes (or necessitates) regionalization'.

3   *For the post-communist countries of CEE, globalization places pressure both to democratize and to put in place market-orientated economic systems.* This statement implies a loosely expressed explanation for both political and economic reforms in CEE along the lines that globalization causes (or necessitates) economic and democratic reforms in the countries of that region.

The overall point is that, in each example, globalization is mustered as a process without a subject, that is, no agent or agents are identified. The result is that we fail to get beyond Hay's first question ('Have we identified an agent or agents?'). To temper the logic of inevitability that these statements suggest, we need to 'seek to restore active subjects to this hypothesised process' (Hay 2002: 114). When we do this, replacing the initial state-ments with the following takes the analysis a stage further:

1   In Western European countries, 'the ability of foreign investors to move capital and assets rapidly from one national context to another undermines the state's capacity to raise revenue to fund the welfare state through corporate taxation' (Hay 2002b: 114).
2   The ability of external actors to apply economic pressure on North American coun-tries undermines their ability to develop – unless they develop a cohesive and goal-orientated regional organization.
3   The ability of external actors, especially the European Union, to apply political and economic pressure on post-communist states in CEE undermined the capacity of authoritarian rule to continue without significant reforms.

Such statements have clear analytical benefits. First, they help us to identify concrete agents with capacity to act. Second, they exchange intangible and potentially confusing references to globalization with a less abstract process. Nevertheless, in the second set of statements, we can note the continued absence of acknowledgement of causal agency to identifiable subjects. A third set of statements serves to place agents back into the analytical frame:

1   'The perception on the part of many western governments that investors are mobile and will exit high taxation environments has driven a process of corporate tax cutting, thereby undermining the revenue basis of the welfare state' (Hay 2002b: 114–15).
2   The awareness on the part of North American governments that external economic actors can undermine their ability to develop economically drives the current process of regional economic integration.
3   The observation by many governments in CEE, which, given that they wanted their countries to join the EU and that the organization's existing member states would not accept undemocratic political regimes and state-dominated economic systems, helped drive a continuing process of multifaceted liberalization.

In this third set of statements, we identify a more concrete set of potential actors that can theoretically impact upon various decisions (welfare expenditure, regional development, political and economic reform) and we noted regional governmental perceptions of the importance of these issues. A fourth set of statements fully includes the influence of agency, replacing the original unspecific statements about the inevitability of the influence of unspecified 'globalization' on governmental decisions:

1   'Government X, acting on its belief that investors will leave high-taxation environments for low-taxation environments, has reduced the rate of corporate tax, with consequent effects for the revenue basis of the welfare state' (Hay 2002b: 115).
2   The governments of Canada, Mexico and the USA, acting on their belief that external economic actors can undermine their chances of economic and developmental progress, move towards enhanced regional integration with consequent effects on their – economic and political – relationships.
3   CEE governments act on the belief that, unless they implement and continue with political and economic reforms, their chances of EU membership would be zero. Consequently, they developed as a priority demonstrative strategies of political democratization and economic liberalization in order, at least in part, to meet the non-negotiable criteria of EU entry.

Conclusion

In the first part of the chapter, we looked briefly at developments in understanding and analysing comparative politics over the last 50 years. We succinctly surveyed some of the key themes, assumptions and contributions. In the second half of the chapter, we examined how we might systematically include external actors in comparative political analysis.

We discussed, first, the significance to political outcomes of both structure and agency and introduced a concept – *structured contingency* – that seeks to capture their interaction; and, second, the importance of identifying as precisely as possible *what* actors need to be taken into account when assessing the impact of globalization on domestic political outcomes in our three categories of states. We saw that attempts to restore notions of agency to a specific process, globalization, often presented without subjects, 'serves to problematise the logic of inevitability that processes of globalization are frequently seen to imply' (Hay 2002b: 113–15). We are now in a position to present our analytical model, a task we shall turn to in the next chapter.

5
External Actors and Domestic Politics

We noted in chapter 4 that various state and non-state cross-border actors can influence domestic political outcomes. Consequently, it is surprising that there have been few systematic and comprehensive analyses attempting to assess the comparative impact of such actors on the domestic politics of various kinds of country. Some observers argue, however, that some kinds of country are more vulnerable than others to the influence of external actors. It is sometimes suggested that many established democracies – especially the economically developed countries of North America and Western Europe – are less vulnerable to the influence of external forces, compared to transitional democracies[1] and some non-democracies[2] (Diamond 2001: 360–1; Oksenberg 2001; Holland 2002). In addition, Hague and Harrop (2001: 47) assert, 'weak states – and, of course, most countries in the world are both small and poor – must accept both the external setting, and their vulnerability to it, as a given'. However, as Risse-Kappen (1995a) notes, it is one thing to propose that various kinds of state theoretically have differing levels of vulnerability to cross-border actors. It is quite another – and more difficult – task to identify precisely how and in what ways external actors can affect domestic political outcomes.

There have been various attempts at model-building in this regard. Putnam's (1988) 'two-level game' model highlights certain links between domestic political and external actors. It has, however, been criticized for focusing attention on governments, while giving less attention to non-state actors. Seeking to broaden the analytical focus in this regard, Moravcsik's (1993) model included a concern with both transnational and trans-governmental actors and alliances.

---

[1] This is because many transitional democracies depend significantly on various external actors for foreign aid and/or for support in campaigns to join regional organizations, such as the European Union.

[2] Non-democracies may be especially vulnerable to the influence of external actors under certain circumstances. This includes a phase when governmental remit diminishes significantly as a result of prolonged political instability or civil conflict, such as recently occurred in Somalia, Haiti and, notoriously, Rwanda. In addition, after 9/11 and the consequential 'war on terror', a non-democracy, Iraq, felt the full brunt of Western displeasure. While one of the stated reasons for the US/UK invasion – the search for 'weapons of mass destruction' – turned out to be spurious, there is a wider issue to note: when they are judged to be sponsors of 'terrorists', governments of non-democracies should legitimately fear Western attention. For example, an earlier 'sponsor of terrorism', the government of Libya, made strenuous attempts after 9/11 to regularize its position with the West – in part by paying billions of dollars in 2003 in restitution to the families of victims of the mid-air explosion over Lockerbie in December 1988 that killed 270 people (<http://www.geocities.com/CapitolHill/5260/victim.html#hit>).

More recently, Risse-Kappen (1995b: 299) has examined a range of domestic/ external interactions. He notes that both transnational and transgovernmental alliances 'can . . . affect the domestic "win sets" and the inter-state negotiations' by aiming to 'by-pass national governments (understood as unitary actors)'. This suggests that 'inter-state negotiations' (Putnam's level I) may actually be inhabited not by state governments per se – but by cross-cutting transnational and transgovernmental alliances. While 'original bargains' may be struck at this level, the state does not simply disappear from the framework – because any international regimes that result are still *inter*-state institutions. The main consequence is that 'state governments have to sign on to the original agreements which then have to be ratified through the processes of domestic politics' (Putnam's level II).

Building on such an understanding, Risse-Kappen reconceptualizes Putnam's original two-level process in what he calls a 'three-level game':

● level I is the realm of transnational/transgovernmental bargaining;
● level II is the sphere of intra-governmental as well as inter-state bargaining over the negotiating results on level I; and
● level III is the area of domestic politics. (Risse-Kappen 1995b: 300)

Informed by Risse-Kappen's conceptualization of the interaction of external and internal actors, table 5.1 shows that the ability of various kinds of external actors to access and potentially influence domestic politics depends to a considerable degree on comparative strengths of state and society in individual countries. The table suggests that the impact of external actors on domestic political structures and processes is not uniform, but depends on countries' differing political and institutional characteristics. For example, the access of external actors may be facilitated when state institutions are 'weak' and those of civil society are 'strong', or at least 'stronger' than those of the state. When a country has a strong (domestic) civil society, it may provide suitable conditions for interaction with various cross-border actors that can be significant for domestic political outcomes.

Following from this, Risse-Kappen (1995b: 300, 281) suggests two hypotheses:

1 'Under similar international conditions, differences in domestic structures determine the variation in the policy impact of transnational actors.'
2 'Institutional structures of governance mediate the impact of transnational actors and state policies.' Note that this can theoretically include not only domestic but also regional structures of governance, for example, those associated with the European Union.

Let us examine how these factors come into play in the context of the various kinds of political system noted in table 5.1:

(1) *State-controlled political structures*. Here, a country's political institutions are state-dominated and centralized, with a weak and fragmented civil society. This arrangement normally offers few, if any, entry points to external actors seeking to gain access to domestic political structures. Access will be extremely difficult – because the state

Table 5.1 External actors and domestic politics

Domestic political system	External actors' access to domestic political institutions	Policy impact in case of access	Likely political system
1. *State-controlled* Examples: China, Vietnam, communist-era USSR, Cuba, North Korea, post-communist Central Asian countries	Most difficult	Profound if coalition with state actors predisposed towards external agents' goals or empowerment of social actors	Non-democracy
2. *State-dominated* Examples: Malaysia, Singapore, South Korea, Zimbabwe, pre-2000 Mexico, Iran, Turkey, Arab countries and many post-communist countries in Central and Eastern Europe	Difficult	Profound if coalition with state actors predisposed towards external agents' goals or empowerment of social actors	Non-democracy/ transitional democracy
3. *Stalemate* Examples: Germany, France, UK, India, Canada, South Africa and EU	Less difficult	Impact unlikely	Established democracy/ transitional democracy
4. *Corporatist* Examples: Japan, Denmark, Germany, Sweden and pre-Chavez Venezuela	Less easy	Incremental but long-lasting if coalition with powerful societal and/or political organizations	Established democracy/ transitional democracy
5. *Society-dominated* Examples: Hong Kong, Philippines and USA	Easy	Difficult coalition-building with powerful societal organizations	Established democracy/ transitional democracy
6. *Fragile* Examples: Russia and many African countries	Easiest	Impact unlikely	Non-democracy/ transitional democracy

Source: Adapted from Risse-Kappen 1995a: Tables 1.1 and 1.2, pp. 23 and 28.

controls all relevant domestic institutions – *unless* important state actors themselves desire external actors' domestic political presence.

(2) *State-dominated political structures.* In this case, there is a set of centralized, state-dominated political institutions, while civil society is relatively weak and fragmented. This is a similar situation to category (1) – although state control is somewhat

less overarching. Consequently, external actors' access should be a little easier, although still difficult, unless state actors want it.

It is important to note that in the contexts of both categories (1) and (2), external actors will seek to modify policy strategies to the target country's specific situation, and some domestic structures should make this task easier than others. Both *state-controlled* and *state-dominated* political structures will, theoretically, make it difficult for external actors to overcome the initial hurdle of gaining access. However, once this barrier is overcome, then the policy impact of such actors can be profound. This is because if powerful state actors are predisposed towards their goals, then external actors may find it possible directly to influence state policies. 'Alternatively, cross-border contacts might serve to empower and legitimise the demands of otherwise weak social groups in relation to various social and political issues', for example, 'environmental, human rights and gender issues' (Risse-Kappen 1994: 186–7; also see Waylen 2003: 173).

(3)   The state–society relationship is characterized by *stalemate*, with both a *relatively* strong state and a *relatively* strong civil society. Such a situation is found not only in certain established democracies – for example, Britain, Canada, France, Germany, India and South Africa – but also, some argue, within the regional context of the European Union (EU).

Within the EU's territorial states, linkages between governing institutions and the public often take place via the medium of various kinds of interest groups. Some 3,000 such 'Euro-groups' are based in Brussels, attempting to intermediate between sections of the public and various EU institutions. Their formal status is recognized by EU decision-makers, as consultation with such interest groups is now officially sanctioned (Etzioni-Halevy 2002). Euro-groups have a presence in some of the more than 70 consultative committees, often featuring mixed memberships of Commission officials, national civil servants and Euro-group representatives. In addition, extensive interest representation also takes place through less structured, informal networks within the EU (Mazey and Richardson 1994). In sum, the EU agenda is open to a variety of interest groups and this has led both to a relatively wide range of policy options and a comparative openness to new ideas on the part of EU institutions.

On the other hand, as Etzioni-Halevy (2002) argues, appearances are to some degree deceptive. This is because it is only at the initial stages of policy formation and the drafting of legislation that such consultation is a feature of decision-making; only at this stage are EU officials *obliged* to consult widely with various interest groups. Moreover, EU officials have no obligation to accept the advice of the Euro-groups and, as a result, the interactive consultative process typically closes up at the point of decision-making (Smith 1999). In other words, there is no guarantee that Euro-groups managing to gain institutional access at the point of policy *formulation* will actually be able to influence policy *implementation*. On the other hand, they cannot be ignored.

Sometimes EU officials seek to mobilize interest groups affected by their policies, consulting with them in order to secure their cooperation – but only for their own purposes (rather than the other way round) (Beetham and Lord 1998). This means that in many cases it is really EU policy-makers who decide which interests to incorporate and how much weight to assign to each of these interests. So the fact that interest groups are consulted does not mean that those serving the interests of, say, the disadvantaged have the same access to policy as those working for the economically privileged, for example, big business. The wider point is that even though the EU attempts to institutionalize balanced consultation between officials and interest groups, its objectives of consultation remain rather limited. While there is effort to balance various interests, participants may only be able to gain access to policies if they have resources to offer. And those with greater resources, such as big business, may well have most influence. Etzioni-Halevy (2002: 210) puts it like this: 'The very fact that there is such a maze of interest groups contending for influence creates a danger of mutual blockage. This is of advantage to the more privileged interests, as it favors the existing situation, thereby protecting privileges already in place.' It also underlines a potential situation of *stalemate* in relation to the relative strengths of state and society in the EU.

(4)   The fourth category comprises countries with institutionalized, consensus-seeking, *corporatist structures*, found in various forms in certain established democracies, including Japan, Denmark and Sweden (Swank 2002). This situation is characterized by both strong state and identifiable society interests, which, rather than endure a situation of stalemate, work consensually to negotiate mutually beneficial political and economic outcomes. In such circumstances, external actors typically have good access to both state and civil society actors.

(5)   In *society-dominated political structures*, individual external actors and collective coalitions have no trouble in penetrating societal and political systems, since they provide multiple channels to influence policies. However, easy access does not necessarily translate into guaranteed policy impact. 'Governments are likely to have less control over the access of transnational actors into the societal and political institutions', but it is not certain that easy access guarantees policy impact. In fact, given the likely 'fragmented nature of the political institutions, the requirements for putting together "winning coalitions" are likely to demand much greater efforts for the transnational actors to be successful' (Risse-Kappen 1994: 197). Put another way, for external actors to have clear policy impact requires them to make quite elaborate efforts not only to build coalitions, but also more generally to foster relations with the political system's significant players.

(6)   The final category comprises states with *fragile political structures*. We noted in relation to *state-controlled* and *state-dominated* political structures that when states closely control their domestic political environments then they are also able to control external actors' access. At the other end of the spectrum of state strength, external actor access should be easier because such countries have weak and fragmented political institutions. However, easy access for external actors does not necessarily translate into significant leverage on state policies. This is because while they may readily penetrate countries with fragile political institutions, they may find that when they gain access there is little institutionally to work with and hence help achieve their goals. This is because the state and civil society are both weak; hence, necessary coalition-building with societal actors is next to impossible and, given organizational weaknesses, bound to fail. Even if external actors do achieve their goals in changing policies, the state is often going to be too weak to execute its decisions.

Our discussion suggests two conclusions at this stage. First, significantly to influence domestic policy-making and policies – that is, to change decisions in a desired direction – external actors need to overcome two hurdles. First, they must gain access to the political decision-making structures of the target state and generate and/or contribute to successful policy coalitions. Second, the ability to influence policy depends on building domestic coalitions with key policy networks that have – broadly or narrowly – the same goals as the external actors. The implication is that the characteristics of domestic political structures will be very important, as they help determine (1) the availability of access points into the political system, and (2) the size of and requirements for winning coalitions. In sum, on the one hand, 'domestic structures mediate, filter, and refract the efforts by transnational actors and alliances to influence policies in . . . various issue areas'; on the other hand, 'the extent to which [external] actors gain *access* to the political systems seems to be primarily a function of the state structure' (Risse-Kappen 1994: 213).

Political Opportunity Structures

The concept of 'political opportunity structure' (POS) emerged in the late 1960s and early 1970s. Initially, the aim was to examine the causes of collective action and the genesis of social movements in established democracies, especially in Western Europe and North America. Scholars were interested in finding out what happens politically when people engage in collective action for identifiable goals within individual countries (Tarrow 1998: 18–20; Kriesi et al. 1992). The concept of POS is characterized by Kitschelt (1986: 58) as 'reflecting specific configurations of resources, institutional arrangements and historical precedents for social mobilization, which facilitate the development of protest movements in some instances and constrain them in others'. He differentiates between its different aspects. First, a POS allows for 'coercive, normative, remunerative and informational resources'. Second, it reflects extant 'institutional rules', reinforcing 'patterns of interaction between government and interest groups, and electoral laws'. 'Institutional rules' include both formal institutional arrangements – extant political and organizational arrangements institutionalized under a ruling regime – and various informal procedures also important for political outcomes. Third, he suggests that the institutional opportunity structure is likely to be relatively static over time, often for as long as a particular form of political regime is in power. Finally, the character of a POS is strongly influenced by its degree of openness to participation. This highlights how important it is that governments are responsive both to the input side (agenda-setting and decision-making) and also in terms of outputs, that is, implementation processes (Kitschelt 1986: 61–3).

   The concept of POS, originally developed in the context of social movement and protest behaviour research, has been extended over time to cover wider areas of participation research. It was initially 'used mainly in the singular, relating to the whole political system. The plural has been applied only in analyses comparing several states' (Nentwich 1996: 3). More recently, the general idea of 'opportunity structures' – used by various kinds of political actor to participate politically – has been used in explanations of how individual political systems function. For example, Mazey and Richardson (1994: 13) claim that the number and range of such structures has increased considerably in many established democracies. This implies that 'every opportunity to participate, every channel into the core of the decision-making (and implementation) system is associated with specific (structural) properties which differ from channel to channel'. The shifting nature of the terms used relates 'to the broadening of the concept in the sense that the main focus on protest movements has been replaced by more general research into all forms of political participation' (Nentwich 1996: 2), including both 'conventional' and 'unconventional' political involvement.

Our interest in political opportunity structures is not limited to the ways – both conventional and unconventional – that domestic actors can seek to influence agenda-setting, decision-making and implementation. We are also concerned with the ways that external actors seek to pursue such goals in the domestic political contexts of our three categories of country. Consequently, we need to examine two separate types of political context: domestic and regional/international contexts, where there are authoritative political institutions engaged in agenda-setting, decision-making and implementation. This suggests the idea of opportunity structures in the plural – with characteristics differing from policy area to policy area, both within countries and regionally/internationally. These 'opportunity structures for participation' (OSPs) are the aggregation of various channels of access – 'conventional and unconventional, direct and indirect, formal and informal, active and passive, policy- and polity-related, implemented and not yet implemented (i.e. innovative) involvement or participation' (Nentwich 1996: 3) – to the public sphere and to the policy-making and implementation processes available to various kinds of political actors.

The Influence of External Actors on Domestic Politics

J. Smith et al. (1997: 66) argue that political opportunity structures – 'factors that facilitate or constrain social change efforts' – are not found only in domestic contexts. This is because not only do 'national states produce structures of opportunities, but [also] intergovernmental and transgovernmental arenas (such as the UN or the EU)'. They also provide structures of opportunity as they facilitate or restrain the capacity of international actors. However, the ability of such actors to influence agenda-setting, decision-making, and implementation both within individual countries and as well as regional/international organizations depends on their ability in two key respects. First, they must have the capacity to interact and work with the established political structures. Second, the external actors must be a part of 'winning coalitions', the constituents of which will in part also be a function of individual OSPs. Variations in the latter can help account for differences in the policy impact of external actors, whether singly or in coalitions. Overall, the nature of extant OSPs can be pivotal in determining to what extent external actors can significantly influence politics at both domestic and regional levels. Remember, however, that as we discussed in chapter 4, structures rarely tell us the whole story. We also need to take into account the influence of contingency, including what individual actors or groups of actors do.

To what extent does globalization facilitate the involvement of external actors in national and regional/international OSPs? Bermeo (2003) observes that at various points in the twentieth century certain domestic developments had profound international significance. For example, the success of the Bolshevik revolution in 1917 'gave leftist movement entrepreneurs in Europe new and highly influential allies' and led to a 'European restructuring', 'the downfall of traditional ruling systems' and 'proximate shifts in ruling alignments' that opened up access to power for new or previously unin-fluential political groups. Forty years later, in the late 1950s, the 'success of the Cuban revolution gave leftist movement entrepreneurs highly "influential allies" in Latin America' (Bermeo 2003: 231–2). Later, in the 1980s, the end of the cold war, the third wave of democracy and factors associated with globalization collectively offered new opportunities for international – state and non-state – actors to seek to influence agenda-setting and decision-making in both domestic and regional/international con-texts. The growing importance of what I shall call 'international opportunity structures for participation' (IOSPs) has led to a research focus on various kinds of transnational and international actors, including: (1) cross-border political parties, (2) international non-governmental organizations (INGOs) and (3) transnational corporations (TNCs). Although their political significance varies, the importance of such actors is related to their ability to exploit both domestic and regional/international OSPs.

It is argued that the degree of success of such actors is linked to *the extent of inter-national institutionalization* that covers specific issue areas. 'International institutionali-zation' refers to the extent to which 'international agreements, regimes or organizations regulate a specific issue-area'. The more a specific issue-area is overseen by international cooperation, then the more likely it is that state boundaries are permeable and hence facilitate external activity (Risse-Kappen 1995a: 6–7). When the OSP is favourable, then actors should be able to press their case more successfully than when it is not. Regional and international organizations, such as the EU, the North American Free Trade Agree-ment (NAFTA) and the UN, can mediate the policy impact of external actors, making 'it easier for international and transnational networks to lobby governments and other representatives' (Martens 2001: 3). Keck and Sikkink (1998a: 2) have identified what they call a 'boomerang pattern' in this regard. This is when 'domestic social actors bypass the repressive state in order to find international allies who can bring pressure on the state in question from the outside'. The boomerang pattern is of particular importance in relation to the EU, the UN and NAFTA, because inter-state relations among member states serve to 'lower' state boundaries, thereby allowing for flourishing cross-border relations. In addition, this is a favourable context whereby such international govern-mental organizations (IGOs) serve as mediators for transnational activity. This aids INGO cross-border access by 'loosen[ing] up or relax[ing] the[ir] political opportunity structure[s]'. This can also serve more generally to 'legitimize transnational activities in the "target state"; actors are less and less treated as "foreigners", but as almost indis-tinguishable from other domestic players' (Risse-Kappen 1995a: 32). In sum, the domes-tic political opportunity structure of both states and IGOs can facilitate or restrict the opportunities of both domestic *and* external actors (Martens 2001).

Scholars have now begun to develop theoretical models to try to explain and account for such international and transnational interactions. Among these is the study of what Keck and Sikkink (1998a) call 'transnational advocacy networks' (TANs). TANs com-prise 'relevant actors working internationally on an issue . . . bound together by shared values, a common discourse, and dense exchange of information and services'. The purpose of TANs is to enable the interaction of various national entities – such as groups, domestic NGOs and/or social movements – with INGOs and/or sympathetic states. Working together, they seek to establish or – if they already exist – develop links to pressurize norm-violating states to amend their behaviour in relation to various issue areas, including developmental, environmental and human rights concerns.

In the remainder of this chapter we examine the significance of various kinds of external actor on domestic political (and political-economic) outcomes in our three categories of countries: established democracies, transitional democracies and non-democracies. We will see that such outcomes reflect the extent to which external actors can interact with significant groups of domestic political actors to pursue collective goals. The implication is that the significance of such external actors will vary from issue to issue and from country to country.

Since the end of the cold war and the deepening of interdependence, various aspects of globalization are judged to be analytically significant in this regard. This is because globalization implies increased significance for a range of international and transnational actors and as a result governments find it more problematic to control their territorial penetration (Watts 2004). While international interactions involve state-to-state contact, transnational relations are 'regular interactions across national boundaries when at least one actor is a non-state agent or does not operate on behalf of a national government or an IGO' (Willetts 2001: 358).

Beginning in the 1970s, there has been intermittent academic interest in the political consequences of transnational relations. In the 1980s, reflecting the rise of neo-realism, such attention all but withered away, although it later re-emerged after the cold war in the 1990s. Now, much consideration is devoted to both international actors – that is, states and transnational actors, a category of actor whose numbers have increased greatly over the last three decades. We start from the premise that a focus on what Risse-Kappen (1995a) calls 'political images of policy making' is useful to highlight the rise to prominence of certain issues and channels of influence in this regard. The identification of various 'images' of policy-making does not imply that a common logic applies to all policy-makers. Rather, it depends considerably on the political characteristics of the polity where policy-makers operate. This suggests that the key political characteristics of a polity, especially whether it is recognizably democratic, influence what policy-makers do and how they do it. The following hypothesis seeks to capture the point:

Countries have variable structural political characteristics that, interacting with perceptions of decision-makers, combine to produce certain kinds of outcome. These factors are analytically central in seeking to explain how various external actors affect political outcomes within countries.

To examine this issue further, we focus next upon three kinds of external actor – international governmental organizations (IGOs),[3] international non-governmental organizations (INGOs) and transnational corporations (TNCs) – to ascertain how each can affect domestic policy-making and outcomes.

The first thing to note, as shown in table 5.2, is that there is a large number of politically significant state and non-state actors. The huge number of actors represented in the table both create and reflect dense cross-border connections, and are instrumental in creating more complex patterns of governance within countries. We have already noted that, theoretically, individual countries' opportunity structures for participation

---

[3] These are supranational bodies that can override national sovereignty. In the context of the EU, such bodies include the Commission, Court, Parliament and Central Bank (Christiansen 2001: 504).

Table 5.2 Types and numbers of international actor

Actor	Number	Examples
States	192 (members of the UN)	Brazil, India, Nigeria, United Kingdom
International governmental organizations	c.250–350	European Union, North Atlantic Treaty Organization, Organization of Islamic Conference, United Nations
Transnational corporations	c.60,000	Coca Cola, Ford, Microsoft, Nestlé, Shell
Single country non-governmental organizations	c.10,000	Freedom House, Médecins sans Frontières
International non-governmental organizations	c.25,000*	Amnesty International, Greenpeace International, Oxfam, Red Crescent

*These are 'active' INGOs, although Anheier and Themudo (2002: 195) note another 22,000 they characterize as 'dead, inactive, and unconfirmed'.
Source: Adapted from Willetts (2001: 357) and Anheier and Themudo (2002: 195).

will mediate such actors' influence. We should also note, however, that the impact of external actors on domestic political environments is an empirical issue.

Let us look next at three categories of cross-border actor – IGOs, INGOs and TNCs – and examine how each can influence politics in our three categories of states.

International Governmental Organizations (IGOs)

Only internationally recognized states can be members of international governmental organizations. Most IGOs were founded after 1945, although some functional bodies were established earlier, for example, the International Telecommunications Union was established nearly a century earlier, in 1865. Several IGOs inaugurated after World War II – for example, the United Nations (UN), North Atlantic Treaty Organization (NATO), the EU and the Organization of Islamic Conference (OIC) – have multiple tasks, including security, welfare and human rights goals.

Willetts (2001: 357) notes that there are more than 250 IGOs. Conceptually, members of an IGO will aim to preserve their formal autonomy while being bound in certain policy-making options as a consequence of their IGO commitments. Precisely how IGO membership can impact upon countries' domestic politics depends on the extent to which countries are enmeshed in IGO networks and their domestic political arrangements.

Established democracies

Some established democracies, notably in Western Europe, belong to hundreds of IGOs, implying myriad contexts whereby the latter can theoretically influence domestic policy-making and outcomes (Hague and Harrop 2001: 49). It is suggested that one of the impacts of extensive IGO membership is a blurring of the boundaries between domestic and foreign policy; and this is likely to undermine governmental cohesion. This is because, as Hague and Harrop (2001: 49) note, multiple IGO membership can lead to 'a club-like spirit . . . develop[ing] among ministers in "their" IGO'. Webber and Smith (2002: 64–5) point out that 'direct contacts between governments usually below the level of the executive policy makers' develop either from functional necessity or as a consequence of more explicitly political pressures. Such transgovernmental coalitions – involving sub-units of national governments – may 'attempt to achieve specific political goals in the "target" state of their activities' (Risse-Kappen 1995a: 8).

In pursuit of common objectives, actors located in specific ministries in different countries may seek to create coalitions against 'rival' ministries within their own governments. This situation can readily occur when a country belongs to many IGOs, because multiple IGO membership may serve to encourage both fragmentation within national governments as well as a shared sense of camaraderie among ministers with similar areas of responsibility. Such transgovernmental coalitions may also function not only to affect the production of government policy, but also to influence 'any subsequent coordination of policy into a joint intergovernmental position. In such circumstances state and coalition actors are numerous and the bargaining calculations of these actors ever more intricate' (Webber and Smith 2002: 65).

Transitional democracies

Complex transgovernmental relations are uncommon away from Western Europe and North America (where the development in the 1990s of NAFTA is a significant stimulus of transgovernmental relations in and between the three member states: Canada, Mexico and the United States). Most transitional democracies, however, belong to relatively few IGOs and, as a result, there are fewer opportunities to develop the kinds of transgovernmental interactions noted above. However, this does not imply that IGOs are necessarily without influence in transitional democracies. For example, the US government has used the carrot of NAFTA membership to encourage Mexico both to democratize and economically liberalize. Further, the EU has encouraged a range of transitional democracies in Central and Eastern Europe (CEE) to reform both politically and economically, with the prize of potential EU membership.

Potential EU membership was also the touted reward in the case of another transitional democracy, Turkey. The EU has sought to use both political and economic conditionality[4] to encourage Turkey's government to reform politically and to improve its human rights regime. Turkey's case illustrates, however, that the application of conditionality can lead to a variety of outcomes. Turkey, on the periphery of Europe, has long aspired to join the EU. For years, the country's relatively poor human rights record gave the EU a defensible reason not to progress with Turkey's membership

---

[4] Yilmaz (2002: 83) defines conditionality as the 'effectiveness, visibility and immediacy of external punishments and rewards'. The EU has employed conditionality since the 1980s to achieve certain foreign policy goals – including good governance, democratization, better human rights, the rule of law and economic liberalization – in numerous transitional democracies and non-democracies.

application. Recently, however, Turkey's democratic and human rights record has demonstrably improved – to the extent that EU membership now seems a realizable ambition.[5] There is, however, another important dimension to note. After the 11 September 2001 terrorist attacks on the USA, EU governments seemed to believe that it was better to have Muslim Turkey in the EU rather than, potentially, part of the anti-Western 'axis of evil'. As a consequence, in early 2003, the European Commission recommended that aid to Turkey should be doubled – from €0.5bn to €1.05bn – in 2004–6. This was a calculated attempt both to encourage Turkey's moderate Islamically influenced government to refrain from military intervention in Iraq as well as concrete encouragement to continue with domestic political and human rights reforms (Osborn 2003b).

Non-democracies

Many non-democracies belong to few IGOs and, as a consequence, there is little potential for the latter to have significant domestic impact. Unlike some former communist CEE countries and Turkey, EU membership was not on the agenda for geographically contiguous non-democracies, such as Morocco, although its government was encouraged to undertake political and economic reforms (Gillespie and Whitehead 2002: 199). More generally, by the early 2000s, a decade of EU democracy promotion efforts focused on North Africa's non-democracies had led to disappointing results. 'North African governments ha[d] contrived either to nullify' such external encouragement 'or to reorient it towards a project compatible with their own objectives' (Gillespie and Whitehead 2002: 192). It is clear that EU encouragement to North African governments to reform politically was no match for entrenched domestic factors who did not share that objective.

Holland (2002) argues that this outcome was not a regional aberration. During the 1990s the EU applied sanctions against thirteen African, Caribbean and Pacific states – all then led by non-democratic governments, and with all but two (Fiji, Haiti) located in Africa. Holland notes (2002: 132) that there were quite similar outcomes: targeted governments seemed rather impervious to externally encouraged reform. This suggests that the use of conditionality does not necessarily produce normatively desirable political and economical changes in unwilling states. What is also needed for external pressure to make a difference is to interact and work with key domestic reformist groups. Consequently, EU conditionality had greater influence in some transitional countries compared to non-democracies because the former had significant numbers of pro-democracy reformers compared to the latter. In addition, no non-democratic country was offered the inducement of potential EU membership, unlike Turkey and some CEE countries; this served as an important means of encouragement to reform

[5] Freedom House (2002: 12) reported that 'Turkey [had] registered forward progress as a result of the loosening of restrictions on Kurdish culture. *Legislators made progress on an improved human rights framework, the product of Turkey's effort to integrate into European structures.* At the same time, political rights were enhanced as the country's military showed restraint in the aftermath of a free and fair election that saw the sweeping victory of a moderate Islamist opposition party' (emphasis added).

politically. In sum, it is plausible to surmise that, if geographical criteria were met, then a democratic transition was a necessary trigger for EU financial aid and, potentially, Union membership (Mair and Zielonka 2002).

International Non-Governmental Organizations (INGOs)

The number of active INGOs has grown more than tenfold in the last three decades – from around 2,000 in the early 1970s to about 25,000 in the early 2000s (Willetts 2001: 357; Anheier and Themudo 2002: 195). INGOs are cross-border bodies, such as Amnesty International, Greenpeace International and the Roman Catholic Church, whose members are individuals or private groups drawn from more than one country. The chief theoretical assumptions concerning INGOs are that states are not the only important cross-border actors in international politics and that INGOs can be politically signifi-cant. This can be noted in the case of collapsed states – that is, where state authority no longer exists – reliant on aid provided by INGOs 'for basic supplies and services' (Hague and Harrop 2001: 47). INGOs can also be executors of policy stemming from various international organizations, including the UN and the EU.

Some INGOs also seek to change state policy more proactively in a variety of – politi-cal, social or economic – areas. The influence of such actors is not assured but depends on two main factors: (1) how skilful they are in infiltrating national policy-making processes and (2) the extent to which a targeted government is receptive to them. Their effectiveness may be augmented when groups of transnational actors link up – for example, in pursuit of political, religious, gender-orientated or developmental goals – to encourage popular pressure for domestic change. This can lead to the development of 'transnational citizen groups' (TCGs).

Partly a function of the global communications revolution, the chief consequence of TCGs is regional or global spread and interchange of ideas and information. To under-stand the social dynamics of TCGs it is useful to perceive the international system as an agglomeration of various issue areas – for example, religious, environmental, human rights, political, gender and development concerns – organized under the rubric of 'social transnationalism'. This is facilitated by multiple linkages between individuals and groups interested in the same goals but separated by large physical distances. Cross-border exchanges of experiences and information and shift of funds not only facilitate devel-opment of TCG strategies but can lead to national, regional and/or global campaigns. This underlines that social transnationalism:

> is not just a matter of individuals and masses who feel conscious of being primary inter-national subjects as they are entitled to civil, political, economic, social and cultural right by positive international law. In the world system these subjects form the international social layer which claims primacy over the diplomatic layer. Today the chances of social transnationalism reside in INGOs whose members cross states and assert 'pan-human' interests such as the promotion of human rights, environmental ecology, [and] international development co-operation. (Attina 1989: 350–1)

Collectively, the agglomeration of TCGs comprises 'transnational civil society' (TCS). Unlike domestic civil society, TCS is not territorially fixed. Instead, according to

Lipschutz (1992: 390), TCS is 'the self-conscious construction of networks of knowledge and action, by decentred, local actors, that cross the reified boundaries of space as though they were not there'. Many component parts of TCS work towards normatively 'progressive' goals, including improved standards of governance, by encouraging popular, cross-border coalitions to challenge government decisions on a variety of issues. TCS effectiveness may be increased when influential organizations – such as Amnesty International, Human Rights Watch and Freedom House – play a leading role (Risse and Ropp 1999: 238). Such INGOs were influential in getting various human rights issues on to international conference agendas, such as a UN-sponsored human rights conference held in Vienna in 1992, and one on gender issues in Beijing (1995).

Established democracies

It is sometimes suggested that it is difficult to draw a neat distinction between demo-cratic and non-democratic states in relation to the influence of INGOs. However, it does seem likely that variations in accessibility of domestic political structures will likely mediate their influence. For example, compared to other kinds of regime, democratic polities normally offer INGOs most assured access to relevant policy-making figures. This is especially the case in relation to countries enmeshed in regional organizations, for example NAFTA and the EU.

Macdonald and Schwartz (2002: 149–50) suggest that a number of North American INGOs, interested in, inter alia, labour, human rights, environmental and women's issues, have sought to 'strengthen their impact through cross-border ties with similar organizations', forming 'major umbrella coalitions', and lining 'up according to their position on issues and not by nationality'. Their common objective is to influence broadly political outcomes by collectively targeting policy-makers, who in some cases may actively seek their advice and support. The development of NAFTA has been a key stimulus to such groups and their activities. For example, the Hemispheric Social Alliance (HSA) brings together leading social movements and trade union federations from various regional countries, including the USA, Brazil and Canada. Their chief aim is to develop alternative proposals for developmentally orientated hemispheric eco-nomic integration. To this end, the first 'People's Summit' was held in 2001 in Santiago, Chile. The meeting brought together around 800 leaders of interested groups from almost every country in the Americas (Massicotte, forthcoming, cited in Macdonald and Schwartz 2002: 151). In sum, the activities of HSA suggest that under certain circum-stances, in this case the development of NAFTA, regional potential exists to develop cross-border ties to improve popular involvement in the formulation of developmental strategies.

However, as Macdonald and Schwartz (2002: 138–9) note, 'formidable obstacles remain' in the achievement of the region's objectives in NAFTA. In the region's various national settings, obstacles are chiefly institutional in character, for example, the author-ity of Canadian provinces to affect trade decisions (Delagran 1992) and the nature of the Mexican legal system. Overall, the notably different political institutions of Canada, Mexico and the USA influence how their roles are executed. For example, Canada has a parliamentary system and multiple, cohesive political parties. It is a federal system, as are the other two countries, but one where provincial authority is relatively stronger.

The United States has a congressional system of divided powers and an established two-party system. Its political parties are rather open, implying considerable scope for individual politicians' personal agendas. As a consequence, local and regional interests have significant opportunities for national-level representation and influence. In Mexico, the situation is different again. Until the December 2000 presidential elections, Mexico had a one-party system with a highly centralized polity and a powerful presidency. Organized along corporatist lines, business, workers and peasants were strongly linked to the ruling party. While already changing, such characteristics were major determinants of Mexico's NAFTA membership debate.

> Party positions on trade during the NAFTA debate thus were not only different in the three nations (and from party to party within each nation), but were arrived at by different processes. In the three countries, NGOs exercised pressure on the parties and directly on the government at different points, with different results. (Macdonald and Schwartz 2002: 138–9)

Regarding the international context, power differences between the three countries were crucial. Perceived US hegemony meant that its interactions, including those coming from its NGOs, were often regarded with suspicion in Canada and Mexico.

This brief discussion of INGO involvement in the development of NAFTA suggests two main conclusions. First, both domestic and regional structures of governance – involving state and non-state actors – can have policy inputs. Second, the 'state world' and the 'society world' need each other: INGOs need states in order to get their preferred outcomes enacted, while states can also find INGOs useful – to gain access to new, policy-relevant ideas, to help create and/or develop international institutions and to monitor regime compliance.

Transitional democracies and non-democracies

Because it is not always easy to draw hard and fast distinctions between these two generic categories of country, we will deal with them together in this section. Yilmaz suggests that in such countries, transnational actors, including some INGOs, are 'mostly beyond either state control or mediation', and have replaced 'state-to-state relations' as their 'principle mode of international relations'. He argues that some such states, including Turkey,

> have been rapidly losing their control over the movements of people, capital and information in and out of their boundaries . . . Transnational companies, and world-wide communication and entertainment networks, have become more influential in controlling the flows of people, ideas and capital from one place to another. (Yilmaz 2002: 82–3)

Mendelson and Glenn (2002: 11) suggest three types of integration that can differently influence the policy impact of INGOs among transitional democracies and non-democracies. They divide such countries into three categories:

1 *Thickly integrated states*, for example, Poland, Czech Republic, Hungary, and Nigeria, significantly involved in regional and/or global organizations.

2 *Thinly integrated states*, for example, Slovakia, Russia, Algeria, less significantly involved in regional and/or global organizations.
3 *Unintegrated states*, for example, Kazakhstan, Kyrgyzstan, Uzbekistan and Tahiti, hardly involved at all in regional and/or global organizations.

Among thickly integrated states, Poland offers an interesting example of the involvement of an INGO – the Roman Catholic Church (RCC) – in the transition from authoritarian to post-communist government. The RCC's transnational activity – in tandem with the trade union Solidarity – was influential in encouraging the resignation of the communist government. Encouraged by the Pope's expressions of support, Polish Catholics gradually became both a counter-culture and an alternative social space to the official communist ideology and channels. This led, in 1980, to the creation of the Solidarity movement that articulated and expressed Catholic social ethics as a counter-statement to those of communism. This not only reflected a significant convergence between national and religious identity in Poland, but also, just as importantly, it symbolized the failure of a communist (secular) identity fundamentally to implant itself in the hearts and minds of most Poles, a people with a cultural heritage firmly based in Christian-Catholic traditions. In sum, Christian-Catholic heritage and traditions were a vital resource in helping create and then sustain resistance in Poland. More generally, the Church's institutional concern with issues of social justice that had first emerged in the 1960s was brought to the fore in the 1980s and 1990s. At that time, it became involved in various momentous global changes, including the breakdown of communism in Eastern Europe and democratization in Latin America and Africa (Haynes 2001b).

Next we examine further examples of INGO involvement in a thickly integrated state (Nigeria), a thinly integrated state (Algeria) and a non-integrated 'state' (Tahiti).[6] In each of them, INGOs have been influential in helping articulate and focus popular, anti-state struggles over various issues in recent years. Such concerns may have been expressed in the rhetoric of environmentalism or feminism or democracy or religion or ethnicity. However, basic issues seem rather similar, whatever the political forms and ideological context. At the core is a tendency to reject power imposed without consultation or responsibility and to demand a fair share of resources for all. Apparent differences between – the angry, mostly young, people of Tahiti who appeared to want to burn down their own capital city, Papeete, in September 1995 following France's decision to resume nuclear testing at Mururoa Atoll; Algerian Islamists, who in 1991 launched a still uncompleted civil war that led, by the end of 2004, to more than 120,000 deaths; and the Ogoni people of Nigeria's anti-state struggle galvanized by the state killings of author and environmentalist, Ken Saro-Wiwa and eight other Ogoni activists in November 1995 – are not as large as geographical distance and professed political objectives might first suggest.

The main characteristic linking these three sets of anti-systemic actors is alienation from unrepresentative political systems dominated by small elite groups. Many powerless people in these three states – including women, young people and national religious and ethnic minorities – seemed to believe that their governments were not sufficiently responsive to their demands and did not adequately incorporate their con-

---

[6] Tahiti is still a colonial possession of France.

cerns into policy-making. In short, their political leaders failed to address their concerns, while their frustrations and exclusions increasingly seemed to chime with extant global currents.

What could the powerless people do about it? While their responses appeared both diverse and politically ambivalent, what they all had in common was, first, they all formed proactive NGOs to contest their political marginality and, second, they sought the assistance of INGOs in pursuit of their objectives. In other words, Tahitian anti-nuclear testing groups, Algerian Islamists and anti-state Ogonis all sought to exploit political opportunities offered by globalization. Each group did this by linking up with sympathetic INGOs to spearhead extra-territorial campaigns designed to elicit sympathy and support from as wide a forum as possible. Both the Ogonis and Tahiti's anti-nuclear testing groups developed strong links with Greenpeace International and Human Rights Watch. Algerian Islamists undertook a different kind of international campaign. Denied electoral success in January 1992 by a military coup, they responded by launching both a civil war in Algeria and a brief bombing campaign on the streets of Paris in 1995. In addition, they became part of a transnational network of co-religionists with two goals: an Islamic state in Algeria and the removal of a perceived US 'imperialist presence' from the Muslim Middle East (Haynes 1997).

These examples emphasize the importance of transnational links for the achievement of national political, social and economic goals. Interaction with INGOs can be especially important as such purposive inter-group relationships often conducted across great distances can have important political results. Not least, they can change the context of politics, offering political actors new possibilities, values and allies. Transnational linkages with various INGOs also offer the chance of widespread publicity for their campaigns. In sum, the development of transnational networks, taking advantage of new communications technologies, helps anti-state groups to tap into wider – regional and global – networks.

Transnational Corporations (TNCs)

Numerous commentators have noted the existence of 'an increasingly interdependent global economy [that] affect[s] politics within national boundaries' (Hague and Harrop 2001: 56–7). TNCs are often singled out in this regard as they are key actors engaged in cross-border import/export activities. Changes in health and safety standards, regulation of communication facilities and governments' general economic policy can obviously affect their ability to trade and to make profits. If the result is likely to be beneficial, then they may not feel the need to respond; but if they expect to lose financially, they may judge it necessary to lobby the foreign government. Willetts (2001: 362) notes four common routes they may take in this regard:

1 Indirectly: the TNC asks its own government to put pressure on the foreign government.
2 Indirectly: the TNC raises a general policy question in an international organization, for example the EU.
3 Directly at home: the TNC lobbies an appropriate diplomatic embassy.
4 Directly in the other country: the TNC lobbies government ministries.

While TNCs are not new, having first emerged in the nineteenth century or even earlier, two aspects of economic globalization have been central to their recent growth in numbers and significance: the internationalization of production and the international- ization of financial transactions as a result of freeing of trade barriers and general growth of the global economy.

Nationalists often condemn TNCs as subversive of national cultures and sovereignty. Trade unions regularly criticize them because of their adaptability, and socialists and anti-globalization activists berate them as amoral instruments of global capitalism. Moving to low-wage economies in pursuit of lower costs, not least to avoid minimum- wage legislation, the activities of TNCs can provide an argument for those favouring international organization. However, when in the early 1990s the EU tried to control their activities, it found it could not realistically prevent them moving from country to country or region to region.

TNCs may organize their production, marketing and/or distribution regionally or globally. Yet, even when they do appear to have clear national interests, it remains the case that their activities are predominantly geared to maximizing international com- petitive position and profitability. Consequently, individual (national) subsidiaries operate in the context of an overall corporate strategy and thus investment and pro- duction decisions may not primarily reflect local or national conditions or considera- tions. For example, many financial organizations such as banks appear progressively more global in scale and orientation; one consequence is that they are able to monitor and respond to developments around the world almost instantaneously. Moreover, new information technology radically increases the mobility of certain economic units – such as currencies, stocks, shares and 'futures'. The consequences of economic globalization make it possible to speak of the emergence of a single global financial market with virtual 24-hour-a-day trading. However, some productive resources – for example, man- ufacturing units – cannot be moved around the globe instantaneously (although they may well only tie themselves to a specific location for about five years: the time it typically takes for investments, say in a microelectronics factory, to generate a satisfac- tory profit).

Markets and societies are sensitive to one another as the Southeast Asian economic travails of 1997/8 made clear. In general, the very possibility of states' pursuing a *national* economic policy is reduced. National governments' monetary and fiscal poli- cies are increasingly dominated by movements in international financial markets, with global foreign exchange trading over $650 *billion* a *day* – that is, twice the total foreign exchange reserves of the US, Japanese and British central banks at any one time. Add to this the dependency of levels of employment, investment and revenue within a country of TNC decisions about the location of their facilities, and it seems clear that governmental capacity to pursue independent macroeconomic strategies is everywhere circumscribed. The consequence is that to a large extent – although *how* large is a subject of controversy – many concepts of national economic policy formulation now seem of doubtful value.

It is not that national rules and policies are obsolete or no longer needed. Rather, it is that they cannot work unless close attention is paid to what is being done elsewhere. National controls and regulations have limited effectiveness if they are at odds with wider international conditions. The outcome is that the globalization of economic rela- tionships has altered the possibility of states' deploying many traditional areas of their economic policy in the face of a global division of labour, widespread absence of capital controls and a global financial market.

However, such loss is not uniform across economic sectors or societies more generally. Some individual markets can, it appears, isolate themselves from transnational economic networks by employing measures designed to restore the boundaries or 'separateness' of markets, extend national laws to cover internationally mobile factors and/or adopt cooperative policies with other countries to coordinate economic policy. In particular, regionalization of sections of the world economy, with economic activity clustering around a number of poles – notably, Western Europe, North America and Japan – provides some ability to try to regulate market trends.

Established democracies

Internationalization of production and finance erodes state capacity to control their own economies. As already noted, TNC responses to changing economic circumstances – including strategies of adjustment to compete with low-cost producers and/or concentration on high-value-added goods tailored to specialized markets – are rarely if ever favourable to national strategies of regulation. Consequently, national regulatory strategies either have to assist the process of adjustment or risk a declining tax base as production facilities move abroad; in the latter case, governments must find less macro and more micro or local regulatory regimes to assist economic activity.

In addition, the apparently quickening pace of technological and economic change implies that substantive 'command and control' regulation is increasingly obsolete. The clear diminution of state autonomy in the sphere of economic policy emphasizes the gap appearing between the idea of a political community determining its own future and the dynamics of the contemporary world economy. Such factors are felt most acutely – but by no means only – in the world's marginal and weaker economies, mostly transitional democracies and non-democracies. However, the post-war demise of the European empires, erosion of the USA's economic position and increases in internationalization of productive capital and finance since the 1970s have combined to leave even industrially developed established democracies with fewer options in terms of economic policy. While this alone does not amount to a direct erosion of an individual state's entitlement to rule its own territory, it does leave them exposed and vulnerable to the networks of economic forces and relations – especially TNCs – ranging in and through them.

Relationships between economic and political power are highly controversial. An emblematic event in this regard was the involvement of an American TNC, International Telephone and Telegraph (ITT), in the successful anti-Allende military coup in Chile in 1973. However, it is important to note, that such overt and violent intrusions into a country's domestic politics are very unusual. Research on TNCs that manage to be effective actors in national, regional and global political contexts suggests that they can achieve their objectives via more subtle – but not necessarily less effective – methods. The activities of the European Roundtable of Industrialists (ERT) is a good example of how such influence acquisition operates in the EU and underlines how corporate interests can influence the policy-making.

The ERT was founded in 1983, with a membership comprising the heads of more than 40 of the most powerful, most globalizing industrial giants, including BP, Daimler-Benz, Fiat, Shell and Siemens. From the foundation of the ERT, its guiding figures have been drawn from among the most powerful and influential industry leaders, including Fiat's Agnelli, Philips's Dekker and Volvo's Gyllenhammer. The ERT provides an agenda-setting role within the EU, encouraging its policy-making institutions, such as the Commission, to pursue policies that the ERT believes will be most beneficial for its members, including the goals of regional (and global) free trade and competitiveness. Overall, the influence of the ERT in the EU highlights a disjuncture between the formal authority of the state and the spatial reach of corporations and their control of systems of production, distribution and exchange. Sklair (2002) notes that the significance of the ERT is to undermine the institutional competence and effectiveness of EU institutions. It also shows how the latter are subject to sustained lobbying and pressure from powerful organizations representing the interests of big business.

Transitional democracies and non-democracies

Many analysts see economic globalization as an unstoppable process – to the point that serious questions are now raised about the relevance and effectiveness of individual countries in trying to manage national economic activities. Fukuyama (1992: 275) argues that, whereas nationalism once fulfilled an integrative role that met the needs of early capitalism, 'those same economic forces are now encouraging the breakdown of national barriers through the creation of a single, integrated world market'. It is a process that seems to follow its own technical and economic logic, facilitated by cross-border mobility of capital, growth in foreign direct investment and increased TNC economic importance. To this must be added the significant amounts of employment, investment and revenue dependent on the decisions of TNCs when choosing where to invest and locate in terms primarily of profitability rather than national considerations. 'In contrast to *national* exports and imports of goods and services, the organization, flow and purview of FDI and global capital, undertaken by . . . TNCs, assume a global market place' (Sen 1999: 62).

What is the role of TNCs in relation to transitional democracies and non-democracies? Most TNCs are no doubt strong supporters, along with Western governments and International Financial Institutions (IFIs), of the Washington consensus, rooted in the belief that the best framework for globalization is a worldwide free market. This form of economic globalization is believed by them to be both welcome and progressive, spreading positive economic benefits to those previously denied them by heavy-handed and damaging state policies. Critics, on the other hand, posit that economic globalization is a cipher for a general Westernization of the global economy, an economic counterpart of the spread of liberal democracy as the preferred global political ideology.

Both economic globalization and TNC influence can be measured in terms of extensiveness and intensity. Expansion of the size of the global economy is probably the most obvious consequence of the end of the cold war, as it has led to the gradual, uneven and still continuing incorporation of nearly all the former socialist countries into the global economy. While it has not (yet) reached the extent premised by the high expectations of the immediate early post-cold war period, it nevertheless seems clear that the end of the First World–Second World economic separation is, potentially, a huge step towards a consolidated global economic system. In particular, the significance of the incorporation of the former Second World is added to by the steady opening up to TNCs of developing country economies. Often under pressure from Western governments and the IMF and the World Bank, many developing country governments have accepted – sometimes under considerable duress – the abandonment of national development strategies based on state-led programmes and import substitution policies, and more or less rejected nationalization. Structural adjustment programme-based development strategies had the effect of further integrating developing country economies into the global economy.

Internationalization of production, finance and other economic resources are importantly expressed through and by TNCs; a process facilitated by the acquisition and retention of political influence within a variety of countries. TNC responses to changing circumstances – including strategies of adjustment to compete with low-cost producers and/or concentration on high-value-added goods tailored to specialized markets – do not obviously favour the efficacy of national strategies of regulation. Consequently, many developing countries find it practically impossible to control the activities of TNCs – not least because the pace and interactions of technological and economic change means that, substantively, states' 'command and control' regulations are almost impossible to apply meaningfully. Consequently, regarding regulatory strategies, developing country governments are faced with a stark choice: (1) assist the necessary process of adjustment to attract TNCs, or (2) risk a declining tax base if TNC production facilities move elsewhere. These factors are especially felt in weaker developing economies and the result is often a gnawing away of individual governments' legal entitlement to rule their own territories (Schulz et al. 2001: 16).

Four interrelated processes can be identified in this regard: first, the increased mobility of financial capital, making it difficult for many states to influence the terms on which they borrow; second, the crucial importance of FDI as a vehicle for exports and economic growth; third, the dramatic perceptual impact of the phenomenon of high growth rates in the East Asian 'tiger' economies on the hopes and anxieties of elites elsewhere in the developing world; and fourth, East Asia's economic travails in 1997/8 – followed by those in Russia, Argentina and elsewhere – that increased the determination of many countries to speed up processes of regional economic integration as a means of becoming less vulnerable to changes in the global economy.

Conclusion

We have seen that globalization is changing, in various ways, political arrangements and configurations within countries. It is often suggested that this amounts to an erosion of the nation-state's formerly 'hard' boundaries and a consequent – albeit a variable – diminution of states' ability to control their domestic environments and hence policy decisions.

In this chapter we have examined a range of cross-border actors in order to ascertain their relative political significance in relation to domestic outcomes. The conclusion is that it is necessary to develop appropriately synthetic analytical frameworks – drawing on the insights of both comparative politics and international relations – to examine how and with what political effects various kinds of cross-border actors can influence policy-making and outcomes in established democracies, transitional democracies and non-democracies. We have also noted that the impact of external actors on domestic political structures and processes is not uniform. Rather, it depends on the nature and characteristics of differing political and institutional arrangements within countries, what we referred to as 'opportunity structures for participation'.

Two overall conclusions can be drawn. First, when international conditions are similar, variances in domestic policy-making structures are instrumental in determining deviations in the policy impact of external actors. Second, institutional structures of governance – domestic as well as regional, for example in relation to the EU – will influence the political impact of external actors.

Part II
Comparative Politics and Globalization: Issues and Processes

6

Regionalization

Regionalization is often said to be a driving force of globalization, influencing both economic and political outcomes (Leslie 1997). The aim of this chapter is to examine selected examples of regional cooperation to help answer the following questions:

- Why do numerous states in various parts of the world now pursue regional cooperation?
- What does regional cooperation imply for comparative political analysis?

In this chapter we look at regional cooperation and globalization and at the new regionalism approach; then we compare two regional organizations: the European Union (EU) and the North American Free Trade Agreement (NAFTA). We focus attention on the EU[1] and NAFTA[2] in order to ascertain the importance of developed regional organizations for comparative political analysis.

Traditionally, comparative political analysis focuses on countries' domestic politics. However, as Risse-Kappen (1995a: 28) notes, 'state autonomy and state control over outcomes is not just a function of domestic structures, but also of the state's position in the international distribution of power'. However, 'the difficult problem' of how to enter state membership in regional and international organizations is often not addressed (Lane and Ersson 1994: 166).

Why do states around the world increasingly seek to involve themselves in regional networks? It would appear that states sign up to such 'treaties and conventions in order to reduce uncertainty about the behaviour of other nations, whether friends or adversaries' (Rittberger 1993, cited in Lowndes 2002: 102). In addition, making decisions about regional cooperation, states are 'steered by the structural constraints (formal and informal) of international political life' (Lowndes 2002: 96). We shall see that this implies two conclusions of importance for both regional political outcomes and comparative political analysis. First, when transitional democracies seek to join developed regional organizations, such as the EU and NAFTA, then the norms of political and economic behaviour that the existing members – in both cases, exclusively established democracies – already exemplify become a condition of membership. Second, in the context of regional organizations, the cross-border actors that are most likely to influence regional

---

[1] In 2005, the EU had 25 member states: Austria, Belgium, Cyprus, Czech Republic, Denmark, Estonia, Finland, France, Germany, Greece, Hungary, Ireland, Italy, Latvia, Lithuania, Luxembourg, Malta, The Netherlands, Poland, Portugal, Slovakia, Slovenia, Spain, Sweden, and the United Kingdom (<http://www.eurunion.org/states/home.htm>).
[2] The NAFTA had three member states in 2005: Canada, Mexico and the USA.

political outcomes are those – such as transnational corporations – that are best equipped to exploit both formal and informal opportunity structures. Other cross-border groups – such as interest groups and political parties – are usually less able to exploit these structures in a consistent and structured way.

Regional Cooperation and Globalization

> Regional cooperation results from new challenges, which governments believe can be better met by means of new regional regulations than by adhering to present national or regional strategies. *Such new challenges make regional cooperation seem 'functionally efficient' and compatible with the 'national interest'. By engaging in new regional cooperation, states create or strengthen a policy domain in which they receive new instruments for dealing with specific actors, situations and processes.* (Schirm 2002: 10; emphasis added)

Regional cooperation is now a global phenomenon. States around the world are increasingly 'enmeshed in networks of important regional . . . political and economic institutions' (Smith 2000: 24). What drives regional cooperation? The quotation above from Schirm (2002) suggests that states expect regional cooperation to help them pursue various objectives, in the context of 'new challenges', including those emanating from globalization. Regional cooperation can be regarded as both 'functionally efficient' and in line with the pursuit of national interests, but it may also lead to development of new regional regimes, with associated regulations, structures and processes.

Hague and Harrop (2001: 50) define a regional organization as a 'specific form of [international governmental organization] IGO in which neighbouring countries join together for common purposes'. Schulz et al. (2001: 5) suggest an analytical distinction between what they call 'regionalism' – that is, 'state-led, purposive structures' – and 'regionalization'. This is characterized by 'change from relative heterogeneity and a lack of cooperation towards increased cooperation, integration, convergence and identity in a variety of fields such as culture, security, economic development and politics, within a given geographical space'. Not only states but also non-state actors can be involved in this process.

It is often observed that increasing numbers of countries adopt cooperative policies with regional counterparts – primarily for economic goals. Many states are said to regard regional economic cooperation as a crucial mechanism to try to regulate the impact of economic globalization, such as volatile global market trends, capital flows, the activities of transnational corporations and protectionism (Hirst and Thompson 1999; Schirm 2002; Webber and Smith 2002). This suggests a close relationship between regional integration and globalization, with the former seen as both a 'shelter from', and 'an accelerator of' global processes (Christiansen 2001: 511).

It is however widely agreed that what may initially appear to be solely 'economic issues' often have wider – political and social – ramifications. For example, developing countries are often said to 'need' regional economic integration – as a key means to increase their capacity to negotiate with 'hostile forces' associated with economic globalization, especially loss of state control of national economies. Many developing countries adopted structural adjustment programmes (SAPs) in the 1980s and 1990s, under pressure from the IMF and the World Bank. A common judgement, however, is that SAPs often turned out to have deleterious domestic effects, with unfortunate economic, social and political impacts. Consequently, developing countries are said to 'need' regionalization as a means to reinforce their capacity to negotiate globalization. If they do not, Roy (1999: 120) contends, then 'the lack of stability and growth will push [them] further into the desperate margins of global society. . . . Regionalism will be the key to the success of globalisation in the years to come.' In short, many commentators judge normatively that developing countries 'should' develop regional cooperation as a vital step to enable them to 'adapt to the process of globalization without being excluded from it' (Heine 1999: 114). So far, however, such attempts have been mostly disappointing.

The New Regionalism Approach

Studies of regional cooperation can conveniently be divided into two phases. During the first period, from the 1950s to the 1980s, the main focal point was Western Europe. The founding of what is now the EU in the early 1950s was explicitly linked to the conditions of the cold war, and the attendant rivalry between the USA and the USSR. After the cold war ended in the late 1980s, there was a shift in analytical emphasis. Academic interest in regional cooperation acquired a new dynamism, captured in a novel term: the 'new regionalism approach' (NRA). The starting point for the NRA was an empirical development: regional cooperation appeared, for the first time, to be a significant phenomenon beyond Western Europe. This was linked to what some observers called a 'restructuring of the nation-state', a result of increased 'interdependence, transnationalization and globalization'. The main issue was 'not the delineation of regions per se, but the processes and consequences of regionalization in various fields of activity and at various levels' (Schulz et al. 2001: 3, 13).

The NRA differs from the 'old' regionalism approach in two main ways. First, the latter is firmly linked to the circumstances of the cold war, a time when regional cooperation in Western Europe was said to be imposed, directly or indirectly, from outside and above, in line with the wishes of the superpowers. The NRA, on the other hand, is concerned with a range of processes whose genesis is within the regions themselves, both from 'above' and 'below'. The analytical inclusion of various kinds of actor – both states and non-state actors – is regarded as characteristic of a wider process. It is a 'heterogeneous, comprehensive, multidimensional phenomenon . . . linked to global structural change, and especially to what is perhaps its dominating feature, globalization'. The focus is on 'state, market and society actors and . . . economic, cultural, political, security and environmental aspects' (Schultz et al. 2001: 4, 7). In short, a key NRA presumption is that the ending of the cold war had significant repercussions for regional cooperation, both within Europe and elsewhere. It led to new opportunities for states to cooperate in various areas, for example, trade and security, while encouraging non-state actors of various kinds to try to influence regionalization structures and processes.

It is often suggested that the EU gave this development a particular impetus, not least with the signing in 1992 of the Maastricht Treaty, which generated much global interest (Postel-Vinay 2001: 94). Partly as a result, the EU is said to have helped more widely to create – albeit unintentionally – what is sometimes called the 'urge to merge' for other regions, primarily as a result of competitive pressures exerted by the Single European Market (SEM). National governments in regions engaged in serious economic competition with Western Europe – such as the Americas and Southeast Asia – were concerned that the facilitation of easier market access for member states within the EU itself would lead to trade diversion at the expense of their exports. As a result, Christiansen (2001) suggests, the linked emergence of 'Fortress Europe'/SEM provided a focused impetus to encourage more dynamic regional cooperation away from Europe.

A second key development associated with the NRA analytical framework is linked to what is seen as a generally increasing analytical significance for various cross-border, especially non-state, actors. The NRA framework suggests that studies of regional cooperation should move beyond a focus on formal regional structures to include informal ones. Until now, studies of regional cooperation have tended to ignore or pay only scant attention to the role of agency, with little attention devoted to various domestic and transnational agents, including interest groups, such as civil society actors and business corporations. In the NRA focus, the emphasis extends from states to 'contemporary forms of transnational cooperation and cross-border flows through comparative, historical, and multilevel perspectives' (Mittelman 1999, quoted in Schulz et al. 2001: 12). Thus the focus is on what Smouts (2001: 96) calls regional searches 'for relevant space for action', directing attention to both the geographical spread of regionalism and the multiple dynamics at work, including both state and non-state actors.

NRA analyses emphasize that some regional milieus – for example, Western Europe and North America – appear to be conducive for building the influence of cross-border actors. The success of such actors – whether acting singly or in coalitions – is in turn said to be linked to the extent to which they manage to develop highly cooperative and institutionalized relationships, both among themselves and with certain domestic actors. This suggests a point of wider relevance to our concerns in this chapter. It is that regional institutions can theoretically have substantial effects on governments' domestic practices, both in terms of policies and in how they define their interests and preferences. Put another way, both state autonomy and governmental control over politics can be significantly influenced when states are embedded in and hence affected by regional structures of governance. The impact on domestic politics of regionally oriented, cross-border actors is likely to depend on the kind of political system the latter encounter, whether an established or transitional democracy or a non-democracy. In other words, as we noted in chapter 5, the characteristics of the political institutions they encounter will affect the ability of external actors, including regionally orientated actors, to penetrate and influence them. In the next section we examine these issues in relation to the EU. Following that, for comparative purposes we consider the situation in NAFTA.

The key issue upon which we focus is the question of what the best examples of advanced regional cooperation – especially the EU and increasingly NAFTA – suggest about the ability of transnational actors to influence policies. What actors are driving the regional projects, with what means, and for what purposes? (Schulz et al. 2001: 15–16). We may expect a 'distinct differentiation [in] the international and domestic conditions under which transnational coalitions and actors are able to influence state policies' (Risse-Kappen 1995b: 310–11).

The European Union

In all its many functions and manifestations, the state remains the central form of political organization in today's world. To be sure, the forces of global interdependence – economic interactions, communications links, environmental spillovers, and the like – are driving sovereign governments to cooperate with one another more than at any other time in history. No country in today's world can claim to be fully self-sufficient or capable of living in complete isolation from the rest of humanity, a reality that places the very concept of national sovereignty in doubt. The everyday realities of international relationships have in some cases led to highly structured attempts to promote cooperation across state boundaries. The most far-reaching of these efforts thus far has been the European Union. (Sodaro 2001: 159)

What uniquely characterizes the EU is its 'mature set of institutions' that make it – 'by some distance – the most developed project of regional integration in the world' (Rosamond 2002a: 498). The current advanced stage of EU development represents a complex process over five decades, a period during which the Union has developed a multifaceted agenda with economic, cultural, security and political goals (Christiansen 2001: 510). Key institutional developments have included the Treaty of Rome (1957), the founding of the European Union (1986)[3] and the Maastricht, Amsterdam and Nice treaties (1992, 1997 and 2000, respectively).

There are clear differences between the EU and other extant examples of regional cooperation. Verdier and Breen (2001: 229) point out that 'although some non-EU countries are also involved in some form of regional organization (European Free Trade Agreement, North American Free Trade Agreement, Mercosur, and so forth), none of these schemes have reached a level comparable to the EU'.

The European Community (EC), forerunner of the EU, was created in 1957. It emerged as a result of the Treaty of Rome that initially involved just six states (Belgium, France, Italy, Luxembourg, the Netherlands and West Germany). Over the next five decades, membership expanded greatly. The advance of European integration has been regarded in various ways by academic observers. For some, the EU is an example of 'turbo-charged globalization', while others regard it more as 'a protective shield against the negative 'fall-out from' globalization' (Christiansen 2001: 511–12). Both interpretations can be invoked to explain and account for the EU's recent – and likely future – expansion.

Until recently, the EU was exclusively a Western European regional grouping of established democracies. However, in May 2004, it expanded both numerically and geographically, to welcome ten new members: Cyprus, the Czech Republic, Estonia, Hungary, Latvia, Lithuania, Malta, Poland, Slovakia and Slovenia. In 2007, two further

---

[3] The Single European Act (SEA) was signed by the then 12 members in 1986 and came into force the following year. The SEA established a single European market (defined as an area without frontiers in which free movement of goods, services, people and capital is ensured), and was the first major revision of the Treaty of Rome three decades earlier. The SEA also allowed for increased involvement of the European Parliament in the decision-making process, as well as qualified majority voting in the Council of Ministers for some policy areas. Finally, the Act included provisions covering collaboration in research and development and in environmental policy.

Table 6.1 Freedom House ratings of new and aspirant EU members

Country	Freedom House ratings, 2003	
	PR	CL
New members from May 2004		
Hungary	1	2
Poland	1	2
Slovakia	1	2
Malta	1	1
Cyprus	1*	1*
Estonia	1	2
Latvia	1	2
Lithuania	1	2
Czech Rep.	1	2
Slovenia	1	1
New members from 2007		
Bulgaria	1	2
Romania	2	2

*These ratings were for the Greek segment of the island.
Source: Freedom House 2003. PR = political rights, CL = civil liberties.

countries, Bulgaria and Romania, are scheduled to join, as table 6.1 indicates. The new, enlarged EU symbolizes the end to Europe's artificial division. Now the organization is a pan-European Union. However, the road to EU enlargement was a drawn-out and complex process, dominating the politics of Europe's pan-regional relations for a decade prior to the actual enlargement. The process began with the first manifestations of Euro-enthusiasm from Poland and Hungary in the early 1990s, a time when both countries were emerging from decades of communist rule. In 1993, the EU officially set out its definition of membership criteria in response to requests to join: aspirant countries must have both democratically elected governments and liberal economies, that is, without too much state control. Shortly after, in early 1994, the first formal EU accession applications were submitted, from Hungary and Poland. Applications then followed from Slovakia, Romania, Bulgaria, Estonia, Latvia, Lithuania, Slovenia and the Czech Republic (Bardi et al. 2002: 227). In addition, at the Helsinki Summit in 2000, Turkey was given the status of being a candidate country for full EU accession.

Political and economic criteria that the EU attached for putative members were important factors in encouraging both democratization (and the consolidation of democracy) and the marketization of their economies. Pridham (2000: 299) lists several 'broad types of influence exerted by the EU on democratization in applicant countries'. These amount to a combined 'carrot-and-stick approach', which features the use of political and economic 'conditionality' in order to encourage putative new members to implement satisfactory political economic policies. The chief incentive for putative members was a 'clear timetable for quick accession to the EU' and 'generous aid, credit and direct investment flows from the member to the candidate countries' (Yilmaz 2002: 73). However, some observers claim that for the new members the objective of joining the EU goes beyond expected economic benefits; it is also seen as emblematic of a redis-covered, shared 'European-ness'. For Hettne, the 'question "what is Europe?" can only be answered by the political process of self-recognition. It is a social construct . . . an idea rather than a territory.' It implies that 'the content of "European" can be defined normatively by: a strong role for civil society, various institutionalized forms such as par-liamentary decision making, and a democratic culture stressing above all individualism and human rights inherent in the individual human being' (Hettne 2001: 38–9).[4] For our concerns, the issue and application of 'European-ness' is important as it sheds light on the question of the ' "de-easternization" of former Eastern Europe – or, as spokesmen for civil society in those countries called it, "a return to Europe" ' (Bogdanor 2003).

EU governing institutions

Politically, the EU is policed by a supranational Commission. It also has a Parliament and a Court to interpret EU laws. Over time, intervention in each other's internal affairs has become the norm for the EU members and, prior to the influx of 10 new members in May 2004, 12 of the then 15 members shared both a central bank and a single currency (the Euro). In addition, during 2004–5 the EU sought to draw up and dis-seminate a constitution. Earlier, in December 2001, EU heads of government, meeting at Laeken, Belgium, had declared that Europe's citizens were 'calling for a clear, open, effective, democratically controlled Community approach' (<europa.eu.int/comm/laeken_council/index_en.htm>). For this reason they established a convention to draw up proposals for a European constitution. It would seek to (1) clarify where power resides, by defining powers of various EU institutions, (2) identify the rights of citizen vis-à-vis the established powers and (3) 'provide an indication of purpose, a rallying cry for the citizen' (Bogdanor 2003). Finally, the EU has 'made progress towards a common foreign policy, most effectively in the Balkan backyard, where trade, aid, diplomacy and a small military component complement each other. Advances have also been made in the Middle Eastern minefield' (Black 2003).

Away from Europe itself, the so-called 'soft power' of the EU – notably, development aid to encourage both nation-building (Iraq) and democratization (in the Middle East, sub-Saharan Africa and Central Asia) – can also be significant. This is in contrast to the 'hard' military might of the last remaining superpower, the USA. However, it is some-times suggested that the two actors can complement each other in the 'post-9/11 Hobbes-ian jungle'. To some observers, the EU increasingly defines itself in the context of its relationship (and rivalry) with the USA. However, being a group of countries rather than a single nation-state, it lacks some of the crucial material and political means to do so. For 'europhiles', EU failure to compete with the USA is due to its slow speed of

[4] Hettne (2001: 40) defines civil society as 'inclusive institutions that facilitate a societal dialogue over various social and cultural borders', while 'identities and loyalties are transferred from civil society to primary groups, competing with each other for territorial control, resources and security'.

integration. 'Europhobes' counter by claiming that the EU's ability to be a global actor is most likely to be strengthened if it remains a group of sovereign states, largely devoid of integrationist aspirations (Black 2003).

Both Europhiles and Europhobes agree on the growing mobility of various kinds of transnational actor in the Union. For example, 'political parties, local and regional authorities, social movements, interest groups, and NGOs . . . are now active, alongside national governments and supranational institutions, on a European scale' (Christiansen 2001: 499). This development is facilitated by the relative openness of the European policy-making process. Uniquely among regional organizations, the EU has developed an increasingly institutionalized framework of interaction, to the extent that a plethora of political groups and/or economic interests can seek to influence Union decisions. The EU is increasingly perceived as a system of multilevel governance, where a multiplicity of supranationally, nationally and/or subnationally focused actors seek to influence outcomes. Hix (2003) claims that some areas of EU politics now look like domestic politics of states and, as a result, there may be a need to turn to approaches drawn from comparative political analysis. Two questions about the EU most obviously draw upon comparative political analysis: what are the key political institutions in the EU? and to what extent are they democratically accountable?

The EU has the following governing bodies:

1   The *European Council of Ministers*. The Council is the predominant governing body of the EU. The ministers – all of whom are cabinet ministers in their respective countries – are chosen by member states to represent them. A president coordinates the Council's work, a rotating position changing every six months. The Council is both an executive and a legislative body, with the final word on most significant issues in the Union.

2   The *European Commission*. This is the executive body of the EU. It puts into effect decisions made both by the Council of Ministers and the European Parliament. It is made up of Commissioners, individually appointed by member states (although they do not represent their home countries, but are supposed to represent the EU only), and given areas of responsibility akin to those presided over by government ministers in domestic contexts. The Commission has a president, selected following a consensual decision by member states.

3   The *European Parliament*. This is the legislature of the EU. Its 626 members are chosen via the ballot box in each member state every five years. It is the only elected institution in the EU. The most recent elections were held in June in 2004, and the next are due in 2009.

4   The *European Court of Justice*. The Court of Justice of the European Communities (often referred to simply as 'the Court') was set up in 1952 under the Treaty of Paris. Its job is to ensure that EU legislation (technically known as 'Community law') is interpreted and applied in the same way in each member state, so that it is always identical for all parties and in all circumstances. The Court has the power to settle legal disputes between member states, EU institutions, businesses and individuals. The Court has an important role in regionalization since it can legally settle disputes in the EU.[5]

[5] I am grateful to an anonymous reader of the manuscript for this point.

5   The *European Council*. This body comprises the heads of member governments. It
    meets a few times a year for discussions about various pressing issues.
6   The *European Central Bank*. This is a coordinating organization. Its key function is
    to bring together the central banks of member states for policy-making in their areas
    of competence (Etzioni-Halevy 2002: 209).

The EU's governing bodies feature a mix of two governmental models. The first is
intergovernmental, with national parties, legislatures and governments functioning as
key supports of EU governing bodies. The second is supranational, with the EU governing bodies (noted above) separate from national political institutions and organizations (Beetham and Lord 1998).[6]

It is sometimes suggested that the first (intergovernmental) model has gained ground
at the expense of the second (supranational) one in recent years. However, this does
not really make a difference in terms of representation, because in the first model, relationships between ordinary people and the EU institutions are indirect; while in the
supranational model they are weak. Combining the two models is thus unlikely dramatically to increase EU institutional representation. However, the picture is by no
means static. According to Etzioni-Halevy (2002: 205), 'European governing institutions
are in constant flux, and suffer from excessive complexity, fuzziness, and ambiguity of
procedures', characterized by 'Euro-jargon' and the use of numerous technical terms
and more than 1,300 acronyms! She suggests, plausibly, that this situation is 'off-putting
for citizens, and makes it difficult for them to understand what is really going on in these
bodies, and what they need to do to link up with them'.

The EU institutions have important political functions, but how do they measure up
as representative bodies? Many observers point to what is called a 'democratic deficit'
– that is, democratic deficiencies that amount to a gap – or a gulf – between aspirations
and reality. While some of the governing institutions of the EU – especially the Parliament and to some extent the Commission – have inbuilt provisions for regularized interactions with ordinary people, it is often suggested that there are major problems in how
these arrangements work. As Etzioni-Halevy (2002: 209) points out, this is not to suggest
that things were designed like this, only to note that this is how they have turned out,
'due to factors beyond the control of anyone in particular'.[7] Research is now addressing 'questions of representation, policy making, and future political dynamics in the EU'
(Gabel and Anderson 2002: 894).

'Euro-groups' and interest representation in the EU

It is important to note that 'national governments are not the sole intermediary between
citizens and policy makers' in the EU (Hooghe and Marks 1999: 79). Citizens from EU

---

[6] This issue is dealt with in detail by Christiansen (2001: 500), Rosamond (2002a: 508–9) and Hix
(2003).
[7] It may be worth noting that the EU is often thought less problematic in this regard than several
other important transnational actors, including the World Bank, the International Monetary Fund,
the United Nations and NATO. In these organizations, no real provision exists for significant
public interaction.

member states can gain entry to EU policy-making agendas and processes through various subnational and supranational channels. One such channel is that incorporating transnational interest groups and political parties. However, we should note that even though there is now an integrated market in the EU, as well as the 'growth of trans-border economic, social and cultural exchange', the development of both region-wide political parties and civil society has been limited by various factors. On the one hand there is the language barrier – no EU-wide *lingua franca* – and on the other, 'national and regional identities' – that is, within countries – 'continue to take precedence over any emerging European identity' (Christiansen 2001: 510). In addition, political parties continue to pay most attention to domestic politics, understandable as this is the location where they will acquire the ability to exercise power if elected.

Within territorial states, interest groups – collectively conceptualized as 'civil society' – are theoretically a key means by which governing institutions can interact with citizens. However, there may be difficulties with such intermediation even on the national level – for example, governments may not listen to such groups, while the groups themselves may be fragmented and thus lack ability to present a strong, united voice. But such problems are said to be greater at the European level (Imig 2002). This is not because of a lack of what are called 'Euro-groups'. An estimated 3,000 are based in Brussels, and share a common aim: on the one hand, to intermediate between citizens and national interest groups and, on the other, to liaise with EU institutions, especially the Commission. Compelled to recognize their legitimacy, aims and concerns, some EU institutions have in-built opportunities for deliberation with Euro-groups. Under the auspices of the Commission, there are some 75 consultative committees with mixed memberships. These are mostly formalized institutional relationships involving Commission officials, national civil servants and Euro-group representatives. In addition, 'extensive interest representation takes place through unstructured, informal networks' (Mazey and Richardson 1994: 48). Such interaction is facilitated by the involvement of some 15,000 'Eurocrats' serving under the Commissioners. They help set policy agendas and implement policies. Although much of the implementation detail is left to the governments of the individual member states, it occurs in the context of general EU oversight. As a result, if there is an issue that cannot be resolved, the European Court of Justice can be called upon to arbitrate.

The ability of Euro-groups to influence outcomes is not always straightforward. Sometimes consultative mechanisms have only limited value. This may be because discussions with interest groups often only take place at the early 'stages of policy formation and the drafting of legislation' and it may not be clear 'what, if anything, comes out of such EU-sponsored consultation'. There is an example from 1986 that is worth noting. At that time, the Commission consulted with various groups in the EU – including trade union representatives, 'artisans' associations, local authorities, activists of various voluntary associations, church leaders, and private individuals' – to discuss local employment initiatives. But it is not clear if the Commission took into account what the groups had to say (Etzioni-Halevy 2002: 208).

The conclusion Etzioni-Halevy draws is that while there are both formal and informal means of consultation with interested parties, this does not necessarily imply transparency in EU decision-making. This is because the Commission – like other EU governing institutions – is not *obliged* to accept interest groups' advice and, as a result, consultative systems may not have much of an impact on the final decisions. Thus there is no guarantee that interest groups – which clearly are able to have a voice at the stage of policy *conception* – are able to influence its eventual *execution*. The implication is that formal consultation processes are pitched more in the favour of EU officials.

Beetham and Lord (1998) suggest that EU officials may prefer to consult with interest groups that are affected by their policies, and discuss with them for their own purposes (rather than the other way round). This is a means to secure the support and cooperation of certain, influential interest groups, and suggests a two-way process. On the one hand, various interest groups seek to influence EU decision-making via institutionalized structures of consultation. On the other hand, EU officials may actively seek support for the policies that they have already determined or at least have clear preferences about. They do this by mobilizing interest groups upon whose backing they can count. This allows EU officials both to determine and include in consultative processes the interests they prefer, and to attach more weight to the views of some interest groups rather than others. For example, 'those serving the interests of the disadvantaged [do not] have the same access to policy as those working for the economically privileged, such as those of corporations and employers' (Etzioni-Halevy 2002: 210).

TNCs and the EU

The issue of the ability of transnational corporations (TNCs) to influence agenda-setting and decision-making in their favour is a common theme in the literature and, as we noted in chapter 5, the nature of connections between TNC economic power and political influence has long been controversial. For example, there was the infamous involvement of an American TNC, International Telephone and Telegraph, in a successful, but bloody, coup against the leftist government of President Salvador Allende in Chile in 1973. However, this was one of a small number of exceptions – not the rule – after 1945. It is far more common for influential TNCs to use less overt means to seek to attain political objectives that also assist their economic interests (Willetts 2001: 362–5).

Rosamond (2002a: 500) notes that in the EU, the 'development of cross-border company organization and activity has effectively created a set of transnational economic actors'. Sklair (2002) highlights the particular importance of 'the oil, automobile, road building, supermarket and other industries'. Some observers claim that while the EU aims to conduct evenly weighted consultations between employers and workers, a fair balance is not always attained. The ability of TNCs to achieve goals seems to be linked to the extent to which they organize themselves effectively. For example, a group of Europe-based TNCs is organized collectively for EU lobbying in the European Roundtable of Industrialists (ERT).[8] The ERT was founded in 1983 by a group of business heads, including Umberto Agnelli of Fiat, Marcel Dekker of Philips, and Volvo's Pehr Gyllenhammer. It chiefly performs an agenda-setting role for global free trade and competitiveness in European institutions and has also developed an institutionalized,

---

[8] The Corporate Europe Observatory (CEO) website contains a series of briefings that collectively illustrate how corporate interests can influence the emphasis of policy-making in the European Union, sometimes with major global implications (<http://www.corporateeurope.org/briefings.html>).

influential position within the EU more generally. The ERT membership now comprises leaders of around 45 TNCs, including BP, Daimler-Benz, Fiat, Shell and Siemens, all of which have both European and global interests.

Bypassing the European Parliament, the European Centre for Infrastructure Studies (ECIS), an offshoot of ERT, is said to have worked directly with the European Commission in establishing the Trans-European Networks (a programme of around 150 environmentally sensitive infrastructure projects). Founded by Fiat's Agnelli in 1994, the ECIS brings together regional and national governments, municipalities, EU institutions, research institutes, banks and corporations. Over the years, close links have developed between ECIS figures and the Commission. How close these links were was exemplified when a former Commissioner, V.-P. Henning Christopherson, joined the ECIS Board when he left the Commission (Sklair 2002: 161).

More generally, some observers claim that corporate interests are highly influential in the making of EU transport policy (Imig 2002). Sklair points to the political efficacy of the coordinated power of TNCs in this regard. It is reflected, he claims, in the failure of EU governments to shift freight and people from private vehicles to public transport and rail freight, despite state claims to wish to do so. He gives two examples. First, Greece makes feta cheese from German milk that is then sent back to the latter country for sale. Second, Unilever now has one huge factory making soap in England, whereas it formerly had a number of soap factories throughout the EU. Naturally, such policies add to major growth in long-distance transport of goods throughout Europe. A further consequence is that while this policy may make 'production much more "efficient" for producers, and in a sense also for consumers' – that is, if the real price of products actually falls with no decline in quality – it is however ' "inefficient" for essential road users and all those who lose jobs, and in the long term, for our relationships with the environment' (Sklair 2002: 161).

'Euro-protest'

Business corporations have, for several decades, employed various informal and formal means to try to influence policy in the EU. More recently, what Imig (2002) calls 'Euro-protest' has also developed. This reflects attempts by some interest groups to seek to influence EU agenda-setting and decision-making. According to Imig (2002: 929), Euro-protest has its roots in the issue of 'European integration . . . highly salient to a growing range of citizens across the continent'. While national and transnational examples of such 'Europe-focused contention' collectively amount currently to only 5 per cent of overall recorded examples of protest, their proportion has been slowly increasing since the mid-1980s. Many Euro-protests are principally motivated by and organized along occupational lines, in defence of jobs lost as a result of European integration.

Euro-protests can be EU-wide in focus, with the aim of combating integration *specifics*. This might include a demand that individual EU governments make more effort to protect domestic jobs. However, as we have noted, development of supranational spheres of governance in the EU offers both novel chances as well as constraints on interest groups seeking to affect outcomes at the European level. Imig (2002: 930) suggests that Euro-protesters are becoming attuned to European issues and, as a result, he claims that a 'European repertoire of contentious action' is emerging. Campaigns can involve transnational actions that feature like-minded actors from EU member states who share collective objectives and act together to try to persuade EU policy-makers to adopt their preferred policies. However, there may be substantial barriers to such actors acting together – not least the lack of a common language of communication. Partly as a result, and despite the 'rapid development of supranational policies and institutions . . . the realm of social movement mobilization – to date – largely has remained focused on domestic politics' (Rosamond 2002a: 508–9). In sum, 'tried and true routines of collective action and familiar institutional patterns continue to attach citizens to their national political systems'. This suggests that while EU governing institutions can be an important focus of interest group attentions, most such efforts at the current time seek to 'express political preferences about Europe . . . in domestic rather than transnational venues' (Imig 2002: 130).

Conclusion

Christiansen (2001: 495) contends that 'the EU emerges as a post-sovereign polity that, despite its imperfections, has firmly established a new form of governance at an intermediate level between the global and the state'. Our discussion has suggested that a slightly more nuanced view might be in order. First, the EU agenda appears to be more consistently open to some interest groups. While the EU's governing institutions may be only patchily responsive to demands from below, they seem more prepared to listen to and liaise with well-organized and influential groups, including those created by and for business interests. Second, while theoretically there is a chain of interactions – for example, via interest groups, parties or elections – most citizens are not necessarily persuaded that using Europe-focused groups is the best way to pursue their own interests. For example, political party groups organized generically in the European Parliament seem to have problems connecting to the voters. This may be because parties do not fight European Parliament elections in a coordinated fashion. Instead, like most voters, political parties in the EU continue to see the national context as the place where power lies and thus where to concentrate their efforts.

A general point is that, like domestic political systems, the EU has various 'opportunity structures for participation' (OSPs). We saw in chapter 5 that a polity's OSP is the aggregation of various channels of access to the public sphere and to the policy-making and implementation processes available to political actors (Kitschelt 1986: 58, 61; Nentwich 1996: 3). The EU has two main forms of regional-level, cross-border intermediation between rulers and ruled: formally, via its governing bodies, and informally, with various kinds of interest group. This suggests a wider point affecting consultation mechanisms in the EU: there may be institutionalized mechanisms designed to enable consultation between EU policy-makers and various interests, but they are not necessarily successful in bringing together the interests they would claim to represent. Participants in agenda-setting discussions may only be in a position to gain access to policies if they have resources to offer. 'Those with greater resources may well have more influence than others. . . . The very fact that there is such a maze of interest groups contending for influence creates a danger of mutual blockage. This is of advantage to the more privileged interests, as it favors the existing situation, thereby protecting privileges already in place' (Etzioni-Halevy 2002: 210).

The North American Free Trade Agreement

The substantial increase in the 1990s of regionally based attempts at institutionalized cooperation among states in various parts of the world led observers to coin a novel phrase: the new regionalism. According to Leslie (1997), this reflected the impact of 'globalization, which transfers economic power from states to private sector entities (from politics to markets) . . . [and] seemingly stimulates the emergence of regional systems'. In addition, as we noted earlier, there was much concern in the 1990s about the emergence of 'Fortress Europe', which provided 'much of the impetus behind the dynamic development of' regional organizations away from Europe (Christiansen 2001: 513).

While many other regional integration attempts away from Europe are in various stages of development, the North American Free Trade Agreement (NAFTA) has made swift progress towards regional economic integration. Founded in 1994, NAFTA is a much smaller regional grouping than the EU. It comprises just three states: the USA, Canada and Mexico. Christiansen (2001: 513) claims that NAFTA 'is the most far-reaching example of a regional cooperation project spanning the North–South divide'. It is also noteworthy because it brings together both established democracies (USA and Canada) and a transitional democracy (Mexico). We might expect that the democratic ways of 'doing' politics in the established democracies would 'rub off' on Mexico, a country that only emerged from non-democratic rule very recently. And, as we shall see, this is indeed the case.

The forerunner of NAFTA was the Canada–US Free Trade Agreement (CUSFTA), dating from 1988. NAFTA is characterized by a considerable asymmetry in the economic size and strength of its members. The lack of uniformity in the member states' economic structures, as well as the glaring differences in levels of development between Mexico, on the one hand, and USA/Canada, on the other, suggested that creating a single free trade area would not be an easy or straightforward task. When NAFTA was inaugurated, the USA made up nearly nine-tenths (88 per cent) of the Agreement's gross domestic product. Mexico contributed just one-twentieth (5 per cent) and Canada one-fourteenth (7 per cent). Given this assymetrical relationship, Schirm (2002: 137) claimed that 'NAFTA – i.e., the US market – is much more relevant to Canada and Mexico than its neighbouring markets are to the USA'. However, while NAFTA's overt *raison d'être* is economic and financial – the abolition of impediments between the three countries to trade in goods and services – it has also had political ramifications by encouraging Mexico's recent move towards democratization.

We noted earlier that the desire of numerous post-communist governments in Central and Eastern Europe to join the EU helped to encourage both democratization and economic liberalization among those countries. There was a similar cause and effect process at work in Mexico, with determination to join NAFTA leading to both political and economic results. This helped to bolster attempts to 'dismantle Mexico's statist economy, which was essential to undermining the economic basis of Mexican authoritarianism' (Delal Baer 2000). This emphasizes how Mexico's governments regard NAFTA membership: as a crucially important means to help the country develop economically, primarily by attracting increased investment from the USA. This would not only contribute to the country's economic growth, but also increase its credibility more generally, both

Table 6.2 Political rights and civil liberties in Mexico, 1972–2003

Year	Political rights	Civil liberties	Status
1972*	5	3	Partly free
1980	3	4	Partly free
1990	4	4	Partly free
1995	4	4	Partly free
1997	3	4	Partly free
1999	3	4	Partly free
2001	2	2	Free
2002	2	2	Free
2003	2	2	Free

*Freedom House data were first compiled in 1972.
Source: <http://www.freedomhouse.org/ratings/allscore04.xls>.

regionally and internationally. Second, NAFTA 'has contributed to greater decentralization of economic and political power, as Mexican states attempt to capture NAFTA-related investment'. Third, 'Mexican political and human rights practices came under greater international scrutiny as a result of the political battle to pass NAFTA in the U.S.' (Delal Baer 2000).

The issue of NAFTA membership resulted in clear signs of increased pluralism in Mexico during the 1990s. In 1991, the then ruling Institutional Revolutionary Party (PRI) controlled 320 seats in Congress. By 1997, this had fallen to 239 seats, which meant that the party lost its congressional majority for the first time. The electoral decline of the PRI was underlined in December 2000, when an opposition candidate, Vicente Fox, a vociferous supporter of NAFTA, won that year's presidential elections. Fox's victory led to improvements in both political rights and civil liberties, as table 6.2 indicates. It also resulted in greater openness in Mexican policy towards civil society consultation in the Free Trade Area of the Americas (FTAA) process.[9] The overall result of these developments, Ottaway (2003: 7) claims, is that 'Mexico can now be classified as a country that experienced a protracted transition, but one could not have classified it that way ten years ago without indulging in wishful thinking or making unwarranted assumptions about the inevitability of democratic outcome'.

How best to explain Mexico's rapid progress from embedded single-party state noted internationally for its sclerotic, undemocratic political system to card-carrying member of the democracy club? Many observers suggest that Mexico's democratization was linked to the strong encouragement it received from its northern neighbours (N. Phillips 1999; Wallis 2001; Philip 2003). In addition, Mexico's PRI government regarded NAFTA membership as the best available means of encouraging increased economic growth. Consequently, despite initial doubts, the government was willing to reform both political and economic systems in order to win the support of the US Congress for Mexico's accession to NAFTA (Wallis 2001). The reasons for US encouragement to reform were

[9]The FTAA Treaty was signed in Quebec City in 2001. The intention is that from 2005 the FTAA will be a regional free trade agreement covering both the Americas and the Caribbean.

also linked to the circumstances prevailing at the end of the cold war. The state department's global view was that democracy and free trade were key goals of the putative 'new world order'. NAFTA was the United States' regional blueprint for the kind of economic-strategic relationship it wished to build as part of its post-cold war global strategy, which – until 9/11 – was built on the twin global goals of democratization and economic liberalization. NAFTA was the regional model for President Clinton's ambition of building a 'Washington consensus'.[10] From the time that Bill Clinton took office in January 1993, this was Washington's consistent message, not only to Mexico but also to Latin America. However, such goals were highly controversial in Mexico at this time, because they might lead to the hitherto unthinkable: undermine or even replace the long-running PRI hegemony built on central political control and state economic monopoly.

The Clinton government warmly welcomed the election of the pro-market Vicente Fox as president in December 2000. The US administration saw Fox as a kindred spirit, a man with whom they could do business. However, it remained to be seen whether President Fox could actually put into practice his proclaimed policies. He promised deregulation, competition and a balanced budget, together with an ambitious social agenda that included a pledge to double education spending, increase subsidies for farmers and build health clinics; in short, a raft of policies and programmes to address the enormous disparity between rich and poor. However, to enact such policies would obviously require a sea change in long-established policies and, as a result, Fox was unlikely to have things all his own way politically. Despite losing the presidency, the PRI still had sufficient congressional seats, in tandem with smaller parties, to block Fox's crucial constitutional and structural reforms. The PRI also retained control of half of the country's 32 state governorships and numerous municipalities. Whether Fox is in fact able to dismantle the inherited structures of PRI rule still remains to be seen.

To conform to the norms represented by NAFTA, Mexico needs urgent progress in a number of areas, including the rule of law to be upheld throughout the country, better civil and human rights and sustained actions to reduce both poverty and inequality. But Fox must resolve significant problems in these regards – not least because to reform both the political and economic system in the ways he has outlined would require stepping on a lot of powerful toes. Mexico's political and economic structures have long centred on the linked power of the PRI and the centralized state. Whether such important structural factors can be overturned through the agency of Fox remains to be seen. An interim judgement in 2004 – that is, midway through his single six-year term of office[11] – might be: tries hard but must do better. In elections to the Chamber of Deputies in July 2003, Fox's party, PAN, had lost a quarter of its seats, declining to 155; meanwhile PAN's great rival, the PRI, had increased its representation to 223 seats, while the leftist Party of the Democratic Revolution (PRD) also did well, nearly doubling its number of seats to 96. Commentators explained PAN's – and by extension,

[10] The Washington consensus was so named because of the uniformity of views about the desirability of both economic and political reforms held by the US government and the IMF and the World Bank: all are based in Washington, DC.
[11] Under the terms of the Mexican constitution, incumbent presidents are prohibited from seeking a second consecutive term of office.

Fox's – disappointing results in the elections to three factors: (1) a well-managed PRI campaign under the leadership of Roberto Madrazo Pintado, which managed to capitalize on public dissatisfaction, (2) high unemployment, at its highest level for 18 months in mid-2003 and (3) relatively low economic growth, expected to be about 2 per cent in 2003 (Cole-Bailey 2004: 165–6).

NAFTA's coordinating institutions

Compared to the EU, NAFTA is less institutionally developed. Member states maintain tight control over trade negotiations, both because of the centrality of trade to their economic agendas and because of the perceived need for secrecy in negotiations. However, while the Agreement's administration largely relies on national ministers, it does have various institutions: the Free Trade Commission, 'Coordinators', Committees and Working Groups, and the Secretariat.

1   *The Free Trade Commission* is the Agreement's central institution. It comprises cabinet-level representatives from the three member countries, Canada, Mexico and the USA. However, the Commission is not an institution in a key sense, as it only holds meetings when required. Its main work is to supervise implementation and further elaboration of the Agreement and to help resolve disputes that arise from its interpretation. The Commission oversees the work of the Committees and Working Groups, as well as other subsidiary bodies.
2   *'Coordinators'* are senior trade department officials designated by each country both to carry out day-to-day management of the organization's work programme, and to seek to implement the Agreement more broadly.
3   *Committees and Working Groups.* There are more than 30 of these bodies, helping to smooth implementation of the Agreement and to provide forums to explore ways of further liberalizing trade between members. The Agreement envisages that further work will be required towards fulfilling the objectives of the free trade agreement, in various areas. These include: trade in goods, rules of origin, customs, agricultural trade and subsidies, standards, government procurement, investment and services, cross-border movement of business people, and alternative dispute resolution.
4   *The Secretariat* comprises national offices in each of the Canadian, US and Mexican capitals. It is responsible for the administration of the dispute settlement provisions of the Agreement. Each National Section maintains a court-like registry relating to panel, committee and tribunal proceedings. The NAFTA Secretariat maintains a 'trinational' website where current information on NAFTA is presented (<www.nafta-sec-alena.org/>).

Interest group representation in NAFTA

NAFTA governing institutions are relatively underdeveloped compared to those in the EU, and regionally focused interest groups do not primarily focus upon them to try to achieve their goals. Instead, various interest groups – including business and 'NAFTA-protest' groups – generally lobby domestically within the member states. What they manage to achieve will be related to the success they have in exploiting in each country's opportunity structures for participation (OSPs). Canada has a federal parliamentary system with multiple, cohesive political parties and relatively strong provincial authorities. As a result, lobbying efforts will be directed at both federal and provincial levels. Mexico has a highly centralized polity with a powerful national president. Interest groups focus their attentions at the national level because while the country has a federal system it has weak provincial authorities. The US political system is different again. It has a congressional system of divided powers and 'porous' political parties, an arrangement offering much scope for 'individual political agendas', while allowing 'local and regional interests considerable opportunity for representation and influence at the national level' (Macdonald and Schwartz 2002: 138–9).

There are several sets of circumstance that NAFTA shares with the EU. First, interest groups in the former sharing common concerns – for example, job protection or environmental damage – have not yet managed to develop an effective network of regional organization, although the existence of a common language in the USA and Canada might be expected to facilitate efforts. Consequently, victories on several labour and environment issues were achieved by 'citizen politics' via domestic organizational efforts. The peculiarities of the US congressional system were important, 'with its openness to district-level influences, the use of "log-rolling" to win support for bills, and the effective cooptation by US administrations of part of the environmental NGO coalition' (Macdonald and Schwartz 2002: 139).

Second, like the EU, domestic politics in NAFTA member states is the main terrain of democratic contestation around trade policy issues. Third, big business is widely regarded as having considerable ability to influence decision-making in NAFTA, just as in the EU. Leslie (1997) suggests that this is linked to the nature of these regional systems. He explains that regionalization can assume different forms, and not all states are affected in exactly the same way. However, seeking to respond to globalization, a strategy open to any regional grouping of national states is to remove barriers among themselves. The more fully integrated a regional economic environment – the most advanced is the EU, followed by NAFTA – then the more facilitative it is both for creating transnational corporations and for enabling them to increase their regional influence. Focusing upon markets of hundreds of millions of people, as in both the EU and NAFTA, TNCs have opportunities both to specialize and to develop advanced technologies. This enables them to create or to exploit economic opportunities and can also lead to them becoming important political actors.

Within NAFTA, 'business interest groups' have been influential in various ways. In the absence of powerful regional institutions, their main focus is the member governments. For many US (and Canadian) business corporations, the opportunity to expand into Mexico's newly liberalized economy was an important motivating factor for action in the 1990s. The adoption of neo-liberal concepts and policies in Mexico was strongly supported by transnational business networks, involving both Mexican and primarily US companies. One example of such a network is the 'Americas Society', based in New York. Its membership includes influential US entrepreneurs, such as David Rockefeller and John Reed (Citibank), and important Mexican businessmen, including Miguel

Alemán and the head of a media conglomerate (Televisa), Emilio Azcarraga (Schirm 2002: 150).

Although business groups are influential, able to organize to take advantage of opportunities resulting from NAFTA's expansion to include Mexico, civil society actors have shown a more patchy response. On the other hand, as in the EU, NAFTA's member governments have been willing to include civil society groups in consultations around trade policy. One key area of current and future discussion is the scheduled expansion of NAFTA into the FTAA. These have focused upon – but not been restricted to – issues linked to the increasing politicization of trade issues and consequent mobilization of interest groups in the member countries. Like their counterparts in EU member states, such actors in NAFTA are primarily concerned with the impact of trade liberalization on jobs, the environment and, increasingly, domestic systems of social regulation. But because NAFTA lacks the type of institutionalized forums that the EU has, notably the Commission and the Parliament, the regional impact of their campaigns has been patchy.

Opponents of the FTAA – including some trade unions and environmental groups – claim that, despite repeated calls for the open and democratic development of trade policy, the expanded NAFTA will be a disaster. This is primarily because of fear of both extensive job losses and serious environmental damage, expected by critics to be a key result of the extension of free trade policies. Critics also claim that despite governmental assurances, the FTAA negotiations have been conducted substantively without citizen input. While the governments maintain that they want to hear citizens' views, opponents claim that this amounts only a widely denounced 'mailbox' mechanism, that is, an electronic 'suggestion box'. They assert that this is mere window dressing, not a substantive mechanism to incorporate the public's concerns into the actual negotiations. At the same time, however, hundreds of corporate representatives are said to be advising FTAA negotiators, with advance access to the negotiating texts. As a result, the anti-FTAA campaign suggests on its website that 'citizens are left in the dark, [and] corporations are helping to write the rules for the FTAA' (<http://www.globalexchange.org/campaigns/ftaa/topten.html>) (Phillips 1999: 82–5).

The issue of citizen access to FTAA negotiations came to a head at the 2001 FTAA Summit in Quebec City. Foreign and trade ministers from the Summit countries agreed to meet with 60 representatives from hemispheric NGOs inside the chainlink fence that separated the dignitaries from the ordinary citizens. Outside, hundreds of representatives of NGOs demonstrated, and were sprayed with teargas for their pains. Critics contend that this indicates that the main aim of government policy is to sidetrack 'actions on issues such as the environment, gender, human rights, labor standards, and democracy to other forums', including institutions of the Organisation of American States (Macdonald and Schwartz 2002: 153). NGOs and citizen groups oppose this policy, arguing that it is not appropriate to try to divide trade and social issues which should be discussed together during the FTAA negotiations. So far, however, there are few signs that the FTAA Committee of Government Representatives – the key institution overseeing the negotiations – is willing to open up and extend the process in the ways that their critics would like to see. It may be that to find a way out of this impasse will require more open and transparent processes of consultation than have so far been adopted.

Conclusion

Our brief survey of NAFTA suggests several conclusions. First, Mexico's recent democratization appears to be linked to pressures emanating from the Agreement's founder members – the USA and Canada. This is significant for the issue of links between globalization and comparative political analysis as it suggests that Mexico's rulers believed that membership of NAFTA was worth the price: economic liberalization and democratization (to the extent that the incumbent regime eventually lost power). In short, free trade helped break down rigid economic and political traditions in Mexico, leading to the institution of both democratic norms and economic liberalization.

Second, what were initially seen as 'only' trade issues in NAFTA have gone beyond narrowly defined economic outcomes to affect a wide range of social and political issues, while informing discussions about its probable successor, the FTAA. In the NAFTA member states, trade issues are defined and underlined along sharply partisan lines. On the one hand are the proponents of free trade, notably the member states and big business. On the other hand are ranged what might be called 'the popular sector', with its concern with what it sees as the unwelcome social, environmental, economic and political results of regional trade liberalization.

Third, widespread involvement of various interest groups suggests that, while excessive optimism about the role of both domestic and transnational NGOs in trade talks would not be unwarranted, it is unlikely that what has been called the era of 'competitive elitism' will soon return. This is because opponents of regional trade agreements are very unlikely to accept passively trade agreements negotiated behind closed doors in meetings of elites. Instead, domestic and to some extent transnational coalitions of actors now mobilize around trade issues and have been successful in affecting popular perception of trade issues, including the free trade assumptions behind both NAFTA and FTAA. The issue has opened up the consultation process in countries in Latin America and the Caribbean in the context of FTAA discussion, where these issues were previously determined by executive fiat (<http://www.crnm.org/ftaa.htm>). Macdonald and Schwartz (2002: 153) aver, as a result of these developments, that although regional 'states . . . continue to control the trade agenda, we may nonetheless be seeing the first stages of a movement toward more participatory and consultative forms of trade agreements and a convergence between "globalization from above" and "globalization from below"'. However, this union is only likely to succeed if it manages to develop thinking 'about ways in which both party and NGO models of political representation, and both national and international politics, can be viewed as synergistically linked, rather than as diametrically opposed realities'.

Conclusion

We noted at the beginning of this chapter that a key aim of virtually all existing regional organizations is to expand trade among member countries in the context of globalization. We have seen that when there are appropriate formal and/or informal institutions – as in the EU and to an extent in NAFTA – then political, social and/or developmental objectives, even when officially of no or minimal importance, can grow in significance in the context of trade talks. For example, the issue of EU enlargement was not only about the economic ramifications of regional augmentation, but also importantly concerned wider political, cultural and social issues subsumed under the heading of what constitutes 'European-ness'.

In our two case studies, we saw that when transitional countries want to be linked – not only economically, but also, by extension, politically and by security issues – to regional established democracies, then they must absorb the political values of the established democracies or be refused membership. This represents a 'process of being incorporated' into relevant regional organizations (Schulz et al. 2001: 260) and puts into effect what Kumar (2000: 137) refers to as the application of 'regional norms'. For example, NAFTA's 'regional norms' demanded that Mexico acted according to what was regarded by the American and Canadian governments as 'good behaviour'. Democracy and economic norms of NAFTA required that Mexico be a free-market democracy, while similar concerns also informed the issue of EU augmentation.

A further point is that states engaged robustly in regional cooperation want both to have their cake and to eat it: they 'attempt to gain the economic advantages of larger and more open markets without sacrificing their political sovereignty' (Hague and Harrop 2001: 52). However, the history of the EU, the most developed regional organization, indicates that advanced regional cooperation can have multiple – economic, political, security and cultural – outcomes (Kumar 2000; Baxter 2002). In addition, when states engage in such regional cooperation, they 'create or strengthen a policy domain in which they receive new instruments for dealing with specific actors, situations and processes' (Schirm 2002: 10). Consequently, national lobbies – both formal institutions and informal organizations – seek to ensure that they have an adequate voice in regional-level decision-making. This is important because, as Coussy (2001: 151) notes, national choices are ignored or devalued if the region becomes 'a means of bypassing national lobbies'. As Leslie (1997) notes, 'it is possible, then, that globalization diminishes the economic role of national states by strengthening firms over governments, while regionalism transfers, in some degree, political control over the economy to supranational institutions'. This implies that politically unaccountable transnational actors, such as TNCs, can have a larger say in regional outcomes than elected representatives.[12]

Finally, developed regional organizations, especially the EU and to a lesser but growing extent NAFTA, can influence the policy impact of transnational actors in two ways. On the one hand, demands of transnational actors for changes in national policies may be legitimized and strengthened by the respective regional regime norms. In relation to the EU we saw this in respect to its policy concerning new members. In North America, on the other hand, NAFTA membership has encouraged Mexico both to democratize and to liberalize economically. In both regional contexts, we can see some evidence of Risse-Kappen's (1995a: 32) claim that 'co-operative and highly institutionalized inter-state relations tend to lower state boundaries thereby allowing for flourishing transnational relations'.

---

[12] In addition, regional economic integration among developing countries may well remain hostage to political and security concerns of the participating countries. The situation will also be affected by prior interest in fuller integration with the global economy through inter-regional trade and investment linkages (Grugel 2000: 124).

7

Economic Globalization

It is often said that economic globalization, reflecting an increasingly interdependent global economy, undermines state capacity to pursue independent macroeconomic and development strategies. The historic process of economic globalization is said both to have broadened and deepened since the 1970s and 1980s. This was a phase of world history characterized by the end of European colonial rule, diminution of the USA's hitherto dominant economic position and significant growth in the internationalization of productive capital and finance. Together, these developments led to powerful global changes – to the extent that even the most powerful industrialized states are said to have declining options in relation to economic policy, including welfare procedures. Today, all states – rich and poor, weak and strong – are exposed to networks of economic forces and relations that range both in and through them. It is often said that the consequence is to reduce – sometimes fundamentally – their ability to pursue autonomous, national economic and developmental policies.[1] Thus the monetary and fiscal policies of all states must take cognizance of the influence of globally orientated economic actors.

Consequences of Economic Globalization

In this chapter, we examine the impact of selected aspects of economic globalization on three categories of states: established democracies, transitional democracies and non-democracies. All governments must attempt to deal with three consequences of economic globalization: (1) the increasing influence of international economic actors, such as transnational corporations (TNCs); (2) the growing integration of national economic systems; and (3) the massive expansion of financial markets and the deregulation and liberalization of trade, credit and currency movements. Let's start by seeing why these actors are important.

TNCs

The concept of economic globalization is strongly informed by the rise to prominence of a key type of economic actor: the TNC. TNCs are sometimes said to be beyond state control because of their ability to move capital, goods and services across national

[1] Todaro (1989: 87) defines economic development as 'the reduction or elimination of poverty, inequality, and unemployment within the context of a growing economy'.

borders. As Sen (1999: 62) remarks: 'In contrast to national exports and imports of goods and services, the organization, flow and purview of [foreign direct investment] FDI and global capital, undertaken by . . . TNCs, assume a global market place.' The importance of FDI is widely noted in the literature as a crucial vehicle and conduit for economic growth in general and for exports in particular. TNCs routinely make significant decisions – about location, employment, investment and revenue issues – that affect outcomes in countries. Yet states – particularly small, weak developing countries – find it difficult to control TNCs – because the pace and interactions of technological and economic change mean that their 'command and control' regulations are increasingly difficult to apply meaningfully. Consequently, states are faced with increasingly stark choices regarding regulatory strategies: what processes of adjustment are necessary to attract and retain TNCs? The fear is that TNC production facilities are at liberty to move elsewhere, with attendant unwelcome impact: declining tax bases and increased unemployment.

TNCs are also said to have wide-ranging political power in some circumstances. One view is to see Western TNCs as complicit in the strategy of powerful Western states, such as the United States, to seek to gain control of the global economy. Second, TNCs are sometimes said to support authoritarian solutions to problems of political and economical instability when they believe it necessary 'to ensure a politically more secure environment for the free movement of capital' (Yilmaz 2002: 82–3). In sum, TNC activities are said to erode state capacity to control national economies and may also have political ramifications (Schulz et al. 2001: 16).

Growing integration of national economic systems

The global economy has greatly expanded since the end of the cold war, not least because of the gradual, uneven, still continuing integration of the former communist countries of Central and Eastern Europe (CEE) into the global economy and financial system. The collapse of the region's communist systems was an important background variable to the global spread of economic liberalization, as it appeared both to exonerate and galvanize market forces. These underlying changes in the international political economy were partly responsible for the advance of market reforms – not only among CEE's former communist countries, but globally. The overall result is that, while it may not yet have reached the extent premised by some in the early post-cold war period, the end of the former economic separation of the First/Second/Third World was a huge practical step towards a fully integrated global economy.

The incorporation of CEE's former communist countries – that is, the former 'Second World' – into the global economy was augmented by a steady opening to the international market of numerous developing economies (that is, the erstwhile 'Third World'). We should note, however, that prior to the end of the cold war, many developing countries had already adopted economic liberalization policies as a result of serious economic problems. These included: balance of payments crises, instability or collapse of national currencies, very high rates of inflation, insupportable fiscal deficits and intolerable levels of international indebtedness. These developments were typically preceded by periods of economic stagnation and/or declining rates of economic growth, leading to growing unemployment and increasing poverty and, in many cases, political instability. This was frequently followed by citizen demands for fundamental political and economic reforms.

Such concerns are central to global financial health and the maintenance of global financial and trade systems. Recent financial crises in Pacific Asia, Argentina, Mexico, Russia and elsewhere raised questions about what can be done to prevent, solve or contain the spread of regional financial crises and what can be done to reduce the debt burden on poor countries. International financial institutions, such as the International Monetary Fund (IMF) and the World Bank, are at the core of efforts to address financial crises. The United States is the major contributor to the IMF and relies heavily on it and the World Bank to promote world economic health. The operations and transparency of these institutions have come under increased scrutiny.

Dozens of affected countries, mostly in the developing world, adopted structural adjustment programmes (SAPs) in the 1980s and 1990s, following pressure from Western governments, the IMF and the World Bank. Economic liberalization and a concomitant rolling back of the state's economic role was a uniform condition for the receipt of significant external economic assistance. The IMF had several aims: (1) to encourage a high level of fiscal and monetary discipline; (2) to advance reforms leading towards market economies; and (3) to encourage free trade, free capital flow and economic cooperation among countries. The overall objective was to strengthen the international monetary system and advance the process of economic globalization. To achieve these goals, the following key steps were necessary:

- cut government spending, including on health and welfare;
- cut wage levels or at least severely constrain wage rises in order to reduce inflation and make exports more competitive (Brecher and Costello 1994: 56–7);
- expand the role of the private sector through privatization of state assets;
- liberalize foreign trade;
- liberalize control of capital, capital movement and money markets, including the lifting of restrictions on foreign investment;
- protect weaker sectors of society by strengthening social safety nets.

SAP-adopting countries abandoned or downgraded national development strategies – that is, those based on state-led programmes and import substitution policies – and rejected nationalization of foreign-held assets. The overall outcome was to integrate such economies more fully into the global economy.

Recent research indicates that under SAPs poverty has actually grown in recent years, most economic 'progress' has occurred in only a small number of countries (some of them with large populations and unusual appeal for foreign investors) and, even in successful cases, many people are actually no better off, and may actually be poorer, than before (Haynes 2005). While the enforcement of cutbacks, privatization and liberalization of capital was a uniform condition to receive IMF aid, the matter of protecting the weaker sectors of society was typically rather vague, rarely enforced to a degree which permitted it to offset the growing inequalities that flowed from SAPs. In sum, SAPs were externally imposed, yet seriously flawed development strategies that often undermined the already weak developmental position of many poor people. As a result, there were widespread calls to reform SAPs, tame financial markets, 'upsize' the state and 'downsize' the single global market (Held and McGrew 2002; Pettifor 2003).

Massive expansion of financial markets

Economic globalization is often said to be an unstoppable process, entrenched and irreversible, to the point that serious questions emerge about the relevance – and effectiveness – of state ability both to manage and direct national economic activities. Fukuyama (1992: 275) contends that, whereas nationalism once fulfilled an integrative role that met the needs of early capitalism, now 'those same economic forces are . . . encouraging the breakdown of national barriers through the creation of a single, integrated world market'. This process follows its own technical and economic logic, and is facilitated by the cross-border mobility of capital. For example, each day, more than $1.6 *trillion* passes through foreign exchanges. To put this figure in perspective, it is about 400 per cent of the combined foreign exchange reserves of the central banks of the United States, Japan and Britain. As a result, oversight of financial institutions and markets has become increasingly challenging. Each day, around the world, particularly in the developed countries of Europe and North America, millions of households collectively have trillions of dollars flowing through financial institutions and markets. Globalization of financial firms and markets – along with constantly advancing technology – has created opportunities for increased efficiencies. But they have also increased the speed and scope of undesirable results, for example, the flow of illegal finances or the spread of financial crises. The global scope of TNCs, along with difficulties in valuing knowledge-based assets, also raises questions about extant accounting and disclosure models. Finally, globalization of electronic commerce not only increases access but also makes it more difficult to protect consumers and businesses from fraudulent and abusive marketing as well as adding to audit, security, backup and disaster recovery concerns.

In sum, the overall result of post-cold war changes was the incorporation of both the former communist countries of Europe and numerous developing states into the global economy. This process produced a qualitative, but as yet incomplete, transformation of the global economy. One of the key characteristics of economic globalization was a sometimes dramatic alteration of the balance of power between state and market. However, the question of the significance of economic globalization is controversial, and various theories have been advanced to understand and explicate the phenomenon.

Theories of Economic Globalization

Globalists and anti-globalists

While there is much agreement about the analytical significance of economic globalization, there is little about what it amounts to for comparative analysis.[2] Most simplistically, debate about the impact of economic globalization is polarized: is it 'good' or 'bad'? One group – the 'globalists' – expresses a generally 'positive' perception of economic globalization. They contend that, following a perception that the end of the

---

[2] This section is based on Haynes 2003c: 1042–5.

cold war would lead to a progressively improving international climate, then it was plausible – even likely – to expect a new era of global cooperation. This would not only involve states and various IGOs, such as the EU and the UN, but also a range of citizens' groups. Collectively, it was hoped, these actors would work together in pursuit of a range of broadly developmental and political goals.

Various Western state and non-state actors together make up an influential group of globalists. Examples of the former include the governments of the USA and Britain, and of the latter, the IMF. Both see economic globalization as a key strategy to stimulate beneficial economic and developmental outcomes. The IMF, as noted above, has three main aims: to institutionalize economic globalization, to ensure greater mobility of capital across borders and to encourage states to move towards balanced budgets. The overall purpose of these objectives is, on the one hand, to provide the potential for general growth and prosperity and, on the other, to increase provision of social services for the poor. However, it is sometimes admitted that while the *potential* benefits from economic globalization are widely, but not universally, accepted, there is also potential for destabilizing risks in those countries unable to withstand globalization's dynamic forces.

Anti-globalists see things quite differently. They see globalization as a series of processes with unequivocally negative consequences, connected to unfair trade practices, production processes that leave the poor worse off, millions of refugees (especially from the poor countries), increasing examples of international terrorism, widespread ethnic and religious conflicts, and the rise of anti-immigration right-wing political parties in Western Europe.

Right-wing populists seek to exploit some local people's fears of an 'influx' of foreigners –as a perceived result of economic globalization – for their own political purposes. While they might be prepared to admit that global free trade theoretically has a good side – lower taxes and cheaper goods – for them this does not outweigh a less desirable outcome. This is that a free(r) labour market would bring with it a higher level of immigration, the consequence, they claim, of massive, uncontrollable population movements from the poor world – for example, North and West Africa and Central and Eastern Europe – to the rich Western European world. (Whether such a movement of labour would actually be beneficial for European economies is rarely discussed.) Notable among the ranks of the anti-globalists are many conservative politicians and their media allies who claim that such population transfers result in often serious 'conflicts between immigrant and established communities in formerly tight-knit neighbourhoods' (Mittelman 1994: 429). Such concerns frequently inform xenophobic populist propaganda, for example, during Germany's 2002 presidential and legislative elections. In sum, while globalists see economic globalization as a key to greater national and international stability and security, anti-globalists see the opposite outcome.

In sum, globalists and anti-globalists fundamentally differ on what they see as the outcomes of economic globalization. Yet both agree that it is having significant effects on domestic political and economic systems. But how significant and in what ways? Cutting across the globalist/anti-globalist divide is a further issue: to what extent is economic globalization a 'non-negotiable, inevitable/inexorable process' (Hay and Rosamond 2002: 152), in the face of which *all* states are helpless. Three sets of views can be isolated in this respect: hyper-globalizationist, globalization sceptic and structural dependency. I will now examine briefly the views of each, before turning to an inspection of the impact of economic globalization upon different kinds of political regime.

Hyper-globalization

Significant debate about economic globalization began in the late 1980s, following the airing of the views of the mostly US business schools' approach. This hyper-globalization analysis took as its main theme the notion that the post-1970s, increasingly integrated world economy, posed a fundamental challenge to the sovereignty of the (nation-)state (Ohmae 1990). The key hypothesis was that economic globalization was a steamroller that would compel Western European states in particular to drop Keynesian-style social democracy (Strange 2003). The wider claim was that national adaptation to economic globalization would require general state acceptance both of an advanced competitive imperative and other neo-liberal policy prescriptions. These would include significant labour market reforms to lessen costs by increasing labour and wage 'flexibility'.

To the hyper-globalizationists, economic globalization was signalled empirically by: (1) the growing significance of TNCs, (2) major growth in foreign direct investment, especially in the advanced capitalist economies and among the East Asian 'tiger' economies, and (3) a globalization of finance. These three developments posed a central challenge to the autonomy and independence of all states, with particular pressure on both social democracy and broadly progressive regulation. Consequently, so the argument went, whether governments liked it or not, economic globalization was resulting in the dominance of (1) the competitive market order and (2) the domestic political consequences of economic neo-liberalism (Strange 2003).

The globalization sceptic

By the 1990s, a powerful critique of the hyper-globalizationists had emerged, principally from the political left (Hirst and Thompson 1999; Hay and Rosamond 2002). It advanced two core propositions opposing the hyper-globalizationist claims: first, the social democratic nation-state with its Keynesian characteristics was not in terminal decline because of economic globalization and, second, the hyper-globalizationist claim of economic *globalization* was empirically incorrect, as substantively it only included the 'golden triangle' of North America, Western Europe and Japan (Hirst and Thompson 1999).

Hay and Rosamond (2002) presented an influential critique of the hyper-globalizationist view. This was that there was little or no role for agency when it came to economic globalization. But, they argued, economic globalization was actually not a steamroller; instead, there was a more nuanced effect, with a role for various agents. Their critical analysis of the hyper-globalization thesis was developed in relation to what they saw as Britain's (New) Labour government's unnecessary surrender to the neo-liberal depiction of economic globalization, but its ramifications are wider. In general, they stressed the significance of ideas and discourse in helping determine accepted contours of the impact of economic globalization on domestic political economies. For example, they argued that Britain's economic and welfare reformist policies since the early 1980s had been not under the *force majeure* of economic globalization, but were the result of the then intellectual hegemony of neo-liberal political parties and social forces inside both state and civil society. In other words, there were no irresistible *structural* constraints on social democracy in Britain imposed by economic globalization. Consequently, there was at least some scope to develop particularistic political-economic projects, such as those of Chavez in Venezuela (Hawkins 2003) and of Mahathir in Malaysia, which seemed to be able to 'flout' to some degree the supposed imperatives of economic globalization *à la* hyper-globalizationist arguments.

In sum, for the globalization sceptics, economic globalization is a force that to a degree can be resisted or moulded. Indeed, it is best perceived as a 'contingent process or tendency to which counter-tendencies might be mobilized' (Hay and Rosamond 2002: 152). This implies that economic globalization neither inevitably implies the diminution of the welfare state nor disallows a 'social democratic' alternative to unalloyed economic liberalization.

Structural dependency

Arguments seeking to deny the inevitability of the impact of economic globalization were followed later in the 1990s by further analyses based on a restatement and rearticulation of structural dependency theory (Coates 2000; Radice 1999). This argument suggested that economic globalization is 'not merely a set of ideas and a dominant discourse' but instead an aggregate 'of structurally imposed imperatives rooted in material relations' (Hay and Rosamond 2002: 152). The core of the structural dependency approach is a radical left view of the economic globalization thesis. Largely concurring with the empirical claims of the hyper-globalizationists, the structural dependency view nevertheless rejects the inevitability of neo-liberalism. In addition, it seeks to critique the positivist analysis via a deeper structural account of the capitalist mode of production (Strange 2003). The structural dependency view claims that recent empirical weakening of reformist politics and political economy, not only in Western Europe but also via structural adjustment programmes in many developing countries, is explicable by the rise to unchallenged global hegemony of emphatically pro-capital class forces. The structural dependency approach to economic globalization makes two key conclusions. Post-cold war economic globalization is (1) a set of ideas and a dominant discourse emphatically favouring capital, and (2) an assemblage of structurally imposed imperatives that are rooted in material relations.

Conclusion

In sum, hyper-globalizationists, globalization sceptics and the structural dependency approach differ significantly in interpretations of the impact and ramifications of economic globalization on countries' domestic economic (and by association political and social) terrains. On the other hand, there is agreement that we need to understand better the political and economic impact of significant border-crossing – state and non-state (transnational actors and international organizations) – actors. This implies that to account for contemporary political (and economic) developments within countries there is a need to bridge the analytical gap between what until now have been separate spheres of endeavour: comparative politics and international relations.

While approaches to economic globalization differ, there is little real doubt that economic globalization is a significant phenomenon with important domestic impacts on states. However, although it is a multifaceted phenomenon, its impact is not uniform, but varies from country to country. It is clear that for all states economic globalization results in a significant loss of economic autonomy. And, as a result, state capacity to perform both established economic and developmental functions is undermined. This is a consequence not only of the advance of the global market but also of the power and influence of international economic actors, including TNCs, to influence state policies.

In the next section we focus upon three aspects of economic globalization:

- the growing integration of national economic systems;
- the deregulation and liberalization of trade, credit and currency movements;
- the massive expansion of financial markets.

We will examine these in relation to a selection of established democracies (the USA, Britain and India), transitional democracies (Poland, Hungary and Turkey), and non-democracies (China and Vietnam). We shall see that outcomes are related to the ability of various kinds of external actor to access and influence domestic outcomes.

Established Democracies

The USA

The United States is the principal architect of an open world trading system. It is the world's largest exporter of goods and services, and is widely thought to have benefited immensely from global trade. Under the circumstances of economic globalization, all governments, including that of the USA, must pay increased attention to three issues: welfare, jobs protection and creation, and industrial innovation.

The General Accounting Office (GAO), the audit, evaluation and investigative arm of Congress, claims that 'globalization is increasing the interdependence of the world's economies and affecting national security and the economic well-being of the American people'. The GAO notes that US exports have grown much faster than the domestic economy: between 1970 and 2000, the USA's gross domestic product (GDP) doubled, while exports rose fivefold. However, the GAO admits that not all people – whether in the USA or elsewhere – have benefited equally from economic globalization, and there is no certainty that they will in the future. Borger (2003b) points out that the 'richest 1% of Americans now own well over 40% of their nation's wealth. It is a skewed distribution that sets the US apart from other modern industrialized nations. In

Britain, widely viewed in America as the embodiment of social stratification, the richest 1% owns a mere 18% of the wealth.'

The current disparities of wealth in the USA are not the results solely of the policies of the current Bush administration. Instead, the country's economic division has been under way for more than two decades, following a long period after World War II of movement towards levelling incomes and wealth. Inequality began to increase sharply from about 1980, a trend driven by a dual development: a boom in stock prices and the decline in the clout of labour unions. In the mid-1990s, welfare reform was instituted under a cooperative agreement between President Clinton and a staunchly Republican Congress. The result was to dismantle much of the welfare system built decades earlier during the years of the New Deal and the Great Society. Under the new arrangements, time limits were set on how long the poor and unemployed could draw social security payments. The aim was to force people back into work, aided by a large number of federally funded job training programmes. In the short term, a mixture of economic boom and social programmes that supported the working poor and retrained many among the unemployed assuaged the harsh impact of welfare reform. After Clinton, George W. Bush largely did away with such programmes, an ideological victim of a regime that, critics argue, 'fundamentally does not believe [that] government should have a direct role in alleviating poverty' (Borger 2003c). These conditions served in general to improve the position of the rich while undermining that of the poor. According to Phillips (2002), one needs to go back over a century to arrive at a parallel era when big money and government were in such a tight embrace.

A second aspect of economic globalization of major relevance to the USA is its involvement in trade agreements. The USA is a member of more than 300 international trade agreements that affect hundreds of billions of dollars in trade and millions of domestic jobs. The mutual dependence of international markets and the US economy is expected to increase even further with China's recent admission to the World Trade Organization and the launching of new multilateral trade negotiations. However, the issue of China's emergence as an economic competitor to the USA is a controversial political issue in the latter country. This is because, over the last few years, US factories in various parts of the country, including Connecticut and Michigan, have closed or relocated to China, from whence 'big retailers and manufacturers produce goods at artificially low prices and sell them for greater profit in the United States' (Garriga 2003).

China's recent emergence on to the global economic scene reflects the fact that it enjoys several key advantages. First, it pays relatively low wages and salaries; second its currency is pegged to the US dollar; and third, it has relatively few effective environmental and healthcare requirements of the kind that American firms must be concerned with (Scherer 2003). The Manufacturing Alliance of Connecticut (MAC) argues that 'manufacturers will not be able to recover because of unfair trade practices from China and other countries, ranging from copyright infringement, patent stealing, child labor and currency manipulation, and lack of attention to the industry by government officials'. The MAC also contends that China's currency is undervalued by up to 50 per cent, allowing big retailers and manufacturers to produce goods in China at artificially low prices and sell them for greater profit in the United States. 'We have been taken advantage of. The big companies and big retailers won't buy springs from me if they are making their products in China. We are not looking for tariffs. We are looking for fairness', says Fred Tedesco, president and co-owner of Pa-Ted Spring Co. Inc. in Bristol,

Connecticut, which employs only 80 people after two years of downsizing. 'This has not bottomed; it is actually getting worse', said Tedesco, who was forced to lay off 40 employees. He added that these factors have given the Chinese a huge advantage, while the quality of Chinese products is improving rapidly. Currently, the US trade deficit with China is $12.7bn (£7.05bn) (Garriga 2003). In 2004, a presidential election year, the loss of manufacturing jobs became an issue of major political significance – not least because many of the regions affected were crucial swing states. An early contender for the Democratic nomination, Richard Gephardt, backed by the United Steelworkers, stressed his long-time opposition to free-trade agreements with Mexico and China, 'and other Democrats are getting behind the issue' (Teather 2003).

Third, turning to industrial innovation, a key issue is globalization of the defence industry. This is driven by falls in governments' military investments worldwide, and follows patterns similar to those found in other commercial sectors. US defence companies are engaged in a wide variety of business arrangements across national borders. For example, some enter into 'offset agreements', that is, developing long-term supplier relationships that change the nature of the market and the composition of the supplier base. The wider point is that globalization has the potential to speed innovation and reduce costs – but it also carries potential threats to the technological superiority of the US military and may require even greater investments in weapons modernization (Nelson 2001).

In conclusion, issues associated with economic globalization impact upon the USA in relation to welfare and poverty, trade agreements and the globalization of the defence industry, and the question, more generally, of industrial innovation. They all require particular attention, while being increasingly difficult to control. In short, economic globalization has made the United States more vulnerable to overseas economic crises. The United States has found it increasingly difficult to maintain control over both critical technologies as well as the industrial base on which US economic and military security depends.

Britain

For EU states, including Britain, economic globalization is said to amount to a process 'of advanced market deregulation' that occurred as a result of 'exposing themselves to the global winds' (Verdier and Breen 2001: 3). Economic globalization also reflects the greatly increased scale of international exchange of goods, services and capital that is said to undermine the autonomous decision-making capacities of states. In the EU, as Allen (2002: 23) notes, 'the shift of fiscal and monetary policy to the European level became codified with the introduction of the physical Euro in January 2002'. This emphasized how hard it was 'to maintain the fiction that national governments retained traditional post-Westphalian domestically-based sovereignty – let alone democratic political accountability – in a globalized EU'. In short, all EU governments – including that of Britain – now experience new pressures on their authority and policy-making capacity, especially in relation to a range of domestic policy initiatives.

All EU member states, including Britain, are very keen to attract foreign capital, in order to raise both output and employment. Britain has lower unemployment than EU member states in the eurozone, an outcome reflecting both the Labour government's 'more expansionary economic policies' as well as the 'apparent acceptance of a low-wage economy as something to boast about (in order to attract inward investment)' (Keegan 2004: 8). This policy is linked to the desire to attract both domestic and transnational capital, a highly competitive and necessary process. Under these circumstances, it makes sense to: (1) weaken labour protection, (2) cut non-wage social overheads and (3) reduce corporate and income tax rates. This is because controllers of internationally mobile funds – including TNCs, wealthy asset-holders and key financial bodies, such as fund managers and banks – have an increasingly powerful tool of 'exit': they can threaten to remove 'their' capital. Such circumstances may encourage states to create, develop or retain policies in line with such actors' preferences (Shaw 2003).

Under the circumstances of economic globalization, all governments, including that of Britain, see three issues as central: jobs protection and creation, industrial innovation and welfare. A key issue is how to reconcile the demands of voters for jobs and welfare with the interests of business that may want to see both lower taxes and less government regulation of their activities. Business is most likely to invest where domestic wage levels are relatively low. However, 'labor instability creates a demand for government to insure workers against market risk through unemployment benefits, government employment, and the provision of assorted social services'. The problem, however, is that 'cross-border capital mobility undermines the capacity of the government to deliver this much-needed insurance' (Verdier and Breen 2001: 229), as capital can move easily to environments where tax rates are most attractive. In short, there are two forces working at cross purposes: rising demand for public insurance and sinking capacity to meet that demand. Under circumstances of economic globalization, markets become more important and, as a result, governments may lose some ability to determine domestic outcomes. This may have political results: citizen loyalty to political parties may decline, along with voter turnout and government stability. Voters may believe not only that politicians have lost the capacity to govern but also that government has lost 'some of its prior relevance to market allocation' (Verdier and Breen 2001: 229). In sum, the range of goals that political actors, both states and parties, can realistically aspire to is said to be circumscribed by the need to have 'policies which reflect not autonomous political processes, but market decisions' (Cerny 2000: 177).

Allen (2002: 1) asks how best to explain the policy choices of '12 out of [the then] 15 European states' that 'elected democratic left governments in the late 1990s'. Why did these governments, including that of Britain, he asks, all of which were no doubt aware of concerns about the 'democratic deficit' and difficulties in maintaining a 'social Europe', not as a result produce 'more explicit left-wing policies'? He contends that this unique grouping of left-led governments could have seized the opportunity to address serious social, economic and developmental problems, including unemployment, regional economic disparities and the issue of qualitative, ecologically sound economic growth. In addition, they might have used their collective strength to force the EU to address democratic deficit concerns, a problem said to be exacerbated by economic globalization and its associated results: privatizations, deregulations and transnational mergers of large European and North American firms.

Allen advances three explanations to account for a recent perceived 'roll back of welfare provision' by social democratic governments in the EU, including that of Britain. Such governments are said to have:

- feared that, if they did not roll back welfare provision, capital and business would find more profitable places to invest;
- rolled back welfare provision because of shifts in their own ideologies – yet they chose to blame it on the conditions 'imposed' by economic globalization; however, governments were unwilling openly to inform the electorate about their changed ideological position because they feared that the latter would reject them at the ballot box;
- rolled back welfare provision because they all 'suffered from a fundamental failure of imagination'. (Allen 2002: 1)

Allen (2002) also argues that these governments suffered not only from weak and tame policy prescriptions but also from a failure of imagination both in terms of ideological vision as well as newer possibilities of governance. This included, at one level, both sectoral and subnational and, at another, supranational governance in the EU. In sum, Allen contends that perceptions about economic globalization undermined the ability of leftist governments in Europe to work together in pursuit of collective social democratic goals and instead led them to seek individualistic solutions. However, Swank's (2002) main research finding, supported by other empirical work in this field (see, for example, Pergher 1998/9), indicates that globalization has actually had less impact on domestic social welfare programmes than is often claimed polemically in accounts such as Allen's. Note however that Swank's argument accepts the view that globalization universally imposes *pressures* on the welfare state but that institutional configurations determine the *response to pressures*.

This reminds us that institutions are not just fixed structures but also dynamic entities. What they do can be informed both by purposeful policy-makers and patterns of understood responses to a wide range of political and policy outcomes. It is important to note that these responses are not spontaneously occurring phenomena but need to be understood, reinforced and continually tested against new challenges. If they are not, state institutions are unlikely to retain the capacity to produce novel economic and political policies appropriate for changing conditions. It is sometimes argued that European leftist governments missed the opportunity in the early 2000s to head a new debate: 'What should be the relationship between state and market – between private and public sectors – in the context of new or renewed institutional governance structures' in the 21st century?' (Allen 2002: 21–3). The importance of such a debate might be gauged from the fact that this was a time when millions of European citizens were expressing, in various ways, concern and unease about the perceived ability of globalization to erode the power of national governments. Nevertheless, there was no real attempt to begin serious and coordinated debate in the Union on the triangular relationship between globalization, the EU and national governments.

India

India is a rare case: an established democracy with a relatively underdeveloped economy. The classic starting point for the link between economic development, democratization and democratic consolidation is the early work of Seymour Martin Lipset (1963). Utilizing contemporary data, Lipset surveyed selected Western democracies, comparing them with a batch of authoritarian Latin American countries. He found that in the former there were consistently higher mean levels of socio-economic development than among the latter. Thus Lipset's famous dictum: 'The more well-to-do a nation, the greater the chances that it will sustain democracy.' However, Lipset established a correlation between prosperity and democracy. He did *not* propose that democracy is the *inevitable* result of a certain level of socio-economic development. In fact, it is empirically easy to see that there is no *inevitable* connection between the level of economic development and the degree of democracy. If this *was* a rule of general applicability, how would economically developing India's half century of democracy be explained, or recent shifts to democracy in poor countries like Ghana or Benin? Consequently, we can assume that there is no simple relationship between socio-economic modernization and the development of liberal democracy.

India has been a democracy since 1947, excepting a brief interregnum between 1975 and 1977 when the country was under a State of Emergency. However, by any conventional criteria, India is an established democracy, not least because of the overall longevity of its democratic regime. Because it has been a democracy for decades, it did not come under pressure from foreign governments to democratize. But India's democratic continuity raises major doubts about at least one important conventional assumption relating to democratization and democratic consolidation: the need for growing national wealth, relatively equitably distributed (Prezeworski et al. 1996). What is India's record in this regard? Poverty reduction was laid down as a central aspiration by the country's nationalist leaders at the time of independence, yet progress has been slow. By the end of the twentieth century, more than 50 years after independence in 1947, India was one of the poorest countries in the world (165th out of 210). It had a GNP per capita of only $430, with more than half of Indians living on less than US$1 a day (World Bank 2000: 230). Chakravarty (1997: 89–90) argues that a consequence of the failure to develop faster economic prosperity was growing concern about the fate of the poor, an issue linked to 'a lot of disillusionment . . . about [democracy's] decline' and its ability to tackle the problem of poverty.

India had a state-dominated economy until the late 1980s. Then, in response both to a debt crisis and external encouragement from various Western governments, including those of Britain and the USA, India embarked on extensive economic reforms. They focused on reformulating the economic and developmental role of the state, in accordance with the then neo-liberal thinking embedded in the notion of the Washington consensus.

Until that time, India's economic characteristics were dominated by a very inward-looking, heavily statist economy. This was justified and defended by a dominant ideological mix of what Callaghy (1993: 194) calls 'socialism, self-reliance, nationalism and Third World pride'. The immediate cause of the reforms was an international debt crisis, although pressures for reform had been building from various Western governments and agencies, including the IMF.

In the 1960s and 1970s, the real annual rate of GDP growth in India was 3.4 per cent, implying a per capita annual growth rate of barely 1 per cent. Growth rates in national output since the mid-1980s have been appreciably higher on average. In the 1990s, average consumption per capita (as measured in the national accounts) has grown at an annual rate of 3.0 per cent, implying about a one-third increase in consumption per capita over the decade. It appears plausible that the economic reforms carried out by India in the 1990s have helped achieve this higher growth. (Datt and Ravallion 2002: 89)

While experiencing respectable economic growth rates from the mid-1980s, India had fallen well behind South Korea, one of the most economically successful of developing countries. Yet in the mid-1950s, both India and South Korea had the *same* annual per capita income – around $340; three decades later, South Korea had surged ahead with a figure *ten times that of India*. With exports accounting for less than 5 per cent of GDP, the Indian government began to realize that – like its counterpart in South Korea – the best way forward was to focus on export-led growth; in effect, to engage with and profit from economic globalization. However, a succession of weak governments in India in the 1980s lacked both the ability and the political will to reorientate the economy. Instead, balance of payments imbalances and inflation and foreign exchange reserves dropped alarmingly. The result was an international debt crisis. By the early 1990s, India's foreign debt was $83 billion, the third highest in the world. Only those of Brazil and Mexico were greater. India's debt service ratio – that is, the proportion of export earnings devoted to paying the interest on foreign debt – was just over 30 per cent, four times that of South Korea's manageable 7 per cent (on a debt of $35 billion) (Word Bank 1995: 200–1, Table 20). On top of this came the Gulf Crisis of 1990–1 (temporarily) leading to higher oil prices and increased price inflation. India's reluctance to restructure economically was finally dispelled in mid-1991 as $600 million was due to be repaid in debt servicing and the government did not have access to such funds. The result was serious economic restructuring which, while leading to rapid growth, nevertheless did very little to diminish already serious socio-economic divisions between rich and poor.

To what extent was India's economic growth in the 1990s and beyond linked to economic globalization? Was the outcome more or less poverty reduction? On the first question, Nayar (2003) argues that 'the critics of globalization maintain that it has the consequence of eroding the economic autonomy of the nation-state'. He contends however that the national autonomy that India is assumed to have had in the past was exaggerated. As we have already noted, the impact of economic globalization is likely to vary with the capabilities of particular states. Analysis of quantitative and qualitative data pertaining to India's situation before and after its involvement with economic globalization suggests that, contrary to the position of the critics, there was erosion of India's economic autonomy *before* the advent of economic globalization. Nayar (2003: 1) argues that, instead, 'India's autonomy grew, relatively speaking, after globalization because of the consequent strengthening of its economic capabilities.'

In conclusion, what impact is economic globalization having on poverty reduction in India? On this issue, evidence is mixed. Prior to the 1990s, evidence suggests that economic growth in India typically reduced poverty, albeit slowly (Datt and Ravallion 2002: 89–90). However, it is difficult to be clear about what happened in the 1990s. Some observers argued that poverty fell more rapidly in the 1990s than previously (for example, Bhalla 2000). Others argue that poverty reduction stalled and that the poverty rate may even have risen (for example, Sen 2001). On balance, it is probable that India maintained its 1980s rate of poverty reduction in the 1990s. However, 'the basic question of measuring India's poverty rate has turned out to be harder to answer than it needed to be because of difficulties with coverage and comparability of the survey data' (Datt and Ravallion 2002: 106).

Transitional Democracies

Transitional democracies – found in Central and Eastern Europe (CEE), Latin America, Africa and Asia – are often also transitional economies. During the 1980s and 1990s, high growth rates in East Asian 'tiger' economies – Hong Kong, Singapore, South Korea and Taiwan – were influential in encouraging numerous countries to embark upon economic reforms, often encouraged by the Washington consensus (the US government, the IMF and the World Bank). There appeared to be links between economic and political reforms, focusing upon the role of the state. Transitional democracies/ economies are, like other states, on the look out for substantial external injections of funds and may seek to open domestic markets to external economic actors and increase exports. In both respects, this connects them to wider processes of economic globalization.

Poland and Hungary

After the cold war, the emergence of transitional democracies and economies in CEE brought a new dimension to the development debate. Initially, in the early 1990s, events in CEE were depicted as confirming that there was no viable alternative to the market economy and the neo-liberal perspective on development. However, over time, the region's transition turned out to be a complex and problematic process, characterized by recurrent economic and political crises 'and a general failure to establish consistent patterns of growth or maintain attraction for international capital' (Dixon 2003: 288). Kurtz and Barnes (2002: 524) contend that in CEE 'results suggest that faith in economic liberalization as a cause of democratization may be misplaced'.

More than a dozen years after the disbanding of the Soviet bloc, there is a wide range of regime outcomes in CEE. Along a spectrum, there are countries now emerging as relatively consolidated democracies (for example, Poland and Hungary) at one end, while others are at the opposite end, for example, Russia and Kyrgyzstan, appearing to exemplify political transformations to differing kinds of authoritarianism. Accounting for these diverse outcomes, apparently emerging from broadly similar predecessor conditions, leads to a focus on the circumstances resulting from the dual collapse of communist party rule and command economies. The role of economic liberalization is often noted in the process of seeking to consolidate the post-communist political regime, including the influence of international political conditionality.

Kurtz and Barnes assert 'that a specific kind of pressure emanating from the international system – strictly democratically conditioned material benefits – can have a substantial positive effect'. But this process is not a straightforward one of diffusion. This is because 'neither economic nor political connectedness to the advanced industrial democracies shows similar benefits'. What is required are 'explicit international pressures backed by material incentives' (Kurtz and Barnes 2002: 526). This suggests that we need to be cautious in our assumptions, for example, that simple external encouragement for economic reform will have the desired effects. A key problem is how to ensure that cutbacks, privatizations and liberalization of capital are taken seriously as a condition for external assistance, while at the same time making sure that there are robust policies in place to protect weaker sectors of society. The issue is complicated further because some transitional countries, such as Russia, have received especially favourable economic assistance from some key external actors, including the IMF and some Western governments. However, while Russia receives generous quantities of aid, there appears to be little attention paid to the 'inadequate efforts to protect the weaker sectors' of the society 'or to the widespread corruption which further diminishes the livelihood of the ordinary and poorer people, and thus increases inequalities'. In short, international pressures can be important, but this only seems to be the case when they are of a specific type: 'strict democratic conditionality applied to important material benefits' (Etzioni-Halevy 2002: 6).

Both Poland and Hungary are widely regarded as transitional democracies well on the way to consolidating democratic regimes (Freedom House 2003: 249–51, 446–50). Both countries became members of the EU in 2004. So it comes as something of a surprise when we note Kurtz and Barnes's (2002: 25) comments: 'The cases of Poland and Hungary seriously undermine the argument that marketization fuels democratization.' On the one hand, since 1990 both countries have constructed increasingly stable electoral democracies. On the other hand, their political regimes are not underpinned by a 'broad array of independent social organizations drawing on the resources of a developing private economy. That is, they have not done it by creating strong "civil societies".'

The examples of Poland and Hungary – where marketization and economic globalization have not clearly stimulated the development of civil society – seem consistent with post-communist regimes in many CEE countries, also characterized by continuation of state-dominated political structures. We noted in table 5.1 that state-*dominated* political structures are like state-*controlled* political systems, except that in the former state control is somewhat less overarching. There is a set of centralized, state-dominated political institutions, while civil society is relatively weak and fragmented. State-dominated political structures will, theoretically, make it difficult for external actors to overcome the initial hurdle of gaining access to the domestic terrain. However, once this barrier is overcome, then the policy impact of such actors can be profound. This is because if powerful state actors are predisposed toward their goals, then external actors may find it possible directly to influence state policies.

In sum, in both Poland and Hungary, there appears to be a surprising lack of organized political activity (Pridham 2000; Cook et al. 1999). Groups such as Solidarity that formed in the euphoric days of 1988–1990 tended to disperse quickly, without establishing roots in society. From above, new leaders shied away from the project of building state–society links, and from below, grassroots pressure to create such institutions has been weak. Employers are said to be in a strong position to thwart attempts of labour to organize (Miszlivetz and Jensen 1998: 87–8). While cross-border contacts could conceivably help to empower and legitimize the 'demands of otherwise weak social groups' in relation to various social and political issues

(Risse-Kappen 1994: 186–7; also see Waylen 2003: 173), it appears that so far economic globalization has served primarily to empower both the state and key economic actors, such as business. In addition, economic liberalization – whatever its economic merits or defects – does not appear so far to be the force for democratization that many expected. Finally, these cases suggest 'that the provision of strong international incentives – in this case the hope of EU membership – has had a felicitous and under-acknowledged effect on the process of democratization, whereas similar multilateral pressure for economic reform lacks the political benefits usually attributed to it' (Kurtz and Barnes 2002: 25).

Turkey

Like Poland and Hungary, Turkey is both a transitional economy and a democratizing country. In Turkey, processes of economic liberalization and deregulation began in 1980, a decade earlier than in Poland and Hungary. Since the late 1980s, Turkey has had:

> a financially open economy with a fully convertible currency. In terms of capital flows, it is far more open [than] many European countries. [Yet] financial liberalization and financial deepening have not resulted in a significant internalization of the markets or in providing useful net transfer of funds. . . . Turkey's liberal financial markets have been facing serious destabilizing effects of financial globalization. The general characteristics of Turkey's finan-cial markets are extreme volatility and fragility. (Arin n/d: 1)

Founded on the collapsed Ottoman empire in 1923, Turkey is a very different example of a transitional democracy from that of Poland and Hungary. It is a populous country of more than 65 million people – 80 per cent are Turkish, with a number of minority peoples, including Kurds – that straddles the divide between Europe and Asia. Its politi-cal history reflects not only the political importance of a centralizing state but also that of the military. Ninety-eight per cent of the population are Muslims, and Islam main-tains a strong social and political position despite the secular emphasis of state policy since the founding of the Turkish republic. But Turkey is actually a second-, rather than a third-, wave democracy, having first democratized in 1950. However, the country was taken over by the military three times over the next few decades – in 1960, 1971 and 1980 – before the latest round of democracy, which began in 1983. Focusing upon Turkey highlights the importance of both structural and contingent factors in both democrati-zation and economic liberalization.

Since the 1970s, Turkey has experienced recurring economic problems that have impacted upon political developments. Turkey enjoyed sustained economic growth during the 1960s, but it declined in the 1970s. A non-oil producer, it felt the impact of rising oil prices that led to severe balance of payments problems and high price infla-tion. By 1975, two-thirds of export earnings were spent on buying oil products, inflation soared to over 100 per cent a year, and, in 1980, an economic austerity programme was introduced to try to deal with these problems. While this led to substantial macro-economic improvements, including improved export performance and falling price infla-tion, the improvements did not last. By the late 1980s inflation had risen again to an annual rate of over 70 per cent. Encouraged by the IMF, the government introduced new, forceful measures to try to deal with inflation. However, it remained high – around 80 per cent in the mid-1990s, before rising to about 100 per cent in 1997. To attempt to deal with the situation, the government introduced a three-year economic stabilization programme, which cut state jobs and led to increased hardship among millions of ordinary people.

The worry for Turkish governments has been that economic problems have tended to stimulate the rise of 'extremist' parties calling for radical solutions – such as fundamental political reforms – to deal with the situation. But radical solutions are often seen as potentially destabilizing and therefore anathema to the self-appointed guardians of the status quo: the military. Whereas in the past, the armed forces would deal with perceived instability by, if necessary, periodically taking over government, increasingly this option was unavailable. This is largely because Turkey is anxious to gain membership of the EU, open only to democracies with good human rights records. Although Turkey was an associate member of the European Economic Community from 1964, relations with its successor, the EU, deteriorated in the wake of the 1980 military coup. This not only dissolved democracy, but also led to serious human rights violations.

The resumption of democracy in 1983 led to a rebuilding of Turkey's links with the EU and the Council of Europe. In 1989, the EU Commission laid down a number of stringent conditions for admission to the Union, including better human rights record and progress towards improved relations with Greece. But Turkey could not fulfil these conditions and so remained outside the EU. In 1995 Turkey and the EU signed a customs union, but the country was again passed over for membership, as it was once more in 1997 when, in principle, several Eastern European states were allowed to join. It seems likely that Turkey's recent military actions against rebellious Kurds had been a factor in the decision to deny it EU membership. In sum, Turkey's desire for EU membership may have encouraged the army not to attempt to take power since 1980, but the inability to deal with various human rights problems and the issue of the Kurds meant that it was still denied its goal to become an EU member. Recently, however, at the EU Helsinki Summit in 2000, Turkey was given the status of being a candidate country for full EU accession.

In conclusion, after nearly two decades of attempted democratization and economic liberalization, Turkey still seems not to have completed its programme of reforms. While there has been a 'commitment to democracy at both elite and mass levels' (Ozbudun 1996: 6), it has proved impossible to institutionalize democracy in a manner commensurate with democratic consolidation. While a high proportion of citizens vote in elections – over 80 per cent on average in the five national-level elections since 1983 – the choices they make have not necessarily helped the cause of democratization, as they tend increasingly to vote for extremist parties, a course of action viewed with disfavour by the armed forces (Günes-Ayata 1994). On the other hand, it seems unlikely that overtly authoritarian government would return to Turkey in the short term, not least because this would make the possibility of EU membership – with attendant economic benefits – impossible to achieve.

Turkey's current situation is characterized not only by its problematic democratization and the aim of joining the EU, but also by the continuing weakness of its economy, despite – or because of – a long period of economic liberalization. Although Turkey has a financially open economy with a fully convertible currency and welcomes external capital flows, as Arin (n/d: 1) notes, 'Turkey's liberal financial markets have been facing serious destabilising effects of financial globalization. The general characteristics of Turkey's financial markets are extreme volatility and fragility.'

Non-Democracies

We focus in this section on two non-democracies, countries that are also transitional economies (TEs): China and Vietnam. We noted in table 5.1 (see p. 95) that both China and Vietnam are countries with *state-controlled political structures*. Such countries have political institutions that are both state-dominated and centralized, with weak and fragmented civil societies. While this arrangement can offer few, if any, entry points to external actors seeking to gain access to domestic political structures, entry and engagement will be facilitated if important state actors welcome the external actors. We noted that this was likely to have a potentially profound policy impact if a coalition is formed with state actors who are predisposed toward the external agents' goals.

The recent emergence of TEs in Pacific Asia – including China and Vietnam – has led to the emergence of a new dimension in the development debate. Earlier, in the 1980s and 1990s, events in CEE were depicted as confirming the then conventional wisdom: there is no viable alternative to the market economy and the neo-liberal perspective on development, captured in the notion of the Washington consensus. However, things have turned out to be much more complicated than originally believed, as both economic and political transitions in many CEE countries have proved to be both complex and problematic.

> What seems to irk critics is how Vietnam has blown off the 'Washington Consensus', that package of policies long advocated by US officials and international institutions as a recipe for wealth. Few quibble with the consensus that opening markets, reducing government control and curbing inflation are good for economic growth. The problem, though, is that many developed-world governments were encouraged to move too hastily. The last five years offered myriad cautionary tales of nations that took the free-market plunge and ended up chastened by speculators. Many also found themselves disappointed by the dearth of long-term foreign investment. And when money did flow in, corruption often flourished as policy makers lined their pockets. (Pesek 2002)

Both China and Vietnam have managed to record high economic growth rates and developmental improvements while not changing their political regimes, as the quotation from Pesek suggests. Dixon argues that this is the result of four main factors: (1) party-states' promotion of growth, (2) establishment of incentives, (3) encouragement of more localized activity and (4) readiness to undertake lucrative economic projects with external actors, including Western TNCs. Significantly, 'the World Bank has suggested that in terms of economic growth, investment and the generation of new enterprise the countries of Eastern Europe could learn much' from both China and Vietnam (Dixon 2003: 288).

Strong party-states in both China and Vietnam have facilitated the engagement of domestic power-holders with agents of economic globalization including Western TNCs, largely on their own terms. However, the ability of even strong party-states to 'control' the impact of economic globalization should not be over-emphasized. One result of the 1997–8 Pacific Asia crisis for both China and Vietnam was that it gave ammunition to those who were 'opposed to the reform process, or at least its speed and consequences' (Dixon 2003: 296). This crisis also affected financial and commodity markets not only in Pacific Asia but also in Latin America and Eastern Europe. Typically, affected countries experienced drops in economic growth rate, and by the early 2000s many had only slow and tentative recoveries. However, Philip (2003) contends that the specificities of the crisis differed from country to country, with differential political impacts. Both China and Vietnam experienced neither policy change nor unexpected regime change, reflecting the strong hold on power of their communist party-states.

On the other hand, it appears that the crisis impacted on the domestic political arrangements of both countries in a specific way, acting to change partisan alignments to some degree that in turn led to a close assessment of the desirability of economic liberalization and connection to the global economy (White and Xiaoyuan Shang 2003: 177–81). The overall point is that the effect of the crisis upon China and Vietnam was both indirect and in practice quite variable. Overall, however, the results of the economic reform process in China and Vietnam and the concurrent opening up to the global economy clearly sets them apart from most Eastern European nations. Importantly, it does not confirm or conform to the dominant neo-liberal view: 'rapid economic growth necessitates the replacement of state planning, privatization and domination of production by approximations to western market structures' (Dixon 2003: 292).

This brief comment on the process of economic liberalization in China and Vietnam leads to the following conclusions. First, both the form and apparent developmental success of China and Vietnam, contrasting with those experienced in many post-communist countries in CEE, can be seen as building on the challenge to neo-liberalism mounted by the earlier generations of Pacific Asian economies, such as South Korea and Taiwan. Second, policies in both China and Vietnam can be seen as 'protecting significant domestic interests and restricting the interaction with the forces of economic globalization' (Dixon 2003: 301).

Conclusion

This chapter has illustrated that economic globalization leads to different results in various countries. A key finding is that it involves diminution of state autonomy in the sphere particularly of economic policy-making. This implies a reduction in state sovereignty, while also encouraging many states to look towards greater economic integration with regional neighbours as a means to contain the perceived deleterious impacts of economic globalization. We also noted that economic globalization, informed by specific events and processes – including the end of European colonial rule in the 1950s and 1960s, the diminution of the USA's economic position in the 1970s and 1980s and the collapse of the communist counter-challenge in the 1990 – was a result of growth in the internationalization of productive capital and of finance. These developments had clear consequences for all states: they all had fewer options than previously in regard to the range of economic policy they could realistically employ. The conclusion is that economic globalization may not (yet) have resulted in an *overt* gnawing away of state sovereignty – but it does lay them open and exposed to networks of economic forces and relations which now range in and through them. However, the precise impact will vary from country to country and be linked to state strength in relation to international and transnational economic actors. In particular, there is no compelling evidence suggesting that European governments were forced to diminish welfare provision as a result of pressures from economic globalization.

8

The Natural Environment

In this chapter we focus upon the natural environment ('green issues') in the context of globalization. We look at comparative outcomes in this regard in our three categories of country. The chapter is organized as follows. First, we examine the background to the contemporary global significance of environmental issues. The second section explores the significance of green parties in domestic politics, and the third focuses on international green actors. We then look at a number of case studies and assess the significance of both domestic and cross-border environmental actors in selected established democracies (Britain, Germany, the USA), transitional democracies (Mexico, Russia) and non-democracies (China, Indonesia[1]). The overall objective is to see how, in relation to green issues, various state and non-state actors seek to exploit political opportunity structures for their advantage.

From Stockholm to Kyoto: 25 Years of Increasing Global 'Green' Awareness

The natural environment, along with human and women's rights, religious conflict, terrorism and (in)security, and the developmental consequences of economic globalization, comprise what is sometimes known as the 'new international agenda' (Webber and Smith 2002: 120). Various problems come under the general heading of green issues, including pollution, animal species protection, desertification, deforestation, nuclear power and GM foods.

Environmental problems first emerged as a contentious global issue in the 1970s, becoming a focus of societal concerns in many countries. The 'first formal awareness of the international dimension' of environmental issues was the United Nations Conference on the Human Environment held in Stockholm in 1972 (Vogler 2001: 192). The conference, attended by 113 countries, drew up 26 Principles calling upon all governments to cooperate in protecting and improving the natural environment. During the 1980s Stockholm's message was reinforced by a series of developments, including the 1984 Bhopal (India) disaster, when an explosion at a factory producing toxic chemicals killed more than 4,000 people; a near-meltdown of the nuclear reactor at Chernobyl, Ukraine, in 1986; the destruction of forests in Europe due to acid rain; an expanding hole in the ozone layer and consequential skin cancers;

---

[1] The case study examines the situation prior to Indonesia's democratization in 1998.

pollution of the seas and overfishing; and global warming, threatening the existence of many low-lying countries and islands. The overall result was that the 1980s became known as the 'decade of the discovery of the environment' (Hadjor 1993: 105).

Consequently, the relationship between people's social and economic demands and the natural environment began, for the first time, to be discussed in a serious and scientific way. The 1992 United Nations-sponsored 'Earth Summit' held in Rio de Janeiro, Brazil, was a tangible sign of growing global concern. More than 100 heads of state and 30,000 bureaucrats and representatives of non-governmental organizations attended. They discussed 24 *million* pages of preparatory documents and sought to make wide-ranging decisions regarding the future of the global environment. The Earth Summit was called specifically to confront two pressing, interlinked problems: environmental degradation and poverty and underdevelopment. Coming just after the end of the cold war, there was expectation that relaxation of international tensions would facilitate progress on these issues. The Earth Summit produced Agenda 21, trumpeted as 'a plan of action to save the planet', and endorsed by representatives of all countries present. Agenda 21 was a compromise between, on the one hand, most Western states (claimed or actual promoters of environmental conservation) and, on the other, many developing countries (advocates of growth, sometimes with apparently scant regard for environmental protection).

Many developing country governments seemed ambivalent about the very principle of environmental protection, perhaps irritated by Western attempts to prescribe universal environmental standards and goals. Many governments claimed that the West's industrial development was the long-term result of often thoughtless environmental exploitation, both at home and in colonial possessions. As the West's development was the result of thorough environmental exploitation, why should that of the developing world be different? The West stood charged with hypocrisy on two counts: (1) concern with environmental protection was seen by many developing countries as a blatant attempt to prevent them from catching up developmentally by adopting the West's own tactics; and (2) while the West professed to deplore environmentally harmful policies, it strongly urged dozens of developing countries to open up their economies to foreign investment and increase exports of agricultural products and timber leading to more environmental damage (Miller 1995).

Agenda 21 reflected this polarization of views. Critics argued that it was no more than an inadequate, aspirational response to public concern, a document without enough teeth to ensure progress. However, despite failure to produce an agreement on tropical rain forest destruction (one of Rio's main concerns), the Earth Summit did give rise to a Framework Convention on Climate Change. This was significant because, as Vogler (2001: 193) notes, it 'marked the beginnings of a systematic international attempt to grapple with the problem of "global warming"', one of the most significant threats with which the human race has had to deal. At the end of 1997, measures were agreed to control emissions of the greenhouse gases held responsible for global warming. In July 2001, despite the withdrawal of the United States from the protocol, 185 countries had agreed in principle limited but concrete measures to try to deal with the problem (Brown 2001).

Domestic Politics and Green Parties

The rise to prominence of environmental issues was followed by the founding of green political parties in numerous countries.[2] The world's first green party, the United Tasmania Group, was formed at a public meeting in Hobart in March 1972, followed two months later by the foundation of the world's first national green party: the Values Party, inaugurated at a meeting at Victoria University, Wellington, New Zealand.

The region where, proportionately, most green parties are found is Western Europe and, as a result, they have been widely studied there. European green parties largely emerged in the 1980s and led to much political science analysis. Key issues included their characteristics, patterns of conflict and structural and institutional processes believed to inspire their development (Rüdig 1990; Doherty 1992). Three main theoretical approaches emerged, with two aims: (1) to further understanding of the parties' formation processes, and (2) to explain why they succeeded or failed as political organizations. While treatments of these issues differed, a clear theme ran through them: in Europe in the 1980s, green parties marked the rise of a new political cleavage.

First, Ronald Inglehart (1990, 1997) developed an analytical framework known as 'postmaterialist value change'. Inglehart argued that green parties expressed a novel political cleavage defined in terms of 'materialist' opposed to 'postmaterialist value systems'. He suggested that events should be categorized as postmaterialist when they involve any one of a broad set of non-market dimensions of public policy, including green issues and human and animal rights. The consequence of changing mass attitudes, he argued, was to strengthen the prospect that contemporary polities would be reformulated to augment the direct political control of citizens. He noted that, from the early 1970s, many advanced industrial democracies – including the USA, Germany and Britain – appeared to have been influenced by changes in people's social priorities. Inglehart labelled these alterations a 'participatory revolution' and a postmaterialist 'culture shift'. The main consequences of these changing popular attitudes was that citizens were more inclined (1) to take available opportunities to directly affect political outcomes and (2) to become less attached to particular parties or distrustful of the parties that had been in existence for a long time (Inglehart, 1990; Tarrow 1998). A further result was that at least some people were likely to employ existing opportunities to engage in direct political participation. In addition, 'politicians ha[d] new electoral incentives to support reforms that increase opportunities for direct democracy' (Scarrow 2001: 653). As we shall see later, this raises the intriguing prospect of the availability and desirability of cross-border political activities, leading to a focus on 'transnational advocacy networks'.

Second, Rüdig offered what he called a 'cleavage-based approach' to green parties. His view of green party development focused on the notion of an 'ecological' cleavage and differed from that of Ingelhart. Rüdig (1990: 16) sought to define what was signifi-

---

[2] The generic term 'green party' can be used by any grouping that chooses to do so. However, there are a number of political parties and movements to which the term is especially applicable. These entities base their formative ideas on what are known as the 'Four Pillars of the Green Party': 'ecological wisdom', grassroots democracy, pacifism and social justice (<http://www.wisconsingreenparty.org/index.shtml>).

cant about green parties by pointing to their 'ecological identity' rather than 'some other social force which is totally unconnected to the material content of their demands'. He also argued that emergence and politicization of various environmental problems was an important reason for green party formation and development, amounting to a 'cleavage in its own right'. The issues that Rüdig raised pointed to an important question: how do the cleavages thought to underlie green party development shape their identity?

Third, Kitschelt (1986, 1988) offered another variant of the cleavage-based approach to green parties, claiming that they amounted to a 'left-libertarian' cleavage, just like an older subgroup of left-socialist parties. He explained the emergence of green parties in Europe via a combination of structural change and resource mobilization theories. For Kitschelt, both green and left-socialist parties have a similar – 'left-libertarian' – ideological orientation. This involves a shared belief in decentralized power structures, often held by a particular set of voters. European green parties were perceived as part of a group of 'new politics' parties, distinctive in that they adhered to this 'new politics' ideology. This was characterized by participatory organization and a support base rooted in the young, well-educated new middle class and/or the 'postmaterialist' stratum of society. The 'new politics' parties differ from the older established parties in four key ways. The latter aim to win power at both national and subnational levels via elected office; have a professional staff of party functionaries and a comprehensive party organization; represent economic interest groups, such as labour or business; and chiefly focus on economic distributive and welfare issues.

In conclusion, central to both the 'new politics' and 'left-libertarian' traditions is the idea that, wherever they are physically located, green parties have certain characteristics that distinguish them from the traditional parties that dominated the political landscape of many of Europe's established democracies from soon after the end of World War II. Europe's green parties, along with other 'left libertarian' parties, are seen as essentially 'postmaterialist' in their attitudinal orientation and behaviour. This is because they reject or downplay the overriding status of economic issues. Instead, they are characterized by a 'negative consensus that the predominance of markets and bureaucracies must be rolled back in favor of social solidarity relations and participatory institutions' (Gunther and Diamond 2001: 30). Because there is no consensus supporting a single comprehensive ideology or set of programmatic preferences, the 'negative consensus' revolves around various issues that are not limited to a single arena. Instead, they inform such parties' agendas, functioning as the lowest common denominator, shared by a diverse group of supporters and activists. Such groups have no barriers to membership; they are open to anybody who wants to involve themselves and this characteristic implies that their activists' social foundations and attitudinal orientations will be very diverse. Strong commitment to direct participation often leads either to weakness or even rejection of centralized organization and leadership or to a rather informal organizational style. Green parties are often rooted in 'loose networks of grassroots support with little formal structure, hierarchy and central control' (Gunther and Diamond 2001: 30). Finally, because green parties stress 'constituency representation' over the logic of electoral competition, shared orientations often facilitate formation of international transnational groupings.

How satisfactory are such characteristics as accounts of reality? Are green parties' identities actually shaped by the character of the new political cleavages thought to underlie their initial formation? One problem with such classifications is that they fail to provide a complete explanation of the often very different strategies adopted by Europe's green parties over the course of their development, not least their links both with the wider 'environmental movement' both domestically and internationally. What green parties often have in common, however, is a relative lack of electoral success. For example, in 2003 there were no green politicians in the elected chambers of national legislatures in the United States, England and Wales, and Canada. Because green parties can find electoral success particularly elusive, they often focus on electoral reform. Duverger's Law says that in plurality and majoritarian electoral systems, the outcome over time is a party system dominated by two 'effective' parties. These parties fight around the ideological centre of the party system with their key aim of attracting and retaining the support of the 'median voter'. The latter exists at the point where the aggregate of voters' preferences reaches an equilibrium, and thus effectively a consensus. Under such systems, there is only one logical outcome: a centrist form of politics, whereby two main parties compete for the centre ground. Preferences of voters who do not share the median position are relatively neglected. Critics assert that both plurality and majoritarian systems can lead to a 'tyranny of the majority' (Lees 2002: 9). In countries with a 'first-past-the-post' electoral system, such as the USA, Canada and England and Wales, green parties – like other smaller parties – traditionally find themselves disadvantaged, facing serious barriers to gaining federal/provincial/regional/state-level seats. In addition, green parties in various European countries – such as the Czech Republic, Hungary, Romania and Slovakia – have so far found it impossible to win seats in national legislatures despite fairly sizeable numbers of votes. Table 8.1 shows election results – for national legislatures and the European Parliament – for member parties of the European Federation of Green Parties (EFGP) between 1999 and 2003. The EFGP has 32 member parties, of which just under half (15) are represented in their national parliaments.

Cross-Border Green Actors

We have seen that the ability of green parties to achieve a measure of electoral success in Europe is linked to the nature of the political system where they compete for power. This underlines that the nature of political opportunity structures is an important factor in enabling actors to access and potentially influence decision-making in domestic politics. Tarrow (1998: 18) suggests that in domestic contexts, green parties and environmental movements emerge when 'dimensions of the political environment . . . either encourage or discourage people from using collective action'. To what extent does globalization facilitate the spread of political influence of international and transnational green actors?

Bermeo (2003: 231–2) observes that 'the timing of . . . public polarization' is 'directly related to changes in opportunity structures'. For example, the success of the Bolshevik revolution during World War I gave leftist movement entrepreneurs in Europe new and highly influential allies. At the same time, European restructuring led to the demise of traditional ruling systems and caused proximate 'shifts in ruling alignments' and opened up access to power. Forty years later, the 'success of the Cuban revolution gave leftist movement entrepreneurs highly "influential allies" in Latin America'. During the 1980s,

Table 8.1 Election results for member parties of the European Federation of Green Parties, 1999–2003

Country/party	Year	National elections			European elections 1999		
		%	Seats	Votes	%	Seats	Votes
Austria/Die Grünen	2002	9.5	17	465,021	9.3	2	260,273
Belgium/Agalev	2003	2.5	0	–	7.5	2	464,043
Belgium/Ecolo	2003	3.6	4	–	8.4	3	525,316
Bulgaria/Bulgarian GP	2001	0.5**	0	21,851**	–	–	–
Cyprus/Cyprus GP	2001	2.0	1	8,129	–	–	–
Czech R./Str.Zelenych	2002	2.4	0	112,929	–	–	–
Denmark/De Gronne	2001	–	0	–	–	0	–
Estonia/Estonian GP	2003	–	0	–	–	–	–
Finland/Vihreä Liitto	2003	8.0	14	223,267	13.4	2	166,801
France/Les Verts	2002	3.2	3	677,933	9.8	9	1,700,000
Georgia/Georgian GP	1999	–	0	14,400	–	–	–
Germany/B-90/Grünen	2002	8.6	55	4,110,355	6.4	5	1,741,000
Greece/Ecologists Greens	2000	–	–	–	–	0	–
Hungary/Zöld Demokr.	2002	3.9**	0	–	–	–	–
Ireland/Comhaont.Gl.	2002	3.8	6	71,480	6.7	2	93,600
Italy/Fed.D. Verdi	2001	2.2	17	911,735	1.8	2	550,000
Latvia/Latv.Zala P.	2002	9.5**	4	93,748	–	–	–
Luxemb./Dëi Gréng	1999	9.1	5	92,186*	10.7	1	108,514
Malta/Alt.Demokrat.	2003	0.7	0	1,950	–	–	–
Netherl./De Groenen	2003	–	0	–	–	0	–
Netherl./GroenLinks	2003	5.1	8	495,802	11.9	4	419,869
Norway/Milj.d.Grønne	2001	0.2	0	3,787	–	–	–
Portugal/Os Verdes	2002	1.2*	2	63,097*	–	–	In coalition
Romania/FER	2000	1.4*	0	140,000*	–	–	–
Russia/Interreg.GP	–	–	–	–	–	–	–
Slovakia/Str.Zelenych	2002	1	0	28,364	–	–	–
Spain/Los Verdes	2000	1.1*	2	300,000*	1.4	0	300,000
Sweden/Milj.d.Gröna	2002	4.6	17	246,392	9.5	2	245,955
Switzerl./Grüne/L.Verts	1999	5.0	9	97,935	–	–	–
Ukraine/GP of Ukraine	2002	1.3	–	338,252	–	–	–
UK/GPEW	2001	2.9	0	166,626	5.5	2	568,251
UK/Scottish GP***	2001	0.1*	–	4,551	0.6	0	57,127
Total			164			36	

* estimated figures.
** in coalition.
*** Elections to Scottish Parliament in May 2003: 7 MSPs and 132,138 votes (6.7%).

Source: The European Federation of Green Parties website (<http://www.europeangreens.org/peopleandparties/results.html>).

developments linked to the end of the cold war, the third wave of democracy and various aspects of globalization led to new opportunities for external actors to seek to influence domestic agenda-setting and decision-making in a variety of areas, including green issues. In recent years, the natural environment has emerged as a key area where cross-border actors seek to influence outcomes. Among these can be noted green parties, environmental non-governmental organizations (ENGOs; a specialized kind of INGO) and TNCs. All are regarded as 'major actors in global environmental politics' (Miller 1995: 35). Let us look next at transnational green parties, before turning to ENGOs and TNCs.

Transnational green parties

Some scholars predict that political parties are in inexorable decline as representative bodies and effective political actors and will largely be replaced by NGOs. Others contend that if political parties manage to incorporate support from new organizations and social movements and adapt their agendas to face new issues, they will retain their niche against the inroads of NGOs. For Tarrow, in either case, the outcome will be affected by 'the institutional context in which both parties and NGOs operate and by the issues they deal with'. 'The ease of organising opinion in representative systems and finding legitimate channels for its expression induces many movements to turn to elections.' Over time, 'a movement turns into a party or enters a party in order to influence its policies. . . . At its most successful, the electoral strategy produced Green parties in parts of northern Europe, parties that rapidly became part of the parliamentary game of politics' (Tarrow 1998: 84). However, despite some often limited successes, green parties have rarely fared well in domestic elections in Europe, often because electoral systems disadvantage them, while many voters still see politics as chiefly about settling traditional questions that focus on economic distributive issues.

Noting that environmental degradation and damage is a global phenomenon, it comes as no surprise to see green parties seeking to organize transnationally, both in regional and wider contexts. In Europe, an umbrella organization, the European Federation of Green Parties (EFGP), was founded in 1993 (<http://www.europeangreens.org>). The EFGP brings together a number of 'environmentalist, ecologist, and Green-Left parties and the Green members of the Green/European Free Alliance group in the European Parliament'. Together, these parties enjoy the support of around 5 per cent of voters in the EU. In 2002, politicians affiliated to the EFGP held 38 of the 626 seats in the European Parliament (6 per cent), one of the 20 EU commissioners and one of the EU foreign ministers (from Germany). EFGP-affiliated parties were also in power in coalition governments in four of the then 15 EU states (Gabel and Hix 2002).

The EFGP seeks to act transnationally in Europe, supporting weak and embryonic European green parties, notably in Southern Europe and various CEE countries. For example, in both Spain and (Greek) Cyprus, green parties are beginning to make (limited) electoral gains, while in Greece and Malta they may do so in the future. In addition, several CEE countries now have relatively well-established green parties. However, materially poor CEE has seen an even slower development of green party success than in wealthier Western Europe. For example, in 2003, the EFGP counted six member parties in the associate countries of CEE (Bulgaria, Czech Republic, Estonia, Hungary, Romania, Slovakia) (Delsoldato 2002). However, none was of major or even moderate domestic political importance, with the partial exception of the Green Party of Slovakia (SZS). In the 1998 elections, SZS was part of an alliance of five parties that eventually succeeded in removing Prime Minister Vladimir Meciar's authoritarian government from power. The five-party alliance SDK polled more than a quarter of the votes (26.3 per cent), and formed the new government along with three other party groups. Four SZS members of parliament were elected. On the other hand, 'as a small party in a very heterogeneous coalition involving 10 separate parties, the bargaining position of SZS was quite weak and [it] had to accept just one junior ministerial appointment, which went to the leader of SZS' (Rüdig 2002: 27).

Away from Europe, the first 'Global Green Gathering', bringing together green parties from around the world, was held in Canberra, Australia, in 2001. The aim was to follow the initial meeting with another in 2005 or 2006, to be held in an as yet unnamed African country. The 2001 Gathering agreed on various organizational matters. First, there was agreement to form a Global Green Network, comprising three representatives from each national green party, and a Global Green Coordination, composed of three representatives from each Federation (Africa, Europe, the Americas, Asia/Pacific). Second, the Canberra Gathering agreed to a Global Green Charter (GGC), a set of fairly loose organizing principals and various joint campaigns.[3] These included a transnational attempt – involving the New Caledonia Green Party, New Caledonian indigenous leaders, the French Green Party and the Australian Green Party – to get the New Caledonian coral reef nominated for World Heritage Status, with a view to protecting it. A second example was a transnational campaign to free Ingrid Betancourt, leader of the Green Oxygen Party of Colombia (Partido Verde Oxigeno). Both Betancourt and Claire Rojas, the party's Campaign Manager, were abducted by a faction of the leftist guerrilla organization, the FARC, in March 2002, while travelling in rebel-held territory. Having spoken at Canberra in 2001, Betancourt was well known. Around the world, green parties lobbied their governments to try to free the two captives. For example, the leader of the Australian Green Party, Bob Brown, went to Colombia, accompanied by Alain Lipietz, an envoy from the EFGP, to try to talk to the FARC. Ingrid Betancourt and Claire Rojas were still prisoners facing death at the time of writing (late 2004), but the combined green parties' efforts on their behalf 'does at least show their potential to unite and campaign jointly' (<www.global.greens.org.au/>). A second important forum for global green parties was the 'Global Green Meeting' held in Johannesburg in 2002. Representatives of green parties from around the world[4] met to discuss, inter alia, the situation of green parties in Africa, the possibility of setting up a web site and strategies to achieve closer cooperation (<http://www.wikipedia.org/wiki/Green_parties>).

In conclusion, green parties increasingly seek to build transnational links both with each other and in relation to regional and/or international forums. So far, results are

---

[3] Discussion of the planned organization took place in several green parties prior to Canberra. Communication between them is mostly by email. Any agreement has to be unanimous. It may in future seek to identify possible global campaigns to propose to green parties around the world. The GGC may endorse statements by individual Green Parties. For example, it endorsed a statement by the US Green Party on the Israel-Palestine conflict (<http://www.global.greens.org.au/spinifex-4.pdf>).
[4] Australia, Taiwan, Korea, South Africa, Mauritius, Uganda, Cameroon, Greek Cyprus, Italy, France, Belgium, Germany, Finland, Sweden, Norway, the USA, Mexico and Chile.

patchy. In part this reflects the fact that green parties – like other political parties – pay most attention to trying to win power in their domestic political environment and, as a result, primarily focus on its specific demands and opportunities. As a result, it will probably be more difficult for political parties than for NGOs to forge durable and effective transnational ties. So far, other than in Europe, links largely seem restricted to irregular opportunities for green parties to present their views to sympathetic audiences. On the other hand, to the extent that political parties are issue-driven, the changing global environment is likely to stimulate them to find new ways of adapting. It is likely that if such adaptation does encompass transnational links, then they are likely to be manifested as forums for exchanging ideas rather than as sources of collective action.

Environmental non-governmental organizations (ENGOs)

Advocates of INGO activity are often optimistic about the potential for their growth and influence in the context of globalization. However, as Keck and Sikkink (1998a: 2) observe, this kind of 'organizing is more likely to succeed in certain issue areas, demarcated by "high value content and informational uncertainty"', such as green issues. This is because international opportunity structures tend to be relatively advantageous for them, for two main reasons. First, 'business does not enjoy at the international level the "privileged position" it does at the level of the nation state'. Second, 'public interest groups', including ENGOs like Greenpeace and Friends of the Earth, may 'enjoy greater advantage there than at the level of national government' (Kellow 2002: 176). This points to the fact that some ENGOs 'play an important role in monitoring state behavior' (Bruehl n/d: 16), while 'structural dependence . . . on capital, and unilateral action is likely to result in high costs for little environmenal benefit' (Van der Heijden 2002: 187).

ENGOs are seeking improvements in relation to the natural environment against a background of national material demands. They tend to advocate international regulation as a consequence of a realization that many states will only take strong actions if there are international agreements to encourage them to do so. Organizationally, ENGOs include individual and/or organizational members from at least two countries and share common norms, modes of political influence and a limited thematic goal; Greenpeace International and Friends of the Earth are often referred to as representing ENGO 'prototypes' (Martens 2001: 1). The rise in significance of such ENGOs in Western Europe and North America since the 1980s is explicable against a backdrop of perceptions of increasingly serious environmental damage, symbolized both by the nuclear energy debate and the neo-liberal hegemony of the Reagan/Thatcher/Kohl governments. From this time, certain green groups have developed into mass membership organizations with hundreds of thousands of members. In the United States, for example, in the 20 years after 1980, collective membership of the three main environmental groups – the National Audubon Society, Greenpeace and World Wildlife Fund (WWF) – together increased from half a million to more than three million. In the Netherlands, Greenpeace and the WWF grew fivefold: from 400,000 to two million members. Meanwhile, in Germany, membership of the leading environmental organizations rose 20 times: from 50,000 to one million members (Van der Heijden 2002: 192).

Growth in the environmental movement in both the USA and Western Europe coincided with a decline in membership of political parties. The overall number of members of political parties in the then 15 EU countries was about 10 million, while those belonging to ENGOs was one and a half times as many: about 15 million. 'In the UK and Germany, the ENGO constituency is twice as large as the total number of party members, while in the Netherlands the total ENGO constituency is more than ten times as high as the total number of party members: 3.7 million vs. 294 000 (from a total population of 16 million)' (Van der Heijden 2002: 193). According to Van der Heijden, 'these figures reflect a shift in the relevance of political parties and ENGOs as vehicles for identification, solidarity, and political involvement of individual citizens'. Imig (2002) interviewed in Brussels representatives of various NGOs, including green groups. He found relative indifference among many of their grassroots memberships to a potential source of political participation: European-level decision-making. The consequence was that ENGOs tended to be relatively insignificant in their lobbying in the EU, as, without much in the way of grassroots support, their efforts normally lacked the clout of the better financed business and professional groups they often opposed (Imig and Tarrow 2001). Overall, Imig (2002: 925) depicts a 'picture of Euro-protest . . . characterized by a handful of dramatic cases of contentious action', although 'the largest proportion of contentious politics' in Europe is 'materialist in nature, involving farmers and workers'. In sum, European 'environmentalists . . . may be developing a range of Euro-centered collective actions, [but] the realm of transnational collective action is still notable for the range of interests that are not represented . . . The empirical record . . . suggests that the emergence of Euro-protests over postmaterial' – including environmental – 'issues is uneven' (Imig 2002: 928–9, 931). On the other hand, there are signs that a current campaign – against the emergent biotech industry – is engendering much popular support across Europe. Underlining Imig's argument about the necessity of securing grassroots support for campaign success, a wide range of environmental and related groups coalesced within the Genetic Engineering Network (GEN), whose members include Corporate Watch, Earth First!, Genetix Snowball, Genetix Food Alert, the Green Party, Friends of the Earth, Greenpeace, the Women's Environmental Network, the Gaia Foundation and numerous wholefood groups and organic farmers (Belsie 2000).

Both the UN and EU offer formal provision for the involvement of NGOs, including ENGOs. Article 71 of the UN Charter provides for 'suitable arrangements to be made for consultation with NGOs concerned with matters within its competence' (<www.un.org/aboutun/charter/>). Moreover, the international arena is more favourable to NGOs because the functions they can perform for IGOs translate into influence. For example, ENGOs can provide lobbying not just at international meetings, but also at the national level where agencies such as the United Nations Environmental Program (UNEP) cannot lobby without violating Article 2(7) of the UN Charter. This Article forbids intervention in matters essentially within the domestic jurisdiction of any state. Furthermore, it is doubtful whether UNEP possesses either the resources or the capacity to be effective in such a role. ENGO transnational activities are for this reason important to the development of multilateral environmental agreements (MEAs). Princen and Finger (1994) note that NGO participation in the development of the 1987 Montreal Protocol (and subsequent MEAs) was actively encouraged by UNEP, and the same pattern can be found in the Basel and Climate

Change MEAs. In addition, Willetts (1996) claims that ENGOs were quite deliberately harnessed to support both the Stockholm and Rio conferences, in 1972 and 1992 respectively, while their access was limited post-Rio in the Commission for Sustainable Development.

A similar pattern is apparent in the EU, where ENGOs are useful to the Commission and can assist with reporting on default of EU regulations and directives by member nations. Such ENGOs are often supported financially by grants from the European Commission (Kellow 2002). Finally, as Tarrow (1998: 195) observes, some EU member states actively encourage ENGOs to take their claims to the EU. In both the EU and the UN, ENGOs may be invited to attend meetings and/or allow their participation in multilateral negotiations because the former can gain benefits – knowledge, ideas and, in some cases, international legitimization – from ENGO cooperation (Martens 2001). In short, IGOs such as the EU and UN not only provide both formal and informal mechanisms to facilitate the involvement of ENGOs but may also set up systems of formal accreditation, including arrangements for them to enjoy 'consultative status' and thus ensure their official recognition by the community of states, granted an official status. They may also be recipients of both symbolic and material resources – including financial aid. However, in both the UN and the EU – in addition to national settings (where what they do is governed by domestic legal arrangements) – the power to influence what ENGOs enjoy depends on their ability to exploit extant political opportunity structures. That is, probably more than at the national level, their ability to be influential depends on their skill in focusing on and adapting to unique features of constraints and opportunity that IGOs offer.

In conclusion, ENGOs can benefit from the opportunities offered by IGO political structures. However, the mobilizing power of the former is dependent on the extent to which they can gain access; and this is a function of what individual states and IGOs allow them. To achieve access, they necessarily 'enjoy a certain receptivity/openness at the [IGO] level and must not be restricted in their efforts to mobilize transnationally' (Marks and McAdam 1996: 273). This implies that those actors 'whose mobilising ability is more historically rooted within the national setting – such as political parties – will face considerable difficulties establishing and developing transnational linkages' (Marks and McAdam 1996: 276). Further, IGOs such as the EU and the UN provide structures that not only provide better access to target states for ENGOs but also enable them to coordinate their activities. On the other hand, IGOs are not mediators between ENGOs and the state but primarily the direct target of their activities.

Transnational corporations (TNCs)

There are currently around 60,000 TNCs. They often claim that they pursue desirable social and environmental goals via free trade and international competitiveness. Processes of globalization are said to have contributed to their growing political and economic significance, largely as a result of deregulation and economic liberalization strategies, implemented domestically by states and internationally by actors such as the World Trade Organization. They are said to be increasingly 'able to influence or modify the policies [even] of large industrialized states'. Smaller developing ones, on the other hand, lack financial muscle and are sometimes seen as little more than pawns in TNC strategies of domination. In terms of green issues, TNCs are 'major environmental actors . . . because they control the bulk of world trade and investment' (Miller 1995: 35).

Sklair focuses on the role of TNCs in relation to four areas with environmental connotations: the Codex Alimentarius,[5] the Multilateral Agreement on Investment (MAI),[6] the global tobacco business and EU transport policy. In relation to the latter, Sklair (2002: 161) notes both the coordinated power and political efficacy of TNCs, and links their influence to the failure of governments in Europe 'to shift the balance from private cars and lorries to public transport and rail freight, despite almost universal rhetoric on the need to do this'. Vidal (2003a) makes broadly the same conclusion when he assesses the influence of Britain's Freight Transport Association (FTA). The FTA has regular meetings with 'ministers, shadow ministers . . . the [House of] Commons transport select committee, and holds receptions "throughout the year" for MPs and members of Britain's upper chamber, the House of Lords'. According to Vidal, FTA representatives also meet regularly with the EU transport commissioner.

Sklair also provides evidence of the capacity of TNCs to work through their home governments to seek to influence international policy-making processes in the EU, UN and NAFTA. He suggests that 'TNCs do work, quite deliberately and sometimes rather covertly, as political actors, and often have direct access to those at the highest levels of formal political and administrative power with considerable success' (Sklair 2002: 171). Overall, 'creating a network of alliances has been very important for the strategies of [TNCs], which have been able to identify political and personal contacts with similar interests' (Miller 1995: 37). For example, TNCs gained access and influence at the 1992 Rio Conference through the Business Council for Sustainable Development (BCSD). This is a group of around 50 chief executive officers or chairpersons of corporations from various sectors, including energy, chemicals, forestry and pesticides. The BCSD leadership is a component of the International Environment Bureau of the International Chamber of Commerce (ICC), a body with observer status at the UN, where it lobbies on behalf of business interests. At Rio, both ICC and BCSD pressed hard to keep attempts to regulate TNCs out of the UN Conference on Environment and Development documents, arguing that free trade was essential to sustainable development (Miller 1995: 38).

Kellow argues that at the international level, the relative advantage of environment and business groups is often the reverse of that which obtains at the domestic level; that

---

[5] 'The Codex Alimentarius Commission was created in 1963 by FAO [Food and Agriculture Organization] and WHO [World Health Organization] to develop food standards, guidelines and related texts such as codes of practice under the Joint FAO/WHO Food Standards Programme. The main purposes of this Programme are protecting health of the consumers and ensuring fair trade practices in the food trade, and promoting coordination of all food standards work undertaken by international governmental and non-governmental organizations' (<http://www.codexalimentarius.net/>).

[6] 'The MAI is a proposed multilateral international agreement that is currently under negotiation at the Organization for Economic Cooperation and Development (OECD) in Paris. If it is passed, the MAI will have a profound impact on the way that governments treat foreign investment in all of the 29 developed country-members of the OECD. [T]he MAI promised to give more freedoms to the TNCs without imposing any compensating responsibilities, and such initiatives are likely to be resumed. [However,] the defeat of the MAI proves that, in the short term at least, it is possible successfully to mobilize opposition in the name of local democracy against capitalist globalization and corporate power' (Sklair 2002: 171–2).

is, it is less significant. While not disagreeing that the increasing importance of globalization has made representation in international arenas more important, Kellow argues that key factors affect the associability of business and public interest groups at that level. They 'are markedly different from those which apply at the level of the nation-state' because 'the "privileged position of business" does not [necessarily] obtain at the transnational level, and [as a result] . . . business frequently prefers the national route' (Kellow 2002: 175). Thus the idea of all-powerful transnational business may be something of a myth. In some circumstances, business can be vulnerable to the power of the environmental movement, for example in relation to nuclear power and genetically modified (GM) foods. The significance of the latter was seen in the early 2000s in relation to the American TNC, Monsanto. Monsanto sought to introduce and market the results of new techniques of genetic modification. However, a campaign led by various ENGOs, including Greenpeace and Friends of the Earth, was able to slow considerably in Europe both public acceptance of GM foods in particular and biotechnology in general. This 'imposed substantial costs on the industry, especially in reducing shareholder expectations of future profits' (Lawson 2002: 132).

Established Democracies

Britain

In 2004, Green Parties in Britain had the most elected representatives – in more influential positions – than at any time previously. These included two Members of the European Parliament, seven members of the Scottish Parliament and one Senator in the State of Jersey. In addition, there were three Green Party Members in the London Assembly, one of whom was in the Cabinet of the Mayor, Ken Livingstone. Moreover, 53 Greens sat on 26 different Principal Authority Councils – including Districts, English and Welsh Counties, Metropolitan and London Boroughs – and are part of the ruling administration on two of them. Finally, the Green Party of England and Wales (GPEW) also had a number of Parish, Town and Welsh Community Councillors. There is also a Green Party Member in the House of Lords (<http://www.greenparty.org.uk/>).

It is clear that these results are not outstanding. It is important to remember, however, that for green parties to profit electorally they need either proportional representation (PR) and/or a close-run election whose outcome leads to the green party being invited to join a coalition government and it agreeing to serve. However, often disappointing electoral outcomes for the GPEW reflect the absence of such conditions. Instead, the GPEW competes within a majoritarian system. The Scottish Greens, its partner party, compete under a different, more sympathetic electoral system, based on PR in elections to the Scottish Parliament, and have achieved some – limited – success.

For both the GPEW and the Scottish Greens, the character of the electoral systems within which they compete has helped to shape strategic debate and change within each party. In the GPEW, such debates reflect realities of operating within a 'first-past-the-post' electoral system; this system makes it extremely difficult for a small party with geographically dispersed support to achieve national representation. No political party in Britain receives state funding, and with the necessity of having to provide a large deposit to stand as a candidate in national elections, the electoral issue is an important organizational, strategic and ideological one for the GPEW. The party has two main options: (1) to try and assimilate the costs of a national campaign with the aim of raising the party's national profile, or (2) to concentrate on local campaigning and activism. Because the British party system offers little in the way of political space for new parties, the GPEW has sought political space outside of the parliamentary sphere. Environmental movements, such as Greenpeace and Friends of the Earth, have been relatively, if sporadically, successful in both influencing policy and raising environmental awareness in Britain. This has brought into question the supposed role and status of the Green Party as the 'political arm' of the environment movement, and its relationship with the major green organizations.

In the early 1990s, a changing political agenda proved disastrous for the GPEW. Following its unexpected success in the 1989 European elections, when it gained 2,292,705 votes (14.5 per cent of those cast) but no seats, the party launched a large-scale initiative with the intention of achieving parliamentary representation. At the 1992 general election, the party fielded a record number of candidates, a policy that cost it a huge amount of money, as results were disappointing: it gained no seats and a smaller proportion of the votes cast than in the previous election. The disappointing results led to factional disputes concerning the wisdom of such a national electoral strategy. In 1997, the party fought just 95 seats but again failed to win any seats. Things got no better in 2001 when its share of the votes was just 0.6 per cent.

The introduction of the Scottish Parliament in 1999, with a partly proportional voting system and the inevitability of voting reform for local councils, led to a better performance for the Scottish Green Party compared to its counterpart in England and Wales. In the May 2003 elections to the Scottish Parliament, the Scottish Greens gained 7 of the 129 seats (5.4 per cent) (<http://www.scottishgreens.org.uk/policies/intro.htm>). For these elections, Scots had two votes: one for a constituency member, one for a regional list. The more constituency seats a party took, the less chance it had of taking a regional seat. Scottish Greens won all seven of their seats in Glasgow. In Glasgow, a city where Labour traditionally takes most of the constituency seats, there seemed to many voters little point in their voting for Labour in the list vote. This meant that at least some voters were prepared to give the Greens a chance (Seenan 2003). Reflecting their electoral gains, the Scottish Greens were offered – and accepted – the 'deputy convenorship of the environment and rural affairs committee' (Mcdonnell 2003).

In sum, in elections to the Scottish Parliament, Scottish Greens benefited from a voting system partially based on PR. This encouraged some voters – especially in Glasgow – to give the Greens an electoral try. Their counterparts in England and Wales had to contend with a first-past-the-post electoral system and as a result did badly in elections.

Germany

Because they are more likely to experience electoral success under such arrangements, green parties often argue for PR. Such systems tend to produce multiparty arrangements where, in most instances, no single party is able to command a majority of votes. (There are exceptions to this, for example, multiparty proportional systems can generate a 'dominant' party – for example, Social Democrats in Sweden – or a majority party:

the Christian Social Union in Bavaria, Germany.) Under PR, it is rational for smaller parties, such as greens,[7] to seek to represent minority interests or ideological positions because they are most likely to sustain such parties (Lees 2002). Under PR, 'the general tone of politics may remain centrist, but the tyranny of the majority is avoided. . . . Therefore it is logical to assume that, under proportional systems, we are more likely to find green parties presented with a relatively benign political opportunity structure . . . to exploit [a] niche in the market' (Lees 2002: 9). In nearly every EU country, and recently in some elections in Britain – Scottish parliamentary elections noted above – PR and other electoral reforms have strengthened the position of green parties and, in some cases, facilitated their parliamentary involvement. Green parties in some European countries – for example, Italy and France – tend to do better or worse depending on the overall performance of parties of the left, with which many voters associate them. However, the first sustained European electoral breakthrough was by the German Green Party more than 20 years ago.

Established in 1979, Germany's Green Party did not achieve representation in the Bundestag, and did not therefore receive recognition as a true party, until 1983, when the party exceeded the 5 per cent hurdle. (In Germany, parties must achieve 5 per cent of the vote to be able to sit in the Bundestag.) The Greens in Germany began as the political arm of a citizen initiative movement, with a platform emphasizing a strong stance on environmental issues. The Chernobyl accident of 1986 was instrumental in significantly improving the Greens' position in opinion polls, and the party began to take votes from the established parties – especially the Social Democratic Party (SPD). This offered the SPD little rational option but to move towards the Green position on environmental issues, especially nuclear power, to try to maintain its share of the votes. But it was unclear what role the Greens would adopt: would it remain a small independent party or seek to make a coalition with the SPD? The question was answered following the elections of 1998, when the SPD formed a government with the Green Party, in a so-called Red–Green Alliance. Their platform focused principally upon opposition to nuclear power, as an expression of anti-centralist and pacifist values traditional to green thought. Later, in 2001, the Greens reached an agreement to end reliance on nuclear power in Germany, while maintaining their part in a coalition government and supporting the chancellor, Gerhard Schröder, in his decision to back the US-led wars in both Afghanistan (2001–2) and Iraq (2003). Although this pragmatism was said to have put the German Green Party at odds with many greens worldwide, it also demonstrated that it (1) was capable of difficult political tradeoffs, and (2) believed it best to stay in government to try to influence policy.

USA

The US electoral system does not favour parties that focus on environmental issues. Historically, the environment has come low down the list of US voter concerns and has typically made little difference to electoral outcomes. However, in recent years, in both the WTO and NAFTA, the US government has been concerned and confronted with a 'new international agenda', including environmental issues, international human rights

[7] Other 'niche' parties include: Farmers' parties, communist parties and various far right parties.

and a wide range of social concerns. In principle supporting the extension of international environmental responsibilities, in practice the US government has often emerged as a major obstacle to global environmental agreements. For example, 'under the Kyoto agreement the EU has agreed to cut greenhouse gas emissions by 8% while Britain has promised to strive for a 12.5% reduction. But the US, the world's largest polluter, has rejected the agreement' (Osborn 2003b).

It is often remarked that the US government is unwilling 'to sign up to the central obligations because of domestic pressures to resist new environmental standards' (Webber and Smith 2002: 120). There is evidence for such a statement: between 2001 and 2004, the Bush administration:

- withdrew the USA from negotiations in the Kyoto climate change treaty;
- launched the Clear Skies initiative under which an estimated extra 42 million tons of pollutants a year will be released over US communities;
- reneged on a pledge to cut power plants' carbon dioxide emissions and modify the Clean Air Act to allow an estimated 17,000 outdated power plants to upgrade without fitting new anti-pollution equipment;
- launched the Healthy Forests initiative to increase logging in regions considered at risk from wildfires;
- announced logging plans for Alaska's Tongass rainforest;
- postponed the deadline by which coal-burning power plants must cut mercury pollution to 2011;
- proposed to amend the Endangered Species Act to allow wildlife collectors to import endangered species;
- sought Congressional approval to drill for oil in Alaska's Arctic National Wildlife Refuge;
- proposed cuts of $1.9 billion in environmental programmes during 2005, including $600 million from the Environmental Protection Agency (Ghazi 2004).

It is also suggested that the Bush administration's environmental policy is strongly responsive to the preferences of its business supporters. While many believed that proposed modifications to the Clean Air Act would represent the biggest defeat for American environmentalists since the Bush administration abandoned the Kyoto Treaty on global warming, the energy industry believed the measures were welcome. It argued that they were essential for maintaining coal-fired power stations. But if they are 'adopted, they would represent a multi-million dollar victory for energy corporations, most of whom are significant Republican contributors, and who were consulted in the drafting of the administration's energy plan by vice-president Dick Cheney in 2001' (Borger 2003a). The proposed modifications to the Clean Air Act came in the wake of victories for US justice department lawyers. They had fought cases against six big polluters in the electric power industry, and had forced them to reduce emissions by more than half a million tons a year. 'However, analysts said that, under the new rules, the six would have won. The trade group representing the companies, Edison Electric Institute, contributed nearly $600,000 to the Republican Party from 1999 to 2002, and had at least 14 contacts with the Cheney energy task force in 2001' (Borger 2003a).

Some ENGOs, including the Sierra Club, operate transnationally with numerous member groups in the United States and Canada (<http://www.sierraclub.org/politics/>). This is atypical: most North American ENGOs focus on domestic environmental issues. However, in the regional context there was concern about environmental issues in relation to NAFTA. Greenpeace and the Sierra Club combined to deliver a forceful critique of the Agreement's likely environmental consequences. This was said to have been a major factor in coalescing popular opposition to the Agreement in the member countries (Canada, Mexico, USA) (Macdonald and Schwartz 2002: 143–4). However, the NAFTA trade agreement is also said to have focused 'concern on protecting the environment against the practices of the other country or countries, not on how environmental interests might band together for their mutual benefit' (Larose 1999).

In the mid-1990s, President Clinton's government was able to create a split among environmental groups through the creation of the NAFTA environmental side agreement (Mumme 1999). In both NAFTA and the embryonic FTAA, US business interest groups – like their counterparts in Canada and Mexico – have sought to exert significant pressure on government over environmental issues (James and Lustzig 2003). On the other hand, as Macdonald and Schwartz (2002: 153) point out, 'there have also been some limited successful challenges from labor, environmental, and other civic groups'. One of the results of such pressure in relation to NAFTA was the Commission for Environmental Cooperation,[8] an initiative of mainly US-based ENGOs, including the Sierra Club (Macdonald and Schwartz 2002: 150).

While some environmental NGOs like Greenpeace and the Sierra Club remained openly critical of NAFTA, the administration was able to win over other ENGOs, including the National Wildlife Federation, World Wildlife Fund, Natural Resources Defense Council, National Audubon Society, Defenders of Wildlife, Environmental Defense Fund and the Nature Conservancy (Audley 1997). Such groups were instrumental in getting the NAFTA environmental side agreement implemented, an outcome that reflected their ability to use the political opportunity structure for their benefit. These ENGOs began to mobilize as early as 1991, three years before NAFTA came into operation, and used their contacts in Congress and with the executive to press their case (Johnson and Beaulieu 1996: 25). 'Their support for the side agreements helped win over some of the former Congressional opponents of the deal' (Macdonald and Schwartz 2002: 143–4).

In sum, in both the USA and North America more generally, ENGO efforts tend to focus on domestic, rather than regional, issues. Transnational activities, with the partial exception of NAFTA-related issues, are underdeveloped. This reflects the fact that domestic opportunity structures often provide a more conducive environment to exercise ENGO influence.

---

[8] 'The Commission for Environmental Cooperation (CEC) is an international organization created by Canada, Mexico and the United States under the North American Agreement on Environmental Cooperation (NAAEC). The CEC was established to address regional environmental concerns, help prevent potential trade and environmental conflicts, and to promote the effective enforcement of environmental law. The Agreement complements the environmental provisions of the North American Free Trade Agreement (NAFTA)' (<http://www.cec.org/who_we_are/index.cfm?varlan=english>).

Transitional Democracies

Russia

As a result of the Soviet legacy, environmental degradation in Russia was often said to be among the worst in the world (Peterson 1993). Following Gorbachev's policies of *perestroika* in the late 1980s, an active, but short-lived, environmental movement emerged – but soon fell into relative obscurity. After the collapse of the USSR, there were constant changes in state environmental institutions. They had often conflicting responsibilities, while the shifting content of environmental legislation produced a very unstable, confusing setting where environmentally concerned citizens, advocacy groups and decision-makers could operate yet found it very difficult to influence outcomes.

Powell (2002) examined the influence of home-grown and cross-border green groups in relation to post-communist Russia. She finds that their success cannot be measured in terms of improvements in the environment or in terms of greater consciousness among national or local decision-makers for environmental issues. Rather, their achievement lies in assisting the – often slow – establishment and development of environmental advocacy organizations in Russia. To some, albeit limited, degree, this has been a factor in helping to establish new democratic channels between civil society and the political elite for participation and the articulation of interests.

However, Powell (2002) also found that external environmental aid has had conspicuously little effect to date on the environment itself or on the implementation of environmental policy. This is for three main reasons. First, it reflects state weakness: the Russian state has exerted little control over industrial and commercial interests and even has a difficult time policing itself. Second, channels for articulating societal interests are still underdeveloped. The state enjoys a high level of autonomy in respect to the mass of ordinary people, and is not accountable to them; generally, democratic processes are either absent or dysfunctional. Third, the link between environmental issues and economic-industrial issues is unbreakable. 'The sheer magnitude of the two types of problems and their connections to each other make addressing only one and not the other an ineffectual way to resolve environmental issues' (Mendelson and Glenn 2002: 16–17).

Despite these factors, Russia's environmental movement is said to be growing, partly because of President Putin's apparent assault on environmental regulations. Acting by decree, President Putin abolished the State Committee for Environmental Protection (SCEP) in 2000, and transferred its responsibilities to the Ministry of Natural Resources, a pro-development agency in charge of licensing exploitation of Russia's minerals and petroleum. This led to charges from environmentalists that Putin was 'putting the goat in charge of the cabbage patch'. One of Russia's leading environmentalists, Svet Zabelin of the Socio-Ecological Union, claimed that this policy was reminiscent of the Soviet era, a time when ministries rubber-stamped their own environmental behaviour: 'During the Soviet period, each ministry had an environmental department, but it was not outside control. . . . Now we are simply [returning to] the same situation – an absolutely Soviet solution.' However, Putin's actions led to a popular backlash: more than four out of five Russians opposed the abolition of the environmental agency. Outside Russia, environmental activists around the world protested to the World Bank about its lending to Russia because of President Putin's decision to abolish the SCEP (Hertsgaard 2000).

Mexico

Like Russia, Mexico has sought to move from an authoritarian regime in recent years. Mexico has a fairly well-established and influential green party, the Green Ecologist Party of Mexico (Partido Verde Ecologista de México – PVEM). The PVEM emerged from a group of ENGOs dedicated to ecological activities that decided that its influence would be limited unless it could influence political decisions concerned with the environment (Tarrow 1998: 84). The ENGOs joined forces to constitute the Ecologist Party, which later became the PVEM. The PVEM entered the national Chamber of Deputies for the first time in 1997 with eight deputies, following two earlier, unsuccessful attempts in 1991 and 1994. The number rose to 15 following elections in 2001 when the PVEM was part of an electoral coalition with the party of the victorious presidential candidate, Vicente Fox. In 1997, the PVEM benefited from divided government at the national level, following that year's federal congressional election. As a result, the long-entrenched PRI dominance came to an end, allowing several smaller parties, including the PVEM, not only to enter the Chamber of Deputies, but also to acquire some power – because of the need to form a ruling coalition to keep out the PRI.

The PVEM was able to benefit not only from a popular desire for the end of PRI hegemony but also because it 'dedicated a lot of effort to indigenous people'.

> [Many PVEM party] leaders are indigenous people and most of them speak native languages; 80% of our candidates in 1994 were native people. The Green Party of Mexico tries to protect the ancestral Mexican cultures as well as their values. We have great respect for them because we believe that they had a harmonious relationship with the elements of the earth: water, land, air and fire. (Jager 1997)

Like in the USA, Mexico's recent environmental policies have been affected by NAFTA membership issues. Mexico is the first country straddling the North America/Latin America divide to join in the US-led project to develop NAFTA, to be followed by the FTAA. Since the early 1990s, Mexico's authorities have sought to shape new policies, in the context of unprecedented institutional changes that both NAFTA and democratization have instituted. As part of the same process, 'pressures from international environmental groups with influence in the political processes in their own countries or in international organizations are also increasing their effectiveness in placing their concerns on the policy agenda in Mexico' (Barkin 1999: 14).

Additionally, NAFTA's environmental side agreement, with its new consultative bodies – institutions that the Mexican government was virtually compelled to accept in exchange for approval of the expanded free trade agreement – provide a mechanism for international oversight. This kind of external instrument was previously unimaginable in Mexican politics. Its establishment offers new opportunities to Mexican environmentalists, such as those in the PVEM, as it can bolster their demand that the government complies with external rules. On the other hand, in spite of new awareness of and sensitivity to environmental issues in Mexico, there are signs of continuing environmental degradation, a result in part of major growth in speculative international financial flows, FDI and enhanced volumes of trade due to NAFTA (Morris 1995: 80–1). The state and business view is that economic growth is the best remedy for environmental problems.

However, while Mexico's entry into the global marketplace has helped foster a sophisticated discourse about protecting the environment, there are still many problems within Mexico's institutional structure that prevent implementation of the advanced regulatory package. Even more serious, however, is the considerable bureaucratic resistance to the efforts of grassroots groups and intermediate ENGOs that together advocate environmentally and socially responsible policies (Philip 1999).

Turning to business, because of commitments undertaken with the signing of NAFTA (and other agreements like the Montreal protocol to protect the ozone layer), there is said to be growing awareness among larger corporations in Mexico of the need to take vigorous actions in relation to the environment, in order to forestall potential government intervention. Consequently, a group of firms has created various institutions to provide a platform to defend their activities. Complementing the efforts of the official National Ecology Institute (INE), an elite group – the Businessmen's Coordinating Council – created the Center for the Study of Sustainable Development (CESPEDES). The aim was to forestall demands for greater regulatory activities by the state. This organization, in turn, encouraged the creation of ecology divisions within the Mexican equivalents of the National Chambers of Trade and Industry (CONCANACO, CONCAMIN, CANACINTRA) (Barkin 1999: 14).

Finally, under NAFTA, the Commission for Environmental Cooperation (CEC) was created as part of a widening process of incorporating environmental considerations into Mexico's policy-making process. Moreover, Mexico's environmental NGO community has had some success in getting its voice heard. It has done this on occasion by ignoring local authorities and appealing directly to international organizations, such as the UN, where NGOs may find a more sympathetic hearing. In Mexico, these changes have become especially important in intensifying the pressures for a fuller consideration of the environmental consequences of economic and trade policies (Wallis 2001).

Non-Democracies

China

Miller (1995: 43–5) notes that, partly as a result of the non-democratic political system in China, the race for economic growth often seems to take very little account of environmental issues. Traditionally, public awareness of environmental protection in China has not been well developed, and China had no ENGOs before the early 1990s. This is despite the fact that there are various environmental protection laws in place and China belongs to various international agreements. However, since the 1986 Chernobyl Nuclear Disaster, a small but growing number of concerned environmental activists in China have sought to play an active role in environmental protection. The significant role of environmental NGOs in developed countries is said to have served as an inspiration to those in China (Wu Chenguang 2002).

The first Chinese ENGO was formally registered on 31 March 1994. It was the Academy for Green Culture, affiliated to the non-governmental Academy for Chinese

Culture, now called Friends of Nature. In recent times, more ENGOs have been established, including Global Village of Beijing, established in 1996. According to news released by the Sino-US environmental NGOs forum in November 2001, there were by then more than 2,000 environmental NGOs in China and millions of participants (<www.china.org.cn/english/2002/Jul/36833.htm>).

China's ENGOs have faced considerable difficulties. There have been constraints in registration procedures and problems caused by lack of funds. According to Liao Xiaoyi, leader of Global Village of Beijing, China's ENGOs find it difficult to raise funds because of anomalies in the tax system. 'Global Village of Beijing has no source of regularly recurring funds. Its basic revenue depends on fees from producing TV programs and these cannot be guaranteed indefinitely' (Wu Chenguang 2002). Overall, China's ENGOs lack influence compared to business, especially commercial activities like logging and trapping whose activities may well run counter to the interests of environmental protection. It appears possible, however, that over time foreign ENGOs may become more influential in China. For example, the World Wide Fund for Nature now has its own office building in Beijing and attracts environmentalists, economists and zoologists (<www.wwf.org.hk/eng/>).

In conclusion, Chinese ENGOs currently focus on three main areas: (1) to educate the public about environmental issues, (2) to promote public involvement in environmental protection and (3) to lobby government on issues of environmental protection policy. They also seek to monitor what is happening in the field of environmental protection and aim to help business enterprises develop greater concern for environmental issues. However, to date their efforts have lacked influence and success. This appears to be the case because government support for them is lacking; it will be crucial if China's ENGOs are to make progress (Wu Chenguang 2002). In conclusion, the slow progress of China's ENGOs reflects the fact that the country's non-democratic political system makes it very difficult for such groups to influence environmental policy-making.

Indonesia

As in China, Indonesian ENGOs found it difficult to influence policy-making under the autocratic regime of General Suharto (1965–98). However, in its last years, political opportunity structures began to open. A coalition of ENGOs was able to influence policy in relation to the country's reforestation policy. This is a crucial issue in a country which has seen its forests swiftly disappearing in recent years as a consequence of economic growth.

In October 1994, local environmentalists began a court case against the government to spark a broad inquiry into the government's Reforestation Fund, whose aim was allegedly to replant trees lost to logging. The lawsuit was brought by the Indonesian Forum on the Environment, Wanana Lingkungan Hidap Indonesia (WALHI), an umbrella group with board members from local business and from multinationals such as IBM (Fisher 1993: 149). WALHI's lawsuit challenged the decision of the then national president, General Suharto, to funnel $185 million from the Reforestation Fund into the coffers of the nation's aircraft industry. According to WALHI, the decision violated the government's conservationist commitment to refurbish Indonesia's vanishing rain forests. The government's defence lawyers maintained that WALHI had no legal standing to bring the suit, as the 'non-government organization does not represent the interests of the general public' and 'the reforestation issue should be aired in parliament, not in the courts' (Cohen 1994: 44).

A confidential Asian Development Bank report commissioned by the Ministry of Forestry reported that just 16 per cent of reforestation funds had been spent in the four years prior to March 1993. It also noted that direct funding of natural forest rehabilitation and conservation activity amounted to only 3 per cent of allocated funding. In other words, in the first half of the 1990s, less than *half of 1 per cent* of funds allocated for reforestation in Indonesia was spent for that purpose. The report commented delicately that 'there is evidence of considerable and increasing flexibility on how funds are spent', although no details were given. Moreover, 'many plantations have been situated in logged-over forest, prompting the clear-cutting of remaining trees so as to create a homogeneous forest suitable for Indonesia's rapidly expanding pulp and paper industry' (Cohen 1994: 44).

Despite the damning report, it appeared that WALHI's conservation message had some chance of getting through to Indonesia's then forestry minister, Djamaloedin Soeryohadikoesoemo. He announced in late 1994 that Indonesia would reduce its timber output by 30 per cent between 1995 and 1999, in the interests of 'sustainable development'. Djamaloedin also expressed interest in pilot projects in community forestry, then in operation in Kalimantan and other areas, thus allowing villagers more responsibility in protecting resources. This may or may not be a sign of the emergence of a primary environmental care policy in Indonesia. A scheme for eco-labelling promised to add conservation safeguards to sell tropical timber in developed country markets like Sweden, Australia, Canada and the USA. This scheme would obviously involve integrating environmental concerns more fully into economic decision-making but, several years later, there were indications that this was not being done (Morris 2001; Aglionby 2001). In sum, this brief account of environmental protection endeavours in Indonesia shows that success is dependent upon political circumstances.

Conclusion

We have seen in this chapter that environmental groups and green parties are found in numerous countries. They have varying amounts of influence at both domestic and regional/international levels. Green parties may enjoy some electoral success when there is an electoral system based on proportional representation. However, this is not the only context where we have noted green groups' influence. We saw that ENGOs can be influential in both domestic and cross-border contexts when they exploit political opportunity structures to their advantage. In established democracies there are institutionalized political structures where green issues may be pursued, although there is no guarantee of success. In transitional democracies, on the other hand, democratic political institutions are less well developed and green interests struggle to be influential. In non-democracies, closed political systems do not allow room either for ENGOs or for green parties – if they exist – to influence outcomes. However, external encouragement – from either state or non-state actors – can be a factor in this regard.

9
Political Culture

What is political culture? Rosamond (2002b: 82) defines it as 'the set of values, beliefs and attitudes within which a political system operates'. For Diamond (1993a: 8) it is 'a people's dominant beliefs, attitudes, values, sentiments, and evaluation about the political system of its country, and the role of the self in that system'. Both definitions underline the idea that political culture does not refer to how specific actors – such as individual leaders – view politics, but rather to 'how people view the political system as a whole, including their belief in its legitimacy' (Hague and Harrop 2001: 79). In short, political culture is a shorthand expression used to denote key values that inform the nature of a political system.

Is it possible to measure a country's political culture? While there is no universally agreed way (Welch 1993), attempts have been made to assess citizens' perceptions of their country's politics and political system by examining opinion polls over time. Such surveys often show that in countries that have been democracies for a generation or more, around 75 per cent of people support the concept of democracy – although not necessarily the practices or the individual politicians in the democratic system where they live. On the other hand, the ease with which public opinion can influence policy decisions varies greatly among democratic states. Political culture plays a role, and so does the particular political structure in a country. Moreover, the effect of public opinion can differ from issue to issue. As a result, even when there are similarities in public opinion across various countries, policy will not necessarily be affected in the same way.

In a cross-country study, Risse-Kappen (1994) found that the more open and decentralized the decision-making system in an established democracy and the stronger the social organizations capable of mobilizing and organizing support, then the more opportunity there was for public opinion to influence policy formulation. But even where public opinion is effective, it tends to set limits to the choices available to policy-makers rather than directly influencing their decisions or the implementation of specific policies. This suggests that the main role of public opinion in this regard is to 'enable elite groups to build coalitions, since interest groups and other societal actors need the support of mass public opinion in order to influence policy decisions' (Light 2000: 98–9).

This points to a key difference between transitional democracies and established democracies: no matter how badly a government does, as a system, democracy is not punished. This can be seen in relation to Spain, a country that democratized 30 years ago, now universally regarded as an established democracy. Public opinion surveys over time indicate that democracy commands the stable support of three-quarters of Spaniards (*The Economist* 2001a). This is in line with other European established democracies but contrasts with the situation in Latin America, a region with many transitional democracies. In mid-2002, that is, 20 years after the commencement of democratization in the region, a Latinobarómetro survey discovered that three-quarters of respondents in only two regional countries – Costa Rica and Venezuela, both democracies for over 40 years – replied affirmatively to the following question: 'Democracy is preferable to any other kind of government' (*The Economist* 2002b). This would appear to indicate that the quality and achievements of particular political regimes are important factors when people are asked to comment on their perceptions of the political systems where they live.

Popular attitudes towards politics are often thought to develop primarily in relation to a country's domestic political attributes. Why then are we devoting a chapter to this issue in the current book, which is concerned with the impact of globalization on countries' domestic situations? A key reason is that globalization is regarded as increasingly significant when assessing countries' political cultures, especially when they change. Most earlier 'discussions of political culture focused on its role within the state – but this tradition now needs supplementing'. Like 'many aspects of politics, [political] culture must [now] be viewed from a global perspective. This is because ideas and images know no boundaries; they travel faster than products and arguably have more impact' (Hague and Harrop 2001: 93). Diamond (2002: 226–7) explains that:

> International actors have a crucial role to play in pressing the necessary reform agenda, in supporting civil society actors who see the need for reform, and in providing the financial and technical resources needed to help construct and enable the necessary institutions. An international vision for reform, with distinct institution-building targets and country priorities, could transform an increasingly precarious global situation. Alternatively, a failure of will or lack of clear vision could squander an unparalleled opportunity to build a truly democratic world.

The significance of globalization on political cultures can be seen since the end of World War II. First, following the defeat of Nazi Germany, there was a determined effort to build a united Europe. This was encouraged by the USA, with individual efforts headed 'by a multinational elite with a strong commitment to the European idea'. This developed over time into what is now often referred to as a 'Western European political culture', primarily characterized by an unswerving commitment to democracy (Anastasakis 2000).

Second, there was an important stimulus from the 1950s and 1960s for studies of political culture. This was a time when numerous former colonial countries – primarily in Asia, Africa and the Caribbean – gained independence. Most such countries were bequeathed democratic systems by departing colonial countries, but few managed to retain them for long. Some observers pointed to what they saw as beneficial legacies for democratic political cultures, left by the colonial administrations. Rueschemeyer et al. (1992) suggest that democratic longevity in some former British colonies, such as India, Jamaica and Trinidad and Tobago, was facilitated by inherited colonial traditions. They are thought to have supplied necessary foundations upon which postcolonial political elites could preside over development of pro-democracy political cultures. Smith (2003: 265) points out that 'moderation, co-operation, bargaining and accommodation' are the key values and orientations associated with pro-democracy political cultures. 'Moderation' and 'accommodation' also imply toleration, pragmatism, willingness to compromise and civility in political discourse.

The length of time available for the dissemination and embedding of such values is important, affecting the degree to which nationalist politicians were able both to acquire democratic values and to disseminate them to the masses. An important factor in this regard was the length of time available to prepare for independence. Where there were swift transitions from British colonial rule, for example, in Ghana, Malaysia, Nigeria and Pakistan, then it typically proved very difficult to inculcate pro-democracy values at both elite and popular levels.

Third, in the mid-1970s, there were democratic transitions in three Southern European countries (Greece, Portugal, Spain), encouraged by the EU and collectively important for kick-starting the third wave of democracy. Each of these countries is now universally regarded as an established democracy with appropriate political cultures.

In sum, since the end of World War II there were three periods – the late 1940s, the 1950s and 1960s, and the 1970s – during which globalization helped to remake political cultures in various countries.

The remainder of this chapter examines: (1) the findings and assumptions of Almond and Verba's *The Civic Culture*, a seminal work on political culture; (2) criticisms of the political culture approach to political analysis; (3) the impact of globalization on political culture; and (4) various case studies, with particular emphasis on the post-cold war phase of globalization.

Almond and Verba's *The Civic Culture*

The argument

Almond and Verba originally coined the term 'political culture' more than 40 years ago in their classic pioneering work, *The Civic Culture* (1963). They understood the term to include orientations people possess towards national political institutions, conventions and traditions. In their view, individual political cultures develop as a result of three factors: *cognition*, *affection* and *evaluation* (that is, knowing, feeling and judging):

- *cognition* involves knowledge and beliefs about the political system;
- *affection* consists of feelings about the system;
- *evaluation* comprises commitments to political values and judgements – that is, by making use of information and feelings – about the performance of the political system relative to those values.

Evaluations may change as a result of empirical experiences, while norms and values are thought to be both deeply embedded and long-lasting, durable orientations towards political actions and the political system. Taken together, cognitive, affective and evaluational orientations amount to what Almond and Verba called the '*subjective*' dimension of politics that inform three – '*objective*' – dimensions of political life: *system*, *process* and *policy*.

1 *System* relates to the nature of the political system and to the governing regime and its political institutions. It involves both *inputs* and *outputs*. The chief inputs are political parties, interest groups and the mass media. The main outputs are legislatures,

executives, bureaucracies, courts (plus the incumbents of these institutions) and the nation itself.

2   *Process* relates politics to the actions, conflicts, alliances and behavioural styles of parties, interest groups, movements and individuals.

3   *Policy* relates to political outputs – that is, decisions – of the political system.

Almond and Verba's key argument is based on differences between what they see as three 'pure' types of political culture: *parochial, subject* and *participant*.

1   In a *parochial* political culture, citizens are only indistinctly aware of the existence of central government – as with remote tribes whose existence is seemingly un-affected by national decisions made by the state.

2   In a subject political culture, most citizens do not see themselves as participants in the political process, but as subjects of the government. This includes people living under various forms of political dictatorship and more generally refers to the extent of both trust and legitimacy that people have in regard to their government.

3   In a *participant* political culture, most 'citizens believe both that they can contribute to the system and that they are affected by it' (Hague and Harrop 2001: 79). People have to be confident that they can achieve something by personally taking part in politics.

Almond and Verba's key argument was that democracy is most stable in certain kinds of society. This is where subject and parochial attitudes provide the foundations of an essentially participant culture. This they called the 'civic culture'. Citizens are sufficiently active in politics in this ideal combination to express their preferences to rulers yet not so involved that they will refuse to accept unpopular decisions. In short, 'the civic culture resolves the tension within democracy between popular control and effective gover-nance' (Hague and Harrop 2001: 79–80).

Drawing on their theoretical assumptions, Almond and Verba drew up a typology of political cultures. Their research for *The Civic Culture* was undertaken in the late 1950s, employing a sophisticated questionnaire designed to distinguish the 'subject' and 'citizen' aspects of five countries' national political cultures: Britain, the Federal Repub-lic of Germany (FRG – 'West Germany'), Italy, Mexico and the USA. At this time, both Britain and the USA were established democracies, Germany and Italy were transi-tional democracies, having introduced democratic political systems after World War II at the behest of the USA, and Mexico was a non-democracy, under one-party state rule since the early 1920s.

According to their findings, civic culture was best exhibited by Britain and the USA, countries with the most solid bases for stable democracy; in the FRG, the base was shal-lower; Italy had very little civic culture, and Mexico hardly any at all. From this, Almond and Verba claimed that (1) a nation's political culture helps to determine both its politi-cal structures and its political behaviour, and (2) that elements of political culture are *relatively* – but not completely – impervious to change over time. They also posited that there is a pattern of political attitudes – a civic culture – that supports democracy whereby 'political activity, involvement and rationality exist but are balanced by pas-sivity, traditionality, and commitment to parochial values' (Almond and Verba 1963: 30). Thus to establish and then consolidate democracy requires a political culture that recognizes the legitimacy of territorial and constitutional arrangements while evincing willingness to accept political outcomes – as long as the established rules of political life (especially electoral rules) are followed.

Almond and Verba were well aware that their assessment of the nature of their five chosen countries' political cultures was a snapshot capturing a position in the late 1950s. Soon after the publication of their findings, the existence of civic culture in both the USA and Britain was called into question as a result of external events – such as the war in Vietnam (1960s and early 1970s) and the steep global rises in oil prices (1970s) – and domestic developments, including the rise of postmaterialism (1960s and 1970s). From the beginning of the 1970s, many advanced industrial democracies – including the USA and Britain – seemed to be affected by alterations in popular social priorities, changes labelled as a 'participatory revolution' and/or a postmaterialist 'culture shift'. As a result, many citizens were said to become more enamoured of opportunities to directly affect political outcomes (Inglehart 1990), while becoming less attached to particular parties or even distrustful of all established parties. As a result of such attitudinal shifts, 'citizens may be more likely to employ existing opportunities for direct political participation and politicians have new electoral incentives to support reforms that increase opportunities for direct democracy' (Scarrow 2001: 653). In sum, in both Britain and the USA, there appeared to be diminished trust in government, characterized by 'a shift away from the civic culture towards a more sceptical and instrumental attitude to politics' (Hague and Harrop 2001: 80). However, this discontent centred more on leaders' and governing institutions' performance than on the democratic process itself.

Criticisms of the Political Culture Approach to Political Analysis

For supporters, the notion of political culture provides the location for political activity within a polity. A society's particular political culture is believed to narrow the range of acceptable attitudes towards various forms of rule, whether democratic or authoritarian. For example, Western countries are said to demonstrate a cultural bias towards democracy. The implication is that the intrinsic worth of democracy is not promoted; it is taken for granted, and this presumption reinforces democratic stability within a polity. In contrast, Muslim countries are said to have fundamentally different perceptions of 'Western-style' democracy: it is 'materialistic, unprincipled and American' (Hague and Harrop 2001: 81). This perception is said to exclude even the *idea* of liberal democracy from mainstream discourse.

Huntington (1991: 73) argues that certain types of political culture – found in Buddhist, Hindu, Muslim and 'Confucian' countries – are inherently anti-democratic. Fukuyama (1992: 217, 236) contends that Confucianism is based on 'hierarchical and inegalitarian' views, while Buddhism 'confines itself to a domain of private worship centring around the family'. Consequently, Buddhists are seen as politically passive in the face of authoritarianism and dictatorship. One strand of Muslim thought – Islamic fundamentalism – is perceived as a 'nostalgic re-assertion of an older, purer set of values' that are comparable to European-style fascism.

Such blanket views may, however, be analytically unhelpful because they lack universality and empirical veracity. For example, predominantly Hindu India, yet with an important (c.11 per cent) Muslim minority, has been a democracy since 1947 (except for a brief period, 1975–7). Predominantly Muslim Turkey, Kuwait, Jordan and Malaysia are all characterized as 'partly free', in our terminology, that is, transitional democracies, as is mostly Buddhist Thailand. Finally, Confucian/Buddhist/Christian Taiwan and South Korea are classified as transitional democracies well on the way to democratic consolidation (Freedom House 2003).

The particular work of Almond and Verba, as well as the general concept of political culture, have also been criticized for other reasons. *The Civic Culture* itself attracted several specific sorts of criticism. While all of these were directed specifically at their study, they could also be used to question various aspects of the political culture approach to politics. As a starting point, many critics have stated that people's political actions are in response more to immediate material needs than to cultural predispositions. Others contend that both class and institutional structures are far more important in fashioning national development outcomes than any notion of a people's political culture. These examples point to a more general criticism of the political culture approach: it is simply not a useful analytical tool because it is highly questionable whether it is possible to separate exclusive and stable orderings of political values, beliefs and understandings. Rosamond (2002b: 88) suggests an 'apparent Anglo-American bias' in Almond and Verba's study, while Samudavanija (1993: 270) contends that their notion of political culture is linked to a specific type of incrementalism and gradualism believed to carry political systems to their 'natural' end: liberal democratic civic culture.

In addition, critics suggest further reasons to reject cultural determinism in relation to a society's political culture. On the one hand, cognitive, attitudinal and evaluational dimensions of political culture may be more flexible and plastic than Almond and Verba believed. Consequently, these dimensions may change (sometimes dramatically) in relation to various factors, including regime performance, historical experience, political socialization, changes in economic and social structure, international factors and/or the overall functioning of the political system itself. Moreover, the deterministic approach appears to condemn non-democracies to more of the same lack of democracy. However, as already noted, there are various examples of countries that, despite apparently 'unsuitable' political credentials, have moved from non-democracy to democracy, including Germany, Italy, Japan, Spain, Greece, Portugal, South Korea and Taiwan.

A second criticism of the notion of political culture is that it is actually rather superficial – unless there is 'independent evidence of what the values of people living in [a] country actually are' (Hague and Harrop 2001: 81). Is it really possible to identify just one 'American' political culture of universal validity in the USA? That is, it may not be very useful to talk of a single undifferentiated 'people' in a country such as the USA that appears to be divided by cultural, ethnic, religious, regional and urban–rural issues. As Diamond (1993a: 8) notes, not 'all social groups share the same political culture, [n]or [are] values and beliefs . . . evenly distributed throughout the population'. For example, within a single country different ethnic and regional groups, as well as specific institutions, such as the military or universities, may have quite different value systems and worldviews, and, depending on societal context, for example, whether an individual is in his or her village, workplace, peer group or religious community, then such values might change in response to one's physical or mental location. Critics suggest that it might be more analytically fruitful to think in terms of political *sub*cultures within a state, nation or region, and seek to assess how they interact politically.

Third, as Almond and Verba acknowledged, political cultures can and do evolve and change. Any attempt, 'no matter how successful, to measure political culture can only be a snapshot of political culture at that particular time' (Rosamond 2002b: 88–91). This implies that we need to take into account a range of both domestic and external factors that may influence how people perceive and react to their political system. Analyses should be sensitive as to how a culture continually evolves in response to political experiences.

Finally, analyses of political culture often pay insufficient attention to the impact of international factors. Or, if they do, they are not consistently applied. 'While no boundary or identity is absolute, at least the one between domestic and international issues has been clear.' But now the supposedly clear boundaries between a set of factors called '"domestic" and another called "international" . . . are difficult if not impossible to maintain' (Pridham 2000: 288–9). In the next section, we focus upon globalization and the remaking of political culture.

Globalization and the Remaking of Political Culture

We noted earlier that analyses of political culture often proceed on the implicit or explicit idea that the dynamic focus of a polity's political developments is primarily the domestic arena. Yet, we have already seen examples where there were clearly external factors of significance in helping to deliver fundamental political changes. Over time, they helped lead to reformulations of popular assessments of political systems, for example, evolution of pro-democracy political cultures in the FRG, Italy and Japan after World War II. However, the domestic focus fitted well with conventional approaches in and to comparative politics more generally, with the international arena merely the background to what 'really' mattered: domestic governance.

Now, as Pridham (2000: 313–14) points out in his study of political change in CEE,

> it is quite obvious that the significance of national boundaries has been 'disappearing' relatively speaking, since by the 1990s we are talking not merely of the more institutionalized state of international organizations and networks but also of the age of new technology and its globalizing effects. National boundaries always were to some extent porous, as shown in external influences on post-cold war Italy and West Germany; but the scope for external influences to determine the course of regime change in those respects has certainly increased over time.

It is one thing to recognize that globalization can theoretically affect political developments within countries, but another to separate out its different aspects and then trace their influence within individual countries. To seek to achieve this goal, it is necessary to start by deconstructing the 'international dimension'. Pridham (2000: 285–6) points out that it is simply not analytically plausible to 'speak of an "international dimension" as such as simply one level alongside others such as democratic institutionalization and the emergence of civil society'. In other words, the 'international dimension' is an unsatisfactorily vague term lumping together various cross-border state and non-state actors, factors and influences that only have one thing in common: their origins are outside of the borders of the country on which we choose to focus. However, given the lack of uniformity and differential impacts of external influences, not to mention the fact that they will rarely act in unison, it is confusing to emphasize 'the international dimension' as though it were a unitary factor. As a result, we need to focus on the influence of separate forms of external influences and how they may affect a polity's political culture. In short, a polity's political culture may be influenced by the international diffusion of values and beliefs.

Scholte (2001: 16) notes that the theory and practice of globalization 'encompasse[s] many norms that govern our lives, including thousands of technical standards and (purportedly) universal human rights. These and an ever-increasing number of other rules have acquired a supraterritorial rather than a country-specific character.' This suggests that in some cases – for example, post-1970s Southern Europe – 'international value diffusion [is] now . . . a profound and pervasive, if subtle factor, in the globalization of both democracy' and pro-democracy political cultures. Such international norms may be especially notable across certain regions, such as Western Europe, because they are the 'most effective international context in which external impacts and influences may be identified and measured' (Pridham 2000: 288–9). This highlights the importance of key norms and values that may be characteristic of a region's political and/or political-economic system. Over time, they can 'spill over' national boundaries and influence polities' internal political developments and, as a result, help to amend existing popular perceptions of politics and political systems.

Jowitt (1993: 22) points to what he calls the 'intermestic' dimension, that is, when 'international issues become national ones'. For example, in relation to democratization and democracy, analysts have pointed to the influence of a general 'international diffusion' of ideas and values and/or an 'international environment' conducive to the spread and embedding of such values and norms. In relation to democratization, Huntington (1991) has pointed to the influence of the third wave of democracy (mid-1970s to mid-1990s), in suggesting that many democratic transitions were set in train and advanced by what he calls the 'snowballing' effect of earlier transitions that then stimulated and provided models for subsequent democratization efforts. Diamond (1993b: 422) notes that this draws attention to 'important elements of strategic thinking and cross-country comparisons in political learning and culture change'.

External influences are not necessarily confined to state actors, and as a result it may be erroneous to construe apparent changes in a country's political norms and values as the outcome simply of common patterns involving greater interdependence between states. To do so would not only overlook national diversities, but would also oversimplify complexities both of regime change and reformulation of popular political perceptions. Some analysts point to two-way interactions between domestic and external variables. The result is that 'political communities can no longer be considered (if they ever could with any validity) as simply "discrete worlds" or as self-enclosed political spaces; they are enmeshed in complex structures of overlapping forces, relations and networks'. While such relations are clearly

structured by inequality and hierarchy . . . even the most powerful . . . states – *do not remain unaffected by the changing conditions and processes of regional and global entrenchment.* . . . Increase[s] in the extensiveness, intensity, velocity and impact of international and transnational relations . . . suggest important questions about the evolving character of political community. (Held and McGrew 2002: 123; emphasis added)

What factors are important here? Consider the following example. In the early 1980s, Turkey had a military government and was, in Freedom House parlance, 'partly free', that is, a transitional democracy. On the fringe of Europe and inhabiting a democracy-promoting regional environment, the country's military leaders were nevertheless confronted with a quandary. Should they comply with emerging regional norms in relation to democracy and, as a result, probably speed up Turkey's application to join the EU? But Turkey's record of violent political polarization – between forces of the left and right – had significantly affected both the country's and the military leaders' political cultures – to the extent that the latter did not believe that 'internal costs of toleration' were lower than 'external costs of suppression' (Yilmaz 2002: 81).

A second example comes from Latin America in the 1980s. Regional countries were strongly encouraged both by the US government and the main regional IGO, the Organization of American States, to democratize and liberalize the mostly statist economies. Critics charge that while many regional countries accepted this advice and undertook both steps, it nevertheless led to diminished forms of democracy. These did not serve to embed democratic norms in most regional countries or lead to the development of pro-democracy political cultures. That is, the scope and range of issues dealt with in the political arena did not usually manage to incorporate sufficiently the concerns of many ordinary people: increased welfare provision, jobs, and more and better political representation.

We can note three main structural impediments to the development of fully pro-democracy political cultures in Turkey and most Latin American countries:

1   *Lack of governmental legitimacy and accountability.* Intent on pursuing the interests of civilian and military elites, governments have ruled with scant concern for the interests of ordinary people.
2   *The nature of agrarian class relations.* Large-scale landowners are an important constituency among civilian elites, especially in many Latin American countries. They have traditionally used their influence with governments to resist significant land reforms. The outcome is huge numbers of economically impoverished and politically impotent landless rural labourers.
3   *The political relationship between state and military power.* Close relationships have developed over time between civilian and military elites in both Turkey and many Latin American countries. In both cases, the armed forces are seen as key defenders of the state from external (foreign governments) and internal (class-based political actors) attack.

The overall consequence is that political systems remained rooted in 'culture[s] of repression and passivity that were antithetical to democratic citizenship' (Karl 1995: 79). This suggests that various anti-democratic norms, values and structures inhibited the development of democracy and pro-democratic political cultures. Consequently, both in Turkey and in many Latin American countries it has proved impossible to reconcile popular demands for democracy with largely undemocratic political histories and cultures, reflecting both continuity and discontinuity with the past. *Continuity* is reflected in:

- unrepresentative, elite-dominated political systems;
- a continuing significant political role for the military in many cases;
- gross inequalities between rich and poor;
- lack of liberal freedoms for ordinary people.

Discontinuity is reflected in:

- strong external pressure, especially from powerful regional governments and IGOs, for sustained economic and political reforms;
- emergence of reformist governments – including that of Mexico's Vicente Fox, Venezuela's Hugo Chavez and the AKP government in Turkey. Each of these regimes came to power promising fundamental political and economic reforms but has found it hard to deliver.

A further conclusion is that international norms – such as, 'Western-style' democracy – do not work on a *tabula rasa* but are influenced by pre-existing, indigenous norms and values. Consequently, external norms can only become embedded when they encounter a receptive domestic terrain. Checkel (1999) points to the importance of what he calls the degree of 'cultural match': international norms can become salient within a polity if they coincide to a considerable degree with pre-existing societal norms, understandings, beliefs and obligations. Domestic discourse not only provides the context within which international norms take on meaning, but also conditions how they operate. When an appropriate cultural match exists, domestic actors are likely to treat the international norm as a given, thus inherently accepting obligations associated with it. For example, 'although Britain and France may face the same international norms . . . the unique national experience of [each] country will make its propensity to follow that norm different'. On the other hand, the fact 'that legitimating discourses are bounded by prevailing domestic understandings should not obscure the dynamic nature of the relationship between domestic and international normative structures' (Cortell and Davies 2000: 73). In short, acceptance, development and persistence of sets of political beliefs among a group of people depend in some way on their pre-existing beliefs.

Development of pro-democracy political cultures depends heavily on 'rather precarious sets of delicate relationships' among, on the one hand, political elites and, on the other, between them and the mass of ordinary people (Pinkney 1993: 86). It is likely to be particularly difficult in some contexts, for example, when the people of a country are divided by serious ethnic and/or religious hostilities, major ideological splits, and/or gross economic inequalities. However, several long-established democracies – for example, in India, Mauritius and Trinidad – appear to have developed pro-democracy political cultures over time, despite the existence of such potential impediments (Ayoade 1988; Mitra and Enskat 1999; Premdas and Ragoonath 1998). Their experiences indicate that to develop pro-democracy political cultures requires that both government and opposition politicians work consensually together, animated by the shared belief that consolidating democracy is a normatively desirable goal. Thus to overcome structural drawbacks requires enlightened, dedicated political leaders who work to ensure that politics does not become a zero-sum game. Table 9.1 summarizes the relationship between international norms and political cultures.

Table 9.1 International norms and political cultures

Political system	National political culture characteristics	Impact of international norms
Established democracy	• Entrenched habits of organization and cooperation among most people • High level of trust among groups – vital to sustenance of democratic institutions and procedures • Political pluralism with numerous independent political parties, NGOs and think-tanks • Much social capital	• Norms about politics and political values underpin political cultures of established democracies
Transitional democracy	• Established political culture that may hinder or impede the development of pro-democracy political culture • Pluralism tends to be fragile, with political parties often forming and disbanding • Civil society organizations are insecurely rooted, often heavily dependent on outside donors • Little social capital	• Norms about politics and political values underpin political cultures of transitional democracies. Over time, they can be remade – partly in response to external influences
Non-democracy	• Denial of meaningful political voice for citizens • Power in hands of small elite group • Regime legitimacy measured in economic terms not in relation to degree of accountability or representativeness • Patrimonialism (that is, personalistic rule) • Little or no social capital	• Norms about politics and political values underpin political cultures of non-democracies. External influences are generally uninfluential

Case Studies: FRG, CEE, Mexico, and Malaysia and Singapore

Analyses of political culture draw attention to presumed sets of attitudes held by citizens towards the political regimes under which they live. It is plausible to argue that globalization can affect individual political regimes, for example, the influence of civil society on existing regimes can be affected by external influences. This 'implies some fairly spontaneous activity at the societal level, or a potential for that'. But this tells us little if anything about the influence of globalization on political cultures. The remaking of political culture may imply a fundamental change that can occur only in certain circumstances, for example, a democratic framework. But to remake political culture takes time. In the meantime, a country's 'political culture is bound to comprise both (being) remade elements and those deriving from the past' (Pridham 2000: 248).

Pro-democracy international norms began to be spread after World War II, especially by states, including the USA, and groups of states, such as the EU. Two general methods were employed. On the one hand, Western countries encouraged transitional democracies to democratize further by material inducements, such as foreign aid. Many cash-strapped transitional countries found it difficult to resist such encouragement – but this does not imply that their political cultures necessarily changed rapidly (Elgström 2000). A second method, employed by the EU in relation to putative new members, was to hold out the possibility of enrolment in the Western European 'club' if they adopted certain agreed political and economic norms. Such efforts were augmented by specific events, including the fall of the Berlin Wall in November 1989, influential in forming an international climate conducive to the development of democracy and pro-democracy political cultures (Ottaway 2003).

To transform a political culture from a non-democratic to a pro-democratic state is an often overlapping five-stage process:

1   *The formal level of regime change.* This first stage involves drawing up a new constitution followed by democratic political institutions, including 'free and fair' elections. External encouragement is very important at this stage, linked to granting or withholding foreign aid dependent on the successful creation of democratically accountable institutions.
2   *Political actors and policy amendment.* This stage is marked by gradual development and consolidation of pro-democracy norms and values among political elites and, as time goes on, among the mass of ordinary citizens.
3   *Economic transformation.* At this stage there may well be an elite/popular split, although it is important for elite and popular views to be in accord. If only elites embrace externally encouraged international norms – such as economic liberalization via structural adjustment programmes – without popular support, then 'they may encounter resistance from a domestic populace that views the norm's tenets as inconsistent with their prevailing values' (Cortell and Davies 2000: 74–5).
4   *Civil society.* Building a strong, united civil society reflects the amount of social capital and is crucial for the development of a pro-democracy political culture.
5   *National identity.* The final stage is where the characteristics of a pro-democracy national political culture are in place, from which no significant political group demurs.

In this section, we examine four case studies:

• the Federal Republic of Germany, showing the evolution over time of a pro-democracy political culture;
• transitional CEE countries, indicating how countries emerging from communism have variable political characteristics and a variety of political cultures;
• Mexico, a transitional democracy, whose political culture has become increasingly pro-democracy, partly in response to external encouragement;
• Malaysia and Singapore, non-democracies claiming adherence to 'Asian values' in opposition to what their governments see as Western-inspired attempts to impose 'alien' political cultures via democratization.

The case studies show that the structures and conditions of globalization have varying effects on internal political cultures that are linked to countries' national particularities.

The Federal Republic of Germany (FRG)

No external government, however conventionally powerful, can for long impose on an *unwilling* foreign country its preferred political outcomes, whether a specific political system or, in the longer term, a preferred political culture. Short-term external interventions can of course temporarily dictate what occurs politically within a country – but such arrangements are nearly always characterized by impermanence. Recent examples include attempts by external actors to impose specific kinds of regime change on, inter alia, post-Saddam Iraq, post-Taliban Afghanistan, Haiti and Somalia.

On the other hand, external encouragement can be a factor in the development of a pro-democracy political culture. We noted earlier that political culture has been studied most intensively in the context of established Western democracies. We also saw that Almond and Verba (1963) undertook their research for *The Civic Culture* in both the FRG and Italy in the late 1950s, that is, little more than a decade after their non-democratic regimes ended. Both countries received post-war encouragement, especially from the United States, to develop democratic political systems which, over time, fed into pro-democracy political cultures.

Two domestic factors were crucial for the development of a pro-democracy political culture in the FRG: (1) societal consensus that democracy was better than any alternative non-democratic political arrangement, and (2) relative lack of serious ethnic, religious, regional or class antagonisms/schisms (Haynes 2002: 30, 47). What was the influence of cultural legacies and institutional impacts in this regard? In the FRG the balance between the two shifted in favour of the latter, so that eventually the outcome in terms of remaking the country's political culture was considerable. In other words, the FRG – with no viable democratic tradition before Nazism – was able to overcome an unfavourable cultural legacy and, within a generation, develop an emphatically pro-democracy political culture.

Because of its imperial and Nazi past, the FRG initially appeared to be an unlikely candidate for development of a democratic political culture. Following unification in 1871, over the next century or so, Germany went through a series of 'shock waves':

- rapid industrialization;
- World War I;
- demise of the monarchy;
- economic depression and hyper-inflation in the 1930s;
- rise and swift fall of the Weimar Republic;
- Nazism;
- country disunification in 1945;
- allied occupation of Berlin;
- reunification.

The FRG began life after 1945 with a political culture characterized by considerable popular scepticism about democracy. In a 1951 public opinion survey, West Germans were asked, 'When in this century do you think Germany has been best off?' Only 2 per cent named the current period, while 45 per cent identified the Kaiser's empire before the start of World War I in 1914 as Germany's best period. Another 42 per cent claimed to believe that Germans had lived best under Hitler before the start of World War II (1933–9). Another survey two years later in 1953 asked: 'Is democracy the best form of government for Germany?' This time, half the respondents said 'yes', illustrating how quickly political opinions and perspectives can change. However, a third survey, also carried out in the 1950s, revealed that more than a third of West Germans would have supported a bid by a new Nazi party to seize power or would have remained indifferent if it occurred. Another third favoured restoring the Kaiser's monarchy. At this time, 'clearly, democracy had to prove itself to most West Germans'. However, during the late 1950s and 1960s, mass attitudes shifted considerably in favour of democracy. Nine-tenths of West Germans said that democracy was the best form of government for Germany by 1970, a transformation explicable at least in part by the FRG's economic successes. This indicates that in 25 years – between 1945 and 1970 – West Germany had undergone both political and economic transformation, as well as 'a thoroughgoing transformations of its political culture' (Sodaro 2001: 519–20).

The profound shift in the FRG's political culture was characterized by several developments: (1) popular support for democracy was bolstered by the country's political institutions; (2) there was considerable political stability; (3) the main political parties shared opinions about political and economic fundamentals; and (4) there was considerable economic achievement over time. Crucial to the development of a pro-democracy political culture in the FRG was external encouragement, initially from the USA and latterly from the EU, especially in the crucial decade after Nazism.

Central and Eastern Europe (CEE)

What was the impact of globalization on the political cultures of post-communist countries in CEE? Przeworski (1995: 3) has drawn attention to the processes of change via globalization in the region. This can be seen in relation to the former communist states' 'strategy of adopting forms of organisation (democracy, market economies and consumption-oriented culture) already existing elsewhere, in the advanced capitalist world' (Pridham 2000: 286–7). The spread of economic liberalization and democracy occurred in a group of countries characterized by one key fact: imposition of externally imposed communist governments for decades.

From the late 1980s, following the political transitions in CEE countries, the EU emerged as the most central and influential external actor. The United States, on the other hand, was in the background. The allure of the EU with its political, economic and cultural norms and allure supplied what Pridham calls 'systemic constraints' for many CEE countries. Many countries in CEE showed a strong interest in EU links even during the early stages of their transitions. 'This had to do with their regime changes being much more demanding and consequently their greater need to look outwards for support' (Pridham 2000: 298).

According to Pridham (2000: 299), the EU exerted six broad types of influence on democratization in CEE applicant countries: (1) 'symbolic', (2) 'the prospect of eventual EU entry', (3) 'the gradual involvement of political elites in the EU institutional framework', (4) 'pressure exerted from the application of democratic conditionality by the EU', (5) 'participation of political and economic elites and groups in transnational networks' and (6) 'binding policy commitments from adoption of the *acquis communitaire*'. In sum, EU accession would demand measurable shifts in political culture at both elite and popular levels, implying widespread respect for the post-communist rule of law, acceptance of the authority of the European Court of Justice in legislative processes and principles of representative government tested in relation to participation in the Council of Ministers and the European Parliament.

'Engagement with democracy-building was particularly true of east-Central Europe and some Balkan countries such as Bulgaria and Romania' (Pridham 2000: 292–3). It is important to note that prior to the imposition of communist rule, countries in CEE had a variety of political cultures, albeit with little or no history of democratic tradition in most cases. Post-communist transitions appeared to be influenced by how groups reconcile ideas and practices common in the international community with their long-held domestic beliefs and customs. In some cases – for example, Poland, Hungary and the Czech Republic – Western European ideas and practices appeared to complement specific local groups' organizational cultures. Consequently, political activists were receptive to them. The point is that 'if ideas and practices help solve specific problems (such as increasing a candidate's electoral chances), local activists are particularly likely to adopt them'. On the other hand, activists and 'NGOs tend to reject, based on a "logic of appropriateness", ideas and practices that appear to compete with local customs and beliefs' (Mendelson and Glenn 2002: 223).

Such influences were notable before the end of communist rule. During the 1980s, various state and non-state actors encouraged both political opposition and, by extension, democratization. For many citizens, Western media, particularly shortwave radio, were one of the few reliable sources of information about politics in the communist regimes and abroad. Foreign radio broadcasts helped to publicize and generate support for the activities of opposition groups. The provision of this sometimes more truthful news and information was, Sadowski (1993) shows, an important factor in constructing or 'reconstructing a culture of criticism, independent thinking, and free discourse', all of which are crucial to the development of pro-democracy political cultures. In addition, 'Western organizations and governments also provided essential material, moral, and political support that helped pioneering human rights and other autonomous organizations press out the boundaries of political opposition and resistance to communist rule' (Diamond 1993b: 422). Finally, Western countries strengthened the aspiration for democracy by providing a model of a successful, democratic alternative to the failed communist system.

It is important to note however that within CEE countries themselves, responses to external stimuli differed from country to country. For example, Dryzek and Holmes (2002: 127) found that many Ukrainians believe that: 'Things like freedom of speech, equality, a free press, participation, minority rights, the right to education, and majority rule are not especially important.' In addition, Diamond (2002) showed that in 1998 not only in Ukraine but also in Russia and Belarus, only a minority rejected 'all authoritarian alternatives'. Further evidence is provided in case studies collected in Batt and Wolczuk's (2002) book. They emphasize how various CEE states (Hungary, Poland,

Estonia, Slovakia, Romania and Ukraine) can still be regarded as in a transitional phase, as they attempt to both maintain and strengthen regional identities by means of new or revised local government structures. The book also indicates that while CEE states' post-communist experiences vary, two key themes link them. First, while it would be wrong to suggest that a nation's political future is wholly determined by its past, it is apparent that previous cultural and social experiments do have a bearing on the point of departure for modern reform programmes. Second, desire to 'return to Europe' acted as a catalyst for change on a number of different levels. In other words, institutional changes were encouraged and nurtured by the collective desire to join the EU. But this implied necessary shifts in political culture, including acceptance of EU economic, political and cultural norms (Pridham 2000: 294–7; Dalton 2002: 205–6; Diamond 2002).

In conclusion, CEE countries underwent democratization at a time – the 1990s – when the political weight of European organizations (above all, the EU) and transnational networks were the most developed they had ever been. It is important to note, however, that their task of system-building (political, economic and in many cases also national) was both immense and unprecedented in scale. Over time, the types of influence that the EU exerted on the democratization of CEE applicant countries appeared, at least in some cases, to be beneficial both for democratic consolidation and development of appropriate political cultures.

Mexico

The Economist magazine reported in mid-2001 the results of a Latinobarómetro[1] survey in 17 Latin American countries; all had undergone processes of democratization since the 1980s. Based on responses from more than 18,000 interviews, it revealed that 'Latin Americans are wavering in their support for democracy; they are disillusioned with privatisation; but they are in favour of free-trade agreements, both among their own countries and with the United States'. The implication is that, as in some CEE countries, Latin America's equally young democracies have not yet necessarily proved themselves for many of their citizens. Commenting on the survey's findings, Marta Lagos, director of Latinobarómetro, noted that 'the more people think the economy is tied to democracy, the more democracy is vulnerable' (*The Economist* 2001a).

Remaking political culture takes time. In the short to medium term, the political culture of transitional countries in Latin America – such as Mexico – is almost certain to include both 'remade' elements, as well as those that have their roots in the past. While Mexico moved from authoritarian to democratic rule over the 1990s, the country is still in a transitional political phase characterized by a plastic political culture (Ottaway 2003: 7).

To remake Mexico's political culture necessarily implies fundamental changes, including elite and popular adherence to democratic institutions, rules and norms. A second Latinobarómetro survey (August 2002) revealed that between 1995 and 2002 popular

---

[1] 'Latinobarómetro is a non-profit organisation based in Santiago, Chile, which has carried out an annual survey of opinions, attitudes and values in Latin America since 1995. The poll was taken by local opinion-research companies in 17 Latin American countries, and involved 18,135 interviews, which were conducted in April and May 2001. The margin of error varied from 2.8% to 5%' (<http://www.economist.com/PrinterFriendly.cfm?Story_ID=709760>).

support for democracy in Mexico increased by 14 percentage points, from 49 per cent to 63 per cent (*The Economist* 2001b).

The current support for democracy claimed by nearly two-thirds of adult Mexicans may come as a surprise when we note that a study of Mexico's political attitudes in the 1980s claimed that, despite liberal constitutional trappings, the country had an authoritarian political culture (Booth and Seligson 1993: 110). Earlier we noted that in the late 1950s, Mexico was a case study in Almond and Verba's *The Civic Culture*. We saw that they categorized respondents as 'parochials', 'subjects' or 'participants', dependent on respondents' differing political attitudes. 'Parochials' were said to expect virtually nothing from the political system, 'subjects' looked to government for outputs and 'participants' were most likely to be 'actively involved on the input side of government' (Almond and Verba 1963: 17–19). 'Participants' were 'expected to form the basis of civil society and hence to lay the foundations of democracy' (Klesner 2001b: 762).

Few 'participants' could be found in Mexico in the late 1950s: less than 10 per cent. A quarter of respondents were classified as 'parochials', and two-thirds as 'subjects'. Klesner (2001b: 763) comments that 'Mexicans who tended to see themselves as "subjects" instead of "participants" were simply reacting rationally to the clientelist institutions that had been created in the 1930s and 1940s.' More generally, structural characteristics of Mexico's authoritarian political culture were, for decades, conducive to the entrenchment of authoritarian rule. The once mighty PRI long had an overwhelmingly important role in public life. Its influence could be noted in terms of its control over many aspects of the public realm, including education, medical care and the media. However, a result was that Mexico's political culture was remarkably supine, with most ordinary people apparently in thrall to the party.

Many Mexicans' perception of the political present is strongly informed by experiences of the past under PRI rule. At the end of the 1990s, Latinobarometer surveys indicate, 95 per cent of Mexicans had little or no confidence in many state institutions, including the judiciary and the police. According to Turner and Martz (1997), the figures for Mexico were the lowest among the eight Latin American countries they surveyed. It seems likely that the perceptions that many Mexicans had about the state's inadequacies were linked to the inability of successive PRI governments to disseminate developmental gains among ordinary people in the country.

It is important to note that Mexicans were not necessarily especially tolerant of authoritarian rule and its associated political culture under PRI rule. Booth and Seligson (1993: 111) conducted a survey in the early 1980s on the political views of 430 urban Mexicans in six northern industrial cities and Guadalajara, Mexico's second largest city. They found that the views of those surveyed 'compared quite favorably to a 1978 sample of New Yorkers, with average intensity of support for democratic liberties scores at levels similar to or only slightly below the New York City respondents'. Such sentiments no doubt informed the significant opposition challenge to and a large vote against the PRI in both the 1988 and 1994 presidential elections (around 50 per cent in each year), culminating in the election of a non-PRI candidate, Vicente Fox, in 2000. Fox's election led to new focuses on deregulation, competition and a balanced budget, together with an ambitious social agenda. This included a pledge to double spending on education, increase subsidies for farmers and build many health clinics.

What of the impact of globalization on Mexico's political culture? The influence of both the USA and NAFTA are significant in this regard. Most observers agree that

Mexico's democratization was strongly encouraged by the United States government, with membership of NAFTA the prize. However, it is often noted that Mexico is one of the countries most affected by free trade policies since the early 1990s, with an associated rise in extreme poverty increase. Mexico is the home of the anti-system Zapatistas, a revolutionary group based in Chiapas state, fervent opponents of NAFTA (Vidal 2003b: 13). A Zapatista rebel stated in the mid-1990s: 'We have nothing, absolutely nothing – not decent shelter, nor land, nor work, nor health, nor food nor education. We do not have the right to choose freely and democratically our officials. We have neither peace nor justice' (quoted in Vidal 1996).

Successive governments in Mexico came to regard NAFTA as the best available means to stimulate increased economic growth. Despite initial doubts, the PRI government was willing to reform both political and economic systems in order to win the support of the US Congress for Mexico's membership of NAFTA. Founded in 1994, NAFTA was the United States' regional blueprint for an economic-strategic relationship it wished to build as part of its post-cold war global strategy of democratization and economic liberalization. However, both goals were politically explosive in Mexico, as they were likely to undermine PRI hegemony built on central control and state monopoly (Philip 1999: 5). In sum, Fox's election led to a raft of policies informing a reformist programme that was not only designed to address the enormous disparity between rich and poor Mexicans but also to build Mexico's economic interactions with other North American countries, especially the United States. It remains to be seen to what extent Mexico develops and sustains a pro-democracy political culture.

Malaysia and Singapore

The final case studies seek to illustrate that political cultures are not only being remade by globalization according to Western, pro-democracy norms. We have seen that to remake political culture is a lengthy business, perhaps spanning a generation. Thus for long periods of time political cultures may be transitional, including both '(being) remade elements and those deriving from the past' (Pridham 2000: 248). Most wealthy countries are established democracies; many economically poor countries are not. In between there is what might be called a 'political transition zone', including countries in the 'middle economic stratum [that] are most likely to transit to democracy, and most countries that transit to democracy will be in this stratum' (Huntington 1991: 31).

In many East and Southeast Asian countries, sustained economic growth in the 1970s and 1980s was followed by an economic malaise manifested in the region's financial crisis of 1997–8. This event encouraged many opposition politicians and democrats to demand fundamental political reforms. But whereas international support for pro-democracy actors, most notably from the government of the United States and from the EU, had encouraged local democrats in their demands for reforms in CEE and Latin America, the events of 1997–8 led to only muted pressure to democratize from such actors. It may be that both the USA and the EU, concerned with forging a free market framework as the basis of globalization, were more interested in political and economic stability than democratization in East and Southeast Asia.

We can see from this that political globalization had two main manifestations in the 1990s. On the one hand, there was a strong trend towards democratization and democracy in some regions, encouraged by various Western actors. On the other hand, there was a strong rearguard action, centred on non-democratic East and Southeast Asian countries, including Malaysia and Singapore. Their governments were in the forefront of arguments to the effect that liberal democracy was suited to some countries but not theirs; instead, their political cultures were rooted in what were known as 'Asian values'. Such claims reflect the contention that Western support of liberal democracy is an international norm that is sometimes likened to 'cultural imperialism or colonialism and [can] cause domestic resistance or rejection' (Cortell and Davies 2000: 73).

Prime Minister Muhammad Mahathir of Malaysia and Lee Kuan Yew, a former Singaporean prime minister, were key proponents of the argument that liberal democracy is actually 'culturally alien' to their countries. They claimed that their countries have different kinds of political cultures and histories that, while differing from each other in precise details, reflect an important collective idea: rather than the individual, the community is of most societal, political and economic significance. This claim is at the heart of the concept of a generic '(East) Asian political culture', that is said to embody various values – including, harmony, consensus, unity and community. They are said to differ significantly from those of 'Western political culture' and its individualistic, self-seeking values.

In Mahathir's view, Malaysia's society is richly imbued with such Asian social and political values. As a result, he claims, government is seen by society as legitimate only when it reflects values associated with the community's particular cultural contours. The political consequence is that the claimed appropriateness of Western-style liberal democracy, with its individualistic premises, is seen as misplaced because it overlooks Malaysia's different, community-orientated, national characteristics. Instead, national political institutions and practices of democracy must necessarily be designed to 'fit' local cultural and social values. The result is said to be a national style of politics based on consensus rather than the conflictual adversarial approach characterizing Western political competition (Maravall 1995: 16).

Like Malaysia, Singapore possesses a distinctive centralized, authoritarian, statist, pragmatic, rational and legalistic political culture (Haynes 2001a: 82, 87). While possessing superficial trappings of British-style institutions, such as parliamentary procedure and bewigged judges, Singapore, its leaders keep reiterating, is not a Western country with a Western political system. Although elections are held regularly, they have never led to a change of leadership. Citizens do not expect that political parties would alternate in power. Nor is there a tradition of civil liberties or of limits to state power. The rulers of Singapore, a former British colony with a multiethnic population, and a country independent only by default, have assumed no popular consensus on the rules of or limits to political action. In sum, Singapore is a city-state with a small group of authoritarian guardians who use their superior knowledge to advance the prosperity of the state and to bring benefits to what they considered a largely ignorant and passive population. Under such circumstances, there is scant opportunity for a pro-democracy political culture to develop; nor do Western-style international norms have much impact, largely because Singapore is too wealthy to require Western aid.

Conclusion

To understand a country's political culture requires an assessment, primarily, of domestically generated historical and ideological factors coupled with the lesser, but still potentially significant, impact of external actors and factors, including globalization. The main findings of this chapter are, first, that political cultures evolve – often over long periods – and cannot as a result be imposed from outside.

Second, after World War II, various state and non-state actors influenced political developments, especially in certain European and Latin American countries. As a result, perceptions of both elites and citizens were influenced by propagation of certain international norms. On the other hand, this does not imply that attempts by external actors to impose their political preferences on weaker ones is necessarily successful. Initially, as the cold war developed, political systems characterized both by direct political as well as more covert interference in the fortunes of domestic actors, worked to the particular disadvantage of left-wing political parties and groups. This led to a somewhat restricted version of parliamentary democracy in Greece. Later, however, Greece was able to 'disengage from the American embrace'. This opened the way not only for Greece, but also for Spain and Portugal, to develop a 'multilateral relationship with the EC that helped to foster democratic rule' (Pridham 2000: 289).

Third, the impact of external influences on a polity's political culture will be most significant when it dovetails with pre-existing indigenous ideas, as the external influence can interact with and help build the organization of society.

Fourth, the degree of popular adherence to certain political cultures – especially pro-democracy political cultures – is linked to economic prosperity. Pro-democracy political cultures most obviously develop in polities enjoying relatively broadbased economic success, with most citizens experiencing increased prosperity. Linz and Stepan (1996) note that increasing welfare expenditures from the mid-1970s in Spain, Portugal and Greece helped to develop their pro-democracy political cultures, with governments using increased tax revenues to expand social policies and enhance societal welfare. Przeworski (1986) points out in addition that maintenance of adequate systems of public assistance has a positive influence on democratic consolidation and the development of a pro-democracy political culture. This is because it both reduces the inequalities among different social groups (a factor said to promote democratic collapse) and helps to curb social unrest.

10
Regime Change
and Democratization

Outside Western Europe and North America, there were few democratically elected governments until recently. Instead, many countries had various kinds of authoritarian regime – including, military, one-party, no-party and personalist dictatorships. During the 1980s and 1990s, the shift from unelected to elected governments was deemed so significant that Huntington (1991) gave it a name: the 'third wave of democracy'. As a result, Waylen (2003: 157) notes, 'competitive electoral politics is now being conducted in a record number of countries. In response to the varied processes of transition, the study of democratization has now dominated comparative politics for nearly 20 years.' A key focus in this regard is to explain varied democratization outcomes. Many analyses point to the importance primarily of domestic factors, although external considerations are also widely noted. In this chapter we examine the impact of the third wave of democracy on comparative political analysis, compare the significance of external and internal factors in this regard, and conclude by focusing upon three transitional democracies – South Africa, Indonesia and Russia – in order to assess comparatively the significance of both internal and external factors in their democratization processes from the early 1990s.

The Third Wave of Democracy

The third wave of democracy followed two earlier 'waves'. The first took place during the last decades of the nineteenth and the first years of the twentieth century, when various European and North American countries democratized. The second began directly after World War II, when several countries, including Italy, Japan and West Germany, moved from authoritarian to democratic rule.

The third wave began with the democratization of three Southern European countries – Greece, Portugal and Spain – in the mid-1970s. Following this, in the 1980s and 1990s, numerous authoritarian regimes in Latin America, Eastern Europe, Asia and Africa also democratized. The extent of these changes is shown by the fact that in 1972 only a quarter of countries had democratically elected governments. Twenty years later, in the early 1990s, the proportion had grown to over 50 per cent, and by the early 2000s, around 75 per cent of the world's nearly 200 countries had democratically elected governments. The situation over time is summarized in Table 10.1.

Explaining the shift from authoritarian to democratic rule

Many scholars suggest that the process of democratization occurs in four stages: (1) political liberalization, (2) collapse of authoritarian regime, (3) democratic transition

Table 10.1 'Free', 'partly free' and 'not free' countries, 1972–2002

	Numbers of 'free' countries	Numbers of 'partly free' countries	Numbers of 'not free' countries
1972	43	38	69
1982	54	47	64
1992	75	73	38
2002	89	56	47

Source: Freedom House 2003. The terms 'free', 'partly free' and 'not free' correspond respectively to the terms used in this book: established democracy, transitional democracy and non-democracy.

and (4) democratization consolidation. *Political liberalization* is the process of reforming authoritarian rule. *Collapse of the authoritarian regime* refers to the stage when a dictatorship falls apart. *Democratic transition* is the material shift to democracy, commonly marked by the democratic election of a new government. *Democratic consolidation* is the process of impressing upon both elites and citizens that democracy is the best way of 'doing' politics.

The four stages are complementary and can overlap. For example, political liberalization and transition can happen simultaneously, while aspects of democratic consolidation can appear when certain elements of transition are barely in place or remain incomplete. Or they may even be showing signs of retreating. On the other hand, it is nearly always possible to observe a concluded transition to democracy. This is when a pattern of behaviour developed ad hoc during the stage of regime change becomes institutionalized, characterized by admittance of political actors into the system – as well as the process of political decision-making – according to previously established and legitimately coded procedures.

Until then, absence of or uncertainty about these accepted 'rules of the democratic game' make it difficult to be sure about the eventual outcome of political transitions. This is because the transition dynamics revolve around strategic interactions and tentative arrangements between actors with uncertain power resources. Key issues include: (1) defining who is legitimately entitled to play the political 'game', (2) the criteria determining who wins and loses politically and (3) the limits to be placed on the issues at stake. What chiefly differentiates the four stages of democratization is the degree of uncertainty prevailing at each moment. For example, during regime transition *all* political calculations and interactions are highly uncertain. This is because political actors find it difficult to know what their precise interests are and which groups and individuals would most usefully be allies or opponents.

During transition, powerful, often inherently undemocratic, political players, such as the armed forces and/or elite civilian supporters of the exiting authoritarian regime, characteristically divide into what Huntington (1991) calls 'hard-line' and 'soft-line' factions. 'Soft-liners' are relatively willing to achieve negotiated solutions to the political problems, while 'hard-liners' are unwilling to arrive at solutions reflecting compromise between polarized positions. Democratic consolidation is most likely when 'soft-liners' triumph because, unlike 'hard-liners', they are willing to find a compromise solution.

A consolidated democracy is often said to be in place when political elites, political groups and the mass of ordinary people accept the formal rules and informal understandings that determine political outcomes: that is, 'who gets what, where, when, and how'. If achieved, it signifies that groups are settling into relatively predictable positions involving politically legitimate behaviour according to generally acceptable rules. More generally, a consolidated democracy is characterized by normative limits and established patterns of power distribution. Political parties emerge as privileged in this context because, despite their divisions over strategies and their uncertainties about partisan identities, the logic of electoral competition focuses public attention on them and compels them to appeal to the widest possible clientele. In addition, 'strong' civil societies are thought to be crucial for democratic consolidation, in part because they can help keep an eye on the state and what it does with its power. In sum, democratic consolidation is said to be present when all major political actors take for granted the fact that democratic processes dictate governmental renewal (Diamond 2002).

Observers have also noted that, despite numerous relatively free and fair elections over the last two decades in many formerly authoritarian countries, in most cases ordinary people continue to lack ability to influence political outcomes (Haynes 2001a). This may be because small groups of elites – whether civilians, military personnel or a combination – not only control national political processes but also manage more widely to dictate political conditions (Gel'man 2003). Under such conditions, because power is still focused in relatively few elite hands, political systems have narrow bases from which most ordinary people are, or feel, excluded. This can be problematic because, by definition, a democracy should not be run by and for the few, but should signify popularly elected government operating in the broad public interest.

In sum, during the third wave of democracy, increased numbers of governments came to power via the ballot box – yet not all of then have strong democratic credentials.

Domestic Factors

The third wave of democracy is a politically significant example of globalization. However, many observers agree that focusing on external factors alone is insufficient to get a full picture of democratic outcomes. It is also important to consider a country's internal political characteristics and assess how they interact with external factors in different political contexts. The democratization literature focuses on three main domestic factors: civil society, social capital and political society.

Civil society

Most examples of democratic transition during the third wave reflect the importance of consistent pressure from 'below' on authoritarian regimes (Rueschemeyer et al. 1992; Haynes 1997, 2001a; Törnquist 1999; Pridham 2000). Such pressure, focused through civil society organizations, not only helps push the limits of newly created political space but can also be instrumental in the process of democratization – especially when civil society links up with representative political parties. In such cases, pressure forces non-democratic governments to liberalize, articulate political reform agendas and, eventually, allow relatively free and fair multiparty elections.

The term, 'civil society' crept quietly and largely unexamined into the literature on political economy in the 1980s. It began to be used in relation to the discourse of opposition leaders and groups in many non-democratic countries, especially the communist countries of CEE. However, civil society is not a new term. Often associated with the German philosopher Hegel (1770–1831), the term began to appear in the literature on Western political philosophy from the time of the emergence of the modern nation-state in the eighteenth century. However, in contemporary usage, 'civil society' refers to 'associations and other organized bodies which are intermediate between the state and the family' (Bealey 1999: 59). These include: labour unions, social movements, profes-sional associations, student groups, religious bodies and the media. Collectively, such entities are thought to help maintain a check on state power and its totalizing tenden-cies; ideally, they amount to an ensemble of arrangements to advance the socio-political interests of society, with the state and civil society forming mutually effective counterweights (Stepan 1988). 'Sturdy' civil societies nearly always stem from strong societies. For Risse-Kappen (1995a: 22), ' "strong societies" are characterized by a com-parative lack of ideological and class cleavages, by rather "politicized" civil societies which can be easily mobilized for political causes, and by centralized social organiza-tions such as business, labor or churches'. In sum, 'civil society' is a key defender of society's interests against state (over-)dominance.

Civil society organizations are not directly involved in the business of government or in overt political management. But this does not necessarily prevent some from exer-cising their sometimes profound influence on various political issues, from single issues to the characteristics of national constitutions. In CEE, many observers highlight the role of civil society in helping to undermine apparently strong communist regimes that uniformly toppled like dominoes during 1989–91. As Pridham (2000: 222) puts it: 'The dramatic experience of Communist system collapse in [CEE] underlined the role that civil society could play in regime change.'

Three broad categories of civil society are identified in the literature. First, there are *weak civil societies*, characteristic of societies fragmented by ethnic and/or religious divi-sions, and found in many African, Middle Eastern and Central Asian countries. In such examples, civil society is ineffective as a counterweight to state power. This is frequently linked to wider problems of governance, such as inadequate popular participation and lack of governmental transparency and accountability. In such circumstances, govern-ments are typically adept at buying off or crushing expressions of discontent. Overall, as Villalön (1995: 24) notes, these circumstances reflect the failure or inability 'of social groups to organize in such a way as to defend and promote their interests', while seri-ously reducing societal capacity to 'counter the state's hegemonic drives'.

Relatively strong civil societies are found in various East and Southeast Asian coun-tries, including South Korea and Taiwan, and some Latin American and CEE nations, including Argentina, Chile and the Czech Republic. *Strong civil societies* are found in most established democracies, for example in India, Germany, Sweden and France. In both categories, civil societies are both vibrant and robust; with numerous civil rights organizations, social movements and local protest groups. One of the differences between 'strong' and 'relatively strong' civil societies is the length of time over which they have developed. Most Western European and North American countries have been states for lengthy periods, and their civil societies have also had a long time to develop, in some cases hundreds of years. On the other hand, Latin American and East Asian countries, while perhaps having been states for long periods, have nevertheless demo-cratized much more recently (Shin 1999; O'Donnell 1994). Countries with such civil societies are also normally nations not seriously divided by ethnic and/or religious schisms. They also tend to be relatively industrialized and urbanized, with well-organized trade unions and politically active working classes.

In sum, in relation to the state, civil society's effectiveness is often linked to:

- societal – especially ethnic and religious – diversity, reflecting the quantity of social capital;
- the level of economic development, urbanization and industrialization.

Social capital

Civil society is said to be most effective when it builds upon society's store of social connections, that is, its *social capital* (Axford 2002a: 134–43). Whereas *human* capital comprises formal education and training, and *economic* capital is material and financial resources, *social* capital is the 'interpersonal trust that makes it easier for people to do things together, neutralise free riders, and...agree on sanctions against non-performing governments' (Törnquist 1999: 95). Robert Putnam (1993) has analysed the importance of social capital in helping build and sustain democracy and argues that the level of trust in a society varies according to the vibrancy of associational life. He suggests that the stock of social capital from both extensive and growing membership in voluntary associations is likely to promote the deepening of democracy (Putnam 1999; Shin 1999: 132). Portes and Zhou (1992) identify two main relational characteristics of social capital: first, what they call 'bonded solidarity', that is, the sense of common nationhood and cultural identity which helps focus group resources. Second, 'enforceable trust' that controls the mutual assistance supplied and demanded, permitting a higher degree of resource-sharing than would be conceivable through more informal channels. This 'bank' of social capital is likely to be undermined by:

- inefficient government performance;
- authoritarian regimes that frown on the growth of societal solidarity;
- widespread societal hardship;
- social disintegration, due in part to development shortfalls.

Under such circumstances, it will be very difficult or impossible to build recognizably democratic political systems.

Political society

To take the next steps from the collapse of authoritarianism, through democratic transition to arrive at consolidated democracy, *political society* needs to be actively involved at every stage. This is because to build a democratic polity requires a great deal of serious thought and action about core institutions – including political parties, elections, electoral rules, political leadership, intra-party alliances and legislatures and most of the relevant work is carried out by political society actors. We should note that while political society is analytically separate from civil society, the two are linked. Expressed through political society, civil society can constitute itself politically to help select governments and monitor their performance in office.

Political society is the 'arena in which the polity specifically arranges itself for political contestation to gain control over public power and the state apparatus' (Stepan 1988: 3). Political parties are the main component of political society. Chances of democracy taking root, Sartori (1991) argues, are bolstered when there are relatively few, not ideologically polarized, political parties competing for power. Autonomous, democratically organized political parties can help to keep the personal power aspirations of political leaders in check. Morlino (1998) argues that such political parties are a crucial key to democratic consolidation, especially when a pervasive pro-democracy legitimacy does not prevail during democratic transition. He also contends that the more rapidly the party spectrum forms during transition, then the more likely is eventual democratic consolidation. When party systems become institutionalized in this way, parties typically orient themselves towards the goal of winning elections through choate appeals to voters. But when the party structure is only slowly established, then citizens may respond better to personalistic appeals from populist leaders rather than to those of parties. This scenario tends to favour the former, who may attempt to govern without bothering to establish and develop solid institutions underpinning their rule.

The main point is that institutionalizing party systems matters a great deal, as they are much more likely to help sustain democracy and to promote effective governance than the likely alternative: amorphous party systems dominated by populist leaders. An institutionalized party system can help engender confidence in the democratic process in four main ways. First, it can help moderate and channel societal demands into an institutionalized environment of conflict resolution. For example, in both India and Costa Rica, the party system helped over time to prevent 'landed upper class[es] from using the state to repress protests' (Rueschemeyer et al. 1992: 281). Second, it can serve to lengthen the time horizons of actors because it provides electoral losers with the means periodically to mobilize resources for later rounds of political competition. Third, an effective party system can help prevent disenchanted groups' grievances from spilling over into mass street protests, likely to antagonize elites and their military allies and help facilitate a return to authoritarian rule ('the need for strong government'). Finally, an effective party system, linked to a capable state, can be important in helping imbue the mass of ordinary people with the idea that the political system is democratically accountable.

In sum, chances of democratization are enhanced when there is: (1) a strong civil society, (2) a relative extensive amount of social capital and (3) a solid political society, with a cohesive party system.

External Factors

Much analytical attention is devoted to processes of democratization at the level of the nation-state. It is also noted that the deepening of globalization after the cold war has focused attention on democratization as a process that cannot be assessed by looking at internal factors alone. As a result, most political scientists would now accept that political outcomes within a polity can be affected by external actors. For example, at the very least, democratization requires that no foreign power, hostile to this development, inter-feres in the political life of a country with the intention of subverting the political system. Whitehead (1993) argues that examples of democratization during the third wave indi-cate that the influence of external actors is always secondary to domestic factors, while Huntington (1991) suggests that such actors can hasten or retard but not *fundamentally* influence – at least not for long – domestic political outcomes.

Three sets of external factor can be noted in relation to regime change and democratization during the third wave of democracy: background factors, state actors and non-state actors.

Background factors

The influence of generally favourable or unfavourable geostrategic circumstances in relation to regime change and democratization are sometimes referred to as 'back-ground factors' in the democratization literature (Haynes 2002). This is not a new phenomenon, and the significance of background factors has been noted in relation to regime change throughout much of the twentieth century. For example, after World War I, President Woodrow Wilson's references to the desirability of 'national self-determination' in relation to the founding of the League of Nations encouraged nation-alists in the Middle East and elsewhere to demand self-rule. A decade later, during the 1930s, tentative moves towards democracy in several Latin American countries could not make headway against a background of regional – and global – economic depres-sion. During the 1960s and 1970s, US fears of the spread of the Cuban revolution led to a regional crackdown on calls for democracy and support for military governments throughout Latin America. More recently, in the 1980s and 1990s, global circumstances (the 'new world order') became more advantageous for democracy, following the unforeseen collapse of Europe's communist regimes. The overall point is that external background factors were influential in relation to regime change in various parts of the world during the twentieth century. However, background factors are never sufficient on their own to lead to fundamental changes of regime unless they interact with what actors in both civil society and political society are doing.

State actors

Pridham (2000: 313–14) notes that 'the scope for external influences to determine the course of regime change . . . has certainly increased over time'. As a result of the influ-ence of globalization, Hague and Harrop (2001: 47) suggest that 'weak states must accept both the external setting, and their vulnerability to it, as a given. The task of their leaders is to manage external influences as best they can.' Jackson (1990: 189, 195) points to the fact that many postcolonial countries are not only weak but also characterized by 'negative sovereignty' with 'adverse civil and socioeconomic conditions'. Conse-quently, they may well be objects of other, stronger, states' policies.

But not even weak states are necessarily powerless in relation to powerful external states. For example, in the 1990s and early 2000s, the only remaining superpower – the

USA – was not able decisively to influence political outcomes in several 'weak' states, including Afghanistan, Haiti, Iraq, Liberia, Nigeria, Somalia and Sudan. All had important 'negative' power resources that lay principally in their potential for 'chaos power', that is, capacity to create or make worse regional problems that powerful countries like the USA might be expected – perhaps in tandem with the UN – to deal with. That is, as we noted in chapter 5, the ability of external actors in this regard is linked to the presence or absence of functioning states in the countries they enter; when functioning states are particularly 'fragile' – as in most of the countries noted above – then even powerful external actors will struggle to implement their preferred policies.

Where functioning states do exist, external state actors may encourage their political preferences through the media of 'political conditionality'. There are two main forms: (1) 'positive' political conditionality to encourage further democratization and (2) 'negative' political conditionality to promote desired political reforms in hitherto unreceptive countries.

From the 1980s, the largest aid donors in quantitative terms – Britain, France, Japan and the USA, plus the Scandinavian countries – sought to encourage both democratization and economic liberalization among countries receiving their aid. These governments, along with the IMF and the World Bank, attached political conditionality to aid, loans and investments to recipient countries. If the latter denied their citizens basic human rights – including democratically elected governments – they would be denied assistance. The reasoning behind political conditionality was partly economic. Western governments and IGOs claimed that economic failures were directly linked to an absence of political accountability. Consequently, without democratization, economic liberalization would not achieve beneficial results.

Crawford (2001) discovered that aid sanctions in the early 1990s effected by the US, Sweden, Britain and the EU were effective in promoting political reform in only 11 of the 29 cases (38 per cent) where they were applied. He concluded that aid penalties were most effective where they added to pressure on governments from internal reform pressures, and that they failed when they met strong resistance from recipient governments or when they threatened donors' strategic or commercial interests.[1] Holland (2002: 132) provides further evidence of the patchy effectiveness of political conditionality. During the 1990s the EU applied sanctions against 13, mainly African, developing countries. Holland notes there were contrasting outcomes in 2 of them: Fiji and Zimbabwe. While the latter's government seemed impervious to external encouragement to reform, Fiji's was not.

The United States is a key player in relation to political conditionality, with both the government and various state-linked bodies, such as the National Endowment for Democracy, actively supporting democratization and economic liberalization (Carothers 2002). This is not a new policy, but has developed from the 1950s. Fifty years ago, newly democratic governments in Latin America, including Costa Rica, Venezuela and Colombia, received financial and diplomatic support from the US government. Later, in the 1970s, US foreign policy goals were reflected in President Carter's human

---

[1] However, it became clear that it was easier to state the desirability of political and economic reforms than it was to achieve them. In many cases, attempts at economic reforms, expressed via structural adjustment programmes, and political reforms, were disappointing.

rights policy, while in the 1980s President Reagan's government promoted democracy as a counter to perceived communist expansionism. In the 1990s President Clinton developed policies linked to political conditionality, a strategy continued by the administration of George W. Bush. During the 1990s alone, successive US governments provided more than $700 million to more than 100 countries to further the course of democratization (Carothers 1997).

Carothers (2002) notes that US state assistance is focused in 'a standard democracy template'. This involves offering financial support to help develop electoral processes and democratic structures, including constitutions and political institutions the rule of law, legislatures, local government structures, political parties, improved civil–military relations and civil society. However, as Leftwich (1993: 612) points out, it takes more than simply external sources of finance to develop democracy. This is because money alone cannot create and embed concrete manifestations of 'good governance', without which democracy cannot develop. This outcome is 'not simply available on order', but requires 'a particular kind of politics . . . to institute and sustain it'.

Superficially, democratization may be encouraged if external actors limit their perusal of the democratic process to elections alone; indeed, some critics argue, international observation of elections seems often the only test used to judge a shift from authoritarian to democratic rule. But when elections are complete, and the attention of the corpus of international observers moves on, 'democracy' is at best partially achieved. Anti-democracy elites may remain powerful, and political systems still have narrow bases, characterized by the survival of 'authoritarian clientelism and coercion' (Karl 1995: 74). In sum, external democracy funding will not be effective if target regimes are able to 'acquire democratic legitimacy internationally without substantially changing their mode of operation' (Lawson 1999: 23).

Critics of political conditionality contend that Western governments and IGOs sometimes focus more on security issues than on democracy. Western aid-donating governments may seek to control the pace of democratization, as 'too much' democracy too quickly can be politically destabilizing and affect the stability of individual countries and their regional neighbours. Aid-donating and aid-recipient governments may share a common interest in limiting the extent of political changes, a theory known as Low Intensity Democracy (LID) (Gills et al. 1993). LID is said to satisfy Western governments' allegedly insincere concerns for democratization in relation to non-democracies by encouraging strictly limited political reform processes. In short, the LID argument is that in some circumstances Western aid-donating governments prefer stable – even if authoritarian – regimes to unstable – even if democratically elected – governments receiving their aid.

An example said to support this contention is that of Uganda, a small country in east Africa (Haynes 2001a). During the 1990s, Uganda's president, Yoweri Museveni, made a successful diplomatic offensive to sell his 'no-party' – that is, not conventionally democratic – political system to the Western aid-donating governments. While neighbouring countries, such as Kenya and Tanzania, were strongly encouraged to adopt multiparty democratic systems, Museveni was able to persuade them that his 'all-inclusive', partyless, system was stable, capable of dealing with violent challenges to the status quo, including from the dreaded Lord's Resistance Army, and willing to make innovative appointments, such as that of Vice-President Specioza Wandira Kazibwe, at the time the highest-ranking female politician in Africa.

In conclusion, it is difficult to be sure about when and why political conditionality 'works', in the sense of demonstrably leading to significant political reforms. It is more clear that aid-donating Western states were often important sources of encouragement to reform at the transition stage of democratization – but less important later. This is because building democratic structure and processes is linked to long-term efforts that are rooted in the development of internal structures and processes.

Non-state actors

A second external source of encouragement for regime change and democratization during the third wave were numerous transnational non-state actors, collectively conceptualized as 'transnational' or 'global' civil society. The concept has three main components. First, like domestic civil society, transnational civil society (TCS) encompasses various, principally non-state, groups with social and/or political goals; groups overtly connected to the state, as well as profit-seeking private entities, such as transnational corporations, are excluded conceptually. Second, such groups interact with each other across state boundaries and are not manipulated by governments. Third, TCS takes a variety of forms, for example, a single INGO with constituent groups in a number of countries, such as Amnesty International or Human Rights Watch, or an organization with a presence in various countries, such as the National Democratic Institute, the National Endowment for Democracy, the American Bar Association and the EU's TACIS and Tempus programmes (Adamson 2002: 191–2; Gagnon 2002: 215–16).

TCS forms an important aspect of the globalization thesis as it challenges the notion that states are always the dominant political and economic actors in both domestic and international contexts. Distinct from the insular concerns of states and most political parties, the 'cosmopolitan' focus of TCS concentrates on direct relationships between people in various countries. The growth of transnational interactions as a result of globalization leads to a growing spread and interchange of ideas and information between constituent groups of TCS. Lipschutz (1992: 390) defines TCS as 'the self-conscious constructions of networks of knowledge and action, by decentred, local actors, that cross the reified boundaries of space as though they were not there'. Thus TCS comprises groups and organizations of individuals in different countries that work together to create dedicated cross-border socio-political communities that pursue common goals via regional or global campaigns and encourage the development of popular, transnational, bottom-up coalitions to challenge unacceptable state policies. TCS therefore seeks the goal of better, more ethical standards of governance by providing the potential for direct links between individuals and groups in different countries.

In Attina's words:

> [T]ransnationalism is not just a matter of individuals and masses who feel conscious of being primary international subjects as they are entitled to civil, political, economic, social and cultural rights by positive international law. In the world system these subjects form *the international social layer* which claims primacy over the diplomatic layer. Today the chances of *social transnationalism* reside in INGOs whose members cross states and assert 'pan-human' interests such as the promotion of human rights, environmental ecology, [and] international development co-operation. (Attina 1989: 350–1; emphasis added)

Attina sees the international system as an agglomeration of different issue areas, including struggles for democracy, human rights, development and environmental protection. What he calls *social transnationalism* refers to the multiple linkages between individuals and groups in different societies yet concerned broadly with the same issues, creating what he labels the *international social layer*. This is a line of contacts between societies operating and underpinning the formal world of supposedly independent states.

Two main questions are asked about TCS:

1 *Why* does it exist?
2 *How* does it manage to influence political outcomes within countries?

Transnational civil society networks are said to exist because their constituents aim for certain goals based on shared conceptions of the public good, known as cosmopolitanism. Networks are bound together not primarily by self-interest but by their shared values, such as a normative belief in the desirability of democracy.

To answer the second question, '*How* does TCS influence political outcomes?', we must recall that a main function of domestic civil society is said to be to try to check the power of the state. But of course there is no world government analogous to those of individual states. Unlike domestic civil society, transnational civil society is not *territorially* fixed, but a field of action whose boundaries can change to suit the requirements of new issues and changing circumstances. In sum, TCS seeks to influence political outcomes by using its network of supporters to apply pressure in various ways on selected governments.

Critics contend that while the concept of TCS is a useful heuristic device to explore the notion of cosmopolitanism and associated interactions, it should be treated with caution. First, domestic civil society serves as a counterweight to the state's power and attempts at hegemony. By analogy, *transnational* civil society should have its counterpoise in a *global* power that imposes, or at least seeks to impose, its hegemony. It is sometimes argued that since the end of the cold war the sole remaining superpower, the USA, has sought to dominate international relations via hegemonic control. However, the logic of this argument is that TCS fights against the USA's attempts to impose its hegemony. Yet, many of the values which US governments perennially claim to hold dear – democracy, human rights, development and security goals – are also those of many groups in TCS.

Second, transnational linkages between various NGOs offer the chance of widespread publicity for their campaigns. The development of heterogeneous networks of diversity and plurality, taking advantage of new communications technologies, helps them tap into global social networks. The increase in cross-border links between such groups has been facilitated by the global communications revolution, expediting the spread and interchange of ideas and information, but it is not self-evident to what degree TCS is influential in terms of amending domestic politics.

Third, critics contend that transnational civil society can be viewed as a device to replicate and perpetuate relationships of domination/subservience that characterize the relationship between powerful and weak countries. The concern is that because the great majority of transnational civil society organizations are located in the rich developed countries, they are not equal partners with counterparts in poorer, developing countries. It is alleged that various US and European groups may seek to perpetuate their views inappropriately in different political contexts with dissimilar philosophies and worldviews.

Conclusion

In conclusion, external state and non-state actors can be politically influential in relation to domestic outcomes in various countries. But their influence will be affected by the domestic characteristics of target countries. In the final section of the chapter we examine these issues in three transitional countries: South Africa, Indonesia and Russia.

Case Studies: South Africa, Indonesia and Russia

Analysts have put forward various arguments about the role of international pressures in fostering democratic development (for a summary, see Huntington 1991). We have already seen that, in relation both to the EU and to NAFTA, sustained and clear external material incentives are believed to have positive impacts on democratization. In this regard, the expectation is that 'consistent and explicit tying of financial and other benefits to progress on democratization can be successful'. While membership in these communities is widely desired by putative member states because of their associated market access and developmental assistance, it is 'explicitly and unwaveringly conditioned on the consolidation of a stable democratic political regime' (Kurtz and Barnes 2002: 529). Consequently, establishment of democratic politics is likelier to be easier in countries – such as, Mexico, Bulgaria, the Czech Republic, Estonia, Latvia, Lithuania, Hungary, Poland, Romania, Slovakia and Slovenia – that are already members of EU or NAFTA or at least have a reasonable hope of becoming a member in the fairly near future.

More generally, Leftwich (1997: 522) has suggested that the pace of democratic progress, especially in aid-hungry countries, would be 'influenced, sometimes to a considerable degree, by various international . . . factors'. However, as Diamond (1999: 273) explains, outcomes have often been disappointing: 'Too many international policy makers have taken electoral democracy as an end state in itself. . . . Some observers seem to assume that democratic consolidation is bound to follow transition in much of the world. . . . These assumptions are false and counterproductive.' The point is that once democratic transitions are complete – typically marked by the first free and fair elections – then both ability and desire of external actors to continue to influence democratization outcomes often appeared to wane. In short, external factors were rarely if ever crucial to outcomes in the post-transition progress of democratization. What is the evidence in this regard in relation to our three case studies, three regionally significant countries that experienced different democratization outcomes: South Africa, Indonesia, and Russia?

South Africa

South Africa's democratization began in 1994. The legacy of apartheid was expected to be a huge impediment to the process, but there are indications of democracy taking root in these inauspicious surroundings. This shows the importance of both internal and external actors and illustrates how the outcome is linked to a range of structural and contingent factors. Apparently unhelpful structural factors – especially half a century of white-dominated, apartheid rule – have been overcome, not least due to the commitment of individual political leaders, especially Nelson Mandela and F. W. de Klerk.

Democratic transition

Prior to the shift to democracy, South Africa was ruled for decades by exclusively white governments. The transformation came in three, swift, stages: collapse of apartheid rule, democratic transition and democratization, encouraged both by domestic and international actors.

Domestically, apartheid had long been embraced by many white South Africans as a way, they believed, to ensure both political order and their domination over blacks and coloureds. But this justification began to evaporate following a serious black insurrection in the mid-1980s. This led to suggestions that the apartheid system, rather than providing order, instead led to serious opposition and unrest, including civil disobedience, strikes and riots. Second, there was pressure from various civil society organizations demanding democracy. Third, the declining economic situation encouraged demands for change. Adding to these domestic sources of pressure were various external factors, including direct (state, non-state, moral, economic, diplomatic, military) pressures, the indirect influence of global economic relations and a key diffusion effect – the collapse of communist rule in CEE.

McGarry (1998: 855) contends that South Africa's democratic transition occurred not because the dominant white group 'came to [its] senses, but because it became sensible for [it], because of the changing environments [it] faced, to reach agreement'. Guelke (1999) argues that President de Klerk's National Party (NP) government calculated that Nelson Mandela's African National Congress (ANC) was seriously weakened by the demise of the USSR and the associated loss of support – to the extent that it would be anxious to negotiate a settlement to the political conflict. A third interpretation of what happened is that the government reached a political settlement, not so much because it became persuaded by the activities of liberal civil society activists (as de Klerk's consistent refusal to apologize for apartheid appeared to indicate), but principally because of changing circumstances at home and abroad.

De Klerk was well aware that the proportion of whites among South Africa's population, which had held steady at around 20 per cent between 1910 and 1960, had dropped to 15 per cent by 1985, and was projected to fall to 11 per cent by 2010. The belief was that this waning demographic presence ultimately would endanger the ability of the white minority to occupy strategic positions in the state apparatus and economy, and to run and staff the institutions of apartheid. McGarry suggests that the looming demographic crisis was an important factor encouraging President de Klerk to put forward the prospect of a negotiated settlement that would be 'indispensable for the survival of the whites as a shrinking minority' (McGarry 1998: 863). In sum, 'South African whites were brought together to negotiate because of a range of domestic crises and diffuse international pressures' (McGarry 1998: 855).

South Africa's democratic reforms were, unusually for Africa, the result of a 'pacted' transition. Under such circumstances, conflicting political groupings 'can neither do without each other nor unilaterally impose their preferred solution on each other if they are to satisfy their respective divergent interests' (Huntington 1991: 141–2). The terms of the pact between the two sides – black and white – involved, at least in the short term, not a majoritarian democracy, but a power-sharing agreement preserving many of the institutions of the former regime and avoiding, critics allege, a meaningful redistribution of economic resources. In addition, transition theory suggests that a precondition for elite-pacted democratization is the preservation of capitalist institutions through the public suppression of 'extremists' and radicals and the incorporation and cooption of political leaders who, if left outside the negotiations, might disturb the balance of the agreement 'moderates' are attempting to construct (Przeworski 1991). Once agreement on the political way forward was reached, however, it proved impossible for the ANC and the NP together to impose their terms on the other interest groups that had been involved in the negotiations. As Kiloh (1997: 318) remarks:

> [f]or a pact to be successful it is necessary for the parties to it to guarantee the support of their followers by buying off or disciplining extremist wings. In South Africa this was not possible as opposition to the agreement came from those excluded by it who had already spun out of control of the two main protagonists.

Contingency was important for the democratic transition in South Africa and, central to this, was the almost unparalleled statesmanship of Nelson Mandela, a man incarcerated for nearly three decades in one of the country's most notorious jails until his release in 1990. The moderate stance of the most important opposition group – Mandela's ANC – was crucial to the government's willingness to negotiate. Although Mandela had suspended the ANC's 'armed struggle' only *after* the start of negotiations, this struggle had actually been rather tame, hardly ever directed against the white population per se. And, unlike the more radical Pan-African Congress, leading ANC figures went out of their way to assuage white fears, reassuring the white community that South Africa belonged to *all* of its citizens. Mandela's moderation also encouraged the development of a desire for limited change among many whites: not only was he a supremely important, although aging politician; there were also fears that his anointed successor, Thabo Mbeki, would be distinctly less accommodating to the white constituency. And, while the ANC insisted on, and ultimately achieved, majority rule, it reassured many whites, including even some among the most conservative Afrikaners, that their culture would be accommodated in the new order. Finally, the ANC's movement away from socialist economics in the late 1980s helped to reassure whites that they could retain private power while releasing their grip on the public variety.

In sum, the pacted transition to democracy in South Africa assuaged fears among many whites that a Mandela-led regime would be 'too radical'; the settlement with the ANC posed little or no existential threat, whether physically or culturally. Taylor (n/d: 9) argues that white and black elites cooperated in helping create a political climate wherein radical changes were impossible.

Political participation and institutions

We noted earlier the positive role of a consolidated party system for democratic progress: it provides a forum for political actors to compete legitimately to exercise the right to control power and the state apparatus (Linz and Stepan 1996). In addition, autonomous political parties can help keep power-holders in check. It is for this reason that political parties are sometimes seen as *the* crucial key to democratic consolidation, especially when, as in South Africa, a pervasive legitimacy has not prevailed during the process of democratization. The point is that the more rapidly the party spectrum forms during transition, then the more likely is progress likely to be towards democratic con-solidation. In inchoate – that is, not consolidated – party systems, voters tend to respond to personalistic appeals rather than party affiliation, favouring populist leaders who govern without attempting to establish solid institutional foundations for their rule.

Following transition, South Africa quickly consolidated its party system under the hegemony of the ANC. The ANC won an emphatic electoral victory in the 1994 elec-tions, winning nearly 63 per cent of the vote on a massive turnout: more than 85 per cent of the voting age population cast their ballots. Mandela was voted president by a unanimous vote of the new Assembly. The ANC underlined its dominance five years later, when, in the 1999 elections, it gained just under two-thirds (66.4 per cent) of the vote. Its dominance was made clear when no other party could muster even 10 per cent of the vote: the leading opposition party, the Democratic Party, achieved slightly more than 9 per cent; the Inkatha Freedom Party managed 8.6 per cent; and the erstwhile governing party, the National Party, gained less than 6 per cent. While the result of the second elections appeared to confirm that South Africa had a party system conducive to democratic consolidation, there were also fears that the dominance of the ANC might lead it to rewrite the constitution – which it could do if it gained two-thirds of the popular vote – and proceed to rule in a manner unhelpful to the well-being of the white minority.

External and economic factors

Apartheid's collapse was facilitated by South Africa's increasingly serious economic position. Strong economic growth in the 1960s and 1970s gave way, in the 1980s and early 1990s, to stagnation and then decline. The declining economic situation was reflected in an average annual *negative* GNP growth during 1985–95 of 1.1 per cent (World Bank 1997: 215). Economic decline, which many believed was linked to the con-tinuation of the apartheid system, because it discouraged both external and domestic investors, threatened whites' material privileges while narrowing governmental options. It not only affected the state's ability to buy off the emerging black middle class but also, given the rising cost of defence expenditures, threw into increasing question the state's ability to defend itself. Finally, international economic sanctions, reinforced by cultural, academic and sporting boycotts, effectively cut whites off from the Western community with which they identified. This made many feel very isolated.

Once in power, ANC plans for large-scale nationalization and redistribution of resources were abandoned and more moderate liberalization of the highly protected South Africa economy substituted. It soon became clear that, following the democratic transition and the installation of the ANC government, many leading figures within the government, including President Mandela, were strongly in favour of a mixed economy. Some observers argue that this strategy was chosen because the 'pro-capitalism' strand within the ANC had become dominant within the party, the spearhead of an emerging black bourgeoisie. Enthusiastically accepting the basic tenets of economic neo-liberalism, the main goal of such people was to acquire a larger slice of the economic cake. However, while a capitalist development strategy suited a powerful group in, and close to, the ANC, who materially benefited from the strategy, it was less clear that many poor black South Africans benefited economically under the arrangements. Sceptics argued that the government's economic policies, with their emphasis on business and the free market, encouraged both corruption and a culture of acquisitiveness at the apex of the government. Such a development, it was feared, was unlikely to be conducive to democratic consolidation, not only reliant on a perception that economic gains were being shared relatively equitably, but also on the institutionalization of a representative political system able to channel and regulate societal demands.

Rather than narrowing the gap between the majority of poor South Africans and the minority rich elite, commentators suggest that democratization led to a widening wealth imbalance in the country. This is most clearly seen in the polarization between a new black elite and the poor black majority: by the early 2000s, that is, more than half a decade after democratization, the richest 20 per cent of blacks acquired nearly two-thirds of all the income brought in by black workers. This led to growing concern, espe-cially among trade union activists, that the government had done too little to redress the legacies of apartheid rule. The government responded, however, that to increase the size of the economic cake so that all South Africans would benefit necessitated a strat-egy which looked to the global picture: to compete, South Africa had to offer an attrac-tive economic context to potential and current foreign investors.

The concern was that, nearly a decade after apartheid rule came to an end, the enor-mous hopes generated by the country's political transition had given way for many poor South Africans to the disappointing realities of frustrated change. The government's response was that nothing would be gained by radical policies of wealth redistribution that would frighten off potential foreign and domestic investors. Mandela's presidential successor, Thabo Mbeki, pointed out that, whatever government was in power, the nature of the country's involvement in the global economy would severely constrain governmental ability to bring about a significant shift in economic resources from the rich minority to the poor majority. South Africa had to compete internationally, which meant that its economy had to be competitive. The problem for political stability however was that although South Africa is the richest African country, at least a quarter of the population – nearly all non-whites – lives below the poverty line. But to provide necessary conditions for large increases in wages and employment which the influential trade union confederation COSATU demanded, it would have been necessary for the economy to grow substantially year-on-year; and this, the government argued, could only be accomplished if businesses and investors remained in the country, and new ones came in.

In conclusion, South Africa's democratic transition in 1994 was the result of both domestic and external pressures. The motivation of the apartheid government to allow democratization, involving the enfranchisement of non-whites, was partly an acknowl-edgment of the importance of the global economy – and South Africa's place within it. But to compete within the global economy it was necessary, the Mandela and Mbeki governments claimed, to put in place conservative economic policies that did not seek to redistribute wealth. Given the skewed nature of the South African economy – with whites receiving the lion's share of available resources – the government's failure to redress the situation led to a decline in support from COSATU, an important trade union ally, which claimed that its conservative policies risked a political crisis.

Indonesia

Following independence from Dutch colonial rule in 1947, Indonesia endured nearly two decades of political instability before power was seized in 1965 by General Suharto. From then, until the latter stood down in 1998, Indonesia experienced decades of political stability, albeit under a regime which, Putzel (1997) claimed, was among the most authoritarian in the world. But things eventually began to fall apart politically. By 1998, as Suharto grew aged and his personal power declined, Hewison (1999: 224) characterized Indonesia's political system as '*crumbling* authoritarianism' (emphasis added). Later that year, Suharto's regime crashed and ushered in a period of political instability and tentative democratization. As in the case of South Africa, we examine the issues under the following headings: (1) democratic transition, (2) political participation and institutions and (3) external and economic factors.

Democratic transition

During Suharto's rule, Indonesia was an example of an East Asian 'developmental state': relatively economically successful, with a stable authoritarian political system. The political changes of 1998 were preceded the year before by a serious economic upheaval, which most observers regarded as pivotal to the fall of Suharto. The outcome was that he was forced to stand down following popular pressure – including street demonstrations in the capital, Jakarta. His temporary successor, B. J. Habibie, tried to make piecemeal reforms, but was soon replaced in 1999 by a popularly elected president, Abdurrahman Wahid.

The decline and demise of Suharto's authoritarian rule encouraged the rise of an increasingly confident, yet fragmented, civil society, temporarily united only by the demand for fundamental political changes. By 2003, five years after Suharto's downfall, the situation was stalemate between, on the one hand, a regime apparently unwilling to countenance fundamental reforms and, on the other, a vibrant civil society seeking to accomplish major political changes but stymied by serious urban–rural, class, regional, ethnic and religious divisions. The possibilities for democratic consolidation in Indonesia seemed to depend very much on whether the idea of democracy could take hold, incorporated into the criteria by which government in Indonesia is popularly regarded as legitimate.

After seizing power in 1965, General Suharto and his regime spent much time and effort on the consolidation of power and, by the 1980s, the government had managed to entrench itself in power. This was accomplished in part by restricting the activities of already tame opposition political parties. In addition, the security and political role of the armed forces, known as *dwifungsi* ('dual function'), was reinforced. Election victories were efficiently organized both for Suharto's political party, Golkar, and for the president himself. In 1983, he was authorized as president – for a fourth term. At this stage, Suharto seemed to be unchallenged, at the pinnacle of his power. However, as

Hewison (1999: 235) notes, the downfall both of Suharto and his regime can be traced to this period. Although political control was constantly asserted, 'economic problems were forcing economic change, including liberalization and market-oriented reforms. These reforms had a remarkable impact on economic power, and provided considerable impetus to political opposition.' Not that this was clear at the time. In the late 1980s the regime seemed not only to have weathered the economic problems but also to be maintaining a tight political control, reflected in the fact that Golkar continued to win elections with huge majorities and, for the first time, to move beyond its long-term reliance on the armed forces. However, signs of limited political competition were reflected in the fact that there was a sudden move to limited competition among the political elites and a destabilizing discussion regarding the post-Suharto succession and political arrangements. More concretely, pressure for change began to surface among certain groups, including students and intellectuals, the press, and some Islamic organizations.

Surprising many, Suharto responded to these demands by speaking of the need for political reform and more open debate. This led to a brief opening of political space, but did not immediately lead to democratization. Instead, perhaps troubled by the eruption of criticism of his rule, Suharto soon moved to reinstate tight control, stating that the existing system would not change. However, the political space, once granted, could not be entirely regained. This was partly because the opposition became increasingly heterogeneous, with critical groups found among both the middle and working classes, and, gradually, protests began to hot up: 1994 saw not only a series of protests in urban centres across the country but also financial scandals involving state figures, and labour unrest. The overall result was that the government's control was increasingly challenged (Törnquist 2001).

While the government sought to continue to limit the political space available to the opposition, its various elements were collectively undermining the foundations of the state's control. From the regime's point of view, the unwelcome situation was exacerbated not only by emerging rebellions, inter alia Aceh, East Timor and Irian Jaya, but also by international criticism of the government's human rights record in these and other parts of the country. Overall, by the mid-1990s the available political space had been expanded, primarily by the actions of the opposition, and a slow democratic transition had begun.

The elections in 1997 coincided with another serious economic downturn which gave further impetus not only to demands for Suharto to resign but also an outburst of resentment against the entire Suharto family and the government. Suharto's survival strategy – gradually to oversee political reforms – was contemptuously rejected by the main opposition groups. Students and Muslim activists led the opposition to demand his resignation and – eventually – got it: on 19 May 1998 Suharto resigned, handing over to B. J. Habibie. Hewison notes that the transition from Suharto's rule 'may have had considerable orchestration by elements within the elite', but this did not prevent reform and the further expansion of political space (Hewison 1999: 238). There was the release of some political prisoners, eventually concessions on independence for East Timor (but not for Aceh), investigations of human rights abuses, and greater freedom for the activities of trade unions, non-governmental organizations and opposition parties. However, over the next three years there was political confusion as regimes rose and fell, while conditions close to civil war were felt throughout several parts of the country. This suggests that Indonesians may have had more political space than for three decades, but the potential for further democratization is unclear.

Political participation and institutions: the political clout of the military

The case of Indonesia illustrates that to achieve democratic stability, the important issue is not what religious or cultural system is in place, rather it is this: is there an 'appropriate' civic culture – characterized by relatively high levels of mutual trust among citizens, with societal tolerance of diversity, and an accompanying propensity for accommodation and compromise? When such factors are present, as some would argue is the case increasingly in South Africa, then they are likely to be encouraged by the work of democratic institutions over time, as they serve to encourage appropriately democratic values and beliefs among ordinary citizens and members of the political class.

For Indonesia, two main stumbling blocks to increased political participation and democratization remain: the attitude of the politically powerful military and the difficulties of achieving national integration incorporating the country's hundreds of ethnic groups. Since independence from the Netherlands in 1947, Indonesia's military has regarded itself as the guardian of the nation-state and, despite democratization, has retained enormous power within state organizations. In short, the military played a powerful, perhaps dominant political role in the Suharto regime and while it is clear that the aim is to reduce its political role, it is not certain how or when this would be managed.

During Suharto's rule, the military was adept at crushing dissenting voices and separatist movements, as well as appointing active or retired officers to hold government jobs, from cabinet members to district heads. Golkar was set up by military officers in 1967 and, relying largely on intimidation and coercion, it won every election for the next 30 years. While the regime of Abdurrahman Wahid (known as Gus Dur), elected to power in 1999, acted to advance civilian control, the military (and police) were still represented in the parliament (in both lower and upper houses). An act of parliament in January 1999 stipulated that the military's seats would be cut in half, from 75 to 38. It was anticipated that by 2009 neither group would have any representation in parliament. However, while Wahid moved to control the military, the results were mixed. So-called 'rogue elements' were believed to be trying to destabilize Indonesia, as there were mysterious bombings and trouble, including in the rebellious island of Aceh and now independent East Timor.

External and economic factors

Suharto's fall was welcomed by both the IMF – which blamed him for the country's serious economic slump – and the government of the USA – which saw his regime dragging Indonesia, and perhaps the region, into political turmoil. Later, the campaign to 'impeach' (dismiss from office) the Wahid government, which saw success in July 2001, was tacitly supported by the US government; it did not believe that he could arrest the national decline. Wahid's successor, Magawati Sukarnoputri, enjoyed some support from the government of the USA, although it was not convinced that she necessarily had the ability to improve things. This was not only because Indonesia's economic future remained cloudy but also because both civil society and the state were weak – hardly surprising in the case of the former, as many civil society organizations were parented by the state. Prior to the economic crisis of 1997, authoritarian politics had been dominant in Indonesia, a position maintained to a considerable degree by the fact that most ordinary citizens placed a high value on political stability and economic growth. This conservatism was facilitated by the fact that during the mid-1960s half a million or more Indonesians had been killed in a civil war between communists and non-communists. Memories of the violence and unrest characterizing that period, the time of rule by President Sukarno, continued to have considerable societal resonance decades later.

In conclusion, it is often suggested that problems of national integration are a serious impediment to the creation of a democratic regime. In Indonesia, subnational identities – including religious, ethnic, linguistic and 'tribal' divisions – have had much 'staying power'. For decades, backed by the military, Indonesian authorities consistently alluded to separatist and ethnic divisions as a key justification for the perpetuation of authoritarian rule. Indeed, as Putzel (1997: 264) presciently noted prior to the fall of Suharto in 1998, it was not 'unimaginable that a quick transition to democratic politics could make Indonesia the Yugoslavia of South East Asia'.

In addition, external support for democratization in Indonesia was undoubtedly significant in bringing pressure on its recalcitrant incumbent regime and helped to provide a favourable international setting for the newly elected government of Abdurrahman Wahid in 1999. However, while Western pressure was an important catalyst in undermining Indonesia's authoritarian regime, following founding elections the West's impact on political outcomes diminished over time. But the overall point is that the importance of Western political conditionality declined, not only in Indonesia, but also more widely. This is because, generally speaking, Western governments became more interested in stability than in democracy in most developing countries.

Russia

As in the cases of South Africa and Indonesia, we examine democratization in Russia under the following headings: (1) democratic transition, (2) political participation and institutions and (3) external and economic factors.

Democratic transition

Following the collapse of the USSR in December 1991, the Russian Federation reemerged as a separate, independent state under the leadership of Boris Yeltsin. Deputies agreed on a declaration of sovereignty from the USSR and amended the constitution to create an elected presidency. At this time, many observers believed they saw the beginnings of democratic policy-making in Russia. In particular, there was the country's most freely elected parliament since 1917, following a new constitution creating a bicameral national legislature, the Federal Assembly. However, the issue that had most united deputies – independence from the USSR – promptly disappeared. Less than two years later, Yeltsin put down an attempted coup by hard-liners in parliament. This was followed by a grab for power by Yeltsin's administration at the expense of the federal legislature. He began to rely almost exclusively on decrees, especially to introduce economic policy changes towards a market system. In October 1993, Yeltsin proceeded to disband both the federal parliament and, later, local legislatures.

Political participation and institutions

In the elections of 1993, 1995 and 1996, Yeltsin and his supporters became increasingly adept and overt in their manipulation of media coverage and violation of campaign spending rules. Kurtz and Barnes (2002: 540) suggest that Yeltsin and his team took the decision to undermine democratic policy in pursuit of a more economically liberal economy: 'It was a clear case of centralizing political power in order to pass the "right" economic policies.' It was precisely that tactic in relation to market reforms, a policy strongly encouraged by Western governments and IFIs, that had made some scholars at the beginning of the post-communist era concerned about the future of democracy not just in Russia but in the CEE region more widely. The issue was that if regional governments, including that of Russia, pursued rapid market-oriented reforms, it would undermine significantly chances of democratization and democratic consolidation. By the early 2000s, it was argued that Russia's federal and local authorities had increasingly targeted civil liberties and human rights, while the state had targeted independent media outlets (Freedom House 2003: 459–60).

Economic and external factors

> Russia's second war in Chechnya, starting in 1999, brought with it a general climate of fear spread by federal authorities under President Vladimir Putin and signalled a retreat from human rights in Russia. (Mendelson and Glenn 2002: 21)

In 2003–4, a series of bomb attacks in Moscow and elsewhere were widely judged to be the work of Chechen separatists. The attacks served to remind both Russians and foreign governments that President Putin had not managed to fulfil his pledge to resolve Russia's internal security problems. This promise had been made in 1999, when he was unexpectedly appointed prime minister, and came amid the carnage of attacks, including bombs in two blocks of flats in Moscow, also widely blamed (despite their denials) on Chechen separatists. President Putin then decided to send the army back into Chechnya. But the conflict was not brought to a speedy conclusion; instead, rather predictably, it got worse. On the other hand, his perceived 'strongman' approach to this security issue helped assure his overwhelming re-election to the presidency in 2004 (Walsh 2004). This was despite the fact that since 2000, the self-acclaimed miracle of Russian economic growth and political stability of Mr Putin's first term had brought little or no improvements in the life of many ordinary Russians, a large minority of whom still lived below the poverty line (Shorrocks and Kolenikov 2001).

Observers saw deployment of post-transition authoritarianism in Russia under President Putin as particularly troubling because of the country's regional and international significance. But this did not appear to worry some of Russia's key foreign allies. According to Mendelson (2002: 243): 'Putin enjoyed nights at the opera and pints of beer with Tony Blair, tea with the queen of England, and was the toast of the town at the July 2000 G-7 meeting in Genoa, although Russia had neither a strong industrialized economy nor a robust democracy.' She concludes that the Russian case suggests that the 'likelihood of successful diffusion of norms may be overstated in the literature'. Western governmental willingness to overlook Russia's apparent non-compliance with various international norms relating to human rights appeared to be related to the Putin government's full support for the post-9/11 US-led anti-terrorist campaign. This led to a new era in US–Russian relations, with significantly improved levels of cooperation, manifested in an apparent reduction of US criticism of the war in Chechnya, moves to accelerate Russia's entry into the World Trade Organization and a greater role for Russia in NATO affairs (Freedom House 2003: 460).

In conclusion, Federov (2000) notes that Western support for the war in Chechnya is but one side of the coin. He suggests that Russians believe that choosing democracy implies much more than adopting a political system that allows greater personal freedom and guarantees greater government accountability. It is also believed to involve exposing Russia to the impact, more generally, of globalization. As a result, Russian culture is opened up to foreign ideas, while the country's economy is both marketized and a subject of foreign competition. While many ordinary citizens no doubt relish greater freedom, they also seem wary of the consequences of globalization, of which democracy is part.

Federov (2000) also contends that Russian fear of globalization is driven by a perception that it is not the result of impersonal forces of the information revolution and the market, but controlled by the United States as part of a more general project for domination of international relations. It is often said in the democratization literature that progress is slowed both by civil society weakness and by poor expression of interests in the political process. Observers note, however, that in the case of Russia the opposite is true. Some interests are very well articulated, and this is what slows down democratization: many important groups believe their interests would be threatened if Russia joined the community of democracies and, with it, the global economy (Robinson 2003).

Conclusion

We have seen that far from being a straightforward process, attempts to develop democracy are problematic, linked to a number of issues. These include the nature of a polity's political culture, the strength and effectiveness of civil society as a counterweight to state power, the political role of the military and the impact of various aspects of globalization.

To be democratically relevant, civil society will not merely be an ordering of elite groups, but will actively encourage involvement from those traditionally lacking political influence: the poor, women, the young, certain minority ethnic and religious groups. But, because such an extension and deepening of democracy will normally be resisted by those in power, then legal guarantees and extensive protections for individual and group freedoms and associational life are crucial, to be secured by and through an independent, impartial judiciary. To increase welfare to those that need it, redistribution of scarce resources is both politically necessary and economically appropriate, while the military must be neutralized as a political actor. Put another way, the consolidation of democracy necessarily implies a conscious effort to redress past imbalances, a course of action necessary so that the mass of ordinary people come to believe that democracy is a better system than alternative ones, such as benign dictatorship.

It is however necessary to separate one form of international pressure – political conditionality – from arguments about the salutary effects of economic linkage to the West or diffusion of norms through participation in democracy-promoting international organizations, such as the EU. A wider point, however, is that external encouragement to democratize cannot be overlooked, but it is not a one-way affair. External encouragement seems to be especially important to the progress of political liberalization and democratic transition, but less so in most cases at later stages of democratization. The case of Russia in particular shows that reductions in Western pressure to democratize may be linked to a specific aspect of globalization: burgeoning political violence and terrorism, issues that recently have become an increasingly important issue for comparative political analysis. We focus upon this issue in the next chapter.

11
Political Violence and Terrorism

So far in this book we have examined forms of political participation that normally operate within peaceful frameworks. We have seen that this is especially the case in established democracies, where it might be said that the ballot has replaced the bullet. In such political systems, governments rarely – if ever – fight each other or kill their own citizens. Elsewhere, it was widely expected that the third wave of democracy (see chapter 10) would lead to major reductions in levels of state-sponsored political violence. What happened instead was both less expected and more complicated. While there were indeed dozens of new democracies (see chapter 10) – many of which conduct politics in a relatively peaceful manner – there was also what has been called the 'globalization of political violence'. The result was that comparative political analysis was now compelled to explain and account for not only political violence within countries, but also links between domestic examples and cross-border political violence, including international terrorism.

This chapter is structured as follows. First, we survey traditional domestic concerns of political violence in comparative political analysis. We then examine the globalization of political violence. This development was inherently connected to the tragic events of 11 September 2001, when around 3,000 people were killed in the United States as a result of international terrorism, as well as subsequent linked bombing outrages around the world. Third, we explore the phenomenon of 'failed states', look at examples from both Africa and the Balkans, and uncover links between failed states and international terrorism.

Political Violence and Domestic Politics

Political violence conventionally falls into three main categories:

- the state against its own people;
- by one social group against another;
- by groups of people aiming to alter government policy in various ways.

In established democracies, political interactions and competition are usually characterized by a lack of violence. This is because prevailing political norms reflect what are often known as 'Enlightenment values', including 'critical rationality and an ethic of pluralism, mutual respect, and an authentic dialogue – to distinguish defensible from indefensible' political interactions (Nardin 2003: 273). Such normatively desirable values can only develop when the great majority of people in a polity believe that they have effective means to influence political outcomes, generally via civil society and political society and explicitly via the ballot box.

State-use of political violence on a large scale is invariably associated with non-democracies. Recent examples include state-directed mass killings in the 1970s in Cambodia under the Khmer Rouge and Uganda under Idi Amin. During the 1980s, thousands of Shias were killed in Iraq under the regime of Saddam Hussein, while in Rwanda in the 1990s, thousands of Tutsis and Hutus were massacred. According to Rummel (1997), state pursuit of absolute power explains why such policies are initiated and employed, thereby creating necessary conditions for 'democide', that is, 'the murder of any person or people by a government, including genocide, politicide, and mass murder'.[1]

When groups of people feel that their demands are not getting through to power-holders because of a lack of appropriate political structures (see chapter 5), some may turn to political violence in pursuit of their goals. Conflicts between groups may be the result of failure to deal with various challenges, including competing ethnic and/or religious demand. If unchecked, such conflicts can develop into massacres, civil war, democide or genocide. Statistically, the worst examples of communal violence have been noted in Africa and Asia, regions that until recently were filled with non-democratic regimes. Often, internal extremes of wealth and poverty are associated with such political violence, 'especially where economic differences are linked to ethnic and/or religious divisions' (Bealey 1999: 260).

Such group conflicts are most common in non-democracies or transitional democracies, but not unknown in established democracies. Various groups – for example, animal rights activists, anti-abortionists, or far-left or far-right political organizations – may believe that their goals cannot be achieved via 'normal' political interactions. But to understand why such people resort to political violence to try to achieve their goals, we need to use conventional tools of political analysis. This implies that it is not necessarily helpful to perceive various forms of political violence, including terrorism, as something that only irrational fanatics undertake. This suggests that political violence may be neither random nor uncontrolled – but a tactical response to what are perceived as unacceptable political circumstances that cannot be otherwise addressed. Thus to threaten or to employ political violence is a way of 'raising the stakes'; it supports rather than replaces conventional ways of 'doing' politics. In short, if conventional forms of political competition leave political conflicts unsettled or unaddressed, then groups may turn to political violence of various kinds and intensities. For example, EU farmers violently block roads and mount aggressive demonstrations; animal rights protesters may violently picket laboratories where scientific tests on animals are carried out; extensive – apparently 'uncontrolled' – violence erupts between Hindus and Muslims in India, leading to deaths and destruction of property. What they have in common is that such outbreaks of political violence are rarely random or spontaneous, but are typically initiated – although rarely personally carried out – by identifiable political leaders.

This also suggests that the notion of 'political violence' is a wide one. It includes a range of activities, such as violent demonstrations, looting, riots, sabotage, group con-

---

[1] For definitions and discussions of these terms, see Rummel's homepage at <http://www. freedomsnest.com/rummel_definition.html>.

flicts, terrorism, rebellion and revolution (Calvert 2002: 302–3). At one end of the spectrum we find disruptive demonstrations, sit-in occupations, road blockages, unlawful wildcat strikes and obstruction of premises. While there are numerous examples of such activities undertaken within countries, there are also recent instances of a small but growing number of what are known as 'Euro-protests' (Imig and Tarrow 2001). These are the result of disaffected Europeans – including farmers, fishermen, construction workers, miners and truckers – who engage in EU-wide protests, sometimes employing low-level political violence to try to influence important political decisions. Such protests may develop because their perpetrators believe that important decisions are increasingly taken supranationally by non-accountable EU bodies (Imig 2002). So far, however, most so-called Euro-protests have taken place within countries rather than transnationally. This suggests that while some Europeans may be troubled by the policy incursions of the EU, they still choose to vent their grievances close to home – by demanding that their national governments act on their behalf. Those that have been most likely to march, picket and strike against EU decisions have done so over jobs and welfare issues. Over time, however, occupational groups have been joined in the streets by a growing range of activists with a variety of goals, including students, peace marchers, environmentalists and anti-racist groups. We can also note in this context occasionally violent anti-globalization protests, for example the 'battle of Seattle' in 1999 (Held and McGrew 2002: 13–17).

In short, there are many reasons why people might use political violence in pursuit of their goals, but most such actions fall short of revolution. For Calvert (2002: 303), 'revolution is violence plus political change: it brings about a fall of government or a change of regime'. Examples of revolution over the last century include the Russian revolution of 1917, the Chinese revolution of 1949, the Cuban revolution of 1959, the Iranian revolution of 1979, and the anti-communist – mostly non-violent – revolutions in CEE (1989–91). Political scientists have sought to develop general explanations of revolution, with three in particular – the French (1789), the Russian and the Chinese – the focus of enquiry. More recently, both the Iranian and Eastern European revolutions have generated much analysis and debate (for a discussion of the causes of revolutions, see Calvert 2002).

Terrorism

While political scientists have written plentifully on the causes and consequences of revolution, the issue of terrorism, its causes and consequences, has only recently become a key focus of attention. Terrorism is both a controversial and a subjective issue, not least because it may be difficult objectively to differentiate between tactics and goals of 'terrorists' ('violence-loving fanatics') and 'freedom fighters' ('romantic idealists'). To try to overcome the inherently subjective connotation of the term, Keohane (2002: 1) suggests a more neutral one: 'informal violence'. This is 'violence committed by non-state actors who capitalize on secrecy and surprise to inflict great harm with small material capabilities', and can be contrasted with state-sponsored or directed, 'formal violence'. For those employing terrorism, the threat or use of violence 'from below' serves to emphasize specific issues, grievances or demands. The aim is to gain concessions from the authorities on certain political issues, such as minority rights and regional autonomy. Human rights organizations, including Amnesty International and Human Rights Watch, have condemned terrorism in countries around the world, including suicide bombings employed by Palestinians in their conflict with Israel, by ETA in Spain and by Kashmiri extremists in Kashmir, Chechen rebels taking hostages in a Moscow theatre, killings by Maoist groups in Nepal and Peru, and kidnappings by the FARC and other armed groups in Colombia.

What is clear is that terrorists are nearly always few in numbers, but are quite capable of spreading fear and insecurity widely among populations. Those who employ terrorism use violence in pursuit of tactical political ends, and have a variety of political goals. What, if anything, distinguishes terrorism from other types of political violence? For political violence to qualify for the epithet 'terrorism', it must feature a particular use of 'techniques, targets, and goals . . . To be effective, [it] must be well-planned and directed – in other words, it must embody political skill. Such acts are intended to coerce a wider target into submitting to its aims by creating an overall climate of fear' (Hague and Harrop 2001: 120). Norris et al. (2003: 3) define 'terrorism' as 'the *systematic* use of coercive intimidation against civilians for political goals'. The reference to 'systematic coercion' differentiates terrorism from more random forms of political violence.

Terrorism can be confined within a country's borders, or it may be internationally focused. Terrorism is domestic when both victims and perpetrators are confined within the borders of a single nation-state. It is international when it involves victims or perpetrators from more than one nation-state. In some cases, widespread domestic group terrorism can develop into civil war, with the objective of undermining and ultimately overturning incumbent political authorities. But where such violence is successfully contained, it may be that group dissent can be focused via more conventional channels, for example, the Irish peace process that, while by no means unproblematic, did lead both formerly violent republicans and nationalists to contest democratic elections in Northern Ireland. On the other hand, the existence of peace negotiations is not necessarily enough to quell political violence, for example, in relation to the Israel–Palestine issue. Since 9/11, much evidence has emerged to indicate that some terrorist groups now operate internationally. The short-term goal of such groups – notably al-Qaeda and its allies – is almost always to try to damage the morale of civilian populations, to destabilize the governments of countries they oppose and to seek to encourage such governments to meet their demands.

To focus upon the approaches, goals and ultimate objectives of those who employ terrorism may help us to define the concept, but still leaves unresolved the issue of which actors use such methods. Norris et al. (2003) note that both states and non-state actors may instigate and use terrorism in pursuit of political objectives, related to extant major societal cleavages, that may be racial, nationalist, ethnic, religious or class-based. Non-state actors employing terrorism undertake such forms of political violence against the state, often through targeting ordinary people. This is 'terrorism from below', the focus of much analysis, especially in Western established democracies. This is partly because many Western governments are intensely interested in finding appropriate ways to deal with terrorism. As part of their strategy, they may sponsor the production of policy analysis on the issue.

It is a fundamental assumption of Western social science that 'normal', 'orthodox' or 'conventional' politics can be understood in terms of the rational pursuit of self-interest. This belief may be inherently assumed, or believed to be shown by political actors' preferences and the degree to which what they do politically appears logically to follow from those preferences. Until the mid-eighteenth century, rationality was believed to be a self-conscious goal; the key issue was how to instil rationality into state-craft while simultaneously dealing with 'the ever-present power of chance, contingency and fortuna' (Hurrell 2002: 195). To what extent can terrorism be understood in these terms? That is, to what extent is terrorism an expression of rational policy in the pursuit of identifiable political goals? Are terrorists simply 'wide-eyed fanatics with unclear or inchoate goals'? Or are they groups of people who rationally decide to adopt terrorist tactics as the only, or best-perceived, way of achieving their political goals?

According to Bealey (1999: 319), terrorism in democratic societies is:

> the violence of desperate men [*sic*] . . . small groups of armed assassins and saboteurs . . . the last resort of those who cannot achieve their aims by persuasion and the ballot box . . . the deployment or threat of terrorist violence represents the ultimate failure of conventional channels of political expression and legitimate forms of authority.

In democratic polities, state responses to terrorism typically focus on applying measures that serve to underline the government's determination not to give way to terrorists and their demands. Instead, the government's stated intention is definitively to imbue terrorists and their tactics with the opposite to what the terrorists intended: to make law and order a highly popular policy and to minimize support for their goals.

Recent examples of terrorist activities have been noted not only in a variety of types of political system, including in established democracies – for example, Britain (Catholics versus Protestants in Northern Ireland), Spain (where the Basque Fatherland and Liberty party [ETA] demands independence for the Basque region), and Israel (Palestinian demands for a homeland). In such contexts, terrorism undertaken by non-state actors is best understood as the breakdown of conventional channels of mobilization, participation and expression; in such circumstances, political violence is used as a mechanism of last resort, intended to polarize conflict. Thus we can note the origins and the characters of, for example, Baader-Meinhof in West Germany; radical groups in Northern Ireland, including the Provisional Irish Republican Army and certain Ulster Unionist organizations; ETA in Spain; and Action Directe in France. Such groups are correctly perceived as terrorists, although it is also important to see their genesis and development linked to the particular character of post-1945 West German, British, Spanish and French politics (Henley and Walker 2003).

Both transitional democracies and non-democracies have also seen the use of terrorism to try to achieve political goals, for example in Kosovo, Chechnya, South Africa and various Central and Latin American countries. In non-democratic societies, that is, where opportunities for political expression are constrained, groups opposing the status quo may undertake terrorist activities as a primary means of expression and not as a last resort. As a result, political groups using terrorist tactics in such contexts may have greater popular support than their counterparts in established democracies. This is especially the case among groups with economic and/or ethnic grievances who do not perceive that they can alter the status quo to their benefit in the absence of appropriate political opportunity structures. Examples include various groups in Central and Latin America in the 1980s and 1990s. During this time, numerous peasants and Indians enlisted on the side of, inter alia, the FARC in Colombia and Peru's Maoist Sendero Luminoso, groups that frequently adopted terrorist tactics in pursuit of their goals (Carpenter 2003).

Regardless of the kind of political system within which they operate, terrorists will have both short-term and longer-term goals. The former include: the intention of 'spreading anxiety and alarm among the immediate victims and their families, as well as the wider public'; eliminating opponents and destroying symbolic targets such as the Pentagon or Arafat's Palestinian headquarters; and generating direct damage on society, such as 'depressing business confidence in Wall Street or discouraging international corporate investors in Lima' (Hurrell 2002: 195).

Longer-term goals of terrorism include 'publicizing issues, communicating demands, and airing grievances to pressure authorities, influence the public policy agenda and gain concessions; undermining the authority of opponents; reinforcing and mobilizing support among potential sympathizers and coalition partners' (Norris et al. 2003: 8). All such objectives are designed to increase the terrorists' political clout, status and/or legitimacy. Finally, terrorism may also be used 'simply to shock, demoralize, or otherwise damage a perceived political enemy. The pursuit of politically symbolic rather than instrumental goals may have characterized those who carried out both the [1995] Oklahoma bombings and the 9/11 attacks on the Twin Towers and the Pentagon' (Norris et al. 2003: 6)

However, it is not only non-state actors that may use terrorism to try to achieve their political goals. Numerous governments have also used 'state terrorism'. Under such a policy, the state adopts the tactics of terrorism in order to try to deal with a troublesome political problem. For example, villages where insurgents live may be destroyed, those who live there massacred, while known or suspected regime opponents are apprehended, to 'disappear' into torture chambers and unmarked graves. 'The official view of such activity is that it is "counter-terrorist". The insurgents claim they are not terrorists but resistance fighters. The line is not always easy to draw' (Bealey 1999: 319–20). Thus we can see that state terrorism is a mirror image of group terrorism that involves coercive intimidation initiated by government authorities against civilian populations, representing 'terrorism from above'.

This form of attempted control is most common among repressive authoritarian regimes, and is by no means a new phenomenon. For example, during the 1920s and 1930s in the USSR under the rule of Josef Stalin, the state undertook a massive purge against its own citizens. During the 1970s and 1980s 'death squads' were used to suppress dissent in various Central and Latin American countries, including Argentina, Chile, El Salvador, Guatemala and Nicaragua. In Iraq, Saddam Hussein's regime gassed tens of thousands of Iraqi Kurds during the 1980s. More recently, the state under the leadership of Robert Mugabe in Zimbabwe employed the Fifth Brigade against the Ndebele people, while Russian troops were widely accused of using terrorist tactics in the war against Chechen rebels (Norris et al. 2003: 9).

Although such state-directed violence is not always labelled 'terrorism', it seems clear that its purpose – whether carried out by militias, intelligence services, police or thugs paid by the government – is to try to suppress dissent and intimidate the government's opponents. Consequently, state terrorism shares many of the characteristics and tactics employed by non-state terrorist groups against the state. In extreme cases, state terrorism can degenerate into outright civil war between competing factions, which can eventually lead to state failure. State terrorism can also be directed against civilian targets located in neighbouring countries, for example where foreign governments are believed to offer safe havens, weapons, paramilitary training or funds to terrorists fighting against such states. For example, during the 1980s the white-minority South African government used military force in an attempt to destabilize neighbouring African states, including Zimbabwe, Mozambique and Tanzania. We should note however that it is not only highly repressive regimes that employ state terrorism; in times of war, terrorist tactics may also be employed by democratic governments. For example, during World War II, the allies fire-bombed various German cities, including Hamburg and Dresden. The purpose was both to destroy enemy morale and to demolish conventional military and other strategic targets. In sum, state terrorism has various purposes designed to maintain the control of the political authorities and to suppress internal dissidence, silence opposition leaders and movements, and reduce or eliminate foreign-based threats. Governments may try to justify their use of such 'counter-terrorism' measures on the grounds of protecting civilians from violent attack.

In conclusion, groups of people may turn to various types of political violence – from demonstrations, through riots to no-holds-barred terrorism – in response to what they may judge to be an absence of suitable (and suitably effective) political opportunity structures. This is a reference to conventional channels through which those with political goals can act to pursue their demands. In addition, repressive states may also use various forms of political violence, including state-sponsored terrorism, to try to achieve rulers' political goals.

The Globalization of Political Violence

The second focus of the chapter is to examine the globalization of political violence in the wake of the events of 11 September 2001 ('9/11'). There is virtual unanimity in the literature that the 9/11 attacks on the United States were a watershed in the debate about political violence because they focused attention clearly on the interaction between domestic and international levels. According to Dartnell (2001: 3), the intersection of domestic and global levels of analysis in this regard is the result of the 'intensity and rapidity of contemporary globalization'. This is also exemplified in the growing numbers of 'failed' states. Because failed states are also unstable states, it leads to external military involvement by the armed forces of neighbouring states. Acting alone or through the auspices of regional bodies, the aim is the same: to try to prevent political violence in failed states from spilling over to destabilize neighbouring countries. In recent years, various failed states – including Afghanistan, former Yugoslavia, Iraq, Sierra Leone, Liberia and Somalia – have become safe havens for various terrorist groups, notably al-Qaeda ('the base'), an intensely anti-Western terrorist network said to have cells in more than 50 countries. Al-Qaeda is also believed to dispense money and logistical support and training to a wide variety of radical Islamist terrorist groups (Gunaratna 2004).

The current globalization of political violence is not novel. It follows earlier developments, for example, during the cold war when both the USA and the Soviet Union developed globalized techniques of state-controlled violence as part of their competition for world domination. Even before that, we can note examples of various actors, such as transnational pirates, that have terrorized ships from the seventeenth century until the present time. Hurrell (2002: 197) also points to political assassinations in Russia, France and Serbia during the 1870–1914 period, and links them to what he calls the first 'wave of globalization and integration'. At this time, processes of globalization served to facilitate 'revolutionary movements' via the 'increased range of terrorist targets that followed from new technology and urbanization (bombs, trains, cities)'. There is a parallel to be noted between global conditions of a century or more ago and those prevailing now: both periods were times of intensive social globalization, with much intercontinental immigration. What characterizes the present time compared to the past is the astonishing reduction in costs of global communications and transportation. In particular, invention of the internet has transformed beyond recognition the ease of communication in 'various arenas, including international terrorism' (Smith 2002: 177). By the end of 2003, there were said to be more than 500 million inter-net users worldwide (<http://www.sbm.com.sa/base/news/500_million_internet_users/ 500_million_internetusers.html>). For users of the internet – including not only terror-ists but also other transnational groups – 'new IT-driven media such as email, the Web and chat rooms present a wide range of opportunities due to their global reach. Tech-nological change, information revolution, and global communications thus enhance the visibility of a variety of once unknown, marginal, illegal, unpopular and unorthodox groups' (Dartnell 2001: 1).

Contemporary international terrorism is said to be in part a consequence of assy-metrical interdependence, with four main effects for both comparative political analy-sis and international relations. International terrorism

- significantly undercuts the state's monopoly of violence;
- exploits the privatization of violence and the instruments of violence;
- flourishes in failed states, that is, in countries where state control is weak or non-existent;
- moves and manoeuvres within the many spaces created by technological globalization.

In the next section we focus upon the links between international terrorism and failed states.

Al-Qaeda, 9/11 and international terrorism

On September 11, 2001 Americans were confronted by an enigma similar to that presented to the Aztecs – an enigma so baffling that even elementary questions of nomenclature posed a problem: What words or phrase should we use merely to *refer* to the events of that day? Was it a disaster? Or perhaps a tragedy? Was it a criminal act, or was it an act of war? Indeed, one awkward TV anchorman, in groping for the proper handle, fecklessly called it an accident. But eventually the collective and unconscious wisdom that governs such matters prevailed. Words failed, then fell away completely, and all that was left behind was the bleak but monumentally poignant set of numbers, 9–11. (Harris 2002)

America's new enemies seem to have no demands. They can't be bought, bribed, or even blackmailed. They only want to strike a blow at any cost. And if a suicide hijacker or bomber really believes that by dying in his jihad (Muslim holy war) he'll go straight to heaven and Allah's loving embrace, what earthly reward could the US or anybody else possibly offer as a substitute? (Sacks 2001)

It is likely that without the 9/11 attacks on New York and the Pentagon, this chapter would have had quite a different focus. This is because both the attacks themselves, as well as those that followed in Bali, Casablanca, Istanbul, Nairobi and Madrid,[2] led to a significant change in perceptions of international relations. No longer was it sufficient to understand states as the only actors with the capacity to inflict large-scale, seemingly random, internationally orientated political violence. The attacks emphasized that international terrorism was an important development that called for a new comparative focus on the many themes of conflict and violence traditionally covered in comparative politics and an examination of links between failed states and international terrorism.

As a result of the tragic events of 9/11, globalization was seen clearly to proffer a dangerous threat of violence from non-state actors – who might be physically located almost anywhere – against the national territories of states. At a stroke, the attacks made it quite clear that geographical space could no longer necessarily act as a barrier to external attack, a notion that had, however, already been seriously undermined by the development of thermonuclear war-fighting capacity after 1945. The al-Qaeda attacks[3] on the Twin Towers and the Pentagon in the USA on 9/11 made the job of those seeking to understand both comparative politics and international relations more difficult. This is because there was suddenly a pressing new challenge to understand the nature of world politics and its connections to domestic politics in a newly emphasized context, that is, when the 'hard shell' was irreversibly crushed. According to Smith (2002: 177), this suggested an important connotation for future chances of world order, because states were 'no longer, if they ever were, the key actors in major international arenas'. Thus the kind of international terrorism exemplified by al-Qaeda does not 'map onto state structures', but 'works in the spaces between them'. That is, the *raison d'être* of international terrorist groups such as al-Qaeda is not defined by territory but by commitments and beliefs. This implies that al-Qaeda is a very different type of organization compared to the state, both in terms of identity and structure. Its structure is the reverse of the modern state characterized by a hierarchy of power and authority, while its identity is equally nebulous.

What was the impact of 9/11 both on the USA and more widely? First, while political violence and terrorism issues were already important areas of concern prior to 9/11, that event provided a distinctive emphasis on international terrorism and its networks, of which al-Qaeda is the most significant, but not the sole, example (Gunaratna 2004). Second, the 9/11 attacks were widely regarded as a profound challenge both to the US government and political analysts who had shared a hitherto apparently unshakeable

[2] A London-based Arabic paper, *al-Quds*, announced it received a letter from a group purporting to be linked to al-Qaeda, the Abu Hafs al-Masri brigade, which claimed responsibility for the attack. It said: 'The death squad [of the Abu Hafs al-Masri brigade] succeeded in penetrating the crusader European depths and striking one of the pillars of the crusader alliance – Spain – with a painful blow' (Tremlett et al. 2004).
[3] For the record, bin Laden has never formally accepted responsibility.

belief in fundamental foreign-policy assumptions noted above. Third, there was a profound impact on Americans' sense of security, as the quotations above from Harris and Sacks – both Americans and journalists – makes plain. In short, it shattered Americans' sense of safety. As Huntington notes, the last time that the continental United States suffered anything at all comparable to the 9/11 attacks was nearly 200 years ago, in 1814. Then, the British burned down the White House. Since then, Americans have lived in an atmosphere of invulnerability from foreign attack. After 11 September 2001, that disappeared.[4]

Fourth, the significance of 9/11 is also to be noted in relation to the unequal global distribution of power, a state of affairs that globalization is often said to make worse. Hurrell (2002: 189) notes that globalization is believed to create 'many kinds of negative externalities, including the reaction of many marginalized groups, the creation of new channels for protest, and, in particular, the facilitation of new patterns of terrorist and other kinds' of political violence. Keohane (2002: 30) contends that the 'effective wielding of large-scale violence by nonstate actors reflects new patterns of asymmetrical interdependence and calls into question some of our assumptions about geographical space as a barrier'. The unequal global distribution of power is said to encourage international terrorism, represented not only by al-Qaeda but also by other Islamist groups, such as the Groupes Islamiques Armées and the Groupe Salafiste pour la Prédication et le Combat (GSPC)/Dawa wa Jihad (Volpi 2003: 125–7). This is not to suggest that there this is something inherent in Islam and its belief systems that encourage political violence, but it is to note that there are extremist and violent elements among the Islamist groups – demonstrated not only by 9/11, but also by subsequent bomb outrages in Bali, Casablanca, Istanbul,[5] Nairobi and Madrid.

Societies around the world responded to 9/11 in broadly cultural terms. Most Western governments, including those of Britain, Italy, Japan and Spain, strongly supported the American people and their government, both in relation to 9/11 and to subsequent wars in Afghanistan and Iraq. Some ordinary Muslims, on the other hand, are said to have seen 9/11 differently: it represented an attempt by Islam to 'fight back' against the USA (in particular) and the West (in general) (Hammond 2003: 83). It seems obvious that 9/11 was calculated not simply to wreak terrible destruction, but also to create a global media spectacle. For some among the mass of 'downtrodden ordinary Muslims', bin Laden was already a hero prior to 9/11. This constituency was an important target audience for the highly visual spectacle of the destruction of the Twin Towers and the attack on the Pentagon. Thus for al-Qaeda a key goal of 9/11 was to grab the attention of ordinary (Sunni) Muslims, and to encourage them to make connections between the attacks and the multiple resentments felt against the USA in many parts of the Islamic world. Manifestations of such resentments include support for unrepresentative rulers in the Arab world, the US-led invasions of Iraq in 1990–1 and 2003, and Israel's treatment of the Palestinians. Together, these issues reflect a depth of hatred in many parts of the

[4] 'Religion, Culture, and International Conflict After September 11. A Conversation with Samuel P. Huntington'. Available at: <www.eppc.org/publications/xq/ASP/pubsID.1209/ qx/pubs_viewdetail.html>.
[5] More than 60 people were killed in bomb attacks in Istanbul in November 2003. Turkish authorities blamed those attacks on al-Qaeda, but after a string of arrests said they had crushed the local Turkish group of militants.

Muslim world, a level of concern that is not restricted to small numbers of religious or political radicals. Exacerbated by years of US refusal to censure Israeli actions in relation to the Palestinians, Muslim resentment is also a result of failure to deal with the privations and humiliations inflicted on Iraq following the downfall of Saddam Hussein in March 2003 and his subsequent arrest nine months later. On the other hand, it is plausible to suggest that the resentment of at least some Muslims actually goes wider than these specific issues. If this is the case, then even if solutions for both the Iraq and Palestine issues are found, this might not in reality undercut the potential for terrorist attacks on the USA and the allies. It 'seems plausible', suggests Hurrell (2002: 197), 'that much resentment has to do with the far-reaching and corrosive encroachments of modernization, westernization and globalization'.

Given that both 9/11 and subsequent terrorist outrages already noted appear to have been perpetrated by Muslims against Western targets, the question can be asked whether they are the beginning of Huntington's (1993, 1996) alleged 'civilizational' conflict between Islam and the West. Some commentators alleged that the 9/11 attacks and the subsequent US response served to make Huntingtonian prophecies appear far less abstract and far more plausible than they had been when first made a decade before.

Samuel Huntington, a US academic, first presented his 'clash of civilizations' thesis in an article published in 1993, followed by a book in 1996. His main argument was that, following the end of the cold war, a new, global clash was under way that, replacing the four-decades-long conflict between liberal democracy/capitalism and communism, was a new fight between the (Christian) 'West' and the (mostly Muslim, mostly Arab) 'East'. The core of Huntington's argument is that after the cold war the 'Christian', democratic West found itself in conflict, especially with radical Islam, a political movement concerned with changes in the political order, united by antipathy to the West, and inspired by anti-democratic religious and cultural dogma encapsulated in the term 'Islamic fundamentalism', a key threat to international stability. Christianity, on the other hand, was said by Huntington to be conducive to the spread of liberal democracy. In evidence, he notes the collapse of dictatorships in southern Europe and Latin America in the 1970s and 1980s, followed by the development of liberal democratic political norms (rule of law, free elections, civic rights). These events were regarded by Huntington as conclusive proof of the synergy between Christianity and liberal democracy, both key foundations of a normatively desirable global order built on liberal values. Others have also alleged that Islam is inherently undemocratic or even anti-democratic. For example, Fukuyama (1992: 236) suggests that Islamic 'fundamentalism' has a 'more than superficial resemblance to European fascism'.

Critics of Huntington's argument have noted that it is one thing to argue that various brands of political Islam have qualitatively different perspectives on liberal democracy from some forms of Christianity, but quite another to claim that Muslims en masse are poised to enter into a period of conflict with the West. That is, there are actually many 'Islams' and only the malevolent or misinformed would associate the terrorist attacks with an apparently representative quality of a single idea of Islam. Second, the 11 September atrocities – as well as subsequent bomb outrages – do not appear to have been carried out by a state or group of states or at their behest, but by al-Qaeda, an international terrorist organization. Despite energetic US attempts, no definitive proof was found to link the regime of Saddam Hussein in Iraq with either Osama bin Laden or al-Qaeda.

Third, the idea of religious or civilizational conflict is problematic because it is actually very difficult to identify clear territorial boundaries to civilizations, and even more difficult to perceive them as acting as coherent units. It has been suggested that Huntington's image of 'clashing civilizations' focuses too closely on an essentially undifferentiated category – 'a civilization' – and as a result places insufficient emphasis on various trends, conflicts and disagreement that take place within all cultural traditions, whether Islam, Christianity or Judaism. The wider point is that cultures are not usefully seen as closed systems of essentialist values, while it is implausible to understand the world to comprise a strictly limited number of cultures, each with their own unique core set of beliefs. The influence of globalization in this regard is to be noted, as it leads to an expansion of channels, pressures and agents via which various norms are diffused and interact.

Finally, the image of 'clashing civilizations' ignores the very important sense in which radical Islamist revolt and al-Qaeda terrorism is aimed primarily *internally* at many governments within the Islamic world that are accused of becoming both corrupt and un-Islamic. Since the 1970s, a general rise of Islamist groups across the swathe of Arab countries and elsewhere is much more a consequence of the failure of modernization to deliver its promises than the result of bin Laden's influence. That is, the contemporary Islamist resurgence – of which al-Qaeda is an integral part – carries within it both popular disillusionment at slow progress as well as growing disgust with corrupt and unrepresentative governments in the Muslim world that have refused to open up political systems to become more representative. Confronted by state power that seeks to destroy or control its communitarian structures and replace them with an idea of a national citizenry based on the link between state and individual, Islamist groups have widely appeared as vehicles of popular political aspirations.

But it is difficult or impossible to be sure about the actual level of support for bin Laden and al-Qaeda in the Muslim world, although there is almost certainly a high degree of anti-US resentment and a general belief that the West is opposed to Islam. Such a perception is fuelled by the US move back towards rather uncritical support for Israel's Sharon government, the invasion of Iraq and subsequent inability to rebuild a viable administration in that country. At the same time, in the USA there are voices that appear to play up the notion of civilizational conflict. For example, Congressman Tom Lantos has stated that 'unfortunately we have no option but to take on barbarism which is hell bent on destroying civilization. . . . You don't compromise with these people. This is not a bridge game. International terrorists have put themselves outside the bonds of protocols.'[6]

Such remarks appear to reflect a deep-rooted tradition in Western international thought that believes it is appropriate to set aside normal rules of international relations in certain circumstances, for example, 'certain kinds of conflict or in struggles with certain kinds of states or groups' (Hurrell 2002: 195). During the centuries of Western imperialism, there were frequent debates about what rights non-Christian and non-European peoples should enjoy. In the centuries of competition and sometimes conflict between Christianity and Islam, there arose the notion of 'holy war' – that is, a special kind of

---

[6] Interview with Tom Lantos (2001) BBC Radio 4, *Today* programme, 20 November 2001, quoted in Hurrell 2002: 195.

conflict undertaken outside 'any framework of shared rules and norms' – as well as that of 'just war' waged for 'the vindication of rights' within a shared framework of values. In addition, there is a further strand of conservative Western thought that 'asserts that certain kinds of states and systems cannot be dealt with on normal terms, that the normal rules that govern international relations have to be set aside'. For example, during 1980s the Reagan government in the USA averred that there was a fundamental lack of give and take available when dealing with communist governments, which meant that it was appropriate that some basic notions of international law could be set aside in such contexts. This conservative tradition is also manifested in the remarks of Congressman Lantos noted above,[7] and suggests that available options are restricted to the choice of 'contain or to crusade'. It also indicates that 'such positions clearly continue to resonate within and around the current US administration' (Hurrell 2002: 193–5).

'Failed States' and International Terrorism

One of the principal lessons of the events of September 11 is that failed states matter – for national security as well as for humanitarian reasons. If left to their own devices, such states can become sanctuaries not only for terrorist networks, organized crime and drug traffickers as well as posing grave humanitarian challenges and threats to regional stability. (Commission on Post-Conflict Reconstruction 2003: 4)

On traditional grounds of national interest, Afghanistan should be one of the least important places in the world for US foreign policy – and until the Soviet invasion of 1979, and again after the collapse of the Soviet Union in 1991 until September 11, the United States all but ignored it. Yet in October 2001 it became the theater of war. (Keohane 2002: 35)

The US government responded to the 9/11 attacks with an assault in 2001–2 on both the Taliban regime and al-Qaeda bases in Afghanistan. At that time, the Taliban government controlled much of Afghanistan, a 'failed state' with a shattered social and political structure. Following more than two decades of constant warfare, the country was a nation in ruins, with numerous towns and cities reduced to rubble, and with its social and political structure destroyed by years of unremitting conflict. These circumstances allowed al-Qaeda to set up bases, with the explicit or implicit agreement of the Taliban regime. According to Thürer (1999: 731), failed states like that of Afghanistan 'are invariably the product of a collapse of the power structures providing political support for law and order, a process generally triggered and accompanied by anarchic forms of internal violence'. In short, failed states (French, '*états sans gouvernement*') are characterized by total or substantial collapse of both institutions and law and order, the consequence of serious and prolonged conflict. Robert Rotberg (2003: 1) notes:

nation-states fail when they are consumed by internal violence and cease delivering positive political goods to their inhabitants. Their governments lose credibility, and the contin-

---

[7] Such remarks did not seem to affect Congressman Lantos's electoral popularity. In the March 2004 Democratic primary in California's 12th Congressional District, he gained 71.6% of the votes cast. His nearest challenger acquired less than 20% (19.8%) (<http://www.lantos.org/>).

uing nature of the particular nation-state itself becomes questionable and illegitimate in the hearts and minds of its citizens.

Former UN Secretary-General, Boutros Boutros-Ghali (1995: 9) described the situation as follows:

> A feature of such conflicts is the collapse of state institutions, especially the police and judiciary, with resulting paralysis of governance, a breakdown of law and order, and general banditry and chaos. Not only are the functions of government suspended, but its assets are destroyed or looted and experienced officials are killed or flee the country. This is rarely the case in inter-state wars. It means that international intervention must extend beyond military and humanitarian tasks and must include the promotion of international reconciliation and the re-establishment of effective government.

Currently existing 'failed states' are invariably former 'Second' or 'Third World' countries that have been affected by three geopolitical factors:

1 *End of the cold war*. During the cold war (late 1940s–late 1980s), the two superpowers often helped to maintain illegitimate or unrepresentative governments in power. The purpose was to preserve them as potential or actual allies. The superpowers often supplied such governments with military equipment.
2 *Heritage of colonial regimes*. Typically, colonial administrations were in power for sufficient time to destroy or seriously undermine traditional social structures, without in most cases replacing them with working constitutional structures and/or effective state identity.
3 *Processes of modernization*. Often serving to encourage both social and geographical mobility, modernization processes were nevertheless only rarely matched by nation-building processes that led to the placing of post-colonial states on firm foundations.

From the political and legal point of view, the phenomenon of the 'failed state' is characterized by geographical and territorial political and functional factors:

1 *Geographical and territorial*. Failed states are inherently associated with both internal and endogenous problems, even though these may incidentally have cross-border impacts. Thus a failed state is characterized by an *implosion* rather than an *explosion* of the structures of power and authority, with a wholesale disintegration and destructuring of the institutions of political authority.
2 *Political*. This refers to the internal collapse of law and order, and the structures that normally guarantee it, rather than the kind of fragmentation of state authority characteristic of civil wars. In the latter circumstances, 'clearly identified military or paramilitary rebels fight either to strengthen their own position within the State or to break away from it'.
3 *Functional*. This state of affairs is associated with the 'absence of bodies capable, on the one hand, of representing the State at the international level and, on the other, of being influenced by the outside world' (Thürer 1999: 731).

Failed states are invariably non-democracies, and the absence of political opportunity structures facilitates state breakdown, failures of political and social stability, degeneration into civil war and, in some cases, the establishment of terrorist organizations, whether domestically or internationally focused.

The US focus upon terrorism in Afghanistan was later extended to another 'failed state': the regime of Saddam Hussein in Iraq. Note that this implies another meaning of the term: that is, an 'aggressive, arbitrary, tyrannical or totalitarian' state, said to have failed according to the norms and standards of current international law (Thürer 1999: 731). Alleged links between Saddam's regime and al-Qaeda were a stated reason for the US-led invasion of Iraq in March 2003 and of Saddam's subsequent arrest in December 2003. However, post-conflict in both Iraq and Afghanistan, there have been as yet inconclusive attempts to rebuild either country as a viable nation-state.

Beyond the specific issues of Afghanistan and Iraq, the 'war on terrorism' has also served to focus attention on other failed states, including Sudan, Sierra Leone, Somalia and former Yugoslavia, countries that are said to 'provide profit and sanctuary to nihilist outlaws' (Mallaby 2002: 2). In the past, when such power vacuums emerged to threaten powerful states' interests, they often had a simple solution: imperialism. But ever since World War II, this option has not been viable – even for the sole remaining superpower, the USA. Now, in the context of the 'war on terror', the established principle of 'anti-imperialist restraint is becoming harder to sustain . . . as the disorder in poor countries grows more threatening' (Mallaby 2002: 3).

In such countries, civil wars are both common and long-lasting. Focusing on 52 conflicts since 1960, a World Bank study in 2003 found that civil wars that started after 1980 on average lasted three times longer than those that had begun in the preceding two decades. The study also noted that when civil wars last longer, the number of countries that become involved in them grows. In addition, the study suggested that the trend towards violent disorder may prove self-sustaining, because war breeds conditions to make new conflicts more likely. The problem is that when states decline into widespread violence, people understandably focus much more on how to survive in the prevailing conditions, while longer term issues of state-building are neglected. Under such circumstances, there are clear, and unwelcome, economic results: savings, investment and wealth-creation all decline, while conditions of instability encourage government officials to benefit from their positions by stealing state assets rather than designing policies that might build long-term prosperity. In short term, during civil wars, a cycle of poverty, instability and violence emerges (Mallaby 2002: 2–3).

Apart from civil wars, other reasons noted for growing violence and social disorder include consequences of rapid population growth. By 2025, the global population is likely to increase from about six billion to eight billion people. The great majority of these extra people will be born in poor countries, some of which are Muslim societies with powerful currents of anti-Western extremism, including Afghanistan, Algeria, Iraq and Pakistan. Others will be born in sub-Saharan Africa, a region with especial demographic challenges, where high birth rates and the AIDS pandemic together threaten in some countries both social disintegration and governmental collapse. These conditions are especially conducive to the growth, organization and support of terrorist groups.

In some cases, terrorists will ally themselves with illegal drug producers and suppliers. Much of the global supply of illegal drugs comes from a small number of countries, including Afghanistan and Colombia. In addition, conflict is also conducive to other forms of criminal activity. For example, Sierra Leone's black-market diamonds are said to have benefited various criminals and terrorists, including former President Charles Taylor of Liberia and a Lebanon-based Islamist organization, Hezbollah. Finally, failed states also pose a challenge to more orderly ones because they increase immigration pressures. Such pressures help to create and sustain lucrative traffic in illegal workers, a business that can also provide profit to criminals or terrorists. In sum, there is much evidence to sustain the claim that failed and failing states together pose significant threats to regional and international order.

Political violence and failed states in Africa and Europe

In the light of the growing number of failed states, the once well-established distinction between self-defence and humanitarian intervention is now much harder to maintain. External military actions in failed states, or pre-emptive attempts to save states from failing, is often judged by both Western countries and 'non-failed' neighbouring states to be sensible and desirable in terms both of self-defence and demands of humanitarianism. Humanitarian concerns are self-evident in situations of civil war or mass killings of civilians. The likelihood of political violence spilling over into neighbouring countries and regions, as well as the fact that failed states are prime breeding grounds for political extremism and terrorism, encourage external actions to seek to resolve matters. As Keohane (2002: 39–40) notes, following 9/11 and the subsequent war on terrorism, 'sound arguments from self-interest are more persuasive than arguments from responsibility or altruism'.

Below we note several cases of external intervention both in Africa and former Yugoslavia, the result of the consequences of civil wars and associated attempts to rebuild state capacities. This reflects the view that if left to their own devices, failed states are not conducive to regional stability and peace. As Mozambique's President Joaquim Chissano said, in the context of efforts to build peace in his own country following a long civil war, 'conflicts, particularly violent conflicts between and within states in other parts of Africa, and in the world in general, are also a danger to our peace and tranquillity. Helping other peoples keep and maintain peace is also a way of defending our own peace' (Harsch 2003: 16).

Since the end of the cold war, many African countries have been beset by serious political violence, with a proliferation of armed conflicts. This development was facilitated by the fact that at that time, the late 1980s, most African countries had a non-democratic government, and military or unelected one-party regimes were common. Such regimes' stability and 'stickability' were undercut by the end of the cold war and the associated growth of both pro-democracy movements and outbreaks of often serious ethnic, religious and other social tensions. During the 1990s and early 2000s, many African countries – including Somalia, Rwanda, Liberia, Sierra Leone, Côte d'Ivoire, Burundi, Sudan and the Democratic Republic of Congo – witnessed the deaths of hundreds of thousands of people, most of whom were civilian non-combatants. Millions more 'succumbed to war-related epidemics and starvation' (Harsch 2003).

It is suggested that traditional peacekeeping missions – normally established to monitor peace agreements between established armies holding separate territories – are not well suited to dealing with Africa's current conflicts, many of which are civil wars or insurgencies, with multiple armed factions and grievances rooted in poverty and inequality. Moreover, even when peace accords are successfully negotiated, it is not always the case that all political and military leaders seem able or willing fully to control their followers. In some countries, such as Sierra Leone and Liberia, local fighters who profited from the chaos of war saw more advantage in continuing to fight than to lay down their arms (Harsch 2003: 14). In Liberia, recent claims were made that some Liberians had links with members of Osama bin Laden's al-Qaeda movement in order to operate an illegal diamond trade. A *Washington Post* article said that an investigation into al-Qaeda financing had uncovered evidence that the governments of both Liberia and Burkina Faso had hosted two senior al-Qaeda operatives who bought diamonds worth US\$20 million (Farah 2003).

A 2003 World Bank report provides contrasting examples of what has occurred in one war-torn African country – Sierra Leone – and another that has enjoyed political stability and economic growth – Botswana. In the early 1970s, both countries enjoyed similar per capita incomes, large diamond resources and potential. Subsequently, Botswana used these resources to become one of the fastest growing economies in the world. Eventually, it became a middle-income country. Diamond resources in Sierra Leone led to a completely different outcome: collapse into civil war, environmental degradation and, for most people, utter poverty. Now, Sierra Leone is at the bottom of the table of national human development. In terms of per capita income, the gap between Botswana and Sierra Leone is now 20 to 1. These examples dramatically demonstrate how much is at stake. For the international community, the challenge consists of shifting the balance to create more examples like Botswana than like Sierra Leone.

Signs are now emerging that political violence in African countries is being tackled with a renewed determination, to the extent that some regional countries have begun to commit their own resources to conflict prevention, management and resolution. The new sense of resolution coincided with the transformation from the Organization of African Unity (OAU) – established in 1963 – into the African Union (AU) in 2002. Under the auspices of the AU, regional conflict resolution and security are set to take a higher priority than in the past. Part of the reasons is that unlike the charter of the OAU, that of the AU explicitly affords the organization authority to 'intervene in cases of war crimes, genocide and crimes against humanity' (<www.africa-union.org/>). Among the AU's new institutions is a 15-member Peace and Security Council, which South Africa's president President Mbeki has identified as 'a collective security and early-warning arrangement to facilitate timely and efficient responses to conflicts and crisis situations in Africa'. In addition, the AU's new development strategy, the New Partnership for Africa's Development (NEPAD), includes the establishment of a new African Peer Review Mechanism. It is designed to promote good governance within African countries, seen as one of the best ways to prevent domestic political conflicts from leading to coups, insurgency or civil war (<www.nepad.org/>).

In sum, African efforts are being increasingly focused to try to deal with the problem of regional instability and conflict. In recent times, there has also been helpful intervention by non-African forces, for example, the involvement of British troops in ending the civil war in Sierra Leone in 2003. This might be described as a form of pragmatic ad hoc multilateralism, involving partnerships and joint action between various external countries, as well as the United Nations and various African peacekeepers. Each of these actors plays different but complementary roles in trying to resolve conflict in Africa.

EU peacemaking in the Balkans

Failed states are not confined to Africa and Asia. Our second case study focuses upon another region, the Balkans, characterized by state failure, serious political violence and links to international terrorism, including the scourge of al-Qaeda. EU and UN efforts in the Balkans indicate that there are practical limitations in trying to globalize political, social and economic norms in post-conflict reconstruction of failed states.

The EU's Balkan Stability Pact is an important vehicle for reconstruction that seeks to ask states in the Balkans to replace allegiance to a traditional conception of sovereignty and to replace it with economic, political and social integration with their neighbours. For Johnson (n/d), external attempts to rebuild failed states in the Balkans has led to two important questions:

1   Is the 'global governance' approach the best one to adopt in aiding post-conflict societies?
2   What are the trade-offs of this approach in terms of securing domestic support and durable reforms?

These two issues help to shape the primary goals of the EU and the UN in the Balkans. Chief among these is the aim to establish a liberal peace among countries in the Balkans, and in particular to deal with three key problems: the resolution of conflicts, the reconstruction of societies and the establishment of functioning market economies. Each is seen to be an important goal in the strategy to avoid future regional wars. The ultimate goal of liberal peace is prosperous stability (Johnson n/d: 3). Moves towards regional integration in the Balkans, as in Western Europe half a century ago, are judged to be a key way both to rebuild failed states and to set them on the road of peace and prosperity. In short, the aim is to (re)build 'the social, political, legal, economic, and security' foundations, in order to 'provide the necessary room for those in the region to rebuild on the ground' (Johnson n/d: 1–2).

How has the Balkan Stability Pact affected reconstruction in the area? One of the chief criticisms of EU efforts has been a tendency to undermine local authority by retaining significant control over the reform process. The tension that exists between the international community and regional states concerning which entity exercises authority over the territory illustrates this struggle. Johnson (n/d: 6) points to four significant results of both UN and EU involvement in the area:

1   Balkan Stability Pact initiatives attempt to de-emphasize traditional conceptions of sovereignty.
2   UN administrative activities in both Bosnia and Kosovo prevent the actual exercise of the state's authority.
3   Such external initiatives serve to wrest control from local decision-makers, while removing local leaders' motivation to reform.

4 'Reform-minded local leaders are forced to try to change their systems of governance knowing they have no discretion as to how and little authority to carry out
changes.'

In addition, EU and UN attempts to rebuild peace and stability in the Balkans do not
appear so far to have come to terms with the problem of international terrorism in the
region. The Balkans is one area where the United States apparently would prefer to
step lightly for fear of upsetting the tenuous peace. On the other hand, US and NATO
intervention was required to establish – and now to enforce – that peace in the republics
of the former Yugoslavia.

President George W. Bush has proclaimed that 'the war on terror' should be 'seamless', that is, Washington expects all countries to assist in fighting the scourge of international terrorism. In return, President Bush promised that the United States would
both 'support and reward governments' that, in his words, 'make the right choices'.
Regarding two polities in the Balkans – Kosovo and Macedonia – President Bush's
demand for a 'seamless approach' to deal with the scourge of terrorism appears to be
at risk of unravelling. Macedonian government officials claimed in 2003 that they were
not receiving the resources they needed to combat terrorism. The Macedonian government claimed that the Bush administration actually showed little interest in pursuing
links they claimed to have uncovered between al-Qaeda and groups allied with Albanian separatists (*The Mercury* 2004). The latter continued to foment trouble in northern
Macedonia in 2004, characterized by frequent incursions from neighbouring Kosovo.
Macedonian intelligence was in regular contact with both the CIA and the FBI; both
organizations were supplied with details of the al-Qaeda relationship with militant
Albanian nationalist groups. This was the case both in neighbouring Kosovo, under UN
protection, as well as in Macedonia, spared a civil war in 2002–3 following the broker-
ing of a peace agreement by NATO between the majority Macedonians and minority
ethnic Albanians.[8]

Intertwined Albanian groups in the region, most of them closely aligned with organ-
ized-crime syndicates, have as their objective the carving out of what they call 'Greater
Albania'. This is envisaged to be an area of some 90,000 square kilometers (56,000
square miles), including Kosovo, Greece, Macedonia, Bosnia, Serbia and Montenegro.
Such groups are said to have been disguised under the cover of dozens of 'humanitarian' agencies spread throughout Bosnia, Kosovo and Albania. Funding came from now-
defunct banks, including the Albanian-Arab Islamic Bank and from Osama bin Laden's
so-called 'Advisory and Reformation Committee', one of his largest Islamist front agencies, first established in London in 1994. According to Kurop (2001) this led to the rise
of a 'narco-jihad culture', a reference to the swift increase in heroin trafficking through
Kosovo, now said to be the most important Balkan route between Southeast Asia and
Europe after Turkey. It is also said to have funded terrorist activity directly associated
with both al-Qaeda and the Iranian Revolutionary Guard. 'Opium poppies, which barely

---

[8] Macedonian officials provided US National Security Council (NSC) aides with a 79-page report
on al-Qaeda activity in the area. The report, which was compiled by Macedonia's Ministry of the
Interior, lists the names of al-Qaeda-linked fighters and outlines the roles of two units, one num-
bering 120 and the other 250, in northern Macedonia (Kurop 2001).

existed in the Balkans before 1995, have become the No. 1 drug cultivated in the Balkans after marijuana. Operatives of two al Qaeda-sponsored Islamist cells who were arrested in Bosnia on Oct. 23 [2001] were linked to the heroin trade, underscoring the narco-jihad culture of today's post-war Balkans' (Kurop 2001).

In sum, as Bodansky (2001) contends, the Balkans have become the most prominent international area for recruiting and training recruits for Osama bin Laden's al-Qaeda network. Feeding off the region's impoverishment and taking root in the unsettled diplomatic aftermath of the Bosnia and Kosovo conflicts, al-Qaeda, along with Iranian Revolutionary Guard-sponsored terrorists, are said to be organizing and training in Western Europe's backyard.

Bodansky (2001) also claims that since the early 1990s, senior leaders of al-Qaeda have regularly visited the Balkans, including bin Laden himself on three occasions between 1994 and 1996. Ayman Al-Zawahiri, the Egyptian surgeon-turned-terrorist leader was in charge of terrorist training camps, with weapons of mass destruction factories and money-laundering and drug-trading networks throughout many Balkan countries, including Albania, Bosnia, Bulgaria, Kosovo, Macedonia and Turkey. From further afield, including Chechnya, came many recruits to al-Qaeda.

Conclusion

In this chapter we have examined forms of political participation characterized by their use of political violence of various kinds. We saw that even in established democracies, political violence is an occasional event, including in recent times examples of international terrorism apparently involving al-Qaeda. It was widely expected a decade or more ago that the third wave of democracy would lead to major reductions in levels of state-sponsored political violence. Instead, what happened – partly as a consequence of the end of the cold war – was both the spread of democracy and the 'globalization of political violence'. As a result, comparative political analysis was now compelled to explain and account both for political violence within countries as well as links between the latter and international terrorism. We saw that the phenomenon of failed states invites external involvement, while at the same time producing circumstances conducive to terrorist activity.

12
Religion

This chapter is organized as follows.[1] First, we examine the relationship between religious and political actors in historic and thematic contexts. We will see that from the seventeenth century, until recently, religion was understood to have lost nearly all its political importance. Second, we focus upon the various kinds of relationship between state and 'church'. Third, we assess reasons why religion is often said to have recently reappeared as an important domestic and international political actor. The final section examines three selected religious actors – Islam, the Roman Catholic Church and Confucianism – and assesses why they are politically important in selected established democracies (Britain and France), transitional democracies (Poland and Spain[2]) and non-democracies (China and Vietnam).

Religion and Politics in Historical Context

Prior to the eighteenth century and the subsequent formation and development of the international state system, religion was a key ideology that often stimulated conflict between societal groups. However, following the Peace of Westphalia in 1648 and the development of centralized states first in Western Europe and then via European colonization to most of the rest of the world, religion took a back seat as an organizing ideology both domestically and internationally.

It is often observed that there is a near-global resurgence of religion in the post-cold war era (see for example Petito and Hatzopoulos 2003). Most observers point to the Iranian revolution of 1978–9 as a key example in this regard, more generally marking the reappearance of religion as a significant political actor. To some commentators, Western Europe appears to be an exception to this trend, with the great majority of regional countries characterized by continuing secularization.[3] This situation contrasts with that in the USA, where secularization is said to be less well advanced, with over

---

[1] This chapter draws extensively on material first presented in Haynes 1998, 2001b, and 2003a. Interested readers will find a large number of relevant sources listed there. For reasons of brevity, I do not include all such sources in the bibliography of the current book.

[2] The focus is upon Spain's transition to democracy from the late 1970s.

[3] It is worth noting, however, that some contend that there is evidence to suggest that religion has never actually disappeared as a political cleavage in Western Europe, with certain issues, including abortion, arousing considerable religion-based controversy. My thanks to an anonymous reader of the manuscript for this point. See Aspalter (2002: 10–11) for a discussion of the role of Christian Democracy in the formation and development of West Germany's welfare state after 1949.

half of Americans claiming to attend religious services regularly. In addition, eight words – 'In God We Trust' and the 'United States of America' – appear on all US currency, both coins and notes. The continuing popular significance of religion in the USA is said to be a cultural issue, deriving in part from the original settlers in the seventeenth and eighteenth centuries, many of whom shared an Anglo-Protestant culture. This has stayed an important cultural factor until now.[4]

After the cold war, there appeared to be increased examples of conflicts character-ized by cultural/civilizational issues, with religion often a key component (Huntington 1993, 1996). More generally, the last two or three decades have seen increased political involvement of religious actors in many countries. Attention is often focused upon so-called 'Islamic fundamentalism', particularly in the Middle East, to the extent that a casual observer might assume that the entire region is polarized between Jews and Muslims. Both groups claim 'ownership' of various holy places, including Jerusalem, while conflict between them is also a result of the plight of the mostly Muslim Pales-tinians. There are also other political issues – including the large number of non-democratic regimes in the region – that have led to widespread political involvement of what I shall refer to in this chapter as 'Islamist' actors.[5]

For example, Algeria has endured nearly 15 years of civil war between the state and Islamists (sometimes also known, especially in the mass media, as 'Islamic funda-mentalists'). The conflict goes back to contested elections in 1991–2. In December 1991, Algeria held legislative elections that most independent observers characterized as amongst the freest ever held in the Middle East. The following January, however, Algeria's armed forces seized power to prevent what was likely to be a decisive victory in the elections by the Islamist Front Islamique du Salut (FIS). Many Western observers assumed that if the FIS achieved power it would summarily close down Algeria's newly refreshed democratic institutions and political system. *The Economist*, a respected London-based weekly news magazine, posed the question on many people's lips: 'What is the point of an experiment in democracy if the first people it delivers to power are intent on dismantling it?' (2 January 1992). The answer might well be: 'This is the popular will, it must be respected whatever the outcome.' Instead, Algeria's armed forces had its own ideas: the FIS was summarily banned, thousands of its supporters were incarcerated and so far more than 120,000 Algerians are estimated to have died in the subsequent civil war.

Islamists are also active elsewhere in the developing world. For example, in Africa, Nigeria is increasingly polarized politically between Muslims and Christians, the failed state of Somalia may eventually have an Islamist government, and Sudan has a gov-erning regime led by Islamists that has conducted a long-running civil war with various opponents.[6]

---

[4] This issue is a key theme of Samuel Huntington's book, *Who We Are: Challenges to American National Identity* (2004).

[5] An Islamist is a believer in or follower of Islam, who may be willing to use various political means to achieve religiously derived objectives.

[6] Contrary to popular belief, some of these opponents are actually Muslims. Critics contend that the true goal of the government is to impose enforced arabization upon Sudan's non-Arab peoples.

However, it is not only Islamists who pursue political goals related to religion. In officially secular India, there have been many examples of militant Hinduism that focused on, but were not confined to, the Babri Masjid mosque incident at Ayodhya in 1992. This event was instrumental in transforming the country's political landscape, to the extent that a 'Hindu fundamentalist' political party, the Bharatiya Janata Party (BJP), grew to swift political prominence. From the mid-1990s, the BJP has served in several coalition governments and until recently was the leading party in government.[7] In addition, Jewish religious parties currently serve in the Sharon government in Israel, while the Roman Catholic Church was a leading player in the turn to democracy in Spain, Poland and several Latin American countries in recent years. In sum, there are numerous examples of recent religious involvement in politics in various parts of the world.

State–'Church' Relations

In comparative political analysis the issue of the relationship between religion and politics is usually seen in the context of state–church interaction. Various models have been presented. However, it is important to note that there is a difficulty in seeking to apply such models universally because the concept of '*church*' derives from an Anglo-American standpoint. It is of most relevance to Western Christian traditions, especially British establishmentarianism – that is, the maintenance of the principle of 'establishment' – whereby one church alone (in Britain's case, the Anglican Church) is legally recognized as the established church. In other words, thinking of state–church relations we may assume a single relationship between two clearly distinct, unitary and solidly but separately institutionalized entities. In this model, there is implicitly *one* state and *one* church, and both entities' jurisdictional boundaries are clearly delineated, with both state and church relatively autonomous actors, but with the former enjoying predominance.

However, in Europe there are different examples to be noted. First, in CEE, communist states presided over – and rigorously enforced – a monolithic unity in state–church relations from the late 1940s to the late 1980s, with the communist ideology officially of much greater importance throughout the region compared to religious worldviews. Second, the leading church in France, the Catholic Church, placed itself on the wrong side of the French Revolution, a decision that led over time to the church losing much of its influence, privilege and moral authority. By the mid-twentieth century, the church in France lacked political influence, and was decidedly subservient to the state. Two points emerge from this brief examination of state–church relations in Europe: state prevails over church and the political saliency of state–church issues has declined over time – but not disappeared completely – in the context of a general process of secularization; that is, there has been a gradual diminution of the influence of religion on public affairs.

Expanding the issue of state–church relations to non-Christian contexts necessitates some preliminary conceptual clarifications – not least because the very idea of a pre-

---

[7] The secular Congress Party emerged as the largest party following the elections of April/May 2004. Following the elections, the breakdown of seats in the 542-seat Lok Sabha was: Congress and allies: 220; BJP and allies: 185; and others: 137.

vailing state–church dichotomy is culture-bound. *Church* is a Christian institution, while the modern understanding of *state* is deeply rooted in the post-Reformation European political experience. In their specific cultural setting and social significance, the tension and the debate over the church–state relationship are uniquely Western phenomena, present in the ambivalent dialectic of 'render therefore unto Caesar the things which be Caesar's and unto God the things which be God's' (Luke 20: 25). Loaded with Western cultural history, these two concepts cannot easily be translated into non-Christian terminologies. Some religions – for example, Hinduism – have no ecclesiastical structure at all and therefore no 'church' is conceptually possible. On the other hand, as we have already noted, India's political landscape was until recently dominated by the 'Hindu fundamentalist' BJP. Moreover, the traditional European-centric, Christian conceptual framework of church–state relations also appears alien within and with respect to nearly all African and Asian societies – whether predominantly Christian, Islamic, Buddhist or Hindu, or with various religious mixes. Only in Latin America is it pertinent to speak of state–church relations along the lines of the European model noted above. This is because of the historical regional dominance in the region of the Roman Catholic Church and the regional creation of European-style states in the early nineteenth century.

The differences between Christian conceptions of state and church and those of other world religions are well illustrated by reference to Islam. In the Muslim tradition, mosque is not church. The closest Islamic approximation to 'state' – *dawla* – means, conceptually, either a ruler's dynasty or his administration. Only with the specific stipulation of *church* as the generic concept for *moral community*, *priest* for the *custodians of the sacred law*, and *state* for *political community* can such concepts be used in Muslim contexts. On the level of theology, the command–obedience nexus that constitutes the Islamic definition of authority is not demarcated by conceptual categories of religion and politics. Life as a physical reality is conventionally thought by Muslims to be an expression of God's divine will and authority (*qudrah*'). The consequence is that in conventional Muslim thinking there is no validity in separating the matters of piety from those of the polity; both are divinely ordained. Yet, although both religious and political authorities are legitimated Islamically, they invariably constitute two independent social institutions. They do, however, regularly interact with each other. The point is that in Islam polity and religion are not necessarily – in fact, they are only very rarely in the current era – fused; instead, there is a wide variety of different patterns to be found, with differing arrangements in place in such countries as Turkey, Saudi Arabia, Malaysia, Jordan and Algeria (Haynes 1993, 1998). In sum, there is a variety of state–church relations. Table 12.1 presents some of the common arrangements, but does not aim to be exhaustive.

The *confessional* church–state relationship has ecclesiastical authority pre-eminent over secular power. A dominant religion – Islam in the countries in this section of table 12.1 – seeks to shape the world according to leaders' interpretations of God's plan for humankind. However, confessional states are now rare. One of the most consistent effects of secularization is to separate religious and secular power, often without regard for the religion or type of political system. However, events in various Muslim countries – Saudi Arabia after the country's creation in 1932, Iran after the 1979 Islamic revolution, and Sudan and Afghanistan in the 1990s – indicate that confessional polities are still a contemporary phenomenon.

Table 12.1 Politics and religion: A comparative model

Confessional	'Generally religious'	Established faith	Liberal secular	Marxist secular
Iran, Saudi Arabia, Sudan, Afghanistan (under Taliban rule, *c.*1996–2001)	Indonesia, USA, Spain, post-communist Poland	England, Denmark, Norway	France, Netherlands, Turkey, India, Ghana	China, North Korea, Vietnam, Albania, USSR (both until 1991)

The overthrow of the Shah of Iran in 1979 was one of the most significant, yet unexpected, political events of recent times, because of the pivotal role of Islam. Unlike earlier revolutions in other Muslim countries, such as Egypt, Iraq, Syria and Libya, Iran's was not a secular, leftist revolution from above, but one with massive popular support and participation. The outcome of the revolutionary process was a clerical, authoritarian regime. However, the Shah's regime was not a shaky monarchy but a powerful centralized autocratic state possessing a strong and feared security service (Sazeman-i Ettelaat va Amniyat-i Keshvar, National Organization for Intelligence and Security, known as SAVAK) and an apparently loyal and cohesive officer corps. Although the forces that overthrew the Shah came from all urban social classes, Iran's different nationalities and various ideologically different political parties and movements, an Islamic Republic was eventually declared. In this process, the *ulama* (Muslim clerics), organized in and by the Islamic Republican Party, came to power, established an Islamic constitution and proceeded thenceforward to dominate the country's post-revolutionary political institutions.

The Iranian revolution was internationally significant in various ways. First, it was the first revolution for 200 years – since the French Revolution (1789). It was also unusual in that the dominant ideology, forms of organization, leading personnel and proclaimed goals were all religious in appearance and inspiration. The guide for the post-revolution Iranian state was the tenets of the Muslim holy book, the Qu'ran, and the *Sunnah* (the traditions of the Prophet Muhammad, comprising what he said, did and of what he approved). While economic and political factors played a major part in the growth of the anti-Shah movement, its religious leadership saw the revolution's goals primarily in terms of building an Islamic state that publicly rejected both materialism and liberal democracy.

Radicals within Iran's ruling post-revolution elite began to lose ground following the death of Ayatollah Khomeini, the revolution's charismatic leader, in June 1989, a few months after the end of Iran's war with Iraq (1980–8). Around this time, it became increasingly clear that Iran's government was in need of foreign investment, technology and aid to help to secure the country's revolution. The lesson appeared to be that even a successful *Islamic* revolution could not succeed in splendid isolation. Iranians, like people everywhere, hoped for improving living standards. It also became increasingly clear that many were not content with islamicization of state and society, a process that many appeared to view as little more than political and social repression behind a religious façade. A self-proclaimed reformer, President Khatami, was elected to office in

1997 in a landslide victory, but found himself caught between the demands, on the one hand, of those wanting social and political liberalization and, on the other, the conservative mullahs. Khatami was unable to resolve the conundrum, and stalemate ensued between reformers and conservatives. In sum, the course of Iran's Islamic revolution, a quarter of a century after the event, indicates that the ruling regime has failed fully to develop its model of Islamic administration, while popular support for the government appears to be in decline.

Second, there are states described as '*generally religious*', including the USA, Indonesia, Poland, and Spain. These nations are said to be guided 'generally' by religious principles, but not tied to *specific* religious traditions. Belief in God is widely regarded as a key base on which the nation should develop. In Indonesia, under the regime of General Suharto (1965–98), this belief was expressed in the concept of *Pancasila*.[8] In the USA, the notion of 'civil religion' reflects a similar concern with religious principles underlying the nation's development. Unlike *Pancasila*, the practice of civil religion in the USA is not formally recognized. Finally, there are several countries, including Spain and Poland, whose national principles include a leading social role for the Roman Catholic Church.

Third, the Scandinavian countries and England are examples of a third category: *countries with an officially established faith*. However, they are also socially highly secular. Over time, the voice of their established churches in relation to public policy issues has become of less significance. In the case of the Anglican Church in England, its voice declined to marginality in the 1970s, before later regaining some significance in relation to societal demands for greater social justice especially under Conservative governments in the 1980s and 1990s.

The fourth model is currently very common: *the liberal secular*. This encapsulates the notion of secular power holding sway over religion, with clear distance, detachment and separation between church and state (Hallencreutz and Westerlund 1996: 2). The state strives to use religion for its own ends, to 'legitimate political rule and to sanctify economic oppression and the given system' of social stratification (Casanova 1994: 49). Secularization policies were widely pursued as a means of national integration in postcolonial multi-religious states, including India, although not always with conspicuous success. In this model, no religion is given official predominance. In fact, in aggressively modernizing countries, including India and post-Ottoman Turkey, modernization was expected to lead inevitably to a high and general level of secularization; hence, the constitutions of these countries are notably neutral towards religion. But things turned out differently: in recent years, both democratization and secularization have worked at cross purposes. Increasing participation in the political arena has drawn in new social forces – in India, they include religious Hindus, Sikhs and Muslims – who, in demanding greater formal recognition of their religions by the state, have been responsible for making religion a central issue in contemporary Indian politics. In Turkey, the Islam-orientated Welfare Party (*Refah Partisi*) achieved power via the ballot box in 1996. Its achievement, followed by that of its successor party, the Justice and Development Party,

---

[8]The *Pancasila* idea is summed up in five principles: (1) Kebangsaan (nationalism), (2) Kemanusiaan (humanism or internationalism), (3) Kerakyatan (representative government or democracy), (4) Keadilan Sosial (social justice), (5) Ketuhanan (monotheism).

which gained power in 2002, indicates that even when secularization is aggressively pursued over a long period, as in Turkey, it does not necessarily imply that the political appeal of religious parties is doomed to disappear (Turan 2003).

Finally, there are *Marxist secular states*. They have a particular kind of relationship with religion, sometimes identified as 'anti-religion'. Communism is synonymous with a particular and dismissive attitude towards religion. In some cases, communist governments have even 'abolished' religion, as in Albania between 1947 and 1990. Most communist regimes, however, permitted religion and 'national religious organizations' to exist, although this was on the understanding that religion was the private, spiritual concern of the individual. This arrangement constituted a promise that the authorities would respect people's religious faith and practice (as long as they did it behind closed doors as a solitary vice not for public view). Communist governments usually sought to use their control of religion as a means to further their objective of total social control. Religious organizations were frequently, as in the USRR, merely liturgical institutions, that is, with no official task other than holding divine services. Numbers of permitted places of worship were typically greatly reduced under communist rule.

Paradoxically, however, even the most strident and prolonged state-communist anti-religion campaigns failed to secularize societies. When measured by the high levels of religiosity and the pivotal role of the Christian churches in the returns to democracy in CEE, as well as the situation in non-communist but mostly secular-leaning Latin American countries and the revival of Islam in formerly communist Central Asia, then it is clear that for many if not most people living in such countries religion retained immense significance. On the other hand, the communist, anti-religion state is not only an issue of historical interest. In the mid-1990s, the Chinese government, rulers of an estimated 1.3 billion people, embarked upon a sustained campaign to 'teach atheism to Tibetan Buddhists', necessary, the government argued, so that Tibetans could 'break free of the bewitchment' of religion (Gittings 1996). Confusingly, at the same time the communist government also sought to resuscitate an ancient Chinese 'religious' tradition, Confucianism, as a means of trying to inculcate what it saw as its desirable qualities during a time of unparalleled economic liberalization.

In sum, there are various types of relationship between 'church' and state in the contemporary world. None, however, has been permanently able to resolve the tension between religion and the secular world. The chief manifestation of this tension in recent times is the desire of many religious organizations not to allow the state to sideline them, as governments – almost everywhere – seek to bite ever deeper into social life, a domain that was once significantly the domain of religion. The result has been that, around the world, religious actors have become concerned with political issues. We turn to this topic next.

Political Involvement of Religion: Novelty or Persistence?

It is high time to make it plain what I mean by the term 'religion'. In this chapter, religion has two analytically distinct, yet related meanings. In a *spiritual* sense, religion pertains in three ways to models of social and individual behaviour that help believers to organize their everyday lives. First, it is to do with the idea of *transcendence*, that is, it relates to supernatural realities. Second, it is concerned with *sacredness*, that is, a system of language and practice that organizes the world in terms of what is deemed holy. Third, it refers to *ultimacy*: it relates people to the ultimate conditions of existence.

In another, *material*, sense, religious beliefs can motivate individuals and groups to act in pursuit of social or political goals. Very few – if any – religious groups have an *absolute* lack of concern for at least *some* social and political issues. Consequently, as Calvert and Calvert (2001: 140) point out, religion can be 'a mobiliser of masses, a controller of mass action . . . an excuse for repression [or] an ideological basis for dissent'. In many countries, religion is an important source of basic value orientations; this may have social and/or political connotations.

It is often suggested that there is growing political involvement of religion in countries around the world. An American commentator, George Weigel (quoted in Huntington 1993: 26), has claimed that there is an 'unsecularization of the world', that is, a global religious revitalization. Thomas (1995: 1; also see Thomas 2003) argues that there is now an unexpected 'global resurgence of religious ideas and social movements . . . taking place at the same time among diverse cultures, in different countries, and in states at different levels of economic development'.

How best to account for such claims? The first thing to note is that there is no simple, clear-cut reason, no single theoretical explanation to cover all cases. On the other hand, the widespread emergence of religious actors with overtly social or political goals is often linked to the impact of both modernization and globalization – that is, historically unprecedented, diverse, massive change, characterized by urbanization, industrialization and abrupt technological developments. In particular, modernization is said not only to have undermined traditional value systems but also to have allocated opportunities – both within and between countries – in highly unequal ways. This led to many people feeling both disorientated and troubled and, as a result, some at least have (re)turned to religion as a source of solace and comfort. In doing so, they aim to achieve a new or renewed sense of identity, to give their lives greater meaning and purpose.

A second, linked set of explanations for what many observers have claimed is a near-global religious resurgence moves away from the presumed consequences of modernization/globalization to an explanation rooted in what is seen as a generalized 'atmosphere of crisis' said to be afflicting many people around the world. The key factor is said to be widespread disillusionment with the abilities of secular state leaders to direct their socio-economic polities to the generalized benefit of their citizens. Their disappointment is also said to feed into perceptions that many among such leaders enjoy power illegitimately, a belief bolstered when they resort to political oppression to remain in power. Adding to this sense of crisis is said to be widespread belief – not only among older people – that traditional morals and values are declining. In sum, the cumulative impact of these factors is said to provide a fertile milieu for the 'return' or resurgence of religion.

This is not to suggest that such explanations necessarily see the influence of religion only in relation to personal and social issues. Indeed, many commentators have pointed to a key *political* result of the 'return' of religion in various parts of the world: numerous highly politicized religious groups, institutions and movements. Such actors are found in many different faiths and sects, but share a key characteristic: the goal of changing domestic, and in some cases international, arrangements so as to (re)place religion as a central social and political influence. They adopt various tactics to try to achieve their goals. Some confine their activities to the realm of political protest, reform or change through the ballot box, others may resort to political violence to pursue their objectives. Overall, 'because it is so reliable a source of emotion, religion is a recurring source of social movement framing. Religion provides ready-made symbols, rituals, and solidarities that can be accessed and appropriated by movement leaders' (Tarrow 1998: 112).

Some critics however pose the following question: how do we *know* that there actually *is* a global religious resurgence? Where is the evidence? Some argue that, rather than a religious resurgence, what is actually happening is instead merely a symptom of increased information as a result of the communications revolution. That is, political religion may simply be more visible now; it does not mean that there is more of it. Smith (1990: 34) claims that 'what has changed in the present situation . . . is mainly the growing awareness of [religious actors with political goals] by the Western world, and the perception that they might be related to our interests'. Tarrow (1998: 115) suggests that various forms of 'political religion' were popularized 'through the mass media. In places as diverse as Iran and the United States, religious figures became adept at using the media to diffuse their political messages.'

In other words, what we are seeing is persistence rather than novelty in various manifestations of contemporary political religion. For example, various religious traditions – for example, Hinduism, Buddhism and Islam – all experienced periods of intense political activity during the first half of the twentieth century in many countries under colonial rule. From the 1920s and 1930s, religion was often used in the service of anti-colonial nationalism, a major facet of emerging national identity in opposition to alien rule. In some Muslim countries – such as, Algeria, Egypt and Indonesia – Islamic consciousness was the defining ideology of nationalist movements. In 1947, immediately after World War II, Pakistan was founded as a Muslim state, religiously and culturally distinct from India, 80 per cent Hindu. A decade later, Buddhism was politically important in, inter alia, Burma, Sri Lanka and Cambodia. During the 1960s and later, both 'Christian democracy' – that is, applying Christian precepts to politics in various countries including West Germany and Italy – and 'liberation theology' – a radical Roman Catholic worldview underlining the importance of social justice ideology using Christianity as the basis of a demand for more equality for the poor – were politically consequential in various countries. Later, from the 1970s until now, religious actors have been politically important in diverse countries, including Iran, Nicaragua, Poland, Spain and the United States.

In sum, what our account suggests is that *opposition* to the status quo is the concern of many religious actors with political goals. We have also seen that this is not a novel development, but linked historically in many cases to European colonization and associated processes of globalization. This suggests that many current manifestations of political religion can be located in historical context stressing *continuity* rather than *change*.

Religion and Globalization

To what extent does contemporary globalization affect the relationship between religion and politics? Do religious actors have a capacity to undermine state sovereignty, that is, to 'talk' directly to religious believers across international boundaries beyond state control? To address these questions we need to start by looking at these issues in the context of historical globalization.

We have already noted that some observers contend that there is a global resurgence of religion. This needs, however, to be seen in historical context. We noted earlier that, over time, religion lost most of its earlier political significance during the development of the modern international system. Prior to that, that is, before the seventeenth century, both Islam and Christianity had been key political actors. Islam had expanded from its Arabian heartland in westerly, easterly, southerly and northern directions for nearly a millennium. As a consequence, vast territories in Africa and Asia and smaller areas of Europe (parts of the Balkans and much of the Iberian peninsular) came under Muslim control. But unable to deal with the consequences of centralized Christian polities in Western Europe – superior firepower and organizational skills – Islam found itself on the back foot. The consequence was a significant reduction in the faith's influence in Europe from the late fifteenth century. Overall, however, despite this setback, Islam elsewhere developed into a holistic religious, social and cultural system, developing into a global religion via the spread of transnational religious communities.

Christendom is another historic example of a transnational religious society that developed under historical conditions of globalization. During medieval times 'Christendom' referred to a generalized conception among Christians of being subject to universal norms and laws derived from the word of God. Later, and contemporaneous with the demise of Islam as a major force in Europe, the movement of Europeans to non-European areas facilitated the growth of a transnational Christian community, albeit one divided by differing interpretations of Christianity. The transnational spread of Christianity beyond Europe was also facilitated by processes of colonization, which began with a search for gold in the Americas by sundry Spanish and Portuguese 'explorers' from the late fifteenth century. This led, soon after, to the establishment in the 'New World' of various Spanish or Portuguese-administered colonies; contemporaneously, different Christian Europeans – British, French and Dutch – gained territory in the Caribbean and in parts of Asia. Thus the spread of Christianity was inextricably linked to wider European expansionism, to become a major component of an emerging web of global interactions. Over time, however, the public and political role of Christianity became increasingly marginal, following the rise to prominence of secular states in Europe and elsewhere. Following the Treaty of Westphalia in 1648 (which ended the religious wars in Europe between Catholics and Protestants), the history of the development of the global state system was primarily the history of clashing nationalisms, with each national group aiming for its own state and with a much reduced political role for religion.

In sum, Christian and Muslim transnational religious communities predated the emergence of centralized secular states. Prior to the seventeenth century religious interactions were pivotal to the emergence of an international system. Both Christianity and Islam grew to become world religions, conveying their associated civilizations around the world via colonization, conquest and the expansion of global trade. Contending religious beliefs were the chief motor of international conflicts, the main threat to peace and security. However, the political importance of religion in international politics became increasingly negligible from the seventeenth century, re-emerging as politically important only in the late twentieth century, encouraged by globalization and the accompanying communications revolution.

The last two decades of the twentieth century was an era of fundamental global political, social and economic changes, associated with the multifaceted processes we have identified under the rubric of 'globalization'. This process not only emphasized consolidation of an increasingly global economy and, to some, the gradual emergence of a 'global culture', but was also manifested in other developments, notably the third wave of democracy and increased focus on human rights. Finally, as we saw above, there were also many examples of the increased political involvement of religion. It is this phenomenon that led to the claim that there was a global religious revitalization, or, as George Weigel put it, an 'unsecularization of the world' (quoted in Huntington 1993: 26).

Weigel did not mean to imply that this was 'only' an *apolitical* respiritualization, but that it was also linked to a generalized re-engagement of religion and politics, a development facilitated by the processes of globalization and encouraged by the communications revolution. As a result, Beyer suggests (1994: 1), we now live in 'a globalizing social reality, one in which previously effective barriers to communication no longer exist'. The development of transnational religious communities was greatly enhanced by ease of inter-personal and inter-group communications, facilitating the spread of their messages and enabling such groups to form regional or global networks (Rudolph and Piscatori 1997). Thus if Wiegel is right and there is an 'unsecularization of the world' with political connotations, we should be able to pinpoint examples of such a process.

To date, however, theoretical literature on transnationalism has devoted little concentrated attention to religious phenomena. This is because transnational linkages and penetration have normally been studied in the international relations literature primarily to assess their impact on questions of political and economic security. The conventional security bias of much of the transnational literature helps explain the lack of references to religious actors. Until the recent emergence of transnational Islamist actors in the 1980s, religious actors were usually regarded as an interesting phenomenon, although remote from the central questions affecting states and state power in international politics. The explanation for this relative neglect lies in a key assumption embedded in the social sciences. One presupposition, especially evident in theories of modernization and political development, was that the future of the integrated nation-state lay in secular participatory politics. The implication was that, in order successfully to build nation-states, political leaders would have to remain as neutral as possible from the entanglements of particularist claims, including those derived from religion. The connotation was that politics must be separated from religion (and ethnicity) so as to avoid dogmatism and encourage tolerance among their citizens. As decades of apparently unstoppable movement towards increasingly secular societies in Western and other 'modernized' parts of the world suggested, over time religion and piety became ever more private matters. The consequence was that religion was relegated to the category of a problem that must not be allowed to intrude on the search for national unity and political stability.

In the light of such conclusions, how is it possible to explain the widespread existence of religious actors with political goals? We have already seen that religious actors can directly affect the internal politics of states and thus qualify state power, as conventionally understood. Globalization is significant in this context for two main reasons. First, globalization facilitates the transmission of both material and non-material factors, and religious actors may seek to use opportunities to spread messages, funds and personnel. Second, our case studies show that the domestic impact of religion is always contoured by particular social and political circumstances in individual countries. To illustrate this claim, first we examine Muslim minorities in two established democracies (Britain and France), before moving to explore the significance of the Roman Catholic Church on democratization outcomes in transitional democracies (Poland and Spain). Finally, we investigate how Confucianism is now employed by non-democratic – officially communist – governments in China and Vietnam to try to allay the impact on their populations of economic liberalization and globalization.

Established Democracies

Britain

Britain is home to approximately 1.6 million Muslims, mostly made up of people from Pakistan, Bangladesh, Africa, Cyprus, Malaysia, the Middle East and, most recently, Eastern Europe (primarily Bosnia). Until the 1960s, Islam remained a relatively obscure religion in Britain, with only a few mosques in several cities, including Cardiff, Liverpool, Manchester, South Shields and London's East End. The situation changed with the expansion of Muslim labour migration in the 1970s. At this time, as a result of a change in immigration policy, British governments halted further labour immigration, while allowing family unification (Nielsen 1992: 2). Thereafter, the Muslim presence in Britain changed from one of primarily migrant workers to social communities in a fuller sense, and contacts increased between Muslim families and the British host society.

During the 1980s, some Muslims – especially so-called 'second-generation' Muslims, the offspring of first-generation immigrants and their spouses – became increasingly politically active. Such people, with British citizenship and familiar with British assumptions about political participation, began to demand what they saw as their rights. At the same time, a backlash began against some British Muslims from certain sections of existing British society, who saw them as a threat to social stability. This was in part because of increased fears of 'Islamic fundamentalism', a consequence both of Iran's revolution in 1979 and the conflict between Israel and the mostly Muslim Palestinians, issues that helped to increase Islamic militancy in many parts of the world.

At the same time, some British Muslims began increasingly to identify with struggles of fellow Muslims in Israel-controlled Palestine and elsewhere, with more radical Muslims organizing themselves into 'a huge web of Islamic associations of various shades of feeling and opinion' (Kepel 1994: 37). These organizations included the Young Muslims, Al Muntada al Islami, Muslim Welfare House, Al-Muhajiroun and Hizb ut Tahrir, and collectively represented a range of Islamic positions. Hizb ut Tahrir was often regarded as the most radical, with around 2,000 members in Britain in the 1990s. Its activists called for Muslim separation from Western society, while employing 'anti-Israel, anti-homosexual, anti-liberal rhetoric' (Dodd 1996).

Some young Muslims were said to be attracted to Hizb ut Tahrir and other radical groups because of their deep sense of injustice. Ansari (2002: 1) suggests that this concern is likely to have increased over time because of 'a huge rise in the number of attacks on Muslims in Britain, increasing threats to civil liberties in the name of security measures, a resurgence in the activities of the far-right in Britain and elsewhere in Europe, and a crackdown on refugees fleeing persecution'. Overall, British Muslims were said primarily to be concerned about two main issues, one domestic and one external. These were, respectively, defence of their culture and religion, especially in relation to their children's education, and terrorism and security issues, especially following the US/British invasion of Iraq to oust Saddam Hussein in March 2003, and the subsequent pacification of the country that saw a handover of sovereignty to an indigenous Iraqi government in June 2004.

Education is a very important issue for most Muslim parents in Britain, who have a strong desire to safeguard their culture among their children. Growing numbers of British Muslims are said increasingly to believe that segregated education is necessary to stop young Muslims drifting away from their faith (Travis 2004). Consequently, many Muslim parents have asked for certain conditions to be met by the education authorities on behalf of their children, for instance the inclusion in the curriculum of teachings of Islam, with school prayer facilities; the right to celebrate the main Muslim festivals, Eid ul Fitr and Eid ul Adha; halal food on offer at school; the exemption of their children from sex education; and an insistence on the wearing of 'modest' clothing, especially for girls (Goulborne and Joly 1989: 92–4). Very often, however, these conditions are not met in state education in Britain, and, as a result, increasing numbers of Muslim children are now being withdrawn from state education. Reflecting this, the number of Muslim schools in Britain increased more than four times, from 24 in the mid-1990s to more than 100 in 2002, now educating more than 10,000 Muslim pupils (Ahmad 2002). A recent ICM survey of 500 British Muslims indicated that if they could, nearly half would send their child to a Muslim school rather than a conventional state school. Since only a small fraction of Muslim children are already in such schools, this represents a huge latent demand for separate religious schooling. The demand is said to be greatest among men, younger families and the more affluent (Travis 2004).

The second key issue of concern to many British Muslims was the war in Iraq in early 2003, and its aftermath. An ICM survey in March 2004 found that there was both a declining desire to integrate with the host culture and people, as well as much resentment about continued Western – especially US and UK – involvement in Iraq, an issue seen by many simply as a 'war on Islam'. The poll also showed that many British Muslims see the continuing 'war against terrorism' as a Western-led war against Islam as a faith and Muslims as a group. Nearly two-thirds (64 per cent) believed that British anti-terrorist laws were being used unfairly against Britain's Muslim community (Travis 2004). (This issue is examined further in chapter 13.)

France

France is home to around five million Muslim inhabitants, nearly a tenth of the population. It is thought that about 50 per cent have French citizenship – although precise figures are unavailable. This is because the French state is officially secular and officials do not ask questions about religion. Many observers would agree, however, that while predominantly Catholic, France now has more Muslims than Jews or Protestants, historically the country's most significant religious minorities. Islam is now probably the country's second religion in terms of numbers of followers.

Growth in the numbers of Muslims in France came, as in Britain, initially by immigration. Although a presence from around the time of World War I, they arrived in significant numbers only in the 1960s, most of them coming from France's former North African colonies, including Algeria and Morocco. At this time, the government granted asylum to hundreds of thousands of Algerians who had fought on the French side in Algeria's 1954–62 war of independence. During the same decade, France also invited immigrant manpower – including Muslims – to meet the needs of a then booming economy. The economic boom fizzled out in the 1970s, but by then there were Muslims in most of France's population centres.

Like Britain, France has had a policy of 'zero immigration' since the 1970s. However, France's Muslim population still increases because of relatively high birth rates, an unknown number of illegal entrants, particularly from Africa, and an exception that allows the reunion of immigrant families. The purpose of the exception makes clear French policy in regard to its Muslims: to legitimize them by integrating them into French society. This policy contrasts with that of Britain, where successive governments' strategy has been multiculturalism.

Successive French governments have sought to integrate Muslims into the existing society. This has implied reducing overt signs of 'Muslim-ness', especially particularistic forms of dress, such as the hijab ('Islamic veil'). The so-called 'headscarves of Creil affair' erupted in late 1989, and focused on the desire of several young Muslim women to wear Islamic headscarves at school in the seaside town of Creil. The affair was portrayed in the French media as an attempt to introduce 'communalism' into schools, a traditionally neutral sphere. To explain the passion that this issue has raised we need to be aware that France is the country where the Enlightenment began, a development characterized by a strong conviction that the common ground for the French is 'rationality'. This implies that religion takes a secondary position. Many French people are highly secular, and perceive visible signs of religious identity – such as the hijab – as highly disturbing because they believe it undermines basic French values.

Around this time in France, as in Britain, Islamic networks were growing, made up primarily of students and other young people, often from the Maghreb. Some wanted to stage a trial of strength by confronting the French state on the sensitive ground of laïcité ('secularism') (Kepel 1994: 40). The issue seemed to strike a chord with many French Muslims who, it appeared, also wanted 'positive discrimination' in favour of Muslim girls in French state schools. The student militants appointed themselves as the spokesmen of 'Islam', and sought to negotiate 'positive discrimination' for practising Muslims that would allow them to withdraw, in some areas, from the laws of the Republic and instead obey sharia law. The Islamic militants found powerful allies, including the hierarchy of the Roman Catholic Church and some Jewish rabbis. Such religious figures supported them because they too were determined to seek a renewal of their faiths in the face of laïcité (Kepel 1994: 41). Eventually, after a long campaign, the French national assembly voted overwhelmingly in February 2004 in favour of a ban on Islamic veils in state schools, despite new warnings from religious leaders that the law would persecute Muslims and encourage fundamentalism. MPs voted 494:36 in favour of banning all 'conspicuous' religious symbols in schools. The law, ratified by the senate in March, came into effect in September 2004 (Henley 2004).

Turning to the issue of the war in Iraq in 2003 and its aftermath, the French government was strongly opposed to the Western-imposed conflict. Did France's large Muslim minority help determine French policy? Such a question is hard to answer, but it does seem clear that President Chirac welcomed the renewed bond between the Muslim community and the rest of the French population that resulted from a common opposition to the war in Iraq, and also the boost to his personal popularity that he would no doubt gain from the anti-war stance.

In conclusion, the conventional view is that France has an 'integrationist' approach to its Muslims, while that of the British is 'multiculturalist'. These are sometimes regarded as irreconcilable opposites, although this view appears too simplistic. While cultural diversity is a legitimate policy goal of any government, it is clear that social exclusion and prejudice must also be addressed. This is especially the case in the absence of legislation dealing with religious, as opposed to racial discrimination. In addition, in varying ways it is clear that the 2003 Iraq war and the subsequent problematic 'peace' were issues that galvanized the attentions of both British and French Muslims. While most ordinary Muslims in both countries – including 75 per cent in Britain (Travis 2004) – abhorred terrorist attacks whoever carried them out, some at least took the issue of the war in Iraq so seriously that they went there to fight against British and American troops ('European Muslims "fighting in Iraq"', 2004).

Transitional Democracies

Until the 1970s, the Roman Catholic Church was widely seen as an 'uncompromising opponent of liberalism and democracy' (Rueschemeyer et al. 1992: 281). This was partly because, in the 1920s and 1930s, the church had dealt with the rise of fascism in Europe by giving at least tacit support to several governments, including those of Spain and Germany, which had espoused the ideology. After World War II the church had enjoyed close relationships with several avowedly conservative Christian Democrat parties in Western Europe, including that of Italy. It was not until the Second Vatican Council of 1962–5 (known as Vatican II) that the Pope and other senior Catholic figures publicly expressed concern with human rights and democracy issues. This expression of papal interest came during a momentous period for world politics: the transition from colonial to postcolonial rule in Africa and the aftermath of decolonization in Asia. It was also the time of the rise of socially progressive Catholic theology, known as liberation theology. The overall point is that over time, the Roman Catholic Church shifted its position on some political issues and eventually became a strong supporter of democracy. This development was reflected in strong support for democratization in several authoritarian countries. In our case studies we give examples from Poland and Spain.

Poland

Nearly 96 per cent of Poland's 36 million people are Roman Catholics (<http://www.catholic-hierarchy.org/country/sc1.html>). Emergence of an institutional Roman Catholic concern with issues of social justice from the 1960s was followed, in the 1980s and 1990s, by a further period of significant international changes: the end of the cold war, the third wave of democracy and intensification of various aspects of globalization. During the third wave of democracy, the church was an important actor in relation to various countries, including Poland, Spain and various African and Latin American nations. Overall, as Witte (1993: 11) noted in the early 1990s, 'twenty-four of the thirty-two new democracies born since 1973 are predominantly Roman Catholic in confession'.

In Poland, the communist state had a policy of 'cultural strangulation' towards religion, designed to choke off its social importance. However, a huge majority of Poles are Catholics, and this turned out to be a significant factor in the country's democratization in the late 1980s. There is an important transnational factor to be noted: the Vatican's role in general and that of the Pope, John Paul II, a Pole, in particular.

Encouraged by the Pope's support, some Polish Catholic activists represented both a counter-culture and alternative social space to the official ideology and channels. This led, in 1980, to the creation of the Solidarity movement that articulated and expressed Catholic social ethics as a counter-statement to those of communism. This reflected not only a significant convergence between national and religious identity in Poland, but also, just as importantly, symbolized the failure of a communist (secular) identity fundamentally to implant itself in the hearts and minds of most Poles, people whose cultural heritage is firmly Christian-based. In short, Poland's Christian heritage was a vital resource that helped create and then sustain opposition to communist rule.

Poland's communist government collapsed in late 1989. Flushed with success, some Polish Catholics, most of them lay people, began to press for the 'reinstatement of ecclesiastical norms in public law' (Martin 1994: 4). But they met with no success – because the majority of Poles did not want it. As Michel (1994: 34) notes, the problem for the church was how to define its place within the post-communist world: 'Everything seems to indicate that it will be a challenge much more difficult than that posed by the Soviet system.' Why should this be the case? The paradox is that while many Poles looked to the church as a nationalist focal point of anti-communism, once democracy was won most shifted their attention to conventional – that is, secular – political opportunity structures – such as parties – to try to achieve socio-political objectives. The diminished influence of the church was clear when several of its aspirations – including opposition to abortion, divorce and the suitability of a former communist for the post of national president in the 1995 election – were decisively not endorsed by most Poles. This represented more generally both a swift and a clear 'distancing of Polish political culture from the church' (Johnston 1992: 71–2). No doubt aware of its declining influence, the church did not bother to sponsor or even overtly support a political party in the following years.

The role of Catholic activists in undermining and bringing down Poland's communist government highlights that in a certain historical period – the 1970s and 1980s – the church had much influence among ordinary citizens. However, the swift decline into political irrelevance in the 1990s – when Catholic views were unable to prevail on a range of political, social and moral questions – suggest that many Poles were content to see the Church fulfil a significant opposition role, especially when it appeared to many that there was no other viable alternative. They were, however, mostly much less willing to afford the Church a key voice following the overthrow of the communist regime and the establishment of democracy and, more generally, pluralist politics.

Spain

Some 94 per cent of Spain's 41 million people are Catholics (<http://www.catholic-hierarchy.org/country/sc1.html>). During the country's democratic transition in the 1970s, the Vatican's intervention was of a different kind from that in Poland. In Spain, the Vatican's alterations to the church's organizational structure and composition of the

Spanish episcopate tipped the balance of forces decisively in the early 1970s in favour of 'the new social Catholicism', a key result of Vatican II. As a result, reformers gained control of the newly created National Conference of Bishops. The church also moved to reduce its links with the authoritarian regime of General Franco in 1971. Overall, these moves reflected not only changes in the church's perception of socio-political issues but also wider changes taking place in Spain's political culture.

During the Franco era (1938–75), the norms and values of civil society and the democratic traditions of liberal Spain were to some degree preserved and transmitted through family, working-class and intellectual networks. These networks formed the basis of the democratic opposition movement that emerged independently of the institutional church in the late 1960s and early 1970s. Unlike, for example, in Poland or Brazil, the church in Spain neither became 'the voice of the voiceless' nor promoter of a renewed civil society (Rueschemeyer et al. 1992: 213). Casanova (1994: 87) explains, however, that the church did contribute to the growth of the democratic opposition in two important, if somewhat indirect, ways. The church offered, first, religious legitimation for democratic principles upon which the activities of the opposition were based, including freedom of expression and association; and, second, its churches and monasteries as relatively protected sanctuaries for some opposition figures. Consequently, opposition activists were able to meet to coordinate diverse sectors of the democratic opposition into a unified movement.

When Franco died in November 1975, important sections of his regime were prepared to accept the legitimacy of a series of 'pacts' that dissolved all-important Francoist institutions, legalized all political parties (including the Communist Party), and permitted elections for a constituent assembly to produce a democratic constitution in 1978. Democracy had been overwhelmingly endorsed by a referendum in 1976 and in the following year a democratically elected – socialist – government achieved power. During these momentous events, the church played a low-key, yet positive, backstage role. It accepted both the reality and the principles of separation of church and state, and of religious freedom, and, as in Poland, declined either to sponsor a 'Catholic' party or to support directly any Christian Democratic parties in post-transition elections.

Casanova (1994: 89) suggests three main factors moulded the Church's position: (1) 'genuine desire for religious peace'; (2) realization that the Catholic community, including clergy, was largely politically pluralistic and thus would not necessarily support a church-backed party; and (3) fear that such a party would be politically insignificant more generally among the electorate, thus perhaps undermining the church's claim that Catholicism was Spain's national religion. In short, the church's stance amounted to recognition of the voluntary principle of religious allegiance in Spain. It also provided evidence that the church accepted disestablishment from the state and the reality of a pluralist society. Put another way, by the 1970s Catholicism had ceased to be Spain's national faith, in the sense that principles of religious faith, national identity and political citizenship were now delinked.

The restoration of a constitutional monarchy in 1978, followed by a series of elected governments, seemed to encourage the church to move again in a conservative direction, straining relations with the state (McEwan 1989: 249–50). However, the number of practising Catholics in Spain was rapidly falling. While over 90 per cent of Spaniards regard themselves as Catholics, little more than a third – 38 per cent – attend mass regularly. Among the young the decline is even steeper, with fewer than 30 per cent

attending Church 'regularly' (Gooch 1996). However, practising Catholics are distributed evenly throughout the population, with an estimated 25 per cent of those regularly
voting for the Socialist Party in elections in the 1980s and early 1990s also practising
Catholics. As Casanova (1994: 89) notes, this signifies that 'there is currently no longer
a Catholic vote susceptible of political mobilization by the church'.

In conclusion, the position and attitude of the Catholic Church towards political
regimes was for a long period one of neutrality towards all forms of government. That
is, government was seen as 'legitimate' if its policies did not systematically infringe the
corporate rights of the church – to religious freedom and the exercise of its legitimate
functions. Under such circumstances, the church would not question the state's general
legitimacy. However, as the examples of the church's recent political involvement in
both Poland and Spain during democratic transitions suggest, the church's view of what
comprised a 'legitimate' government underwent significant change in the 1970s. Hence-
forward, its views were rooted in recognition that 'legitimate' governments have clear
responsibilities to their citizens to afford them democracy and other human rights.

Non-Democracies

According to Kurth (1999), Confucianism was in terminal decline in the last quarter of
the twentieth century. Its ideas and principles were said to be unable to withstand that
which accompanied globalization the onslaught of 'foreign' ideas – such as democracy
and individualistic human rights. Recently, however:

> the principle sources of resistance to globalization and to the grand project of the United
> States have become several of the great religions. Especially strong in their resistance have
> been revivalist Islam and a developing neo-Confucianism, known for promoting 'Asian
> values'. . . . [They] correctly see the globalization led by the United States to be closely con-
> nected with secularization and therefore to be a threat to themselves. (Kurth 1999)

Confucianism is culturally and politically influential in several East and Southeast
Asian countries, including China, Hong Kong, Japan, Singapore, Taiwan and Vietnam.
It has long been an important influence in Chinese and Chinese-influenced attitudes
towards life, suggesting patterns of living and standards of social value, while providing
a backdrop to Chinese political theories and institutions. Confucianism is a set of philosophical understandings, which some observers regard as a religion, which developed
from the teachings of Confucius, a Chinese philosopher who lived from 551 to 479 BCE.
Key teachings are concerned with principles of good conduct, practical wisdom and
'proper' social relationships. Recently, Confucianism has aroused interest among
Western scholars because the ideas it represents are widely regarded as an important
component of the concept of 'Asian values' (see chapters 9 and 13). Fukuyama (1992:
325, 217) regards Confucianism as both 'hierarchical and inegalitarian', a 'value system
most congruent with Oriental authoritarianism'.

In this section, we focus on China and Vietnam, countries where Confucianism is traditionally an important cultural and political factor. Following their communist revolutions, modernizing leaders in both places regularly proclaimed that their countries'
developmental backwardness was due to Confucian traditions (Manion 2000). Conse-

quently, they committed themselves to eradicating its ideas and values and to replacing them with communist-style modernization. Recently, however, leaders of both countries have sought to use the ideas and values of Confucianism to try to deal with perceived domestic consequences of economic globalization. That is, both governments now proclaim the desirability of Confucianism to help guide their countries' development. This is surprising, not least because both countries are still officially communist.

China

Although Confucianism became the official ideology of the Chinese state in the historical past, it never existed as an established religion with a church and priesthood. Chinese scholars honoured Confucius as a great teacher and sage, but he was not worshipped as a personal god. Nor did Confucius himself ever claim divinity. Unlike Christian churches, the numerous temples built to Confucius were not places in which organized religious groups gathered to worship. Instead, they were primarily designed for annual ceremonies, especially on the philosopher's birthday. Several attempts to deify Confucius and to proselytize Confucianism failed because of the essentially secular nature of the philosophy.

The success of the communist revolution in China in 1949 was followed by an anti-Confucianism campaign, directed by the state, claiming that the philosopher's ideas were a key reason for the country's economic and developmental backwardness. Recently, however, after decades of scornful criticism of Confucianism, China's leaders have begun to proclaim Confucius as the country's most prominent sage, and in 1999 lavish state-led celebrations were held to mark the 2,550th anniversary of his birth. According to Bezlova (1999), there were both international and domestic reasons for this policy change. Regarding external issues, China's rulers believed that key Confucian virtues – including benevolence and tolerance – would be useful in helping China 'in shaping its international image as an important purveyor of peace'.

Domestically, China's leaders were concerned with the adverse effects of economic liberalization at this time. As a result, they launched a programme to try to re-educate the Chinese people in Confucian values. The campaign was accompanied by officially sponsored excursions into political philosophy with Confucianism harnessed to desirable prescriptions for politics and economic growth, based on its principles of harmony, consensus and order. The overall aim was to try to eliminate or at least reduce the kinds of adversarial activity associated by at least some of China's leaders with economic liberalization.

Waldron (1998) argues that China has always been a state with an ideology, not least because its territory – about the same size as that of the United States – is too large to rule by force or by appeals to local interests. While communism was once regarded as a potential ideology for modem China in the way that Confucianism had been for 2,000 years of pre-modern China, that is, an 'internalized cultural basis for common action', it is now said no longer to persuade either the educated, many of whom acknowledge that Marxism is intellectually bankrupt, or the masses, 'whose possible one-time faith in communist class morality and the Marxist secular apocalypse of revolution and abundance has long since been swept away by the misery and famines the Communism actually brought' (Waldron 1998: 331). In these circumstances, Confucianist ideas and values are deemed to be an alternative ideology of control of stability.

Vietnam

Vietnamese culture has been strongly influenced by Chinese traditions, including Confucianism. The northern half of what is now Vietnam was ruled as a Chinese province until the tenth century CE, and over time, until the nineteenth century, became increasingly Confucian in character. From then, however, the influence of Confucianism declined, as a consequence of first French colonialism and, later, communist rule.

As in China, Vietnam's leaders have recently re-embraced Confucianism, because several of its main values – hard work, high rate of savings, sacrifice today for future generations – are deemed highly relevant for the country's current phase of economic development, known as *doi moi* ('renovation policy'). Also like China, this turnaround followed a period of several decades when Confucianism – along with Vietnam's other main religious traditions, Buddhism and Catholicism – was tightly controlled by the state, in favour of the secular ideology of communism.

This followed the rise to power of the communist Viet Minh in North Vietnam in 1954, followed by reunification of the whole country under communist rule in 1975–6. In 1980, Vietnam's post-reunification constitution was promulgated, in a similar form to that of the Soviet Union, but with at least a few democratic ideals, including secret ballot elections. Overall, however, the Communist Party would continue to dictate what it considered to be the best for everyone. The constitution was revised slightly in 1992, both to reflect the impact of economic reforms – that is, *doi moi* – that had begun in 1986, and to acknowledge a reduction in the party's role in governing. The overall aim was to retain political and economic stability, thus actively facilitating the *doi moi* process.

In recent years, the Vietnamese economy, like that of China, has become transformed from a centralized and planned economy, heavily based on imports, to a market-orientated one, with high rates of economic growth in both countries. Lee Kwan Yew, former prime minister of Singapore, has said that Confucian values have to be preserved even when a society reaches its highest development stage. He claimed that by employing some of the philosophy's main principles, Confucianism had helped various East Asian countries – including Singapore, South Korea and Taiwan – to become 'Asian dragons' in the 1990s (Pesek 2002). The apparent lesson this suggests – that Confucianism is an important ideology to deal with instabilities generated by swift economic liberalization and growth – was also accepted by the rulers of still officially communist Vietnam. While top priority was given to economic reform in order to create a multi-sector market economy regulated by the government, it also needed to consolidate both the legal environment and to renovate both party and state structures (Dixon 2003). In this context, Confucianism was a readily available, culturally appropriate set of values that the government believed would enable the country to deal with the consequences of both domestic economic liberalization and globalization. As a result, the government sought to emphasize traditional values of stability, hard work, a high rate of savings and willingness to sacrifice today for the benefit of future generations.

Conclusion

In this chapter we have examined both historic and thematic relationships between religious and political actors. We saw that, although once highly politically consequential, religion lost most of its political importance between the seventeenth and late twentieth centuries. What some commentators see as a resurgence of religion with political consequences has prompted many to ask why it has now reappeared as an important domestic and international political actor. Part of the suggested reason, we noted, was that many religious actors now pursuing political goals link their concerns to the consequences of modernization, especially secularization. We examined three sets of actors – Islam, the Roman Catholic Church and Confucianism – to explain why religion has become politically and socially significant in various parts of the world in recent years.

We should also note, however, that the issue of religion in and on politics is a complex one. A contrast can be drawn between differences that divide secular democratic (Weberian/Schumpterian) politics – essentially rule-governed where there is consensus about the rules – and religious politics as 'ideological' politics. In this regard, we can note examples not only from the contemporary era – notably involving Islam – but also from Europe's historical past before and after the Reformation. It is not however clear – and this is one area where the complexity comes in – to what extent religion as a political actor is concerned with spiritual issues alone, or where – and how and in what ways – other, more material, concerns also make their impact on what religious actors do politically. In the context of globalization, there is evidence of both spiritual and material issues involving the attention of transborder religious actors (Haynes 2001b, 2003b).[9]

---

[9] I am grateful to an anonymous reader of the manuscript for encouraging me to expand on this point.

13
Human Rights

During the cold war the relative lack of power of the United Nations had left the way free for the superpowers – the USA and the USSR – to cultivate allies without much overt concern for human rights. Following the end of the cold war and the onset of a new phase of globalization, there was renewed emphasis on human rights. This concern was expressed both in the 'New World Order' proclamations of George Bush, Snr in the early 1990s, and in the 'progressive globalization' rhetoric of Tony Blair and George W. Bush. Materially, concern was expressed via Western support for democratization and accompanying human rights. It was however clear that, following the end of the cold war, new human rights problems had emerged, for example, involving ethnic and/or religious minorities in various countries, including former Yugoslavia and Rwanda. Particularly egregious cases attracted external humanitarian intervention (Harrop and Hague 2001; Webber and Smith 2002).

The changing mood in relation to human rights was also reflected in the international community's determination to implement war-crime tribunals following the Gulf War (1990–1), Rwanda (1994), Sierra Leone (mid-1990s–2002) and the conflicts in former Yugoslavia (1993–2001). The notoriety of major recent examples of violations should not draw our attention away from well-documented improvements in human rights elsewhere, for example, in Latin America and some Asian and Eastern European countries. Such improvements were sometimes seen as symptomatic of a rediscovered universalism that resurfaced after the cold war, having first appeared soon after World War II. More generally, there was renewed emphasis on human rights issues in North–South relations, with various actors – Western governments, the EU, the IMF and the World Bank – all becoming more assertive in demanding improvements. Sometimes, as we saw earlier, these demands were articulated in the idea of 'political conditionality', designed to test democracy and human rights observance.

Increased concern with human rights issues did not simply reflect greater attention from some governments but also the influence of both international and transnational networks. The post-cold war era was notable for a growth in networks connecting domestic civil society actors and international human rights organizations – such as Amnesty International, Human Rights Watch and Freedom House – whose aim was to monitor states' observance of human rights. Their influence is said to have grown partly as a result of 'various developments arising from the rise of new technology and its growth in global connections' (Pridham 2000: 295). Moreover, the spread of television, radio and Western-style education were seen as important in this regard (Risse 2000). The overall result of these developments, Bealey (1999: 141) contends, is that 'any country's claim that the way it treats its subjects is no one else's business has now become a relic of a past age'.

The focus of this chapter is on human rights, especially political rights and civil liberties. It starts from the premise that four aspects of globalization helped focus attention on human rights:

1 *The collapse of communist governments in Europe.* In the name of fighting communism during the cold war, Western governments often turned a blind eye to allies' poor human rights records. Once communism in Europe was 'defeated', however, Western pressure increased on human rights abusing governments.

2 *Growth of international and transnational human rights organizations.* Cross-border campaigning organizations, such as Amnesty International and Human Rights Watch, work interactively with domestic civil society groups. Together they encourage governments that violate human rights to reform and adopt international human rights norms and regimes.

3 *International economic integration.* Moves towards economic integration facilitated the movement of capital, labour and goods across national boundaries, while increasing international economic competition. This led to growing importance of market forces that, while encouraging greater economic efficiency, also served to diminish many poor people's already weak economic position. Widespread adoption of structural adjustment programmes in many developing countries also led to widespread failure to fund adequate welfare programmes.

4 *Transformation of production systems and labour markets.* Economic globalization is often said to weaken the ability of organized labour to pressurize governments to enforce labour standards, such as minimum wage levels.

In sum, developments associated with globalization helped to increase attention on human rights issues, while often encouraging demands for more and better human rights.

The chapter is organized as follows. First, we examine what may comprise 'human rights'. Then we look at whether human rights can be 'universal' by examining the debate between, on the one hand, 'Western' individualistic conceptions of human rights, and, on the other, collective interpretations represented by 'Asian values' and Islamic conceptions of human rights. The third section focuses upon the influence of transnational and international actors in relation to changing human rights regimes in transitional democracies and non-democracies. The final section investigates human rights in an established democracy (the USA), a transitional democracy (Russia) and a non-democracy (China). It also assesses the impact of 9/11 on human rights issues.

What are 'Human Rights'?

Human rights issues comprise an important aspect of what Webber and Smith (2002: 120) call the 'new international agenda'. While virtually all governments claim consistently to uphold and defend their people's 'human rights', it is not necessarily clear *what* human rights they are referring to. In short, what are 'human rights'?

Fukuyama (1992: 42–3) offers a list of what he terms 'fundamental' rights, that fall into three categories:

1 *Civil rights*. These involve, 'exemption from control of the citizen in respect of his person and property'.
2 *Religious rights*. These amount to, 'exemption from control in the expression of religious opinions and the practice of worship'.
3 *Political rights*. These focus on, 'exemption from control in matters which do not so plainly affect the welfare of the whole community as to render control necessary', including the right of press freedom.

Note that Fukuyama does *not* identify positive economic and social rights, such as 'freedom from want', but, instead, focuses upon what individual citizens *should* be allowed to do, free from state interference. Ajami (1978: 28–9) identifies three human rights which, he argues, if one is to allow for cultural diversity, amount to the 'maximum feasible consensus'. The first two are civil and political rights, the third is an economic and social right:

● the right to survive;
● the right not to be subjected to torture;
● the right to food.

Ferguson (1986: 211) seeks to identify 'universally accepted . . . basic or primary rights, which apply regardless of cultural differences or social order'. Like Ajami's list, Ferguson's includes: the right to life and the right to freedom from torture, slavery or summary execution. In addition, he contends that, *if* a state has the resources, other desirable rights include: freedom from hunger, a minimum standard of living, and basic education and health care for all.

In sum, Ajami and Ferguson agree that the right to food and the right to life are interdependent human rights, necessary for people to live a minimally satisfactory human life. Fukuyama, on the other hand, seems to deny the veracity of this interdependence. But what all three commentators have in common is an agreement that human rights, whether 'positive' (for example, freedom from want) or 'negative' (for example, preventing the state from doing something that curtails individual rights), are both inherent in the individual as well as socially derived by development. This is a way of saying that, for example, certain political freedoms may not be possible without some reasonable degree of economic and social development. Such concepts are, however, notoriously subjective and, we shall see later, their interpretation is at the core of recent human rights controversies, especially in parts of Asia and the Muslim world.

Despite some lapses, Western governments are usually judged, especially by Western commentators, to have better human rights observance records than other states. Why is this the case? Charged with poor human rights records, non-Western governments often argue that their society's conception of rights is different from that of the West. In the latter, *individualistic* conceptions of human rights have long been dominant (exemplified in Fukuyama's list above). Alternative *collective* interpretations, on the other hand, were privileged in socialist and many non-Western countries (shades of this are inherent in Ferguson's interpretation). Many such governments long sought to defend what many Western commentators saw as arbitrary and/or harsh treatment of some individuals and groups by arguing that their actions were justified in the name of the *collective* good. According to Sodaro (2001: 3), such human rights abuses included:

'violations of fundamental democratic freedoms, such as the freedom of speech and the right to vote, the arrest and torture of political dissidents, mass atrocities committed in times of civil war or unrest, religious and ethnic persecution, the abuse and repression of women'.

Various studies have indicated that certain factors – including, regime type, economic development and the presence of armed conflicts – are typically important factors determining the extent of human rights violations (Henderson, 1991; Poe and Tate, 1994; Poe et al. 1999). One of the most commonly noted political explanations is that democratic regimes are much less likely to engage in repression than are non-democratic regimes (Poe and Tate, 1994; Poe et al. 1999). A related point is made in studies that show that a military presence in government is positively associated with repression (Poe et al. 1999). In addition, not only do democracies rule with less repression, but they also do a better job than non-democracies in promoting economic and social rights (Pinkney 2003).

The central role of real or perceived threats is further confirmed by research on human rights violations occurring during processes of transition to democracy. Fein (1995) suggests that there may be more serious human rights abuses – what he terms 'murder in the middle' – when non-democratic states make the transition to democracy. Snyder (2000) has also argued that ethnic conflict as well as related human rights violations are most likely to occur during the early stages of a transition to democracy. When such violations have been especially egregious – for example in Somalia, Rwanda, Burundi, former Yugoslavia, Russia – they have tended to attract external attention, but this does not necessarily imply that external interventions can on their own amend extant human rights regimes.

Cultural Relativity

Our discussion so far has begged an important question: to what extent are there universal human rights and, if so, what are they? Some governments claim that beyond a bare minimum, very few rights can logically have *universal* application. For example, while (nearly) everyone would agree that it is wrong to kill people without justification or let them starve wilfully, should states *guarantee* citizens the right, for example, of a house, paid holidays and potable water? They are, of course, highly desirable, but are they 'rights'? What if, as in many developing countries, states do not have the financial means to provide such goods to all their citizens? Are they still 'rights', or merely 'highly desirable public goods'?

Apart from the issue of economic and social rights, there is also debate about culturally derived interpretations of human rights. Some argue that because individual cultures have culturally rooted rights, there can be few truly *universal* rights. Consequently, when non-Western governments are accused of systematically violating the human rights of (some of their) citizens, they may respond that they cannot justifiably be judged by 'inappropriate' Western, individualistic conceptions of human rights – but only by the standards of their own cultures and societies. Does this defence hold water? The issue is problematic, as it involves the issue of the appropriateness and applicability of *cultural relativity*.

Cultural relativity is the idea that because different cultures have differing cultural reference points, it is not appropriate to judge all societies according to one, universal standard. That is, individual cultures have their own norms and rules of social and individual behaviour and, consequently, *which* human rights are observed is said to be a function of a society's unique cultural characteristics and history. Consequently, so the argument runs, it is not appropriate for those from other cultural milieus to pronounce judgement, because their different worldviews preclude them from objective assessment of another culture and its associated human rights norms. However, if the logic of the applicability of *universal* rights is denied, then governments claiming to have roots in *specific* cultures acquire a free hand to apply human rights regimes as they see fit – provided they do not violate their society's cultural norms, which, of course, the government itself identifies.

What is the evidence that there are *universal* human rights? The concept of universal human rights is often linked to the promulgation of the Charter of the United Nations (1945). The UN Charter states that all people have 'fundamental human rights', and declares that discrimination on the grounds of sex, religion and race is inherently repugnant. A dedicated proclamation about human rights – The Universal Declaration of Human Rights (UDHR) – appeared in 1948, and identified a range of political rights and civil liberties, as well as economic, social and cultural rights.

The UDHR seeks to develop the idea that there *are* universal human rights, appropriate to *all* cultures. Observers point out that three developments can be taken as evidence of the UDHR's claims to universality. First, several non-Western governments signed the UDHR in 1948. Second, numerous postcolonial developing countries joined the UN in the 1950s and 1960s, and several demanded changes to the UDHR. As a result, the Declaration was redrafted and presented afresh in 1966. The reformulated document had three important revisions: (1) a rejection of the right to property and to full compensation in the event of nationalization; (2) a toning down of the individualistic basis of the 1948 Declaration; and (3) an acceptance of the principle that, on occasion, it might be necessary to set aside individual rights in the national interest – for example, during war.

Third, since 1966, numerous people from around the world have appealed to the principles of the UDHR in their struggles against non-democratic governments. Over time both ordinary citizens and governments have implicitly or explicitly accepted principles enshrined in the UDHR as the basis of good governance. It follows that, logically, governments cannot then claim the 'right' to pick and choose among human rights, enforcing those they like, ignoring those they do not. On the other hand, controversy about the issue has remained. While the *concept* of human rights has become both accepted and internationalized, there is much less agreement about what a desirable human rights regime should comprise.

Two main 'alternative' conceptions of human rights have recently been articulated: 'Asian values' and the Islamic interpretation of human rights. Both rose to prominence at a time when Western governments were seeking to apply what they called 'international' principles and practices of human rights – that is, Western-orientated, individualistic perceptions. In many cases, such human rights were expressed via policies of *political conditionality* in relation to various transitional democracies and non-democracies. Some governments on the receiving end of such policies, notably in the

Islamic world and in parts of East and Southeast Asia, claimed that political conditionality was no more than an attempt to promulgate and spread Western individualistic human rights, such as liberal democracy.

Individualistic Conceptions

According to Ahmed (2003), there are six key philosophical assumptions that underpin what he calls 'modern human rights'. In fact, this is a list of the main characteristics of an individualistic conception of human rights:

1   Discrimination and persecution of individuals and groups on the basis of caste, colour, creed or any other ascribed basis is morally repugnant and therefore unacceptable.
2   Individuals are free human agents and therefore have a right to autonomy vis-à-vis state and society.
3   States must recognize and confer constitutional and legal entitlements upon individuals that can enable them to enjoy human rights.
4   Adequate provisions should be made in law to enable individuals to seek redress of human rights violation.
5   In case of the failure of a state to respect human rights, international bodies should be competent to examine such complaints.
6   Respect for human rights will result in stability, peace and prosperity within state boundaries, regionally and internationally.

The Western notion that individuals have fundamental human rights dates back to the writings of Locke and Rousseau. Such concerns were the basis of key late eighteenth-century statements, including the US Bill of Rights and the French Declaration of the Rights of Man and of the Citizen. Both Europe and the Americas currently have conventions proclaiming the indivisibility of the human rights of the individual. The European Convention for the Protection of Human Rights and Fundamental Freedoms was proclaimed in 1950. This was followed in 1978 by the American Convention on Human Rights, with validity in both North and South America. Both European and American human rights regimes were strengthened by the existence of a Commission and a Court. These developments underpinned European and American claims as to the appropriateness and desirability of individualistic human rights regimes.

Collective Conceptions

'Asian values'

The 'East Asian' view of human rights is captured in the concept of 'Asian values', a view associated with a number of East and Southeast Asian countries, including Malaysia, Singapore and China. Regional political leaders, such as former prime ministers Muhammad Mahathir (Malaysia) and Lee Kuan Yew (Singapore), contend that individualistic human rights associated with 'Western culture' and its individualistic, self-seeking values are 'culturally alien' to their countries. They claim instead that their countries have different cultures and histories reflecting the importance of the community or the collective, not the individual. These cultural characteristics are said to be embodied in an array of desirable socio-political values: harmony, consensus, unity and community. In Mahathir's view, Malaysia's society is richly imbued with such social and political values. As a result, he claims, human rights regimes are seen by society as legitimate only when they reflect the community's collective values. Consequently, national human rights regimes must necessarily 'fit' local cultural and social values (Maravall 1995: 16).

Critics of the 'Asian values' view argue that its key feature is authoritarianism (Diamond 1999; Zakaria 1997; Enberg and Ersson 1999; Christie and Roy 2001). Engberg and Ersson (2001) attack models of 'Asian values' and the use to which regional governments seek to use them. They contend that they are no more than a cloak for continuing authoritarianism and the narrow political interest of the rulers. Zakaria (1997: 28) contends that many regional governments professing to defend 'Asian values' are actually 'illiberal democracies', characterized by: 'democracy, liberalism, capitalism, oligarchy and corruption'. This suggests that regional regimes may well have political systems with periodic, relatively free and fair elections – along with some meaningful rules and regulations to determine their conduct and content – but also lack many individualistic, liberal freedoms. Such rulers may wield power with little reference to other political institutions, while ordinary citizens may enjoy only a relatively narrow range of civil liberties and political rights. Finally, Christie and Roy (2001) also focus upon the politics of human rights in East and Southeast Asia and conclude that the concept of 'Asian values' is no more than an attempt to perpetuate authoritarian political and human rights regimes.

Whatever the merits of the 'Western values' versus 'Asian values' debate, some regional groups in East and Southeast Asia began to demand Western-style, individualistic, human rights in the late 1990s. The catalyst for this was the region's economic downturn in 1997–8. For decades, regional non-democratic governments, such as those of Singapore, Malaysia and Indonesia, had consistently contended that suppression of individualistic human rights, such as freedom of speech, were a necessary price to pay for economic growth and development. However, the economic downturn made it plain that their authoritarian development models were fallible. Some regional leaders, including Mahathir, suggested that local human rights groups were acting at the behest of foreign governments. Hewison (1999: 231) claims however that 'demands for the opening of political space, with calls for increased democracy in Southeast Asia, are not originating in the West or among western-influenced actors, but have domestic causes'.

In sum, perhaps the core dynamic in relation to human rights in East and Southeast Asia lies not in differing cultural approaches but in the processes of social change and economic development, which creates new political dynamics and tensions. The most important tension may not be between 'Western' and 'Asian' values, but that involving modernization and tradition (Christie and Roy 2001: 6). We have noted that globalization processes can enable domestic groups to work with transnational human rights organizations to pursue various goals, including improved human rights. However, the regional diversity of East and Southeast Asia is not necessarily best treated by a macro-approach based on a dichotomy between 'Asian values' and 'Western values', which suggests that the important dynamic is not necessarily between these two approaches. It is, instead, that many regional governments seem to view human rights groups with great suspicion, and may be tempted to commit human rights violations in the name of national stability and security. On the other hand, human rights regimes have recently improved in several regional countries, including South Korea and Taiwan (Freedom House 2003: 308–11, 540–3).

'Islamic' human rights

There are two key Western complaints in relation to the observation of human rights in the Arab Muslim countries of the Middle East: (1) generally poor human rights regimes; and (2) serious democratic shortfalls. Both are said to be linked to the strong regional influence of Islam (Huntington 1991; Fukuyama 1992; Diamond 1999). Speaking at the 10th Non-Aligned Summit Conference held in Jakarta, Indonesia, in 1992, Egypt's foreign minister warned the West against interference in his nation's internal affairs on the pretext of defending human rights. Was this simply a pretext, a desire by the Egyptian government to deflect Western attacks on their poor human rights record by playing the 'cultural relativity' card?

The social importance of Islam cannot be denied: every country in the Middle East region, with the exception of Israel, has a population that is at least 89 per cent Muslim (Beeley 1992: 296–7). What impact does Islam have on regional human rights observances? The first point is that Islam is both premised and rooted in the emphatic importance of collective over individual rights; in other words, there is a high regard for social solidarity within Muslim countries. The Muslim community – the *umma* – is a 'compact wall whose bricks support each other'. The role of the individual 'is not merely to act so as to ensure [the community's] preservation, but also to recognise that it is the community that provides for the integration of human personality realised through self-abnegation and action for the good of the collectivity' (Vincent 1986: 42). As far as girls and women are concerned, if they do not wish to court social opprobrium, they must act within norms of behaviour sanctioned by Muslim conventions.

Second, in Islam, the 'language of duty seems more natural than that of [individual] rights' (Vincent 1986: 42). That is, because of the primary importance attached to obedience to God, in Islam rights are seen as secondary to duties. Via his mouthpiece the Prophet Muhammad, God is said to have laid down rules of conduct fourteen centuries ago. Since then, Muslims have sought to serve God by thorough obedience to divine rules. As Vincent (1986: 42) notes, if rights are thought of as 'freedoms' then in Islam 'true freedom consists in surrendering to the Divine will rather than in some artificial separation from the community of God . . . rights remain subordinate to and determined by duties.'

Contemporary governments of Muslim countries typically claim divine sanction both for the existence of their regimes and for their policies. Critics contend however that this is a potential or actual justification for harsh or arbitrary rule, policies used to justify denials of democracy, freedom of speech and harsh treatment of women (Owen 1992). There is, however, an emergent trend among some educated Muslims and revisionist *ulama* (theological teachers) questioning the poor position of women and of non-Muslim minorities in some Muslim countries; these are areas, it is claimed, that have seemed for a long time to be outside the Islamic critical gaze. Islamic revisionists feel that 'many Muslims confuse some inherited traditional cultural values with Islamic values' (Saif 1994: 63). We focus upon this issue in more detail in chapter 14.

Despite current concern with the position of females and minorities, there are several reasons why it is unlikely that individual rights will soon take precedence over collective rights in the Arab Middle East. First, regional societies are conservative. Second, incumbent political elites do their best to ensure the continuity of the status quo. Since independence, political elites in the Middle East, often in alliance with the military, have striven to modernize their political systems, while retaining a tight grip on power. The avowed aim in, for example, Syria and Tunisia, has been to build nation states along Western lines. As a result, the status of Islam has been downplayed and religious professionals either incorporated into the ruling elite or, if not, their power was neutralized. The result was a modernist superstructure balanced uncomfortably upon a substructure deeply rooted in traditional beliefs, with Islam the cement holding the social system together. Elsewhere, in the region's more socially and religiously traditional countries, such as Saudi Arabia, United Arab Emirates and Morocco, governments have sought with varying degrees of success to deepen their Islamic credentials and limit the spread of what they regard as Western ideas (Haynes 1998: 125–47).

This brief survey of the Muslim view of human rights in the Arab Middle East leads to similar conclusions to those drawn above in relation to East and Southeast Asia. The core dynamic in relation to human rights in the Arab Middle East does not necessarily lie in different cultural approaches but in the dynamics and tensions created by processes of social change and economic development. That is, as in East and Southeast Asia, the most important is not necessarily between 'Western' and 'Islamic values' but between modernization and tradition. Unlike in East and Southeast Asia, there is very little indication that human rights groups in the Middle East have made much progress, except in a limited extent in relation to women's rights (see chapter 14). Many regional governments are said to view human rights groups with intense suspicion and their regimes are often especially prone to human rights violations.

What are the chances of things changing? Clark (1997: 187) is sceptical about how pervasive – and potentially applicable – is the Western conception of individualistic human rights in the Middle East. He notes the World Conference on Human Rights in Vienna (1993), an event that highlighted resistance to Western conceptions of human rights from an alliance of Muslim and East Asian countries. At Vienna, they joined in a confident counterattack against Western assumptions of a claimed 'international' human rights regime based on liberal and individualistic values. Clark concludes by suggesting there is little or no evidence to suggest that the distance between the different cultural conceptions of human rights is narrowing, and more to indicate that polarized conceptions of human rights are now an established aspect of international relations.

The Internationalization of Human Rights?

The recent swift growth in the non-governmental sector both in the Western and non-Western world has led to growing academic interest in the issue (Haynes 1997). Regarding human rights, a sizeable literature has emerged that focuses upon international and domestic human rights groups and their networking activities. Generally, it sees their activities as an increasingly influential factor in relation to regime change (Smith et al.

1997; Risse et al. 1999). This literature also draws attention to such actors' policies in relation to building connections between local and international levels (Keck and Sikkink 1998a). These connections also emphasize that the traditional separation between 'Westphalian sovereignty' and the norm of non-intervention in internal affairs is being eroded. In addition, the resulting challenges to the status quo 'presuppose the emergence of alternative networks and discourses'. From the '1980s, international human rights organizations, but also Western states and international organizations have increasingly taken up such requests for support and supplemented pressure "from below with pressure from above"' (Schmitz 2002b: 150). In short, most of the relevant literature contends that cross-border human rights organizations have become increasingly influential – particularly because of interactions with domestic groups – in helping to improve human rights regimes in various countries. This emphasizes that cross-border interactions need to be taken seriously without overlooking continued importance of domestic politics in relation to human rights regime change.

After the cold war, according to Cardenas (2002: 54):

> international actors have defined and promoted the concept of NHRIs [National Human Rights Institutions], making it costly for states not to create them, and provided governments with the technical capacities to set up these institutions. Without this web of international activities, the rise of NHRIs may not have been possible in the first place.

She also contends, however, that NHRIs are founded primarily 'to satisfy international audiences; they are the result of state adaptation'. The international origins of NHRIs, however, have a paradoxical effect: 'most NHRIs remain too weak to protect society from human rights violations at the same time that they create an unprecedented demand for such protection' (Cardenas 2002: 1).

Cardenas contends that post-cold war circumstances were conducive to the development of government-created NHRIs, largely as a result of pressure from international actors. After the cold war, transnational alliances – the result of alliances between domestic civil societies and transnational NGOs and international organizations – are said to have led to improved human rights norms in various countries. Brozus et al. (2002: 4) contend that these transnational alliances could decisively contribute to more favourable domestic conditions for the promulgation of human rights to the extent that 'transnational alliances between INGOs or IGOs and domestic NGOs may compensate for unfavorable domestic structures'. This is because

> provision of material and [non-material] resources from international and transnational actors can help domestic interest groups to gain access and more influence. Often this transfer mechanism contributes to more open political systems, the enhancement of political capacities of both state and society and the overall empowerment of non-state groups. Regarding domestic salience, the constant influx of ideas from the global level may contribute to incremental adaptations of national norm-sets. Transnational actors [can] thus act as agents of political modernization. (Brozus et al. 2002: 7)

According to Schmitz (2002a: 13):

> principled non-state actors such as Amnesty International have begun to spread . . . UN norms by building transnational networks across state lines and into many domestic

societies. They leveled the playing field between the rulers and the ruled by giving the latter access to the opportunities provided by international institutions.

Can the socialization of 'international' – that is, Western – human rights norms be successful in the absence of favourable domestic conditions? Risse-Kappen (1995a) notes that ideas about human rights do not 'float freely'; instead, their applicability is supported or hindered by two more or less enabling or constraining filter variables: domestic structure and domestic salience (Cortell and Davis 1996). In this context, *domestic structure* refers to state–society relations and the political capacities of states in the issue area of human rights. The concept encompasses three sub-variables: 'capacity', 'openness of the political system' and 'strength of civil society'. *Domestic salience* refers to the extent of 'fit' between 'compatibility of ideas and norms on the international level and domestic ideas and norms'.

Risse et al. (1999: 6, 19) present what they call a 'spiral model' of the internalization of human rights norms and practices, with a focus on 'the right to life (incorporating the right to be free from extrajudicial execution and disappearance) and freedom from torture and arbitrary arrest and detention'.

The spiral model incorporates the influence of transnational human rights regimes on what Risse et al. call the 'normalization' of state policy. It seeks to explain variations in different states in the degree of internalizing norms in relation to human rights via a five-step model of regime change. Adaptation to these norms is said to be the result of a socialization process during which IGOs link up with domestic human rights activists to pressurize norm-violating states to change their behaviour. IGOs, such as the UN or the EU, are said to be particularly important because they institutionalize standards by passing the necessary resolutions. More generally, they can also be important in relation to specific various issue areas – such as the position of minorities – as much relevant discussion often takes place within IGO frameworks and structures.

Contributors to Risse et al.'s (1999) edited book apply the spiral model to a range of comparative case studies in order to analyse the process by which human rights discourses become internalized on a societal level, ultimately surfacing in both the language and the behaviour of individual states (the case studies concern Chile, Czechoslovakia, Guatemala, Indonesia, Kenya, Morocco, the Philippines, Poland, South Africa, Tunisia and Uganda). The overall purpose is to try to specify the conditions under which international human rights regimes and the principles, norms and rules are internalized and implemented domestically and, thus, how more generally they affect political transformation processes.

The spiral model specifies three modes of interaction, involving three processes: instrumental adaptation and strategic bargaining; moral consciousness-raising, 'shaming', argumentation, dialogue and persuasion; and institutionalization and habitualization (Risse and Sikkink 1999: 5). They appear in five consecutive phases of what Risse and Sikkink (1999: 17–35) call the 'spiral model of norm socialization':

- Phase 1: Repression and activation of network;
- Phase 2: Denial;
- Phase 3: Tactical concessions;
- Phase 4: Prescriptive status;
- Phase 5: Rule-consistent behaviour.

Phase 1: Repression and activation of network

The government presides over a repressive situation. Domestic societal opposition is too cowed and/or fragmented to challenge significantly its human rights policy, although domestic human rights organizations may attempt to document violations in order to inform the international community. If or when these domestic advocacy networks succeed in bringing attention to their cause, there is a transition into the second phase of the spiral model: *denial* (Risse and Ropp 1999: 237; Risse and Sikkink 1999: 22).

Phase 2: Denial

To make an impact, the transnational advocacy network must accumulate sufficient information on state-sanctioned repression. However, even if the norm-violating state is put on the international agenda of the human rights network, the state may well refuse to accept the validity of prescribed international human rights norms (for example, as we saw above in relation to 'Asian values' or Islamic conceptions of human rights). Consequently, it will deny that domestic human rights practices should be subject to international jurisdiction.

Once human rights abuses are brought to the attention of the international community, the norm-violating state is placed in the position of having to respond to the accusations of repression. While some repressive governments care little about international pressures, norm-violating states tend to respond in one of two ways: they either deny the human rights charges with which they are confronted, or they question human rights norms legitimacy in general, arguing that state sovereignty should supersede concerns over human rights. However, not all repressive states go through the denial phase. For example, in the case of Tunisia, Gränzer (1999: 120–1) argues that Prime Minister Ben Ali skipped over this phase of denial and moved directly into phase three (*tactical concessions*). The Tunisia case highlights two very important aspects about the spiral model: first, not every country will necessarily go through each phase, and, second, the length of time in which states go through these phases will be dependent on the strength of the opposition, human rights networks and the state itself (Risse and Roppe 1999: 243; also see Risse 2000).

Phase 3: Tactical concessions

To achieve one of three goals – to deal with international pressures, (re)gain military or economic assistance, or lessen international isolation – the norm-violating government may seek cosmetic changes – including temporary improvements – to try to derail international criticism. During this phase, 'shaming' of the norm-violating government becomes an effective communicative tool of the transnational advocacy network. However, state leaders who start 'talking the human rights talk' may not fully understand that as a result they can become 'entrapped' in their own rhetoric, leading to what Risse (2000) calls 'controlled liberalization'.

Movement to this phase is also linked to the strength of human rights networks and state vulnerability to external pressure. This stage is said to be most important in achieving the goal of sustainable, enduring human rights improvements. At this point, governments begin to enact policies aimed at curbing human rights abuses; some may also begin to include human rights language into domestic political discourse. The importance of this phase was especially noticeable in the case of South Africa. David Black (1999) shows that the government's improved concern with and respect for human rights ultimately brought about both deconstruction of apartheid and transition to democracy. The chief impetus for change in this case was said to be the international community's ability to isolate and 'shame' South Africa's government (Risse and Roppe 1999: 243–6).

Phase 4: Prescriptive status

This is the *prescriptive point* in internalization of human rights norms and practices. Norm-violating states are confronted with strongly activated human rights networks and growing internalization of human rights norms, a situation that eventually compels the state permanently to liberalize human rights policies or at least to accept substantive constitutional or governmental changes. The impact of these networks can perhaps be most strongly felt when their continued efforts ultimately lead to a regime change, for example in South Africa.

At this stage, the relevant actors regularly refer to human rights norms to describe and comment on their own behaviour and that of others. Indicators for this phase are reflected in domestic political changes, while the government:

- no longer denounces criticism as 'interference in internal affairs', but engages with their critics in a dialogue;
- ratifies international and/or regional human rights conventions, if the latter exist;
- embeds human rights norms in domestic laws;
- introduces national human rights institutions, institutionalized mechanisms for ordinary citizens to complain about human rights violations.

Phase 5: Rule-consistent behaviour

Phase 5 signifies sustainable changes in human rights conditions, with international human rights norms fully institutionalized domestically. Enforced by the rule of law, norm-compliance becomes a habitual practice of actors, and human rights norms are considered to be internalized.

Probably the greatest asset of the spiral model is its systematic demonstration of the process through which human rights norms become internalized into state practice by states with histories of human rights violations. In addition, its social constructivist approach demonstrates the important role of domestic opposition groups in first mobilizing and then encouraging change. Coupled with domestic groups' relationship to transnational human rights networks, this helps clarify the underlying dynamics that can pressurize oppressive regimes to alter their behaviour and curb human rights abuse.

The spiral model does however have its weaknesses. First, while Risse and Sikkink (1999: 6) claim that it 'is generalizable across cases irrespective of cultural, political, or

economic differences among countries', its explanatory power appears greater in relation to weak and poor countries that rely heavily upon international developmental
assistance. Governments of more powerful countries seem generally less vulnerable to
the impact of combined domestic/transnational pressures to improve human rights.
Second, their book fails to discuss the human rights position of major powers – such as,
Russia, China, the USA and Britain, preferring to focus upon countries that appear vulnerable to external pressures. This is the case even when major powers – such as China
and Russia – are consistently identified as norm-violating states (Freedom House 2003:
141–7, 458–65).

Third, Risse and Ropp (1999: 268) argue that their book's 'case studies confirm that
pressure from major powers toward compliance with human rights norms is uniformly
the result of both shaming and lobbying activities by transnational advocacy networks'.
They offer South Africa, the Philippines and various Eastern European countries as
examples. However, this seems to suggest that the causal mechanism that compels major
powers to act is due to the influence of cross-border advocacy networks. But this is problematic. If it were correct, then how could the lack of impact of such actors be explained
in relation to, for example, the Russian government's policy in Chechnya, Chinese
human rights strategy after the Tiananmen Square incident of 1989, or the United States
with regard to the death penalty? The point is that if transnational advocacy networks
are as consistently influential as the spiral model maintains, then the international community would be expected to have successfully mobilized in relation to the above issues.
But it did not. The lack of mobilization seems to suggest that major powers themselves
need to be active in international efforts to promote human rights norms.

Fourth, the model may be more useful in helping explain what happens during political transitions than after them. There is evidence to suggest that in some cases, once
international attention has moved on, then progress in relation to human rights may
diminish (Cardenas 2002). Or, put another way, over time, international – that is,
'Western', individualistic – human rights norms may be amended through the influence
of extant cultural, social and political structures in non-Western countries.

In sum, the spiral model provides a substantial contribution to the study of human
rights norms and practices, but does not fully provide a complete or 'universal' explanation of domestic internalization of human rights among all norm-violating states. The
spiral model may be more relevant in relation to less powerful states and less so in
regard to more powerful ones.

Case Studies: USA, Russia and China

We have seen that the spiral model asserts that governments of both transitional democracies and non-democracies will be encouraged by a coalition of domestic and trans-
boundary actors to improve their human rights regimes. We have also noted that human
rights norms do not 'float freely'. Instead, they are supported or hindered by more or
less enabling or constraining filter variables. In this section, we examine three case
studies: the USA, Russia and China. They were chosen to help us assess the comparative significance of domestic and non-domestic actors in relation to human rights norms
in our three categories of country: established democracies, transitional democracies
and non-democracies.

The USA

All established democracies institutionalize an impressive array of human rights norms and practices, and the USA is no exception. According to Freedom House (2003: 588), 'the United States began the modern worldwide movement for freedom and self-government'. Citizens of the United States enjoy a wide range of civil liberties protection through federal legislation and court decisions. Commentators have claimed, however, that black Americans have found it particularly difficult to attain certain human rights, especially political rights. For example, Mcdonald's (2003) account of black voting in the American South notes that there was a brief era of post-Civil War enfranchisement that ended in the 1890s. Over the next 70 years, however, blacks were effectively disenfranchised. It was not until the Voting Rights Act of 1965 that a new black electorate was created and, as a result, a new era of electoral democracy began. Mcdonald (2003) shows, however, that this optimistic view of political progress is at variance with reality. His focus is on Georgia, supposedly one of the more progressive Deep South states. He aims to show that the 1965 Voting Rights Act did not of itself produce the changes its authors had hoped for and a generation of scholars has trumpeted. Instead, Mcdonald argues conclusively that there were as many similarities as dissimilarities in Southern white attitudes to black suffrage not only during 1865–1964, but also after 1965. He also shows that there were undoubtedly significant changes following the enactment of the 1965 legislation – but this was the result of a continuing struggle to make its terms a reality rather than voluntary acceptance of the intent of the law by all Southern whites.

However, the 1965 Voting Rights Act led to varying results in different US states. Such variations were partly a result of the fact that the United States does not have a national human rights institution whose job it is to protect and promote domestically human rights norms agreed internationally. There are, however, local human rights commissions – in Alaska, Illinois and New York – as well as a number of civil rights commissions. In general, as Cardenas (2002: 14) notes, 'these institutions tend to have a relatively narrow mandate and focus primarily on issues of non-discrimination'. For example, New York City's Commission on Human Rights, established in 1962, is 'procedurally similar to other human rights commissions, and receives regular visitors from the United Nations and international human rights NGOs'. In addition to local commissions, the United States also has two national human rights bodies: the State Department's Bureau of Democracy, Human Rights, and Labor, and the House of Representatives' Subcommittee on International Operations and Human Rights. But, as Cardenas (2002: 15) notes, 'these institutions are devoted almost entirely to promoting human rights through foreign rather than domestic policy'. This suggests that successive US governments have judged human rights promotion to be a foreign policy not a domestic issue.

Cardenas (2002: 55) contends, however, that the United States – 'the hegemonic power in the human rights arena' – should do more to 'promote the creation of its own local human rights commissions and ensure that their mandates explicitly reflect international human rights norms'. Overall, the unique nature of American rights culture has interacted with the USA's long-standing habit of exempting itself from international human rights obligations and international legal frameworks to produce an 'American

Exceptionalism' in relation to various areas, including freedom of speech and economic and social rights. It is also the case that US views in relation to human rights norms are shaped more by domestic discourse than by trying to conform to international conventions. Brimmer (2002: 22) notes that American 'acceptance of international regimes ebbs and flows with the regular cycles of American domestic politics'. When US politics at home 'are inclusive and interested in social progress', then American governments tend to be interested in participation in international regimes, including some forms of economic, social and cultural rights. On the other hand, when US domestic policy is more 'conservative', it is interested in 'protecting existing conditions, or stopping a perceived erosion of economic or moral standards'. Under such circumstances, US 'policy tends to be more interested in preserving scope for unilateral action'.

Addressing the issue of US human rights norms in relation to international factors, it is impossible to ignore the impact of 9/11. Since then, the US government's human rights concerns at both home and abroad have been dominated by the country's response to the terrorist attacks. In terms of foreign policy, the 9/11 attacks stimulated the successful US invasion of Afghanistan in order to remove from power the Taliban, while also providing a catalyst for the American attack on Iraq in 2003 in order to get rid of the human rights-violating Saddam regime.

Domestically, the aftermath of 9/11 was also influential for human rights issues. For both the US government and the American people, the 9/11 attacks led to an end of the perception that the USA was fundamentally protected by a formidable defensive perimeter, comprising two components: (1) military protection and (2) geographical distance from potential enemies. After 9/11, reflecting justifiable fear of further attacks, the US government's overriding priority was protection of American citizens. Perceptions of the growing threat of terrorism within the country's borders created widespread public concern, fuelled radical changes in US security, counter-terrorism and foreign policies, and, some commentators claim, undermined Americans' civil liberties. The US government's reactions to terrorism included both a reinforcement of its powers and increased reliance of citizens on government for security (Keohane 2002). Following 9/11, the Bush administration created the Department of Homeland Security, and put into effect policies designed to improve intelligence-gathering, security at US borders, the prevention of bio-terrorism and reserves of medicines.

Some critics claimed that the US government sought to reassert its power over its citizens and the country's borders by the removal or curtailment of basic human rights. Amnesty International (AI) expressed its concerns that the post-9/11 'war on terror' was being used as an excuse to deny human rights at both home and abroad. AI claimed that the 'war on terror' led many Americans to reflect upon the fundamental values on which the USA was founded: freedom of speech, freedom of religion, respect for human dignity, justice for all and tolerance. For AI, it was imperative that the United States should stand for the principles of unalienable, universal rights. If it did not, then those who waged war on human rights would have won the battle against freedom.

AI's concerns were expressed in relation to several areas: torture, discrimination, justice and the rule of law, detainees and civil rights:

- After 9/11, the US government appeared to condone and in some circumstances even commit acts of torture.
- Across the USA, rights of individuals of Middle Eastern descent and of immigrants and racial minorities generally were being severely curtailed.

- Basic rights – protected not only in the US Constitution's Bill of Rights, but also by international law, as well as enforcement of human rights laws in other countries – were being denied after 9/11.
- The American government detained thousands of people in the USA and around the world in pursuit of the 'war on terror'. Many people were held without charge or trial in violation of fundamental due process rights.
- The Central Intelligence Agency (CIA) was given permission to tap the telephones of US citizens. The Federal Bureau of Investigation (FBI) and other police agencies were allowed to conduct 'sneak and peak' searches of people's homes and offices. A new definition of 'domestic terrorism' was introduced, broad enough to include political protests, in the Patriot Act of October 2001 (Amnesty International 2003a).

In sum, the US government sought after 9/11 to justify various counter-terrorism measures, including the Patriot Act, on the grounds that they were necessary in order to protect American citizens from violent attack. No longer did the US government speak primarily of law enforcement and justice, but of self-defence and war. To many critics, this 'war' appeared to be increasingly waged outside the norms of human rights and international humanitarian law. As President Bush put it at a press conference on 17 September 2001, in the fight against terrorism 'there are no rules' (Hurrell 2002: 185).

Russia

We noted above that the spiral model of Risse, Ropp and Sikkink (1999) identifies the importance of the interaction of international and transnational actors with domestic civil societies to produce improvements in human rights norms. There is empirical evidence in relation to CEE that, as Thomas (1999) contends, international human rights norms do matter. It is often observed that human rights instituted by the Helsinki Final Act (1975) directly contributed to the disintegration of communism in the former Eastern bloc. This result dealt effectively with the arguments of sceptics who were dubious that such international norms can substantially affect domestic outcomes. Thomas argues that the Final Act transformed the agenda of East–West relations and provided a common platform around which opposition forces could mobilize. Without downplaying other factors, Thomas also notes that norms established at Helsinki undermined the viability of one-party communist rule and thereby contributed significantly to the largely peaceful and democratic changes of 1989, as well as the end of the cold war.

Given the empirical evidence of the impact of international and transnational actors in relation to improved human and political rights in CEE from the mid-1970s, it is surprising to note that an improved situation did not necessarily apply everywhere in the region. Although Russia's government generally respects the human rights of its citizens in some areas, its overall record has worsened since the early 1990s. The political rights/civil liberties position improved to 3/4 in 1993, before declining to 5/5 in 2003 (Freedom House 2003: 458).[1]

---

[1] See chapter 1 (p. 17) for details of Freedom House ratings of countries' democratic position in terms of political rights and civil liberties.

In relation to political rights, Russians can change their government democratically. However, according to the Organization for Security and Cooperation in Europe, both the 2000 and 2004 presidential votes were marred by irregularities (<http://www.osce.org/documents/odihr/2004/06/3033_en.pdf>). In addition, parliamentary elections held in December 2000 were said to have failed to meet international standards, although the voting process was technically well run. Opposition parties found that their ability to compete electorally was undermined by criminal charges and threats of arrest or actual arrest against major financial supporters of opposition parties, as well as seizure of party materials from opposition parties. Although the constitution provided for freedom of speech and the press, the government put pressure on media outlets critical of the Kremlin. Some observers claim that recent presidential elections have provided the authorities with greater impetus to control the operation and content of print and broadcast media (Freedom House 2003: 458–65).

Morosov (2002: 2) pinpoints the decline in the position of human rights in Russia to 1999, noting that it coincided with NATO's invasion of Yugoslavia and the conflict in Chechnya. More generally, it is often noted that the Russian government's human rights record was especially poor in relation to its conflict with Chechen separatists. Amnesty International has claimed that federal security forces have demonstrated little respect for basic human rights in Chechnya. From the mid-1990s, there were numerous, credible reports of serious violations, including many reports of unlawful killings and of abuse of civilians by the Russian government as well as Chechen fighters in the Chechen conflict. There were also reports of both government and rebel involvement in politically motivated disappearances in Chechnya. In addition, the government placed restrictions on the activities of both NGOs and INGOs in Chechnya (Amnesty International n/d).

More generally, there were widespread credible reports that law-enforcement personnel were prone to engage, often with impunity, in torture, violence and other brutal or humiliating treatment. Prison conditions in Russia were judged to be extremely harsh and frequently life-threatening. Police corruption remained a considerable problem, as did apparently arbitrary arrest and lengthy pre-trial detention. A new Code of Criminal Procedure (2002) led to some improvements, although considerable problems remained. Government protection for judges from threats by organized criminal defendants was said to be inadequate, while a series of alleged espionage cases were reported in 2002–3, causing concern about the lack of due process and the influence of the Federal Security Service (the FSB) in court cases. In addition, authorities continued to infringe on citizens' privacy rights. Authorities, primarily at the local level, restricted freedom of assembly and imposed restrictions on some religious groups. Societal discrimination, harassment and violence against members of some religious minorities remained problems. Local governments restricted citizens' freedom of movement, primarily by denying legal resident permits to newcomers from other areas of the country. Government institutions intended to protect human rights were relatively weak but remained active and public (Freedom House 2003: 458–65).

The declining human rights situation in Russia might have been expected to garner international opprobrium. Instead, there was little overt concern expressed by the governments of Western countries. The main reason for this may have been the changed international circumstances after 9/11. Like the USA, Britain and other Western countries, Russia was seen to be facing the threat of terrorism, primarily from Chechen separatists. Consequently, there were considerable changes in the US approach to the war in Chechnya and, more generally, in US policy towards Russia. The Russian president, Vladimir Putin, gave strong support to the US-led 'war on terror'. Putin accepted US military deployments in the territory of several Central Asian countries, formerly constituents of the USSR, provided very useful Russian help in Afghanistan and shared intelligence with the USA. These moves helped to create a new belief in the USA that a cooperative relationship with Russia was both possible and desirable. In addition, both countries had a strong interest in cooperating against Sunni Islamist extremism and terrorism. In the case of Russia, the aim was to prevent regional instability and upheaval in Central Asia and the Caucasus, a potential result of growth of Islamic fundamentalism. Closer links between the USA and Russia were also reflected in strong ties between the latter and NATO. As a result, a NATO-Russia Council was established in May 2002, and terrorism was identified as one of several areas for consultation and cooperation (<http://www.nato.int/terrorism/>).

China

According to Freedom House (2003: 143), 'China is one of the most authoritarian states in the world. Opposition parties are illegal, the CCP controls the judiciary, and ordinary Chinese people enjoy few basic rights.' In addition, each year thousands of Chinese citizens are put to death under a legal system plagued with corruption and secrecy. While the rest of the world moves toward abolition, Chinese authorities only continue to expand the application of the death penalty. According to Amnesty International (2004), 'an average of 15,000 people per year were executed, judicially or extrajudicially, by the government between 1997 and 2001'. AI also contended that the main death penalty targets were poor and marginalized groups, including ethnic minorities, migrant communities, political dissidents and so-called 'separatists'. Following 9/11 and the consequent US-led 'war on terror', the Chinese authorities targeted Muslims in the Xinjiang Uighur Autonomous Region. Political dissidents were regularly labelled 'terrorists', and 'sentenced to death, regardless of whether they have used or advocated violence, and regardless of whether they have been implicated in any crime' (Amnesty International 2003b).

China's human rights record was called into question in the West following the international outcry and internal fallout from the Tiananmen Square incident of June 1989, when an unknown but substantial number of people were killed by state authorities. In response to the post-Tiananmen outcry, the Chinese government published the 'Human Rights in China' White Paper in 1991. The document claimed that China was incorporating human rights perspectives into its laws and policies. It also noted that human rights perspectives in China were informed by the country's 'painful history and present social and economic needs'. The government stated that its core response to human rights was to put initial priority on citizens' rights to subsistence and economic development. This was said to be a precondition to the later attainment of all other human rights. The White Paper also implied that the system's stability was the highest priority of China, as without it there was no certainty that rights to subsistence and development could be provided. The implication was also that, in common with other versions of 'Asian values', individual human rights were subservient to those of the collective;

the latter's rights would definitely not be sacrificed for those of the former (Human Rights Research and Education Center, n/d).

Contemporaneous with publication of the White Paper, China began to champion an Asia-wide perspective on what it saw as the primary right: the right to development. The Chinese participated in every session of the governmental experts group organized by the UN Commission on Human Rights to draft the Declaration on the Right to Development, and made positive suggestions until the Declaration was passed by the 41st session of the General Assembly in 1986. It also supported the United Nations Commission on Human Rights in conducting worldwide consultation on the implementation of the Right to Development (Human Rights Watch 1999).

Later, in December 1991, China engineered the organization of regional preparatory conferences before the 1993 Vienna Conference on Human Rights, and gained a key achievement for 'Asian values'. Many Western countries had opposed the regional conferences. They claimed that because human rights were universal, regional conferences were not needed. A China-led resolution, signed by 49 governments, at the March 1993 Asia Preparatory Conference in the Bangkok Declaration, stated that the 'aspirations and commitments of the Asian region' were emphasized in various expressions of 'Asian values'. The document downplayed the concept of the universality of human rights. The Bangkok Declaration also included recognition that 'while human rights are universal in nature, they must be considered in the context of a dynamic and evolving process of international norm-setting, bearing in mind the significance of national and regional particularities and various historical, cultural and religious backgrounds' (Report of the Regional Meeting for Asia of the World Conference on Human Rights 1993).

A decade later, in March 2004, the United States government decided to introduce an anti-China motion at the Geneva-based United Nations Commission on Human Rights (CHR). The *People's Daily* newspaper, official mouthpiece of the Chinese government, reacted with defiance:

> Thanks to China's reform and opening-up drive over the past two decades, the Chinese people's living standard has greatly improved and the country's legal and social security systems have undergone substantial upgrades. . . . Chinese people are now enjoying unprecedented liberty and personal rights. The progress can be seen not only in the improvement in fulfilling people's basic needs and economic, social and cultural rights, but also in the strengthening of democracy and the legal construction, expansion and maintenance of civil and political rights. . . . Promises to protect private property and guarantee human rights were added to the Constitution earlier this month after the Communist Party of China proposed the amendments last year. (<http://english.peopledaily.com.cn/200403/25/eng20040325_138463.shtml>)

Kent (1999: 247) argues that, over the 1971–98 period, China exhibited gradually changing attitudes towards UN human rights institutions. She contends that China was socialized within ten years of the Tiananmen Square incident into 'an acceptance of basic international human rights procedures'. On the other hand, she notes, China's government was unwilling to apply those norms domestically. Considering the importance of China in international politics and its prominent role in the debate about 'Asian values', Kent's study reconfirms the results of initial research on the effects of norm socialization: governments want to be seen to be complying with international norms, even when their own cultural and political histories, as in the case of China, lead them to different interpretations of international norms. Until the US attack on China's human rights situation in March 2004, the government had managed for years to avoid condemnation in the CHR. It had achieved this via two strategies: (1) expending considerable political resources on cultivating supportive governments, and (2) putting in place its own version of human rights observance based primarily on the collective right to development (Donnelly 1998: 128).

Conclusion

Implementation of international human rights norms into domestic practices of states is only sustained when governments become convinced that such an interpretation of the rights constitute part of their collective identity as a modern member of the international community. Overall, however, despite the impact of globalization, the primacy of the state in relation to human rights norms has not necessarily changed. What has altered is that states often try to adapt to international human rights challenges by deploying innovative strategies, and thereby claiming to embed international norms in their domestic structures and processes. However, while the intent is both to assert and retain state control, results can be unexpected: social demands can emerge that states are not necessarily inclined or equipped to meet. Even so, in most cases state attempts to co-opt human rights discourse have impeded a genuine national human rights debate, as well as an exchange of competing ideas about *which* human beings are entitled to *what* resources.

Finally, the impact of 9/11 on human rights regimes in various countries around the world appears to be significant, not least in the various methods that states have adopted to fight 'terror'. This context has highlighted alternative human rights approaches, such as those expressed in alternative conceptions, notably 'Asian values' and Islamic interpretations of human rights, in relation to Western, individualistic norms. Under globalization, the latter can appear to be embryonic – if hotly contested – global norms.

14
Women and
Political Participation

It is often noted that the political position of women is nearly everywhere subservient to that of men. Around the world, political structures and processes are increasingly examined to try to ensure that they accord an equality of opportunity to women, and in numerous countries, questions of women's power and authority are widely debated (although rarely resolved). More generally, gender issues are now widely considered to be an important aspect of politics, raised at all levels of political thinking, both within countries and internationally. Seeking to explain strengths and weaknesses in relation to women's representation, analysts often examine: cultural norms in relation to gender differences, political socialization and adult gender roles (Sapiro and Farah 1980); and the strength of the women's movement in individual countries, as well as regionally and internationally.

Pettman (2001: 582) notes that both comparative political analysis and international relations have generally 'been taught and theorized as if women were invisible: as if either there were no women in world politics, which was only men's business; or as if women and men were active in and affected by world politics in the same ways, in which case there would be no need to "gender" the analysis'. Now, however, there is an emerging area of feminist scholarship in relation to both analytical foci, while gender issues are also a focus of transnational politics (see, for example, True and Mintrom 2001). Overall, 'feminist understandings and women's organizing provide us with perspectives that contribute a more inclusive view of globalization' (Pettman 2001: 582).

We have already seen that some aspects of globalization, notably perceived negative impacts of economic globalization, are believed to promote anti-democratic tendencies. Other aspects of globalization, however, may offer novel opportunities, both for formal political participation as well as for popular democratic influence, to make an impact on political outcomes both within countries and internationally. Analysts point to two particular aspects of globalization in this regard. First, there is greater popular mobility. This is said to increase chances for people from different cultures to interact and learn from each other. Second, the communications revolution associated with globalization has led to much quicker and cheaper ways to communicate over long distances. This led not only to globalization of various forms of media but also to rising levels of interest in global issues. Together, these developments have encouraged groups and individuals – including women's organizations – to communicate and interact both within and between countries (Hutchings 2002; True and Mintrom 2001). In addition, as Deane (2002: 176) notes, women now play a newly prominent role, for example in Pakistan and elsewhere in South Asia, 'as editors and owners of news organizations'.

This chapter is organized as follows. First, we examine how gender issues are examined in comparative political analysis. The focus is usually upon domestic issues, especially women's representation in legislatures and their role in civil society. We will also focus upon national, transnational and international women's organizations. Many observers believe that this is an important factor to take into account when assessing chances of improvement in women's domestic political position. This is because, working with domestic groups, INGOs can help encourage governments to focus upon gender issues. We shall also see, however, that, as Risse-Kappen (1995) put it, such ideas do not 'float freely'. We have already noted the same point in relation to various other issues – such as human rights, democratization and the environment: external actors can only significantly influence domestic outcomes when their ideas link up with those held domestically and there are appropriate political opportunities to put the ideas into practice. As Worsley (1999: 36–7) suggests, globalization is not a one-way street. All societies are open to foreign ideas – whether borrowed or imposed on them – but they 'always have to be adapted to existing, local cultures. The result is a dialectic; not imposition or the bland acceptance of ideas imported from abroad, but a synthesis of cultures, a hybridity.'

Finally, we will examine gender issues in selected established democracies (Britain and Norway), transitional democracies (Russia, Poland and Hungary) and non-democracies (Arab countries, with an emphasis on Kuwait). The case studies were chosen in order to compare and contrast the various types of political system in regard to gender issues, as well as to assess the comparative influence of external and domestic factors in this regard.

Gender and Comparative Politics

Gender-based prejudice is prevalent throughout much of the world, despite legal and other measures to overcome inequalities. The World Bank (2001: 117) suggests that to improve matters, 'extra efforts' must be made 'to raise awareness about culturally based attitudes . . . towards women'. This is because 'values, norms, and social institutions' that traditionally privilege men can also serve to reinforce persistent inequalities between males and females that in turn can become the basis of severe deprivation and conflict.

Feminist agendas focus upon the lesser political position of women compared to men. According to Gelb and Palley (1996: 2), feminism 'is a movement seeking to operationalize self-determination for women in political, economic and social roles'. Feminist concerns are increasingly reflected in political analysis, leading a growing number of political theorists explicitly to consider the issue of gender equality when assessing comparatively the nature of individual political systems. As a result, it is now common for contemporary theories of politics to relate explicitly to gender issues. However, feminist scholars still critique the mainstream majority of both comparative politics and international relations analysis for the high level of alleged 'gender-blindness' (Coole 1988; Dahan-Kalev 2003). Gender-blindness relates to the fact that some political theories have little or nothing to say about the participation of women in politics, including transitions to and consolidation of democracy and, more generally, the gendered nature – or lack of it – of political structures and processes. However, away from the analytical mainstream, assessments of women's involvement in political processes – including political transitions – are now both extensive and varied, increasing significantly since the late 1980s (Rai 2005). According to Waylen (2003: 157), most authors of such gendered analyses would see their work 'as lying directly within the discipline of politics and the sub-discipline of comparative politics'.

Women are said to face two key problems when they seek to increase their political position. The first is the difficulty of securing an enhanced public role for women, especially in societies characterized by cultures that traditionally consign females to the domestic sphere. The second is the importance, more generally, for women to adopt activist roles in civil society in order to help them achieve feminist goals (Rai 2005). Examinations of the political position of women in various societies often fall into two general areas: female representation in national legislatures and in domestic civil societies.

Female Representation in National Legislatures

Pettman (2001: 584) notes that in all countries women are 'under-represented in formal politics, as heads of state or parliamentary representatives or executive bureaucrats'. Nowhere do women achieve 50 per cent representation in national legislatures (see table 14.1). The main reason for this state of affairs in Britain, Marsh (2002: 34) contends, is that: 'White men with money, knowledge and power do have a privileged position in the British polity.' Removing the adjective 'white' from this sentence gives Marsh's statement universal validity, as male pre-eminence in politics tends to perpetuate itself.

Beyond the issue of the preponderance of men in positions of power, Hague and Harrop (2001: 112) note four further factors that limit women's political participation and representation:

1   Traditionally, females have had less formal education than males – although this situation is now reversed among the young in many established democracies.
2   Interest in formal politics – such as, involvement in election campaigns – may be limited by familial responsibilities, notably childbearing and homemaking responsibilities.
3   Some women are said to 'lack the confidence needed to throw themselves into the hurly-burly of formal, male-led politics'.
4   Many females 'still face the high hurdle of discrimination from sexist male politicians'.

It is often suggested that a key way to tackle gender inequality is to increase female political representation in decision-making bodies that, in turn, would increase women's empowerment and enable females to assume their rightful place in society. (The term 'empowerment' refers to the acquisition of the awareness and skills necessary to take charge of, and to make the most of, one's own life chances.) In this case, empowerment refers to a process whereby women increasingly make decisions by and for themselves in order, as far as possible, to shape their own destinies. To achieve political empowerment requires full participation in decision-making structures and process at all levels: local, national and international.

Table 14.1 indicates that there are 26 countries where, in 2004, women filled a quarter or more of the seats in lower or single houses of parliament. According to Freedom House (2004), 17 of the 26 (65 per cent) are established democracies, 8 of the remain-

Table 14.1 Women's representation in lower or single houses of parliament: 25% or more

Country	Date of most recent election	Seats	Number of women	Women (%)
Rwanda	09/2003	80	39	48.8
Sweden	09/2002	349	158	45.3
Denmark	11/2001	179	68	38.0
Finland	03/2003	200	75	37.5
Netherlands	01/2003	150	55	36.7
Norway	09/2001	165	60	36.4
Cuba	01/2003	609	219	36.0
Spain	03/2004	350	126	36.0
Belgium	05/2003	150	53	35.3
Costa Rica	02/2002	57	20	35.1
Argentina	10/2001	256	87	34.0
Austria	11/2002	183	62	33.9
South Africa*	04/2004	400	131	32.8
Germany	09/2002	603	194	32.2
Iceland	05/2003	63	19	30.2
Mozambique	12/1999	250	75	30.0
Seychelles	12/2002	34	10	29.4
New Zealand	07/2002	120	34	28.3
Vietnam	05/2002	498	136	27.3
Grenada	11/2003	15	4	26.7
Namibia	11/1999	72	19	26.4
Bulgaria	06/2001	240	63	26.2
Timor-Leste**	08/2001	88	23	26.1
Turkmenistan	12/1999	50	13	26.0
Australia	11/2001	150	38	25.3
Switzerland	10/2003	200	50	25.0
United Kingdom	06/2001	659	118	17.9
United States	11/2002	435	62	14.3

* South Africa: the figures on the distribution of seats do not include the 36 special rotating delegates appointed on an ad hoc basis, and the percentages given are therefore calculated on the basis of the 54 permanent seats.
** Timor-Leste: the purpose of elections held on 30 August 2001 was to elect members of the Constituent Assembly of Timor-Leste. This body became the National Parliament on 20 May 2002, the date on which the country became independent, without any new elections.
Source: Adapted from Interparliamentary Union, 'Women in national parliaments' (<http://www.ipu.org/wmn-e/classif.htm>). Data correct on 31 May 2004.

ing 9 are transitional democracies, and one – Cuba – is a non-democracy. This suggests that women are more likely to achieve relatively high levels of representation when they live in established or transitional democracies. Note that data covering the United States and United Kingdom – 14.3 per cent and 17.9 per cent respectively – are included for comparative purposes. Table 14.2 indicates, however, that lower or single houses of parliament in various established democracies have less than 10 per cent female membership.

Table 14.2 Women's representation in lower or single houses of parliament in established democracies: 10% or less

Country	Date of most recent election	Seats	Number of women	Women (%)
Panama*	05/1999	71	7	9.9
Hungary	04/2002	386	38	9.8
Malta	04/2003	65	6	9.2
Thailand	01/2001	500	46	9.2
Sao Tome and Principe	03/2002	55	5	9.1
Ghana	12/2000	200	18	9.0
Greece	04/2000	300	26	8.7
Brazil	10/2002	513	44	8.6
India	04/2004	541	45	8.3
Benin	03/2003	83	6	7.2
Japan	11/2003	480	34	7.1
Republic of Korea	04/2000	273	16	5.9
Mauritius	09/2000	70	4	5.7
Antigua and Barbuda	03/2004	19	1	5.3
Sri Lanka*	12/2001*	225	10	4.4
Belize	03/2003	30	1	3.3

* At the time of writing, July 2004, data relating to the gender composition of national legislatures following elections in Panama and Sri Lanka, in May and April 2004 respectively, were not available.
Source: Interparliamentary Union, 'Women in national parliaments' (<http://www.ipu.org/wmn-e/arc/classif300104.htm>). Data correct at 31 May 2004.

It has often been argued theoretically that a 'critical mass,' ranging from 10 to 35 per cent, of women in national legislatures is needed before major changes in legislative institutions, behaviour, policy priorities and policy voting occurs (Studlar and McAllister 2003: 233). Critical mass theory suggests that:

> when a group remains a distinct minority within a larger society, its members will seek to adapt to their surroundings, conforming to the predominant rules of the game. . . . But once the group reaches a certain size, . . . there will be a qualitative change in the nature of group interactions, as the minority starts to assert itself and thereby transform the institutional culture, norms and values. (Norris 2002: 38)

Assuming that women and men politicians differ in their underlying values, policy priorities and legislative styles, critical mass theory contends that when women's membership of parliaments improves from 10 per cent upwards – perhaps eventually reaching 30, 40 or even 50 per cent – then there is likely to be a transformation in the institutional culture, political discourse and policy agenda of affected countries. That is, the claims of critical mass theory depend on there being underlying differences in the values, attitudes and behaviour of certain identifiable groups (Bratton 2002). In relation to women, it can only operate if female politicians hold norms and values that are clearly different from those of men. For example, women might be expected to hold certain issues to be of importance – public spending on education, parliamentary questions about childcare, or attention paid to constituency service – while men, on the other hand, are believed to be interested in different issues, such as defence spending, foreign policy issues and parliamentary debate. Some studies demonstrate that women do make a distinct contribution to the policy agenda in legislatures in North America, Western Europe and Scandinavia, but elsewhere the evidence is unclear (Bratton 2002).

An article by Studlar and McAllister (2003) examines one of the less-explored dimensions of the concept of critical mass. They ask the following question: 'Is there a process by which women reaching a critical mass of the legislature accelerates the election of further women?' Using data from both the Interparliamentary Union and the International Institute for Democracy and Electoral Assistance, they examine this question in relation to 20 industrialized democracies over the 1950–2000 period. Their results indicate that improvements in women's representation are actually incremental – it is not critical mass that increases the speed of the election of women to legislatures. They conclude that, far from being clearly demonstrated, critical mass theories need empirical testing (Studlar and McAllister 2003: 233).

While critical mass theory claims that once the proportion of women in legislatures reaches a certain point then we might expect the political agenda to change, there is a prior problem to resolve: how to secure and then maintain an influential public role for women in societies where females may have long been consigned to the domestic sphere. To attempt to redress the imbalance, three key steps are suggested. First, it is important to have influential political parties with appropriate activists and ideologies. According to Waylen (2003: 173), parties with certain ideological characteristics are more likely to field women candidates in elections than others. In both Latin America and CEE parties identified with the left tend to field more women candidates in winnable positions than those identified with the right. It also appears to be the case that the more institutionalized parties are, the more likely it is that they would field women candidates, for example, the Labour Party in Britain from the mid-1990s.

Second, active, reformist-orientated, social movements can be influential. In this regard, the role played by women activists, particularly women who identify themselves as feminists, both within autonomous women's sections and within the mainstream of parties, is central.

Third, enhanced female representation is facilitated by certain political processes. To achieve enhanced representation for women, a suitable electoral system is helpful: for example, 'the party list version of proportional representation, a method that allows party officials to select a gender-balanced set of candidates' (Hague and Harrop 2001: 112; Waylen 2003: 169, 173). In addition, a trio of more general, institutional steps are also linked to enhanced female representation in national parliaments: the electoral system, quotas and turnover of legislators.

Regarding the nature of the electoral system, Blais and Massicotte (2002: 15) contend that 'women do best under the party list version of proportional representation, a method that allows party officials to select a gender-balanced set of candidates'. For example, when New Zealand switched to a more proportional system in 1996, the proportion of women legislators increased from 21 per cent to over 28 per cent.

In addition, quotas can ensure that women make up a certain proportion of a party's candidates or, more radically, of its elected representatives. Quotas are easily applied with party list proportional representation, but even in constituency-based electoral systems it is possible to require both genders to be included on a district short-list. The reasoning behind gender quotas is twofold. First, there is a clear case to be made on the grounds of equity. Second, it is often suggested that the entry of more women into legislatures would help to change mainstream policy agendas (Hazan 2002: 115–17). Today, in numerous countries, various adaptations of Nordic quota policies are in operation, 'and the policy of quotas has become one of the most fervently debated means to secure women's presence in political life' (Skjeie 1998). As the World Bank (2001: 120) notes, 'efforts are underway in at least 32 countries to increase women's political representation by reserving seats for them in local and national assemblies'. For example, in Germany, the Social Democratic Party has established quotas for women, while in Norway, the leading parties introduced quotas as early as 1973. In Argentina, women must now legally comprise at least a third of candidates on national election lists. In South Africa, women of the ruling African National Congress have achieved considerable success arguing for institutionalizing women's participation in the country's post-apartheid political organizations (Marais 1998: 170). At the local level, India reserves for women one third of local council seats, and in Pakistan women must by law fill 6 – of the 21 – seats on local councils (McCarthy 2001b).

Finally, there is the issue of turnover of legislators. Low turnover, as in the United States Congress, 'creates a recruitment bottleneck which enables men, once elected, to remain in post for decades. . . . If most incumbents will be reselected, then it is safe to say that most reselected incumbents will be male.' In the United States, in spite of robust demands for greater inclusion of women, candidate composition for elected legislatures is still over-represented by males (Hague and Harrop 2001: 112; also see Hazan 2002: 115).

In sum, seeking to achieve political representation on a par with men, women frequently encounter barriers at three levels: the entry level, the candidate selection level and the general election level. In terms of candidate selection, the imbalances that exist cannot be redressed by variations in candidacy requirements, by inclusiveness of the 'selectorate', or by the existence of a particular voting system. Instead, it is necessary to assure the functional representation of women through mechanisms such as quotas. As a result, the number of women candidates and level of women's representation can be raised. In established democracies where women's representation is low – see table 14.2 – it can be successfully increased. In countries where it is relatively high – see table 14.1 – it can be raised even higher (the experience of the Nordic countries is proof of this). Such quotas are rarely found at the systemic level; rather they are the decisions of particular parties. Thus, the level of candidate selection is usually the most crucial factor for getting women into elected office.

Female Representation in Civil Society

Domestic civil society

Many gendered analyses are interdisciplinary, often focusing on the nature and identity of particular women's movements. Such actors tend not to be regarded as of central importance in the comparative politics/democratization literature as they tend to be seen as part of a social movement perspective (Haynes 1997). In this book, we have repeatedly emphasized that such a view is not necessarily unimportant or marginal. This is because outside formal political structures and processes in the realm of civil society, millions of women around the world organize both in social movements and in domestic and international NGOs. Through such mechanisms women are increasingly actors at both national and international levels, even though they are not necessarily recognized as such in either the comparative politics or international relations literature (Pettman 2001: 584). Rai (2005) points to the importance of a politically activist role for females in civil society networks within, and increasingly between, countries.

The literature notes two main kinds of women's organizations: 'feminist' and 'feminine' organizations. First, feminist groups often have memberships comprising primarily 'middle-class, university-educated women who . . . defy the classification of passive, voiceless and tradition-bound' women (Marchand 1995: 61). Here, feminism is innately political because it picks out and problematizes the fundamentally political relationship between gender and power. Second, there are the 'feminine' groups, concerned primarily with various mostly material concerns, from consumption issues to questions of women's economic status.

Feminist groups pursue what are known as 'strategic' objectives, while feminine groups are said to aspire to more 'practical' goals (Molyneux 1985; Jaquette 1989; Alvarez 1990; Safa 1990). According to Alvarez (1990: 25):

> feminist organizations focus on issues *specific* to the female condition (i.e. reproductive rights), feminine groups mobilize women around gender-related issues and concerns. The cost of living, for example, is one such issue. . . . Women . . . may organize to protest the rising cost of living because inflation undermines their ability to adequately feed, clothe, and house their families.

Waylen (1993: 574) notes that the unitary category of 'woman' – undifferentiated by, for example, race, class, or nationality issues – is not helpful intellectually when seeking to analyse the socio-political impact of women's groups. One way of seeking to deal with the problem is to divide women's groups between those which conceptualize their chief concerns around 'practical' gender interests, such as economic survival, and those involved in 'strategic' gender interests associated with more feminist objectives. It is important to note however that such categories are more for analytical convenience than anything else; in practice, there is much blurring between categories. Nevertheless, there may be fairly clearly defined social divisions between those involved with the practical concerns of the feminine organizations and those belonging to the feminist groups. On the other hand, many urban working-class women's organizations may well not only address 'bread and butter' survival issues, but also concern themselves with issues like domestic violence and reproductive rights, interests they share with feminist groups.

However, the feminine–feminist dichotomy is not only a heuristic device; it is also employed by some women – especially in developing countries – to denote the class position of activists. Middle-class, educated women involved in 'women's issues' may well classify themselves as feminists, and poorer, less-educated women may reject the 'feminist' label (Alvarez 1990; Marchand 1995). Yet, as Safa (1990) points out, an initial involvement in 'practical' interests often leads on to a concern with more 'strategic' questions. Fisher (1993: 103) asserts that the 'distinction between feminist and [feminine] organizations is beginning to blur in some countries, as middle- and lower-class women define their common interests'. Perhaps the best way to conceptualize the issue is not to try to dichotomize the types of group, but rather to see them on a continuum with a large middle area where concerns are both practical *and* strategic. The benefit of concentrating on the middle ground is that it allows us to overcome the private/public dichotomy whereby 'practical' concerns are relegated to the *private* sphere and 'strategic' issues to the *public* realm of politics.

Usually, when gender is discussed as a political issue, definitions of what is 'political' are based on this kind of public/private division. Women are often designated as uphold-ers of the private foundation of the political world of men. Yet one of the main cata-lysts for the emergence of the women's movement in the West in the 1960s – with the slogan 'the personal is the political' – was dissatisfaction with the outcome of demo-cratic politics in terms of the (lack of) progress in bettering the position of females. The aim of the women's movement was – and for many activists still is – to build a more active, *participatory* democracy at both institutional and personal levels. To achieve these aims it would be necessary to organize to change both interpersonal relations between men and women and the nature of the prevailing political order which fails fully to incorporate women and their demands.

Transnational civil society

Gender concerns were firmly put under the global spotlight in the 1990s via a series of UN-sponsored global conferences: human rights (Vienna, 1992), the natural envi-ronment (Rio, 1992), population (Cairo, 1994), human development (Copenhagen, 1995), women and gender (Beijing, 1995) and social development (Geneva, 2000). Their cumulative effect was to help shift both international and domestic agendas from the relatively safe area of 'women's issues' to mainstream political, economic, social, envi-ronmental and military issues.

This suggests that the external environment often impacts upon the domestic insti-tutional context of gender issues (Pettman 2001; True and Mintrom 2001; Ackerley and Okin 1999; Waylen 2003: 172). From the early 1960s, the international women's move-ment helped to change perspectives – first in the West and now increasingly in the devel-oping world – about the political, social and economic position of women. The 1980s and 1990s also saw a growth in the number of women's groups both domestically and transnationally, taking 'advantage of the series of United Nations conferences to form a thick weave of interconnections' (Florini and Simmons 2000: 10).

International organizations and international women's conferences can influence domestic policy agendas in two main ways. First, they can bring pressure to bear on gov-ernments – for example to establish state women's bodies. Second, they can support in various ways domestic women's groups and movements. For example, international support is said to have been significant for the expansion of influence of women's groups in Latin America from the 1970s. In addition, the aim of many countries in CEE to join the EU resulted in external pressures to adopt measures such as equal treatment direc-tives associated with the *acquis communitaire* (McMahon 2002; Richter 2002).

Florini and Simmons (2000: 10) contend that 'women have become increasingly active in [the] world of cross-border efforts'. The New York-based International Women's Tribune Center (IWTC) is the contact and referral office for more than '25,000 groups in 150 countries, 94 per cent in the Global South' (<http://www.iwtc.org/>). While it is clear that such a large number of groups will have numerous individual goals, what they have in common is a key objective: to transform local conditions or domestic institutional domains – such as the household, the community or the neighbourhood, where women find themselves confined to domestic roles – into political spaces. True and Mintrom (2001: 27) argue that transnational networks composed largely of non-state actors – including women's international non-governmental organizations and the United Nations – have been the main actors furthering the spread of 'gender mainstreaming'.[1] Their findings support the claim that transnational networks, in particular transnational feminist movements, have facilitated the spread of gender mainstreaming mechanisms.

In sum, ideas generated at the grassroots can spread to, and influence, international diplomats and policy-makers and, in turn, ideas adopted in international forums can easily affect people's thinking and their daily lives. Overall, whether governments are less or more democratic, institutions of civil society and NGOs can play an important role in the transmission of information and ideas from the grassroots level up through regional representatives to the level of international conferences and policy-making.

Established Democracies

In each of the case study sections, we examine the relationship of gender issues to political outcomes in respect of women's participation in conventional politics, and gender policy as a result of the legislative involvement of women.

In the first section, focused on established democracies, we look at the contrasting cases of Britain and Norway. We see that embedding gender issues on legislative agendas in Norway was the result of a long-term policy to increase the numbers of women in decision-making positions. The case of Britain shows a contrasting situation. There, the policy to increase the representative position of women is of more recent origin. Thus far, the extent to which gender issues have become consolidated as key issue areas of legislative focus is not clear.

Britain

Women's participation in conventional politics

From just 23 female MPs in 1983 (3.5 per cent), the number of women members of parliament (MPs) grew to 120 (18.2 per cent) following the general election in 1997, before declining slightly to 118 (17.9 per cent) in 2001. Coming to power in 1997 with a land-

---

[1] 'Gender mainstreaming is a globally accepted strategy for promoting gender equality. Mainstreaming is not an end in itself but a strategy, an approach, a means to achieve the goal of gender equality. Mainstreaming involves ensuring that gender perspectives and attention to the goal of gender equality are central to all activities – policy development, research, advocacy/dialogue, legislation, resource allocation, and planning, implementation and monitoring of programmes and projects' (<http://www.un.org/womenwatch/osagi/gendermainstreaming.htm>).

slide victory, the 'New' Labour government actively sought to pursue the goal of promoting greater numbers of women MPs. Beetham et al. (2001: 51) note that 'in comparison with the recent past, the current proportion of women in the UK parliament would seem to mark a significant advance'. However, the figure looks less impressive when compared with some other European nations, especially the Scandinavian countries, or in Britain itself in the devolved assemblies in Scotland and Wales.[2] It is even less estimable when we bear in mind the proportion of women in the population as a whole: slightly more than 50 per cent.

Gender policy

It is often suggested that positive discrimination in favour of women is a necessary step in order to raise different concerns in legislatures compared to the men-dominated past (Norris 2002: 39). We noted above that, according to critical mass theory, the expectation is that when women's representation in national legislatures reaches around 15 per cent, then we might expect to see evidence emerging of an alteration in institutional culture, political discourse and policy agenda. As we shall see below, this is precisely what happened over the course of time in Norway from the early 1970s. On the other hand, the recent increase in the number of women MPs in Britain can be seen as a test case for critical mass theory. What evidence is there that the traditional situation of gender marginality in British politics is being amended as a result of the fivefold increase in the number of women MPs since the early 1980s?

After decades when there were fewer than 30 women at Westminster, the 1997 general election and subsequent contests in Scotland, Wales and in relation to the European Parliament saw unprecedented progress in Britain. The main reason for this change was positive discrimination in Labour Party parliamentary recruitment process. Sodaro (2001: 412) explains that 'in an effort to increase the number of women in Parliament, Labour in the 1990s adopted a candidate selection procedure aiming at electing women to half the party's seats in the Commons in future elections'. In addition, as Norris (2002: 55–6) notes, 'constitutional reform has altered the structure of opportunities for women in the new elected bodies in Scotland and Wales, without the barrier of established incumbents'. In sum, 'The growth of women in office has . . . altered the symbolic face of the British political elite'.

Certain mechanisms underpin the recent progress in the representation of women in British politics. Norris (2002) points to the extent and nature of attitudinal and behavioural differences between women and men in the House of Commons, and observes encouraging implications for legislative priorities and political debates to make them more gender-orientated. Overall, she is cautiously optimistic about the gradual emergence and development of political deliberation processes that appear to give greater voice to, and hence seek both to address and represent, the interests of British women.

[2] 'The numbers of women elected to both bodies increased as a result of the 2003 elections. In the National Assembly for Wales, 30 of the 60 members elected were women, up from 25 women in the previous election. In the Scottish Parliament, the number of women increased from 48 to 51, or about 40 per cent of members. These figures put Wales and Scotland near the top of OSCE countries in terms of the proportion of women in Parliaments' (OSCE 2003: 15).

Norris underpins her claims with data – derived from the 1992 election in Britain – suggesting that when compared to men in each of the main parties (Labour, Conservative, Liberal Democrats), women were slightly more supportive of both feminist and 'left-wing' values. She also notes however that in each case 'the gender gap was modest, and overall party rather than gender proved the strongest predictor of values and attitudes' (Norris 2002: 39).

Under such circumstances it is probably unlikely that the augmentation in numbers of women representatives has so far had a significant impact on the policy agenda or ethos of parliamentary life. In other words, the fact of having more women in the parliament has probably not (yet) transformed the political agenda and the dominant political style at Westminster. On the other hand, a consistent gender gap has been noted in relation to the major parties in terms of some policy issues. These are 'gender-related values', with 'significant implications for sex equality in the labour force and home. If these issues become more salient, as women move from a skewed to a tilted minority at Westminster, then critical mass theory suggests that this will gradually become evident in legislative priorities and political debates' (Norris 2002: 56).

Women in Britain won the vote on equal terms with men in 1928, yet equality is still an issue. It is important to note that although the goal of increasing the numbers of women MPs is gradually being achieved, women in Britain still face considerable obstacles when trying to increase their political, economic and social positions. The diminished position of women compared to men in the United Kingdom is reflected in the following statistics, recently compiled by the Equal Opportunities Commission (2003: 1):

- women working full time earn on average 19 per cent less per hour than men working full time; those working part time earn 41 per cent less per hour than full-time men;
- 75 per cent of women work in the five lowest paid sectors;
- more than 50 per cent of parents have no access to flexible working hours;
- only one in seven children under the age of 8 has a childcare place;
- men want to spend more time with their children, yet currently work some of the longest hours in the European Union;
- the average woman in retirement will have an income just over half that of a similar aged man;
- in 2001–2, around 24,000 people took a case of sexual discrimination or equal pay to an Employment Tribunal;
- women hold less than 10 per cent of the top positions in FTSE 100 companies, the police, the judiciary and trade unions;
- police are called out to more domestic violence incidents than any other kind of incidents. Every week, two women are killed by their partners or their ex-partners.

The conclusion is that much more progress needs to be made in Britain before it is possible to talk meaningfully about equality between men and women. The recent increase in numbers of women in the House of Commons, in regional assemblies and in the European Parliament may eventually lead to significant changes, but at the moment it is too early to tell.

Norway

Women's participation in conventional politics

Table 14.1 indicates that in Norway over a third (36.4 per cent) of legislators were women in 2004, a figure that increased from less than 10 per cent in the early 1970s. The case of Norway appears to confirm the applicability of critical mass theory in relation to women's issues. This is because in Norway gender concerns are now mainstream political issues, focusing on various concerns, including representational politics, labour market politics, body politics and care politics (van der Ros 1994).

Skjeie (1998) explains that since the mid-1980s, women in Norway 'have participated in close to equal numbers with men in formulating cabinet decisions'. In addition, in relation to 'the organizational leadership of most Norwegian political parties there are only small differences in women's and men's participation, and most major parties have elected women party leaders over the course of the last decade'. The main reason for this is that:

> Norway's policy on women's political participation rests on a widely shared political credo. The core of this credo can be summarized as follows: gender constitutes an important political category that needs to be fully represented; and women's political interests and orientations cannot, and should not, be viewed as merely equivalent to men's political interests and orientations. (Skjeie 1998)

There are two sources of the increased political role for women in Norway. We have already noted the first: a strong belief rooted in Norwegian culture that women *should* enjoy equality with men. This logic worked its way into circles of party leadership among Norwegian political parties from the early 1970s, a development linked to the emergence of a new feminist movement. The latter put forward the argument that increased rights for women was commensurate with group interests based on the collective good, rather than on individual fairness. According to Skjeie (1998), this was an important factor in legitimizing increases in women's representation. Unlike in many countries, in addition, the Norwegian feminist movement argued that the most viable strategy for empowering women was integration into the existing political structures and process. As a result, the women's movement began to work actively with women in different political parties to promote their access to established institutions of decision-making. This goal was achieved in three ways: careful argumentation, coordinated campaigns, and the clever use of party competition. The consequence was that 'feminist ideas on gender-structured interests came to influence the attitudes of political elite' (Skjeie 1998).

Gender policy

According to van der Ros (1990: 530), Norway is a 'Nordic welfare state' where 'the state has taken over the guardianship of women from individual men'. She bases this view on the fact that women are closely connected, both as social clients and as voters who give legitimacy to state policies. Large numbers of women are public employees: the state employs nearly half (45 per cent) of women working outside the home while, overall, 70 per cent of state employees are women.

Skjeie (1991: 128) claims that Norway's political culture changed during the 1980s. At that time, Norwegian women managed to define gender as a politically relevant category that guaranteed them representation in the public decision-making bodies. Such concern for gender composition of different public commissions was acknowledged in Norway from the 1970s. Overall, women's participation in politics increased the state's concern for the situation of women, and affected gender policy. Various social and welfare policies were implemented to facilitate the combination of work and family: the number of day-care places almost doubled in the 1980s, while parental leave was extended, with fathers eligible for four weeks' minimum leave.

Conclusion

In Britain, the representation of women increased from the mid-1990s. Unlike Norway, however, gender equality in public life is not yet established. The growth in numbers of women in elected positions has altered the representative mix of the British political elite, but it is less clear to what extent it had a significant impact on policy agendas or the culture of parliamentary life. The point is that British party politics has not altered that much, while evidence suggests that British politicians ideologically differ in relation to party more than to sex. This is especially true in terms of core cleavages, such as the economy and foreign policy. On the other hand, according to Norris (2002: 56), there are policy issues with a consistent gender gap in each of the main parties. This includes issues with 'significant implications for sex equality policy in the labour force and home. If these issues become more salient . . . then critical mass theory suggests that this will gradually become more evident in legislative priorities and political debates.'

Transitional Democracies

Recent literature on gender and political transitions divides into two main areas. First, there is the part played by groups of women in the demise of non-democratic regimes and the ensuing shift to democratizing regimes, involving competitive electoral politics. Waylen notes, however, that 'this is fairly well-worn ground . . . sometimes . . . overly voluntaristic'. That is, many accounts focus on women's social movements and accompanying mobilizations, but 'without always giving sufficient consideration to their interaction with different institutions'. Waylen also observes that women's movements frequently employ a ' "wide and adaptable strategic repertoire", comprising different alliances and actions over multiple political venues' (Waylen 2003: 158). This suggests that in order to examine fully gendered aspects of political transitions and their aftermath, we should look at interactions that women's movements have with changing domestic and external political contexts, and levels of representation of women in post-transition legislatures.

The second area of analysis is concerned with the results of transitions in terms of gender outcomes. To assess the latter, we need to be aware of wider – historical, cultural and institutional – contexts. In this section we examine the situation in relation to women in Russia, Poland and Hungary.

Russia

The Soviet constitution created history by proclaiming women's equality. Ambitious communist rhetoric and the existence of large and well-organized women's groups did not mean, however, that socialism's promise of gender equality was fulfilled. In the USSR, women were not only paid less than their male counterparts but also barely represented in positions of power. Women were able to establish mass organizations only under the direction of the Party. The Communist Party created a number of social organizations that enjoyed nominal autonomy, but they all depended on the state for both funding and personnel, and, in the case of women's groups, functioned more as a means of social control than of female empowerment. During *perestroika* in the late 1980s, while official women's organizations continued to elevate an ideal of Soviet womanhood, activists came together to inaugurate the first independent women's movement in the USSR since the 1917 revolution. Now, in Russia, women are again socially and legally disadvantaged, with protection and rights they officially enjoyed in the former Soviet Union a fast-receding memory. According to Diamond (1999: 243) there are signs in Russia of 'deterioration in the political and social status of women after the transition'.

Women's participation in conventional politics

> Because democracy is new in Russia, it has not developed a political culture based on the principles of civil society. As a result, women continue to be repressed; the majority of unemployed are women; and the mass media still support the notion that women's role is limited to that of wife and mother. In short, democracy in Russia still has a masculine face. (Shvedova 1998)

Women in Russia are under-represented within elected bodies. Currently, women occupy just 44 (9.8 per cent) of the 450 seats in the lower chamber of the Russian national legislature elected in December 2003. This compares to the 13.5 per cent of seats that they occupied in 1993. Then, it may have been possible to talk of a critical mass emerging in relation to women's representation, but this is not now the case (Golosov 2001: 45).

How best to explain the decline in women's representation in Russia over the last decade? It is sometimes suggested that obstacles to women's representation are best explained in terms of cultural norms or, more specifically, gender differences in political socialization and adult gender roles (Sapiro and Farah 1980). Golosov (2001: 45) notes that similarly designed studies in Russia are few, but they tend to reach similar conclusions. Another factor said to be influential is the strength of the women's movement (Shvedova 1998).

Gender policy

Three major issues have been identified in relation to gender equality issues in contemporary Russia: transition to a market economy; development of democratic institutions and responsive government processes; and serious domestic violence against women. Let us look at each area.

Regarding gender equality and the economic transition, we can note that in Russia, women have long been an integral part of the paid labour force, essential to the functioning of the economy. Many Russian women have a high level of educational attainment, often higher than many Russian men. During the USSR, women amounted to half the labour force. However, inequalities still existed, with women concentrated in so-called 'female' industries and jobs. As a result, they were prohibited from many types of work, with few in management positions; and their average wages were much lower than men's. Moreover, childcare and work were commonly regarded (especially by men) as the responsibility of women (Shvedova 1998).

The transition to a market economy increased inequalities. Many women lost their jobs, the result in part of the impact of the transition on the sectors in which females predominated (such as textiles and services). Growing inequalities also resulted from what many observers saw as the result of discriminatory dismissals and practices in retraining and recruitment to new jobs. Competing for scarce jobs, men were typically given precedence over women in both the public and the private sector. Finally, the problem of inequality was made worse by new labour standards that failed to provide equal protection for women and by the collapse of childcare provisions (Standing 1994).

Turning to the second area, women's marginalization is also taking place in politics. As we have already noted, there has been a sharp fall in the number of women in parliament (from about a third in the Soviet period to less than 10 per cent in 2004). In addition, women are under-represented in decision-making positions in government ministries and other key institutions. A key concern is that the under-representation of women in political and bureaucratic institutions leads to decision-making that does not take account of women's needs and interests (Shvedova 1998; Posadskaya-Vanderbeck 1998).

A third area of concern in relation to gender policy is that of domestic violence. Amnesty International (2004b) notes a shocking level of violence against women in Russia. Figures indicate that partners or relatives kill more than 14,000 Russian women each year. The AI report documents the failure of the government, the police and the criminal justice system to provide women with the protection of Russian law. Obstacles to lodging complaints, reluctance to investigate and prosecute, and biases against complainants characterize the approach of law-enforcement agencies.

In a climate where the state is seen as unable or unwilling to act on behalf of women, advocacy by women's organizations can be particularly important in gaining attention for women's views and concerns, defending their rights and generating public debate on equality issues. Consequently, women's organizations in Russia are regarded as potentially crucial in identifying gender equality issues and strategies to deal with extant concerns.

Following the demise of the USSR, the women's movement in Russia has expanded enormously to include numerous organizations and institutes, notably the Women's

Movement of Russia (WMR) founded in 1996. The WMR has branches in 62 regions of the Russian Federation and 194 collective members. According to the WMR website, it 'cooperates with women's and other public organizations and parties, which uphold the interests of women, family and children, and with legislative and executive authorities' (<http://www.owl.ru/win/women/wmr/indexe.htm#objectives>). Their interests include research into gender-related problems and issues, as well as 'advocacy about policy and legislation, employment and training services, rape crisis centres and a range of other matters'. The WMR and other women's organizations also play a key role in representing the concerns and aspirations of women and in generating public debate about women's rights and gender relations. This role is particularly important in the current context because of the marginalization of women from political and economic life in the transition process and the current scope of changes.

The present development of the women's movement in Russia has its roots in the Soviet period when Russian feminists often met with indifference and hostility at home. However, some were 'able to forge ties with women in the United States and Western Europe' (Mendelson and Glenn 2002: 13). Richter (2002) has analysed the efforts of transnational feminist organizations and donors to support the growth of a network of women's organizations in Russia in terms of three issue areas: (1) tasks that the organizations and donors seek to accomplish (for example, building NGO infrastructure, public advocacy or community outreach), (2) identity of beneficiaries (that is, individuals or organizations) and (3) terms of involvement (comparing, for instance, grants to individuals or organizations for a specific project with multidimensional grants to enable organizations to accomplish a range of services).

Richter (2002) observes that in Russia, international support of women's organizations has been a mixed blessing for the construction of civil society. In many ways international engagement has made it possible for the women's movement simply to survive. Although some independent feminist organizations – such as the WMR – would have endured without outside assistance, Western money was very important in helping sustain their operations. In addition, political successes of some women's organizations ensured that each of the three major power centres of the Russian government – the Duma (parliament), the Federation Council[3] and the presidential apparatus – has a committee or commission devoted to issues concerning women and families.

But in creating a cadre of professional activists involved in their own networks, norms and practices, international assistance has to some degree increased the distance between the rest of society and the Russian women's movement. That is, while the NGO sector was strengthened, the effect on civil society was unclear. Civic associations became more institutionalized and professionalized, while frequently becoming transformed into hierarchical, centralized corporate entities valuing their own survival more than a proclaimed social mission. Dependence on international assistance tended to compel them to be more responsive to outside donors than to internal constituencies. As we shall see next in the case of Poland and Hungary, by selecting feminist organizations over other women's organizations, donors assisted those whose goals were, from the outset, more firmly based in the transnational network than in Russian society. Their

---

[3] The Federation Council is the upper chamber of the Federal Assembly – the parliament of the Russian Federation, first elected 12 December 1993 simultaneously with the adoption of the new Constitution.

dependence on that network had the unintended consequence of removing incentives to mobilize new members and of fostering competition for grants, resulting in mistrust, bitterness and secrecy between and within organizations.

Poland and Hungary

Women's participation in conventional politics

Until 1990, the communist countries of CEE had the highest female representation of any region. In 1950, it was 11.7 per cent and in 1985, it was 26.6 per cent. It fell to 11.2 per cent in 1990 and a decade later, in 2000, it was 10.9 per cent. The reason for this negative development was simple: during the communist regime, it was a goal that the composition of the parliament should mirror the composition of the population. Thus, a strict quota system was used. However, it is important to note that the communist parliaments could not legitimately be compared to legislatures in democratic states, in terms of their powers and functions. That is, political power was located elsewhere, especially in the politburo; very few women were found there. When the states became post-communist countries, female representation dropped. Thus it is clear that gender quotas were used during communist rule for certain symbolic purposes; and that this regime has had no lasting effects. Neither Poland nor Hungary is close to levels of female representation achieved during the communist regime, although the former does better than the latter: in Poland, in 2004, women occupied 93 of the 460 seats (20.2 per cent) in the Sejm (lower house). In Hungary women occupied just 9.8 per cent (38 out of 386) of seats in the country's single chamber legislature in 2004 (<http://www.oska.org.pl/english/womeninpoland/inparliament.html>).

Gender policies

Since the fall of communism in 1989 the process of democratization in both Poland and Hungary has proceeded at comparable rates. As we noted above in relation to Russia, women in Poland and Hungary have experienced similar challenges. Political and economic changes in the 1990s and early 2000s exacerbated existing disparities between men and women, and in varying ways women in both countries suffered disproportionately from political uncertainty and economic restructuring. Also as in Russia, the post-communist political culture led to a patriarchal backlash in Poland and Hungary as their societies struggled to reestablish their traditional cultures. Yet despite their initial similarities, the diverse and fairly well-developed landscape of women's NGOs in Poland look dramatically different from the still fledgling and unorganized activities in Hungary.

McMahon (2002) has assessed the strategies of international foundations and NGOs for helping the women of Poland and Hungary respond to the challenges posed by the transition to democracy and the market in the post-communist period. She distinguishes strategies in terms of the identity of the beneficiary (infrastructural assistance to organizations versus human capital development); the terms of involvement or method of transfer that the international NGO has used (proactive or imposed strategies versus reactive or responsive ones, and elite-centred versus mass-focused approaches); project-based strategies in terms of their orientation to process or to produce; and short- versus long-term involvement.

The effectiveness of INGO strategies, McMahon finds, is constrained in these two countries by variations in governmental support for the sector, the strength of indigenous NGO culture and traditions, and the different challenges facing women in these countries. A dozen years after communism's demise, the landscape of women's organizations in Poland differs tremendously from that in Hungary. In Poland, infrastructural assistance has had a large influence on the number and the diversity of women's organizations that were established after 1989 and that continue to exist, including the National Council of Polish Women, the Women's Rights Centre, and the PSF Women's Centre/Polish Feminist Association.

Hungary has attracted fewer international donors and international actors to the plight of women's advocacy, although the Soros Foundation of Hungary is a major source of external funding. Polish women's NGOs appear to be better organized and far more active outside the capital than their Hungarian counterparts (Mendelson and Glenn 2002: 13).

In conclusion, McMahon (2002) provides evidence of the power of transnational networks in relation to women's organizations in Poland and Hungary, and she also highlights many of the complexities associated with the issue. She argues that INGOs have been crucial to institution-building and that the strongest NGOs in Poland and Hungary are those that have had support from external sources. On the other hand, international involvement has not been the sole driving force in the development of women's organizations. Indeed, its effect has been paradoxical. While international involvement has increased the pace of the process of building a nascent women's lobby and served to promote development of feminist consciousness, it also led to the creation of women's NGOs in both Poland and Hungary that neither depend upon nor seek to support local women or national governments.

McMahon's analysis also underlines that INGOs generally need states and their institutions to substantiate and codify their demands into law. Transnational organizations may critique the practices of states in, say, the field of women's or human rights, but they also require states to create political and legal frameworks that facilitate setting up the rule of law, as well as civil and political rights, within which such issues can be addressed. Women's groups that demand gender justice and corresponding state protection, as well as appropriate institutions for protection of women's rights, need to work with state-dominated political structures and processes in order to try to amend them.

Non-Democracies

Arab countries

Women's participation in conventional politics

No country in the Arab world is an established democracy, and the picture of women's representation in extant legislatures is a generally depressing one. According to Wide (2002: 3), female representation in North Africa and the Middle East increased from

Table 14.3 Regional averages of women in parliaments

	Single house or lower house (%)	Upper house or senate (%)	Both houses combined (%)
Nordic countries	39.7	–	39.7
Americas	18.5	18.2	18.5
Europe – OSCE member countries including Nordic countries	18.1	15.3	17.6
Europe – OSCE member countries excluding Nordic countries	16.0	15.3	15.9
Asia	15.5	13.6	15.3
Sub-Saharan Africa	14.6	12.8	14.4
Pacific	10.9	20.5	12.2
Arab states	6.0	7.5	6.4

Source: Interparliamentary Union, 'Women in National Parliaments' (<http://www.ipu.org/wmn-e/world.htm>). Data correct at 31 May 2004.

1.5 per cent in 1950 to 6.7 per cent in 2000. However, the growth was mainly due to just a couple of countries, rather than a positive development in all. Among the region's Arab countries, only Syria and Tunisia – with 12 per cent and 11.5 per cent respectively – have reached a relatively high level of female representation (<http://www.ipu.org/wmn-e/arc/classif300104.htm>). These examples are, however, unusual, because parliaments in the Arab world are nearly always totally dominated by men (AbuKhalil 1994: 127–37). For example, in Kuwait, women still do not even have the right to vote, while in the United Arab Emirates, all MPs are appointed – and women are not eligible to take part in the competition for selection. Overall, Arab women's entry into the arena of conventional politics is generally problematic. As table 14.3 indicates, the Arab countries collectively have the lowest regional average of women members of parliament in the world: 6.2 per cent.

Various mechanisms intended to enhance women's legislative presence have been suggested, aspects specifically required for a 'critical mass' in various political institutions generally and in parliament particularly. There are arguments for and against quotas (reserved seats), as well as the potential impacts of different electoral systems. Mechanisms have also been suggested for women to enhance their legislative performance, via what is known as 'the rules strategy', with three main pillars: learning the rules, using the rules and changing the rules (AbuKhalil 1994). The idea here is that various – written and unwritten – rules govern a great deal of the interaction within and without parliaments. Thus for women to increase their influence they need to understand not only what the rules are, but also how to use them for their own benefit.

Gender policies

Arab women rarely hold public positions of authority and are prohibited from holding religious offices. As a result, according to Reveyrand-Coulon (1993: 97), Arab women constitute a 'subordinated group'. In the Arab world, women are often expected to remain at home to run domestic affairs and rear children, rather than to seek a wider role in society. In short, there are said to be cultural and social factors that inhibit women in Arab countries from organizing meaningfully in pursuit of collective self-interest. Such factors are sometimes thought to explain especially egregious examples of the subordination of females in Arab countries. For example, in March 2002, 50 schoolgirls in Mecca, Saudi Arabia, were burned to death and dozens more injured in a fire at their school. Religious police are said to have 'prevented the girls from leaving the building because they were not wearing headscarves, and had no male relatives to receive them. They also reportedly prevented rescuers who were men from entering the premises' (Amnesty International 2004b: 1).

Earlier, in Iraq in 1990, a proclamation was issued by the then ruling Revolutionary Command Council, announcing that 'any Iraqi (male) who kills *even with premeditation* his own mother, daughter, sister, niece, or cousin for adultery will not be brought to justice' (Ekins 1992: 76; emphasis added). A third example comes from Jordan, a Muslim kingdom torn between strict religious and ethnic traditions and swift modernization. There, at least a quarter of all premeditated murders in the mid-1990s were so-called 'honour killings': that is, women were murdered by male relatives for a variety of allegedly 'immoral' types of behaviour, from 'flirting' to losing virginity before marriage (Sabbagh 1994).

Some commentators suggest that Islam is the common factor that explains such behaviour towards females, as well as the generally lowly position of women in Arab countries. For Parpart (1988: 209), it is the influence of Islam, especially 'through purdah or ritual seclusion', that serves to constrain 'female economic and political activities'. Others contend that because interpretations of Islam differ from country to country then links between the status of women and the faith are necessarily both complex and varied. Held (1993: 23) notes that various factors, including 'regime ideology, power relations within the family, low literacy rates and employment opportunities . . . play a determining role'.

Overall, according to Karam (1999: 3), in trying to improve their political, economic, and social position, Arab women generally face five main challenges:

1 *Economic position*: Many Arab women are both poor and illiterate. These factors comprise major hurdles in Arab women's attempts both to spread awareness and to access necessary opportunities for social and political development.
2 *Culture*: Cultural factors are important, especially the idea that an Arab woman's place is in the home. In addition, most existing political institutions suggest the existence of a male-dominated and male-oriented culture.
3 *Freedom of association*: Many Arab women face problems linked to freedom of association. This can seriously affect ability to organize, especially in the NGO sector, reducing the ability for Arab women to 'network' both within their own countries and internationally.
4 *Political parties*: Men dominate most political parties, and their interests and concerns reflect this fact.
5 *The media*: The role the media plays in Arab countries in promoting the interests of women and of female politicians is problematic.

The importance of many of these issues can be illustrated by the case of Kuwait, an Arab country of over two million people, 85 per cent Muslim (Sunni 70 per cent, Shi'a 30 per cent). In Kuwait, women lack the right to vote and to run for office. Consequently, the 50-member national assembly has no woman among its constituents. Recently, however, the government has expressed its backing for women's rights. Liberals in Kuwait are now said to be 'hopeful that the national assembly will pass legislation granting women political rights sooner rather than later, perhaps even before the next election scheduled for 2007' (Berkowitz 2004).

According to Freedom House's annual worldwide survey of political rights and civil liberties, *Freedom in the World 2003*, Kuwaiti women 'are legally disadvantaged in matters of marriage, divorce, and inheritance, must have the permission of a male relative to obtain a passport; and cannot confer citizenship on their children' (p. 314). However, Berkowitz (2004) suggests that there are several reasons, rooted in the country's culture and history, to believe that not only is suffrage now within sight for Kuwaiti women but also that they may soon acquire increased civil rights. This judgement is based on the fact that, while Kuwaiti women are excluded from political life, they have an increasing presence in professional life. Women hold senior positions in various areas, 'in journalism, at the universities, in private business, in medicine, and in government ministries'. Overall, women comprise about one-third of the country's labour force.

This development is explained by the fact that in the late 1960s the government adopted a policy that women should be integrated into the work force. In addition, the government made education compulsory for all Kuwaiti children up to the age of 14, including girls; and women were admitted to the University of Kuwait. Numerous women availed themselves of newly available educational opportunities; and many did well – better than most boys – at both school and university. Many chose professional careers. Mughni (2000) notes that the inclusion of large numbers of educated women into the labour force is gradually altering preconceived perceptions about women.

Mughni (2000) notes that Kuwaiti women have formed numerous professional, educational and welfare associations. Through these organizations, she contends, Kuwaiti women are beginning to have a considerable and direct impact on the shape of their society. As a result, they are starting to develop what she calls 'habits of freedom' that encourage the activists among them to pursue their political rights and civil liberties. This campaign is headed by Kuwait's main women's organization, the Women's Cultural and Social Society (WCSS), founded in 1963. The WCSS seeks to overturn an election law from 1963 that provides the legal basis for excluding women from politics, as it provides electoral rules and regulations that cover only Kuwaiti men. The WCSS believes that the election law is contrary to Kuwait's constitution. The preamble to the latter proclaims a devotion to 'democratic rule', while article seven declares that 'Justice, Liberty and Equality are the pillars of Society' (<www.kuwait-info.com/sidepages/state_constitution.asp>). The WCSS pursues its goals through various means, including conferences, attempts at consciousness-raising and lobbying members of both the national assembly and the government.

In recent years, the WCSS's campaign has been encouraged by external support, notably from various UN bodies and INGOs, including the Once and Future Action

Network.[4] This suggests that, potentially, international organizations can play a role in promoting women's political rights and participation in the Arab world. International organizations can: (1) assist in enhancing democratization endeavours, (2) facilitate access to knowledge/information and technology, (3) encourage concerted efforts to collect more gender-segregated data and (4) provide training and know-how, and promote further necessary research (Karam 1999: 26–8).

Conclusion

We have seen in this chapter that gender policy outcomes can vary considerably depending on the issue, the actors and the context. The socio-economic and political position of women seems to be dependent upon a number of factors. The case studies highlighted two factors necessary to improve the political position of women: (1) sufficient political and social space for them to organize and (2) a strong desire among them to work collectively. A third factor may also be important: international encouragement that can help pressurize governments to improve policies in relation to women and gender issues.

Two overall conclusions suggest themselves. First, vehicles of women's empowerment rarely if ever threaten the state's paramount position. What they *do* do, however, is alarm many men who feel that their relatively privileged positions are thereby undermined. Second, chances of women achieving political goals seem more likely in democratic or democratizing environments; this conclusion is borne out by our case studies. However, as far as transitional democracies and non-democracies are concerned, external encouragement may be important – but only if such encouragement fits well with domestic concerns. When international participation appears to undermine local NGO efforts, it can make them seem too much influenced from outside. However, as Ackerly and Okin (1999: 158) note, linking national and international gender concerns and movements 'has challenged previously heuristically useful distinctions between national and international NGOs and demonstrated that their combined activism can be effective internationally'.

[4] In April 2004, the Once and Future Action Network consisted of 115 member organizations from all regions of the world. The membership is made up of professional associations of women scientists, to technology institutions, to international agencies, to development NGOs working with women at the grassroots level (<http://www.wigsat.org/ofan/ofan.html>).

Conclusion

I started this book with a key presumption: the world significantly changed after the cold war. This was marked by the fall of the Berlin Wall in November 1989, the consequential demise of the Soviet bloc and subsequent global emphasis on economic liberalization, democratization and 'Americanization'/'Westernization'. We have seen that aspects of globalization – for example, pressures for more and better human rights, a protected natural environment and enhanced female political participation – have significantly impacted upon domestic political systems and political economies in various countries around the world. We can conclude by noting that all states have in some way been touched by the consequences of the growth of post-war interdependence and by the end of the cold war. We have also seen, however, that one of the most dynamic and potentially influential developments over the last few years has been the rise of various cross-border actors and forces – such as those epitomizing 'Asian values' and self-proclaimed champions of Islam, such as Osama bin Laden – that in part define themselves in opposition to globalization, regarded as a malign, Western-controlled, -dominated and -led process that is believed to seek to undermine, even destroy, specific non-Western ways of life.

The first problem we encountered was how to operationalize the concept of globalization in order to make it amenable to analysis. Globalization is often presented as both a subjective and an abstract notion, so attempts to isolate its particular effects are problematic. Complicating the issue is the difficulty of separating out, on the one hand, *objective* effects stemming from globalization and, on the other, *subjective* perceptions of political decision-makers regarding globalization and its effects. To overcome the problem of abstraction, we started from a simple premise: in various and variable ways, globalization helps shape the nature of relationships between various actors both within and between countries.

It seems uncontroversial to claim that globalization is changing, in various ways, political, social and economic arrangements and configurations within and between states. Although a variable process, this amounts to erosion of the state's formerly 'hard' boundaries and a consequent – yet variable – diminution of states' ability to control domestic political and economic environments and hence policy outcomes. In other words, globalization is responsible for increasing the absorbency of state borders, to enhance the potential – and, in many cases, actual – influence of external actors on various domestic outcomes.

We also saw that the last two decades of the twentieth century experienced growing consolidation of a truly global economy and gradual – albeit highly contested – materialization of an 'Americanized' or 'Westernized' 'global culture'. It was also a period of quite profound political developments, especially widespread democratization and steady, if uneven, advance of individualistic human rights. In addition, a continuing communications revolution helped underpin and promote these processes of globalization. The result was that in the early twenty-first century we inhabit a 'globalizing' social reality, where previously effective barriers to communication no longer exist. The drastically increased ability of individuals and groups to develop inter-personal and inter-group communications has strongly encouraged the development of various kinds of international and transnational actor. This not only helped to spread various messages – in relation to, for example, gender issues, human rights, democracy, religion and economic development – but also enabled like-minded individuals and groups to link up and interact across state boundaries.

But the $64,000 question is this: do the various processes of contemporary globalization collectively amount to something qualitatively different compared to what existed before? And, if so, to what extent and in what ways is it significant for comparative political analysis? My intention has not been to claim that the present phase of globalization is absolutely without precedent – but to offer evidence for the assertion that it is a heightened phase of an earlier, historically generated development. We noted that at various points in the twentieth century certain developments – for example, the Bolshevik revolution of 1917 and the end of World War II in 1945 – had profound international significance, which in turn influenced global outcomes over time, rather in the manner of a pebble tossed into a pond with the resulting ripples spreading out after the event. I argued and provided evidence to support the contention that the end of the cold war, the third wave of democracy and economic globalization collectively provided new opportunities for globalization (that is, international – state and non-state – actors) to seek to influence agenda-setting and decision-making in domestic, regional and global contexts. Such actors did this by seeking to exploit what I called *international opportunity structures for participation*. This in turn highlighted a new research focus on significant transnational and international actors; in this book, we have paid attention to three such sets of actors: international governmental organizations (IGOs), international non-governmental organizations (INGOs) and transnational corporations (TNCs).

This did not mean that, for analytical purposes, we could usefully regard the nearly 200 extant states as an undifferentiated mass. It was useful to divide them into three broad categories: established democracies, transitional democracies and non-democracies. We worked on the premise that differing political arrangements within countries can influence the domestic impact of globalization.

We also saw that various impacts of globalization are of both theoretical and empirical relevance for comparative political analysis and, as a result, it is inappropriate to 'do' comparative political analysis concerned only with the traditional modus operandi: domestic political structures, processes and actors. Our discussion led to two significant conclusions in this regard. Significantly to influence domestic policy-making and policies – that is, to change decisions in a desired direction – external actors need to overcome two hurdles. On the one hand, they must gain access to the political decision-making structures of the target state and generate and/or contribute to successful policy coalitions – groups of actors that have the power to overcome opposition to their desires and force compliance with their wishes. On the other hand, their ability to influence policy outcomes depends on building domestic coalitions with key policy networks that have – broadly or narrowly – the same goals as them. The implication is that the characteristics of domestic political structures will be very important, for they help determine: (1) the availability of access points into the political system and (2) the size of and requirements for winning coalitions.

In the second half of the book, we turned the focus to examine the influence and contributions of various external actors in relation to a range of issues: regionalization, economic globalization and development, the natural environment, political culture, regime change, political violence, religion, human rights and gender issues; collectively, we characterized these issue areas as the 'new international agenda' and examined them via selected case studies in each chapter.

We saw that the access and consequent influence of various kinds of external actor were facilitated when state-controlled political institutions are relatively 'weak' and civil society is relatively 'strong', an arrangement characteristic of many transitional democracies. This observation enabled us to draw two further conclusions: (1) When international conditions are similar, variances in domestic policy-making structures are instrumental in determining deviations in the policy impact of international and transnational actors, and (2) institutional structures of governance – domestic as well as international, such as those associated with the EU, and less significantly in relation to NAFTA – moderate the impact of external actors on domestic political outcomes.

Regarding policy-making, while the precise impact of external actors differs from country to country, from evidence presented in this book I conclude that small, economically weak, countries – few, if any, are established democracies – are in general less able to control such actors, especially compared to 'stronger', established democracies. Transitional democracies tend to inhabit a middle ground in this regard. The overall, and significant, consequence is that a key assumption of traditional comparative political analysis – confined political territories, with nation-states and national economies, are governed autonomously by sovereign states – is no longer absolutely valid for all countries. We also saw that because of globalization, all states are now subject to a multiplicity of external influences, and governments must make policy in a global context characterized by imprecise and shifting power structures. These developments make it imperative to develop appropriate analytical tools to explain and account for the results of globalization's intrusion on domestic terrains.

This obviously impacts upon the realm of comparative political analysis. Typically, as Waylen (2003) notes, a comparative politics research cycle goes through four stages. First, scholars produce single-country case studies. Second, researchers examine a small group of case studies, usually in an identified region, such as sub-Saharan Africa, Latin America or CEE. The third stage is that of hypothesis-testing, when analysts examine two or three case studies comparatively. The approach I adopted in this book was characteristic of the fourth stage of the research cycle, with the intention to 'draw evidence from [a] range of different studies and suggest some tentative conclusions. . . . This kind of comparative analysis [allows] us to discern any broad patterns that might contribute to . . . theory building' (Waylen 2003: 158).

In terms of theory-building, we sought to assess the variable influence of various agents of globalization as well as the relative importance of structure and agency. We did this by assessing the significance to political outcomes of both structure and agency and introduced a concept – *structured contingency* – to capture their interaction. We saw that it was important to identify as precisely as possible *what* actors need to be taken into account when assessing the impact of globalization on domestic political outcomes in our three categories of states. In addition, attempts to restore notions of agency to a specific process, globalization (too often presented without specific subjects), served 'to problematise the logic of inevitability that processes of globalization are frequently seen to imply' (Hay 2002b: 113).

I argued that structured contingency is a useful concept to help understand the array of outcomes that we saw in the pages of this book. Structural legacies were seen to be important factors when political actors search for new rules of political competition, especially in post-authoritarian systems. In other words, there is no *tabula rasa*: no regime, whatever its stated ideological proclivities or goals, democratically orientated or not, can ever hope to erase all historically produced political and societal behaviour. What structures did I have in mind? While they vary from country to country, we saw that every nation has historically established patterns of power ('structures') involving regular, systematized interaction between power-holders and the mass of ordinary people, an arrangement reflected in a country's extant political rules and institutions. The latter include both *formal*, fixed structures of public life – such as laws and electoral systems – and *informal* ones: in every polity, these are the 'dynamics of interests and identities, domination and resistance, compromise and accommodation' (Bratton and van de Walle 1997: 276). In short, in all states political actors are aware that political competition is moulded by various formal and informal structures, effectively presenting a range of *realistic* alternatives so that political actors are predisposed to select certain courses of action rather than others.

While problems of representation can theoretically be addressed by developing strong, formal political institutions, in many countries – especially transitional democracies and non-democracies – inherited, undemocratic structures of power will be of great political significance in moulding political outcomes. As we saw in relation to our various case studies featuring transitional democracies, to establish and then consolidate democracy is always a very difficult, slow and non-linear process. This is primarily because coexisting power-holders are often arrayed against democratization – or at best lukewarm in relation to it – as they fear the consequences it may have on their own positions. This underlines the fact that democracy cannot logically 'be run by the few as in oligarchies or autocracies; nor should it be guided by intelligence or professional expertise apart from the people' (Shin 1999: 137). In sum, to understand outcomes in both transitional democracies and non-democracies, we necessarily focused upon such countries' institutional variations – while also taking into account *underlying political dynamics*: that is, how and with what results individuals and groups gain access to political power and what they do with it.

This is to underline the importance of human agency. A concern with structures does not mean that we should ignore the equally crucial role of what political actors *do* in helping determine outcomes. For example, when leading political actors sincerely value democracy, that is, when the *idea* of democracy as a desirable political outcome serves as an important factor informing political decision-making, then, gradually, democracy can be built – even when unpropitious conditions, such as a weak economy or a politically active military, make that outcome initially seem very unlikely.

Evidence from our case studies underlines the importance of the interaction of structures and human agency in determining political outcomes. Decisions taken by highly significant political figures – such as Pope John Paul II in relation to democratization in Spain and Poland from the late 1970s, President Mikhail Gorbachev and a change of political direction in the USSR in the mid-1980s, Nelson Mandela's decision to work with apartheid government in South Africa from the early 1990s, and President Bush's post-9/11 response to Saddam Hussein's Iraq, al-Qaeda and by extension generally global terrorism – all emphasize the often vital contribution of human agency in determining political outcomes.

We also paid much attention to the impact of what I conceptualized as political globalization, especially the third wave of democracy from the 1970s. The importance of the issue derived from the fact that there was something important happening at the global level to encourage democratic transitions around the world at a certain time. This not only included global events and developments ('the diffusion effect'), but also specific encouragement from foreign aid donors. It was widely expected that various international actors would significantly influence the pace of democratic progress, especially in poor, aid-dependent countries.

After the cold war, democracy and how to achieve it in non-democracies became an urgent focus of Western attention. Individual Western governments, especially the USA and EU member states, as well as various International Financial Institutions (IFIs), such as the World Bank and the IMF, attached 'political conditionalities' to offers of aid and investment. From now on, regimes that denied their citizens human and civil rights were to be refused funding. The reasoning was that economic failures were seen to be linked to an absence of democracy and political accountability. Without significant and progressive political changes, economic reforms would not produce desired results. However, as Diamond (1999: 273) noted, outcomes were generally disappointing: 'Too many international policy makers have taken electoral democracy as an end state in itself. . . . Some observers seem to assume that democratic consolidation is bound to follow transition in much of the world. . . . These assumptions are false and counterproductive.' Typically, once democratic transitions were over – symbolized by the initial free and fair elections – then in most cases foreign actors' interest waned or moved on to something else, such as international terrorism.

Overall, the influence of globalization cannot be denied when seeking to assess its influence on comparative political outcomes. But this does not imply that pressure or encouragement from external actors – whether to democratize, institute or change a human rights regime, or pay more attention to gender issues – is inevitably one-way traffic that eliminates the ability of powerful political actors from seeking to oversee and direct events in the direction they prefer.

Globalization, Fragmentation and Comparative Political Analysis

Looking at the data and evidence produced in this book regarding, inter alia, human rights, the natural environment and female political participation, a fundamental question emerges: with increasing pressure for individualistic human rights, gender equality and environmental protection, not to mention the political culture of democracy (rule-based politics, essentially), is it possible to conclude that the impact of the current phase of globalization is, in macro-historical terms, a progressive movement in human affairs? While there are no doubt short-term costs, can we regard globalization on balance as a progressive trend in human affairs? Or should we conclude that, all things considered, globalization is a retrogressive development, even if there are short-term benefits? In other words, what do the data presented in this book allow us to conclude about the balance sheet of globalization?

Various commentators, such as Francis Fukuyama (2004), have returned a mixed verdict on such questions by suggesting that the growing number of failed states generally erodes security arrangements while intensifying globalization of world economic processes. Certainly, the issue of failed states – that is, where no central government is in control of a national territory – is now perhaps the most significant issue in relation to globalization. This is because failed states are said to be a key source of many of the world's most serious problems, from poverty, AIDS and drugs to terrorism. Since 9/11, the ability to create strong, functioning polities from failed states has risen to the top of the agenda of the international community. This is because state-building has become a crucial matter of global security.

While the problem of failed states and the need for state-building has existed for many years, it has been regarded as particularly urgent since 9/11, from which time the United States has sought to wrestle with its responsibilities in Afghanistan, Iraq and elsewhere. The problem however is that formation of proper public institutions – such as an upright police force, honest courts, working schools and medical services and a cohesive, effective strong civil service – is characteristically difficult to achieve. While material resources, experts and technology can easily be sent across borders, it is agreed that to build states involves methods that are not easily moved *tout court* from place to place.

Apart from the issue of failed states and their interaction with globalization, what does the balance sheet of globalization look like? The pervasiveness of economic globalization in the early 2000s can be measured both in terms of its *extensiveness* and its *intensity*. Accretions to the former seem the most obvious consequence of the end of the cold war, with the gradual and uneven integration of the former Soviet bloc into the world economy and financial system. Although this has not progressed as far as the high expectations of the early 1990s ('New World Order' rhetoric), nonetheless the demise of the First World–Second World economic divide must be accounted – in its potential – a giant step towards a genuinely global economic system. The significance of this is great – especially when juxtaposed with the recent but steady opening to the international market of many developing economies. Under pressure from both the IMF and the World Bank, many developing countries accepted development strategies based on structural adjustment programmes that had the effect of integrating them into the increasingly globalized economy. The implication was that in most such cases governments abandoned national development strategies based on state-led programmes and import-substitution policies, while giving up on nationalization policies.

However, it is more on the basis of the *intensity* of globalization in the early 2000s that the economic theorists tend to rest their case. According to such arguments, the trends in this direction are now so entrenched and irreversible that they have raised questions about the relevance – and effectiveness – of individual countries as meaningful aggregations in terms of what to think about, much less manage, economic activity. Not only is this growth of economic globalization said to be exponential, but it is claimed that it follows its own technical and economic logic. Even those who offer a more balanced account of what is happening (see for example Hirst and Thompson 1999) concede that in the absence of a clearly defined security agenda, economic integration has a momentum of its own. The manifestations of this intensification of globalization are deemed to lie in the global mobility of capital, the growth of foreign direct investment, and the role of TNCS; all these factors, we have seen, are interconnected. However, it is simply impossible to come up with a definitive conclusion about the normative desirability of this outcome, as opinions are too polarized.

Moving beyond economic globalization, it is possible to be a bit clearer about outcomes. We have seen that processes of globalization are expressed in changed imagery of international relations, with the main emphasis on various aspects of global order and security (including the natural environment, human rights and democracy). But note that such images are not in themselves novel – as they first captured popular attention in the 1970s via the work of scholars such as Keohane and Nye (1977) – although they have intensified in recent years. In other words, the most conspicuous feature of the new international situation is the number of issues that transcend national frontiers. Put another way, limits on national autonomy imposed by the 'balance of terror' during the cold war are now supplemented by a subtler, more structural form of erosion caused by processes of political, cultural, technological and economic globalization.

Evidence for globalization of a global political/human rights order is, by its nature, more difficult to come by than in the economic realm. To the extent that it can be quantified, we can note in particular the growth in numbers of INGOs, expressed normatively in the development of transnational/global civil society. Whereas in 1990 there were about 5,000 INGOs in existence – including environmental, human rights and social movements – by the early 2000s there were around 25,000 'active' INGOs (Anheier and Themudo 2002: 195). This was a fivefold rise in little more than a decade; increasingly, such INGOs are said to play an important role in an emerging regime of global governance, as transnational civil society actors cut across national and regional boundaries.

On the other hand, there is a strong reservation to note about the existence of a globalized political order. That is, it is hardly possible to speak of a *single* world order, as there is a dual order fundamentally fragmented on North–South lines: on the one hand, a liberal democratic order and, on the other, a non-democratic world *dis*order. Put another way, there are two coexisting zones: the first contains most of the world's power wherein no country faces substantial or significant military danger to its autonomy; the second, where 85 per cent of the world's population live, is characterized as a zone of turmoil, with growing numbers of 'failing', 'failed' and 'collapsed' states (Rotberg 2003; Fukuyama 2004).

This division touches upon the extent of both democratization and a more general globalized human rights order, enabling us to characterize globalization as a fundamentally progressive development. We started this book with a key premise: the end of the cold war ushered in conditions favourable to a new respect for universally recognized human rights. The emphasis on such rights in the New World Order rhetoric of the early 1990s reinforced this impression. Moreover, since during the cold war both the USA and the USSR had, for their own *realpolitik* reasons, supported authoritarian, rights-denying governments that egregiously violated their own citizens' rights – like those of Saddam Hussein in Iraq or Jean Claude 'Baby Doc' Duvalier in Haiti – then removal of conditions associated with the cold war should have facilitated emergence of conditions favourable to generalized improvements in this regard. In addition, determination on the part of the international community to implement war-crime tribunals, in association with the wars in Iraq, former Yugoslavia and Sierra Leone, also appeared to be symptomatic of a rediscovered universalism first encountered in the aftermath of World War II and exemplified by the founding of the United Nations. Yet further evidence of the move in this direction was the greater emphasis that came to be placed on human rights issues in North–South relations: in short, not only was liberal democracy triumphant in the ideological competition of the cold war but it also became increasingly assertive in demanding change in political behaviour in much of the developing world (Haynes 2001a).

We also need to note, however, scepticism as to how pervasive, universalist and realistic was the claimed potential for success of the post-cold war democratization/human rights regime (Gray 2004). For example, the expressed wish to punish war criminals, some critics argued, often proved stronger than the international community's will to do so.[1] Overall, there appeared to be little to indicate that the gulf between different conceptions of human rights was narrowing – and much to suggest that they had instead become part of the substance of international relations, a continuation of political intercourse by other means.

Such developments were symptomatic of what are known as 'fragmentationist' tendencies in globalization. As Gray (2004) notes, 'the collapse of communism in the early 1990s [presaged] a resumption of traditional ethnic, nationalist and religious conflicts both within and between countries'. Was this development simply the result of the conditions propelled by the end of the cold war? Or was it a reaction to a longer-term and more fundamental process of historical change? Put another way, were manifestations of fragmentation simply a – temporary – effect of the end of the cold war? Or were they instead symptomatic of the transformations that swept away the bilateral order that had characterized the post-World War II era until the late 1980s?

Since the end of the cold war, there has been a clear strengthening of *counter*-global trends as opposed to that of Western-championed individualistic rights, such as democracy and improved position for females. Often this is manifested in the form of so-called 'religious fundamentalism' or ethnic chauvinism. Thus growing economic integration, driven by technological change and global competition, is counterbalanced by political disintegration, linked to religious and/or ethnic instability, tension and conflict, fuelled by deepening developmental polarization between developed and developing worlds (Haynes 2005). Such issues exacerbate regional and global security concerns.

One argument is to see increasing fragmentation of the international system as a direct consequence of the loss of cold war structures of control, leading to an increasingly unruly and anarchic world. Some argue that what we now have is a world without US primacy, an environment characterized by growing violence and disorder (Halper and Clarke 2004). As regards the developing world, the effects of globalization are ambiguous. Whereas superpower competition had in the past resulted in attempts to control regional conflicts – to ensure that they would not draw in their superpower patrons – then the end of the cold war was a form of liberation. This new freedom came, however, at a price: the removal of the restraining conditions of the cold war led in time

---

[1] An alleged Serbian war criminal, Radovan Karadzic, was wanted in late 2004 for 'assault, crimes against humanity, crimes against life and health, genocide, grave breaches of the 1949 Geneva Convention, murder, plunder, [and] violations of the laws or customs of war' (<http://www.interpol.int/public/Wanted/Notices/Data/1995/47/1995.47747.asp>). He appeared to be living openly in Serbia, yet the 'international community' seemed powerless to extract him and put him on trial.

to declining real interest by the West in the developing world – except in the case of failed states (Afghanistan, Iraq, Sierra Leone, Yugoslavia) where there seemed to be clearly unwelcome implications for US and/or Western security.

However, it may be too simple to regard all manifestations of fragmentation as a mere by-product of the end of the cold war. Despite the resurgence of fragmentationist tendencies – such as religious, ethnic and nationalist forces, expressed both within and between countries – it is implausible to suggest that there is imminent danger of a generalized collapse of states or unstoppable attacks on state sovereignty. This is because globalization is not a wholly autonomous force that has historically been shaped, encouraged and thwarted by wider currents of international relations. It has also been mediated through the activities of states. Today, states continue to enjoy structural powers from their economic activities and continue to provide a framework within which the globalized economy functions.

In the longer term, rather than envisaging that globalization will bring the state system to an end, it may be that the most realistic comment is that international relations will encourage a reformulation and rebalancing of the relationship between the state and globalization. State functions changed considerably over the course of the twentieth century and in some cases the practitioners of state power have tapped new sources of legitimacy. Overall, perhaps the best judgement is to anticipate a new accommodation between state power and the forces of globalization, rather than the outright victory of one over the other.

On the other hand, the fragility of many states in the international system is now clear. Indeed, it is now obvious that, despite its many inequities, the cold war sustained and supported a number of states that later failed or collapsed. This not only includes the post-imperial fragmentation of the Soviet Union and Yugoslavia, where a number of ethnic, religious and nationalist groups are still struggling over the carcasses of the collapsed state. In Africa, various countries – including Angola, Liberia, Rwanda and Somalia – have essentially ceased to exist as sovereign entities. Such states enjoy little or no popular allegiance, and other forms of sub-state or supra-state identity have tended to try to fill the ideological vacuum. Clan, tribe, ethnos, religion and nation have all vied for the allegiance of communities and have asserted their pretensions through intolerance, violence and conflict; and such developments are encouraged by transnational interactions between like-minded groups in different countries. Communal conflicts now assailing many parts of the developing world – especially various sub-Saharan African countries – are the direct outcome of these struggles for identity and attempts to secure territorial bases for their consolidation; often they are fuelled by cross-border, transnationalist support from external actors.

Liberal political theory has been singularly unsuccessful in providing coherent explanations for the recurrence and virulence of these elemental struggles. The most common liberal reaction is a cosmopolitan disdain for the seeming return to a primitive tribalism. The sources of the liberal failure of imagination can best be seen in its proposed models of a social contract, such as those once outlined by John Locke or John Rawls. In these accounts, there is no hint of conflict, as the pre-social nation decides through a process of consensus upon a liberal polity. Although this 'veil of ignorance' is a philosophical contrivance, it does reflect the way liberal thinking tends to overlook the highly coercive and conflictual process by which most states have been formed. Only in very rare cases, such as in England, has the state-building process been relatively conflict-free, due to a variety of factors, not least because the process took place over the course of centuries rather than just the decades that were allowed to many post-colonial developing countries. In the latter, both political liberalization/democratization and economic modernization 'should' concurrently take place. It is sometimes over-looked that earlier states-in-formation only managed to gain their Weberian monopoly on the legitimate use of violence through coercion of their peoples into a common culture and by forcefully subduing other claimants to power. In addition, such earlier state-building – as in England – did not have to contend with the kind of globalizing pressures we noted in the chapters of this book.

This highlights how many developing countries are currently engaged in a struggle of state-building, faced with serious economic, political and social problems in order to build strong, centralized polities. Many also have the additional problem of contending with unhelpful, artificial state borders. The most extreme examples can be found in sub-Saharan Africa, where the postcolonial borders rarely captured any pre-existing politi-cal entity but, rather, a multiplicity of segmented communities with their own distinctive identities. As a consequence, most Africans have no deep – many do not even have superficial – loyalty to their designated states, a fact clearly illustrated by the many mass migrations which continuously take place on the African continent, a process seemingly exacerbated in many cases by globalization. As a result, many legally sovereign states in Africa frequently amount to nothing more than a lucrative source of revenues for competing elites representing one subgroup or another. In such circumstances, despite the efforts of Western governments, IFIs and INGOs, attempts to introduce and develop democratic electoral processes and more equitable economic outcomes have resulted merely in the circulation or a perpetuation of ruling elites rather than a genuine trans-fer of popular power. Most recent democratization processes – encouraged by forces connected to globalization in, inter alia, sub-Saharan Africa, Latin America, Asia and CEE – must, unfortunately, be seen in this light.

The problem of building strong states on divided, segmented societies is not a problem limited to sub-Saharan Africa or elsewhere in the developing world. Continu-ing inter-ethnic conflicts in the former Yugoslavia and Soviet Union show that, even in Europe, the process of nation-building in some polities is incomplete. Underlying these tragedies is a fundamental problem: there are few examples of multinational and mul-tiethnic democratic states that can serve as useful models. Those often mentioned – Switzerland and Belgium – actually have highly specific historical roots, while the futil-ity of seeking to transfer their specific political structures was cruelly exposed by the failure in the 1990s of the Vance-Owen plan for Bosnia-Herzegovina. The reality is that the examples of liberal multiethnic societies, of which India is the most notable example in the developing world, are the exception, not the rule. Elsewhere, the dynamic typi-cally works towards making the people fit the state rather than the state the people – and this necessarily entails varying degrees of compulsion or expulsion. In this context, a process of political liberalization/democratization can, unless very skilfully engi-neered, only contribute to the ensuing violence. Even in countries where a considerable degree of integration and centralization has taken place, past fears of breakdown of social stability can act as a powerful deterrent against political liberalization. An impor-tant example comes from China, where the present communist leadership enjoys con-siderable political capital by referring to popular fears of a return to the political conditions characterizing the end of Manchu imperial rule more than 60 years ago, a time when the deprivations of warlords and political anarchy destroyed the lives of millions of people. Elsewhere in Asia, political leaders use other justifications for continued authoritarianism, including an allusion to the desirability of the Confucian tradition of political order and stability. In this context, promotion of political changes via globalization can be successfully portrayed as a neo-imperialist imposition that, if adopted, would serve fatally to undermine hard-won social solidarity and strength. Moreover, the argument that economic prosperity in East Asia would be threatened by political liberalization provides additional support to the perpetuation of authoritarian rule.

There are, therefore, a number of reasons relating to the intrinsic weakness of states in many parts of the world that limit or at least complicate the potential of globalization to propel democratic and economic reforms. And, even when adopted, such reforms do not unproblematically change the illiberal nature of society; often, they will only perpetuate the exclusive possession of the state apparatus by small unrepresentative elites. In addition, processes of political and economic liberalization – even if strongly encouraged by an array of external state and non-state actors – can be expected to harden rather than weaken existing social cleavages, based on ethnic, religious and/or national grounds. In such cases, the perceived or actual weakness of the state will provide a strong legitimating justification for the continuation of non-democratic rule. In short, despite globalization, authoritarianism remains a live and viable option for many countries away from North America and Western Europe.

In the course of this book we have seen that both the pace and extent of political and economic changes in many formerly authoritarian countries – notably in those European countries anxious to join the EU – were strongly influenced by various external factors. We also saw that both democratic and economic reforms in the former Second and developing worlds became a focus of Western attention after the cold war, yet outcomes were variable. Western governments and IFIs, such as the World Bank and the IMF, attached political conditionalities to aid and investment. And, as a result, governments denying human and civil rights to their citizens were to be denied such external funding. It is now widely admitted, however, even by the IFIs themselves, that externally imposed economic reforms demanded such radical economic reforms that the outcome was typically socially damaging and politically destabilizing, even encouraging greater executive concentration of power in order to make the unpalatable reforms enforceable (Halper and Clarke 2004: 256–7). The final word on globalization and its impact on comparative political analysis is that the former has everywhere impacted upon how we understand the latter, but that the outcomes are by no means obvious or uniform. It is possible to establish models for analytical and heuristic purposes, but to understand what occurs in individual countries we need to apply models with both care and precision, while taking into account the specificities of individual polities' historical, culture, political and economic structures and processes.

References

AbuKhalil, A. (1994) 'Women and electoral politics in Arab states', in W. Rule and J. Zimmerman (eds.), *Electoral Systems in Comparative Perspective. Their Impact on Women and Minorities.* Westport and London: Greenwood Press, pp. 127–37.

Acharya, A. and Stubbs, R. (1999) 'The Asia Pacific region in the post-cold war era', in L. Fawcett and Y. Sayigh (eds.), *The Third World Beyond the Cold War. Continuity and Change.* Oxford: Oxford University Press, pp. 118–33.

Ackerly, B. and Okin, S. M. (1999) 'Feminist social criticism and the international movement for women's rights as human rights', in I. Shapiro and C. Hacker-Cordón (eds.), *Democracy's Edges.* Cambridge: Cambridge University Press, pp. 134–62.

Adamson, F. (2002) 'International democracy assistance in Uzbekistan and Kyrgyzstan: Building civil society from the outside?', in S. Mendelson and J. Glenn (eds.), *The Power and Limits of NGOs. A Critical Look at Building Democracy in Eastern Europe and Eurasia.* New York: Columbia University Press, pp. 177–206.

Adelkhah, F. (1999) 'Transformation of mass religious culture in the Islamic Republic of Iran', in J. Haynes (ed.), *Religion, Globalization and Political Culture in the Third World.* London: Macmillan, pp. 93–111.

Aglionby, J. (2001) 'Fisherman driven to illegal logging as pulp factory poisons river', *Guardian,* 26 June.

Ahmad, I. (2002) 'The needs of Muslim children can be met only through Muslim schools', *Guardian,* 22 May.

Ahmed, I. (2003) 'The human rights standpoint', *Daily Times,* 3 August. Available at <http://www.dailytimes.com.pk/print.asp?page=story_3-8-2003_pg3_3>. Accessed 31 March 2004.

Ajami, F. (1978) *Human Rights and World Order.* New York: Institute for World Order.

Allen, C. (2002) 'Social democracy, globalization and governance: Why is there no European left program in the EU?' Occasional paper, Minda de Gunzburg Center for European Studies, Harvard University, Cambridge, MA, USA. Available at <www.ces.fas.harvard.edu/working_papers/ChrisAllen.pdf>. Accessed 1 October 2004.

Almond, G. (1993) 'Foreword', in L. Diamond (ed.), *Political Culture and Democracy in Developing Countries.* Boulder, CO: Lynne Rienner, pp. ix–xii.

Almond, G. and Powell, G. B. (1996) *Comparative Politics Today. A World View,* 6th edn. New York: Harper Collins.

Almond, G. and Verba, S. (1963) *The Civic Culture. Political Attitudes and Democracy in Five Nations.* Princeton: Princeton University Press.

Almond, G. and Verba, S. (eds.) (1980) *The Civic Culture Revisited.* Boston: Little, Brown.

Alvarez, S. (1990) *Engendering Democracy in Brazil.* Princeton, NJ: Princeton University Press.

Amnesty International (2003a) 'The War on "Terror"'. Available at <http://www.amnestyusa.org/waronterror/>. Accessed 1 April 2004.

Amnesty International (2003b) 'Death Penalty in China'. Available at <http://www.amnestyusa.org/abolish/world/china/>. Accessed 1 April 2004.

Amnesty International (2004a) 'China'. Available at <http://www.amnestyusa.org/countries/china/index.do>. Accessed 1 April 2004.

Amnesty International (2004b) 'It's in our hands: Stop violence against women'. Available at <web.amnesty.org/aidoc/aidoc_pdf.nsf/Index/ACT770012004ENGLISH/$File/ACT7700104.pdf>. Accessed 6 April 2004.

Amnesty International (n/d) 'Chechnya – human rights under attack'. Available at <http://www.amnesty.org/russia/chechnya.html>. Accessed 1 April 2004.

Anastasakis, O. (2000) 'Extreme Right in Europe: A comparative study of recent trends', Discussion Paper No. 3, The Hellenic Observatory, The European Institute, London School of Economics and Political Science. Available at <http://www.lse.ac.uk/collections/hellenicObservatory/pdf/AnastasakisDiscussionPaper3.pdf>. Accessed 1 March 2004.

Anheier, H. and Themudo, N. (2002) 'Organizational forms of global civil society: Implications of going global', in M. Glasius, M. Kaldor and H. Anheier (eds.), *Global Civil Society 2002*. Oxford: Oxford University Press, pp. 191–216.

Ansari, H. (2002) *Muslims in Britain*. London: Minority Rights Group International.

Arblaster, A. (1999) 'Democratic society and its enemies', in P. Burnell and P. Calvert (eds.), *The Resilience of Democracy: Persistent Practice, Durable Idea*, special issue of Democratization, 6, 1, pp. 33–49.

Arin, T. (n/d) 'Financial markets and globalization in Turkey', University of Istanbul, Faculty of Economics. Available at <http://www.sba.luc.edu/orgs/meea/volume1/arin.html>. Accessed 19 February 2004.

Aspalter, C. (2002) 'Worlds of welfare capitalism: Examining eight different models', Research Center on Societal and Social Policy Research Paper Series No. 6, University of Hong Kong. Available at <http://www.rcssp.org/RCSSPeightmodels.pdf>. Accessed 14 July 2004.

Attina, A. (1989) 'The study of international relations in Italy', in H. Dyer and L. Mangasarian (eds.), *The Study of International Relations. The State of the Art*. Basingstoke: Macmillan, pp. 344–57.

Audley J. (1997) *Green Politics and Global Trade: NAFTA and the Future of Environmental Politics*. Washington, DC: Georgetown University Press.

Axford, B. (2002a) 'Political participation', in B. Axford, G. Browning, R. Huggins and B. Rosamond, *An Introduction to Politics*, 2nd edn. London and New York: Routledge, pp. 120–58.

Axford, B. (2002b) 'The processes of globalization', in B. Axford, G. Browning, R. Huggins and B. Rosamond, *An Introduction to Politics*, 2nd edn. London and New York: Routledge, pp. 524–62.

Axford, B. (2002c) 'Individuals: Is politics really about people?', in B. Axford, G. Browning, R. Huggins and B. Rosamond, *An Introduction to Politics*, 2nd edn. London and New York: Routledge, pp. 15–56.

Ayoade, J. A. (1988) 'States without citizens: An emerging African phenomenon', in D. Rothchild and N. Chazan (eds.), *The Precarious Balance. State and Society in Africa*. Boulder, CO: Lynne Rienner, pp. 100–18.

Bale, T. and Roberts, N. (2002) 'Plus ça change . . . ? Anti-party sentiment and electoral system change: A New Zealand case study', *The Journal of Commonwealth and Comparative Politics*, 40, 2, pp. 1–20.

Bardi, L., Rhodes, M. and Nello, S. (2002) 'Enlarging the European Union: Challenges to and from Central and Eastern Europe – Introduction', *International Political Science Review*, 23, 3, pp. 227–33.

Barkin, D. (1999) 'Free trade and environmental policymaking in Mexico', *Borderlines*, 7, 9, pp. 14–15. Available at <http://www.americaspolicy.org/borderlines/PDFs/bl60.pdf>. Accessed 25 February 2004.

Barnet, R. and Cavanaugh, J. (1994) *Global Dreams: Imperial Corporations and the New World Order*. New York: Simon & Schuster.

Bartlett, D. and Hunter, W. (1997) 'Market structures, political institutions, and democratization: the Latin American and East European experiences', *Review of International Political Economy*, 4, 1, pp. 87–126.

Batt, J. and Wolczuk, K. (eds.) (2002) *Region, State and Identity in Central and Eastern Europe*. London: Frank Cass.

Baxter, J. (2002) ' "Another Africa is possible". Social movements organize to challenge dominant economic policies', *Africa Recovery*, 16, 1, pp. 18–19.

Baylis, J. and Smith, S. (eds.) (2001) *The Globalization of World Politics. An Introduction to International Relations*, 2nd edn. Oxford: Oxford University Press.

'BBC's world service. America is not the problem – Bush is', *Guardian*, 19 June 2003.

Bealey, F. (1999) *The Blackwell Dictionary of Political Science*. Oxford: Blackwell.

Beeley, B. (1992) 'Islam as a global political force', in A. McGrew and P. Lewis (eds.), *Global Politics. Globalization and the Nation State*. Cambridge: Polity, pp. 293–311.

Beetham, D. (1999) *Democracy and Human Rights*. Cambridge: Polity.

Beetham, D. and Lord, C. (1998) *Legitimacy and the European Union*. London: Longman.

Beetham, D., Bracking, S., Kearton, I. and Weir, S. (2001) *International IDEA Handbook on Democracy Assessment*. The Hague: Kluwer Law International.

Belsie, L. (2000) 'Could biotech help the environment?', *Christian Science Monitor*, 27 June. Available at <http://www.monsanto.co.uk/news/ukshowlib.phtml?uid=5315>. Accessed 25 February 2004.

Benewick, R. and Donald Hemelryk, S. (2003) 'Treasuring the word: Mao, depoliticization and the material present', in R. Benewick, M. Blecher and S. Cook (eds.), *Asian Politics in Development. Essays in Honour of Gordon White*. London/Portland, OR: Frank Cass, pp. 65–82.

Berkowitz, P. (2004) 'An oasis. Kuwaiti women make progress', *National Review Online*, 3 March. Available at <http://www.nationalreview.com/comment/berkowitz200403030936.asp>. Accessed 7 April 2004.

Bermeo, N. (2003) *Ordinary People in Extraordinary Times. The Citizenry and the Breakdown of Democracy*. Princeton and Oxford: Princeton University Press.

Beyer, P. (1994) *Religion and Globalization*, London: Sage.

Bezlova, A. (1999) 'Beijing embraces Confucian communism', *Asia Times Online*, 19 September. Available at <http://www.atimes.com/china/AI15Ad01.html>. Accessed 18 March 2004.

Bhalla, S. (2000) 'Growth and poverty in India: Myth and reality'. Available at <http://www.oxusresearch.com/economic.asp>. Accessed 23 February 2004.

Biorcio, R. and Mannheimer, R. (1995) 'Relationships between citizens and political parties', in H. D. Klingemann and D. Fuchs (eds.), *Citizens and the State*. Oxford: Oxford University Press, pp. 206–26.

Birch, S., Millard, F., Popescu, M. and Williams, K. (2002) *Embodying Democracy: Electoral System Design in Post-Communist Europe*. Houndmills and New York: Palgrave Macmillan.

Black, D. (1999) 'The long and winding road; International norms and domestic political change in South Africa', in T. Risse, S. Ropp and K. Sikkink (eds.) *The Power of Human Rights. International Norms and Domestic Change*. Cambridge: Cambridge University Press, pp. 78–108.

Black, I. (2003) 'We don't do war', *Guardian*, 23 May.

Blais, L. and Massicotte, A. (2002) 'Electoral systems', in L. LeDuc, R. Niemi and P. Norris (eds.), *Comparing Democracies 2. New Challenges in the Study of Elections and Voting*. London/Thousand Oaks, CA/New Delhi: Sage, pp. 40–69.

Bodansky, Y. (2001) *Bin Laden: The Man who Declared War on America*. New York: Crown Publishing Group.

Bogdanor, V. (2003) 'Europe needs a rallying cry', *Guardian*, 28 May.

Booth, J. and Seligson, M. (1993) 'Paths to democracy and the political culture of Costa Rica, Mexico, and Nicaragua', in L. Diamond (ed.), *Political Culture and Democracy in Developing Countries*. Boulder, CO: Lynne Rienner, pp. 107–38.

Borger, J. (2003a) 'Bush's pollution charter. Republican supporting energy firms set to escape controls on emissions', *Guardian*, 23 August.

Borger, J. (2003b) 'Long queue at drive in soup kitchen, *Guardian*, 3 November.

Borger, J. (2003c) 'Why America's plutocrats gobble up $1,500 hot dogs', *Guardian*, 5 November.

Borger, J. (2003d) 'US moves to high terror alert', *Guardian*, 22 December.

Boutros-Ghali, B. (1995) 'Concluding statement by the United Nations Secretary-General Boutros Boutros-Ghali of the United Nations Congress on Public International Law: Towards the Twenty-First Century: International Law as a Language for International Relations', 13–17 March, New York.

Bratton, K. (2002) 'Critical mass theory revisited: The behavior and success of token individuals in state legislatures'. Available at <courses.smsu.edu/sgu646f/pls319/bratton.pdf>. Accessed 6 April 2004.

Bratton, M. and van de Walle, N. (1997) *Democratic Experiments in Africa*. Cambridge: Cambridge University Press.

Brecher, J. and Costello T. (1994) *Global Village or Global Pillage: Economic Reconstruction from the Bottom Up*. Cambridge, MA: South End Press.

Brimmer, E. (2002) *The United States, the European Union, and International Human Rights Issue*. Washington, DC: Center for Transatlantic Relations.

Brown, C. (2001) 'Human rights', in J. Baylis and S. Smith (eds.), *The Globalization of World Politics. An Introduction to International Relations*, Oxford: Oxford University Press, pp. 599–614.

Brozus, L., Take, I. and Wolf, K.-D. (2002) 'Assimilation of patterns and goals of political regulation as a consequence of globalization?' Draft paper prepared for the CPOGG Workshop at Schloss Amerang, 1–3 November. Available at <www.cpogg.org/paper%20amerang/Lars%20Brozus,%20Ingo%20Take,%20Klaus%20Dieter%20Wolf.pdf>. Accessed 16 October 2003.

Bruehl, T. (n/d; c.2002) 'The privatization of international environmental governance'. Available at <http://www.fu-berlin.de/ffu/Lehre/pkgec/Paper_Bruehl.pdf>. Accessed 12 December 2003.

Bueno de Mesquita, E. (2003) 'The quality of terror'. (Department of Political Science, Washington University). Unpublished paper. Available at <www.artsci.wustl.edu/~ebuenode/PDF/terror_quality.pdf>. Accessed 11 January 2004.

Burnell, P. (1998) 'Arrivals and departures: a preliminary classification of democratic failures and their explanation', *Journal of Commonwealth and Comparative Politics*, 36, 3, pp. 1–29.

Callaghan, J. (2003) 'Social democracy's big problem: Economic globalization or hard times?' *European Political Science*, 2, 2. Available at <http://www.essex.ac.uk/ECPR/publications/spring2003/research/callaghan.htm>.

Callaghy, T. (1993) 'Vision and politics in the transformation of the global political economy lessons from the Second and Third Worlds', in R. Slater, B. Schutz and S. Dorr (eds.), *Global Transformation and the Third World*. Boulder, CO: Lynne Rienner, pp. 161–256.

Calvert, P. (2002) *Comparative Politics. An Introduction*. Harlow: Longman.

Calvert, S. and Calvert, P. (2001) *Politics and Society in the Third World*, 2nd edn. Harlow: Pearson Education.

Cammack, P. (1997) 'Democracy and dictatorship in Latin America, 1930–80', in D. Potter, D. Goldblatt, M. Kiloh and P. Lewis (eds.), *Democratization*. Cambridge and Milton Keynes: Polity Press in association with the Open University, pp. 152–73.

Cantori, L. (2003) 'Democracy from within Islam', *The CSD Bulletin*, 10, 2, pp. 1–2.

Cardenas, S. (2002) 'Adaptive states: The proliferation of national human rights institutions'. Carr Center for Human Rights Policy, Working Paper T-01-04. Available at <www.ksg.harvard.edu/cchrp/Web%20Working%20Papers/Cardenas.pdf>. Accessed 1 November 2003.

Carothers, T. (1997) 'Democracy without illusions', *Foreign Affairs*, 76, 1, pp. 85–99.

Carothers, T. (2002) 'The end of the transition paradigm', *Journal of Democracy*, 13, 1, pp. 5–21.

Carpenter, T. Galen (2003) *Bad Neighbor Policy. Washington's Futile War on Drugs in Latin America*. New York and Basingstoke: Palgrave Macmillan.

Casanova, J. (1994) *Public Religions in the Modern World*. Chicago and London: University of Chicago Press.

Cerny P. (2000) 'Globalization and the disarticulation of political power: Towards a new Middle Ages?' in H. Goverde, P. Cerny, M. Haugaard and H. Lentner (eds.), *Power in Contemporary Politics*. London, Sage, pp. 170–86.

Chakravarty, N. (1997) 'Indian democracy. Reflections and challenges', *World Affairs*, 2, 1, pp. 80–90.

Chalmers, D. (1993) 'Internationalized domestic politics in Latin America, the institutional role of internationally based actors', unpublished paper, Department of Political Science, Columbia University.

Chandhoke, N. (2002) 'The limits of global civil society', in M. Glasius, M. Kaldor and H. Anheier (eds.), *Global Civil Society 2002*. Oxford: Oxford University Press, pp. 35–54.

Chandler, D. (2003) 'Cosmopolitan paradox', *The CSD Bulletin*, 10, 2, pp. 12–14.

Checkel, J. (1999) 'Norms, institutions, and national identity in contemporary Europe', *International Studies Quarterly*, 43, pp. 83–114.

Chiriyankandath, J. (2005) 'Human rights in an unequal world', in J. Haynes (ed.), *Palgrave Advances in Development Studies*. Basingstoke: Palgrave.

Christiansen, T. (2001) 'European and regional integration', in J. Baylis and S. Smith (eds.), *The Globalization of World Politics. An Introduction to International Relations*. Oxford: Oxford University Press, pp. 495–518.

Christie, K. and Roy, D. (2001) *The Politics of Human Rights in East Asia*. London: Pluto Press.

Clapham, C. (1988) *Third World Politics. An Introduction*. London: Routledge.

Clark, I. (1997) *Globalization and Fragmentation*. Oxford: Oxford University Press.

Clark, I. (2001) 'Globalization and the post-cold war order', in J. Baylis and S. Smith (eds.), *The Globalization of World Politics. An Introduction to International Relations*. Oxford: Oxford University Press, pp. 634–47.

Coates, D. (2000) *Models of Capitalism*. Cambridge: Polity.

Cohen, M. (1994) 'Culture of awareness', *Far Eastern Economic Review*, 17 November, p. 44.

Cohen, S. (2001) 'Decision-making, power and rationality in foreign policy analysis', in M.-C. Smouts (ed.), *The New International Relations. Theory and Practice*. London: Hurst and Co., pp. 38–54.

Cole-Bailey, M. (2004) 'Mexico', in D. S. Lewis (ed.), *The Annual Register 2003*, Bethesda, MA: Keesing's Worldwide, pp. 165–7.

Commission on Post-Conflict Reconstruction (2003) 'Play to win'. Final report of the bi-partisan Commission on Post-Conflict Reconstruction, Washington, DC/Arlington, VA: Center for Strategic and International Studies (CSIS) and the Association of the US Army (AUSA). Available at <http://www.csis.org/isp/pcr/playtowin.pdf>. Accessed 5.11.03.

Compton, R., Jr. (ed.) (2002) *Transforming East Asian Domestic and International Politics. The Impact of Economy and Globalization*. Aldershot/Burlington: Ashgate.

Conaghan, C. (1995) 'Politicians against parties: Discord and disconnection in Ecuador's party system', in S. Mainwaring and T. Scully (eds.), *Building Democratic Institutions: Party Systems in Latin America*. Stanford, CA: Stanford University Press, pp. 434–58.

Cook, C. (2001) 'Globalization and its critics', *The Economist*, 27 September.

Cook, L. J. and Orenstein, M. (1999). 'The return of the left and its impact on the welfare state in Russia, Poland, and Hungary', in L. J. Cook, M. A. Orenstein, and M. Rueschemeyer (eds.), *Left Parties and Social Policy in Postcommunist Europe*, Boulder, CO: Westview, pp. 47–108.

Coole, D. (1988) *Women in Political Theory*. Wheatsheaf Books: Sussex.

Cortell, A. and Davis, Jr., J. (1996) 'How do international institutions matter? The domestic impact of international rules and norms', *International Studies Quarterly*, 40, pp. 451–78.

Cortell, A. and Davis, Jr., J. (2000) 'Understanding the domestic impact of international norms: A research agenda', *International Studies Review*, 2, 1, pp. 65–87.

Coussy, J. (2001) 'International political economy', in M.-C. Smouts (ed.), *The New International Relations. Theory and Practice*. London: Hurst & Company, pp. 140–54.

Crawford, G. (2003a) 'Promoting democracy from without: Learning from within (Part I)', *Democratization*, 10, 1, pp. 1–20.

Crawford, G. (2003b) 'Promoting democracy from without: Learning from within (Part II)', *Democratization*, 10, 1, pp. 77–98.

Cronin, A. K. (2004) 'Behind the curve. Globalization and international terrorism', in R. Howard and R. Sawyer (eds.), *Defeating Terrorism. Shaping the New Security Environment*. Guilford, CT: McGraw-Hill/Dushkin, pp. 29–50.

Dahan-Kalev, D. (2003) 'The gender blindness of good theorists: An Israeli case study', *Journal of International Women's Studies*, 4, 3, pp. 126–47.

Dahl, R. (1989) *Democracy and its Critics*. New Haven: Yale University Press.

Dalton, R. (2002) 'Political cleavages, issues and electoral change', in L. LeDuc, R. Niemi and P. Norris (eds.), *Comparing Democracies 2. New Challenges in the Study of Elections and Voting*. London/Thousand Oaks, CA/New Delhi: Sage, pp. 189–209.

Dartnell, M (2001) 'From Action directe to pax electronica: Context and method in the analysis of anti-government groups'. Paper presented at the conference, 'Trajectories of Terrorist Violence in Europe', Minda de Gunzburg Center for European Studies, Harvard University, March 10.

Datt, G. and Ravallion, M. (2002) 'Is India's economic growth leaving the poor behind?', *Journal of Economic Perspectives*, 16, 3, pp. 89–108.

Deane, J, with N. Mue and F. Banda (2002) 'The other information revolution: Media and empowerment in developing countries', in M. Glasius, M. Kaldor and H. Anheier (eds.), *Global Civil Society 2002*. Oxford: Oxford University Press, pp. 171–90.

Delagran, L. (1992) 'Conflict in trade policy: The role of the Congress and the provinces in negotiating and implementing the Canada–US Free Trade Agreement', *Publius: The Journal of Federalism*, 22, pp. 15–29.

Delal Baer, M. (2000) 'Lessons of Nafta for U.S. relations with Mexico'. Testimony of Chairman and Senior Fellow, Mexico Project, Center for Strategic & International Studies to the United States Senate Subcommittee on Western Hemisphere, the Peace Corps, Narcotics and Terrorism, 27 April. Available at <http://www.csis.org/hill/ts000427baer.html>. Accessed 16 February 2004.

Delsodato, G. (2002) 'Eastward enlargement by the European Union and transnational parties', *International Political Science Review*, 23, 3, pp. 269–89.

De Luce, D. (2003) 'Student protesters warn leaders to allow free speech or risk confrontation', *Guardian*, 30 June.

Denny, C. (2002) 'Tough love in tatters', *Guardian*, 9 August.

Diamond, L. (1993a) 'Introduction: Political culture and democracy', in L. Diamond (ed.), *Political Culture and Democracy in Developing Countries*. Boulder and London: Lynne Rienner, pp. 1–33.

Diamond, L. (1993b) 'Causes and effects', in L. Diamond (ed.), *Political Culture and Democracy in Developing Countries*. Boulder and London: Lynne Rienner, pp. 411–35.

Diamond, L. (1993c) 'The globalization of democracy', in R. Slater, B. Schutz and S. Dorr (eds.), *Global Transformations and the Third World*. Boulder and London: Lynne Rienner Publishers and Adamantine Press, pp. 31–69.

Diamond, L. (1996) 'Democracy in Latin America: degrees, illusions, and directions for consolidation', in T. Farer (ed.), *Beyond Sovereignty: Collectively Defending Democracy in the Americas*. Baltimore, MD: John Hopkins University Press, pp. 53–85.

Diamond, L. (1999) *Developing Democracy. Toward Consolidation*. Baltimore and London: Johns Hopkins University Press.

Diamond, L. (2001) 'Is Pakistan the (reverse) wave of the future?', in L. Diamond and M. F. Plattner (eds.), *The Global Divergence of Democracies*. Baltimore/London: Johns Hopkins University Press and the National Endowment for Democracy, pp. 355–70.

Diamond, L. (2002) 'Consolidating democracies', in L. LeDuc, R. Niemi and P. Norris (eds.), *Comparing Democracies 2. New Challenges in the Study of Elections and Voting*. London/Thousand Oaks, CA/New Delhi: Sage, pp. 210–27.

Diamond, L. and Gunther, R. (eds.) (2001) *Political Parties and Democracy*. Baltimore and London: Johns Hopkins University Press.

Dillman, B. (2002) 'International markets and partial economic reforms in North Africa: What impact on democratization?', in R. Gillespie, R. and R. Youngs (eds.), *The European Union and Democracy Promotion: The Case of North Africa*, Special issue of *Democratization*, 9, 1, pp. 63–86.

Dixon, C. (2003) 'Developmental lessons of the Vietnamese transitional economy', *Progress in Developmental Studies*, 3, 4, pp. 287–306.

Dodd, V. (1996) 'Jews fear rise of the Muslim "underground"', *The Observer*, 18 February.

Doherty, B. (1992) 'The Fundi-Realo controversy: An analysis of four European green parties', *Environmental Politics*, 1, 1, pp. 95–120.

Doig, A. (1999) 'In the state we trust? Democratization, corruption and development', *Journal of Commonwealth and Comparative Politics*, 37, 3, pp. 13–36.

Dominguez, J. and Giraldo, J. (1996) 'Parties, institutions and market reforms in constructing democracies', in J. Dominguez and A. Lowenthal (eds.), *Constructing Democratic Governance: Mexico, Central America and the Caribbean in the 1990s*. London: Johns Hopkins University Press, pp. 3–41.

Donnelly, J. (1998) *International Human Rights*. Boulder: Westview Press.

Dower, N. and Williams, J. (eds.) (2002) *Global Citizenship. A Critical Reader*. Edinburgh: Edinburgh University Press.

Dryzek, J. and Holmes, L. (eds.) (2002) *Post-Communist Democratization: Political Discourse across Thirteen Countries*, Cambridge: Cambridge University Press.

Dunne, T. and Wheeler, N. (eds.) (1999) *Human Rights in Global Politics*. Cambridge: Cambridge University Press.

The Economist (2001a) 'An alarm call for Latin America's democrats', 26 July. Available at <http://www.economist.com/PrinterFriendly.cfm?Story_ID=709760>. Accessed 12 November 2004.

The Economist (2001b) 'Democracy clings on in a cold economic climate', 15 August. Available at <www.latinobarometro.org/articulos2.html>. Accessed 12 November 2004.

Ekins, P. (1992) *A New World Order. Grassroots Movements for Global Change*. London: Routledge.

Elgström, O. (2000) 'Lomé and post-Lomé: Asymmetric negotiations and the impact of norms', *European Foreign Affairs Review*, 5, pp. 175–95.

Engberg, J. and Ersson, S. (1999) 'Illiberal democracy in the Third World – An empirical enquiry'. Paper presented at the workshop: 'Democratic consolidation in the Third World: What should be done?', ECPR Joint Sessions of Workshops, University of Mannheim, March.

Engberg, J. and Ersson, S. (2001) 'Illiberal democracy in the "Third World": An empirical enquiry', in J. Haynes (ed.), *Democracy and Political Change in the 'Third World'*. London: Routledge, pp. 35–54.

Equal Opportunities Commission (2003) '75 years on: Equality for women and men today?'. Available at <www.eoc.org.uk/cseng/policyandcampaigns/talking_equality.pdf>. Accessed 1 November 2003.

Ethier, D. (2003) 'Is democracy promotion effective? Comparing conditionality and incentives', *Democratization*, 10, 1, pp. 99–120.

Etzioni-Halevy, E. (2002) 'Linkage deficits in transnational politics', *International Political Science Review*, 23, 2, pp. 203–22.

'European Muslims "fighting in Iraq"' (2004) *Herald Sun*, 16 March. Available at <http://www.heraldsun.news.com.au/common/story_page/0,5478,7775572%5E1702,00.html>. Accessed 16 March 2004.

Falk, R. (2002) 'An emergent matrix of citizenship: Complex, uneven, and fluid', in N. Dower and O. O'Neill (eds.), *Global Citizenship. A Critical Reader*. Edinburgh: Edinburgh University Press, pp. 15–29.

Farah, D. (2003) 'Liberian is accused of harboring Al Qaeda', *The Washington Post*, 15 May.

Fedorov, Y. (2000) 'Democratization and globalization: The case of Russia', Rule of Law Project, Global Policy Program, Working Paper #13, Carnegie Endowment for International Peace. Available at <http://www.ceip.org/files/publications/pdf/federov.pdf>. Accessed 8 March 2004.

Fein, H. (1993) *Genocide: A Sociological Perspective*. London: Sage.

Fein, H. (1995) 'More murder in the middle: Life-integrity violations and democracy in the world', *Human Rights Quarterly*, 17, pp. 170–91.

Ferguson, J. A. (1986) 'The Third World' in R. J. Vincent (ed.), *Foreign Policy and Human Rights*, Cambridge: Cambridge University Press, pp. 203–26.

Figueres, K. Olsen de (n/d) 'A people marching – women in parliament in Costa Rica', in International Institute for Democracy and Electoral Assistance [IDEA], *Women in Politics: Beyond the Numbers*. Available at <http://www.idea.int/women/parl/studies2a.htm>. Accessed 14 August 2003.

Fisher, J. (1993) *The Road from Rio. Sustainable Development and Nongovernmental Movements in the Third World*. Westport, Connecticut: Praeger.

Florini, A. and Simmons, P. (2000) 'What the world needs now?' in A. Florini (ed.), *The Third Force. The Rise of International Civil Society*, Tokyo and Washington, DC: Japan Center for International Exchange/Carnegie Endowment for International Peace, pp. 1–17.

Freedom House (2002) 'Freedom in the World 2002. Liberty's Expansion in a Turbulent World'. Available at <http//www.freedomhouse.org/research/survey2002.htm>. Accessed 1 July 2003.

Freedom House (2003) *Freedom in the World 2003*. Lanham, MD: Rowman & Littlefield.

Freedom House (2004) 'Freedom in the World 2004. Table of Independent Countries Comparative Measures of Freedom'. Available at <http://www.freedomhouse.org/research/freeworld/2004/table2004.pdf>.

Fukuyama, F. (1992) *The End of History and the Last Man*. Harmondsworth: Penguin.

Fukuyama, F. (2001) 'Social capital, civil society and development', *Third World Quarterly*, 22, 1, pp. 7–20.

Fukuyama, F. (2004) *State Building: Governance and World Order in the 21st Century*. London: Profile Books.

Gabel, M. and Anderson, C. (2002) 'The structure of citizen attitudes and the European political space', *Comparative Political Studies*, 35, 8, pp. 893–913.

Gabel, M. and Hix, S. (2002) 'Defining the EU political space. An empirical study of the European Elections Manifestos, 1979–1999', *Comparative Political Studies*, 35, 8, pp. 934–64.

Gagnon, V.-P. (2002) 'International NGOs in Bosnia-Herzegovina: Attempting to build civil society', in S. Mendelson and J. Glenn (eds.), *The Power and Limits of NGOs. A Critical Look at Building Democracy in Eastern Europe and Eurasia*. New York: Columbia University Press, pp. 207–31.

Garriga, M. (2003) 'Factories looking for fairness', *New Haven Register*, 22 July.

Geertz, C. (1973) 'Thick description: Toward an interpretative theory of culture', in C. Geertz (ed.), *Interpretations of Culture*. London: Fontana.

Gelb, J. and Palley, M. (1996) *Women and Public Policies*. University of Virginia Press.

Gel'man, V. (2003) 'Post-Soviet transitions and democratization: Towards theory building', *Democratization*, 10, 2, pp. 87–104.

Ghazi, P. (2004) 'No contest', *Society Guardian*, 25 February, p. 13.

Giddens, A. (1998) *The Third Way*. Cambridge: Polity.

Gillespie, R. and Whitehead, L. (2002) 'European democracy promotion in North Africa: Limits and prospects', in R. Gillespie and R. Youngs (eds.), *The European Union and Democracy Promotion: The Case of North Africa*, Special issue of *Democratization*, 9, 1, pp. 192–206.

Gillespie, R. and Youngs, R. (eds.) (2002a) *The European Union and Democracy Promotion: The Case of North Africa*, Special issue of *Democratization*, 9, 1.

Gillespie, R. and Youngs, R. (2002b) 'Themes in European democracy promotion', *The European Union and Democracy Promotion: The Case of North Africa*, Special issue of *Democratization*, 9, 1, pp. 1–16.

Gills, B., Rocamora, J. and Wilson, R. (eds.) (1993) *Low Intensity Democracy*. London: Pluto Press.

Gilpin, R. (2000) *The Challenge of Global Capitalism: The World Economy in the 21st Century*. Princeton, NJ: Princeton University Press.

Ginsberg, B. (1982) *The Consequences of Consent*. Reading, MA: Addison Wesley.

Gittings, J. (1996) 'Tibet faces an atheist crusade', *Guardian*, 26 October.

Glasius, M., Kaldor, M. and Anheier, H. (eds.) (2002) *Global Civil Society 2002*. Oxford: Oxford University Press.

Golob, S. (2002) ' "Forced to be free": Globalized justice, pacted democracy, and the Pinochet case', *Democratization*, 9, 2, pp. 21–42.

Golosov, G. (2001) 'Political parties, electoral systems and women's representation in the regional legislative assemblies of Russia, 1995–1998', *Party Politics*, 7, pp. 45–68.

Gooch, A. (1996) 'Spanish Church denies leading flock to polls', *Guardian*, 22 February.

Goulborne, H. and Joly, D. (1989) 'Religion and the Asian and Caribbean minorities in Britain', *Contemporary European Affairs*, 2, 4, pp. 77–98.

Gränzer, S. (1999) 'Changing discourse: Transnational advocacy networks in Tunisia and Morocco', in T. Risse, S. Ropp and K. Sikkink (eds.), *The Power of Human Rights. International Norms and Domestic Change*. Cambridge: Cambridge University Press, pp. 109–33.

Gray, J, (2004) 'History bites back', *New Statesman*, 814, 5 July, p. 48.

Green, D. and Luehrmann, L. (2003) *Comparative Politics of the Third World. Linking Concepts and Classes*. Boulder and London: Lynne Rienner.

Grugel, J. (2000) 'State and business in neo-liberal democracies in Latin America', in H. Smith (ed.), *Democracy and International Relations*. Basingstoke: Macmillan, pp. 108–25.

Guelke, A. (1999) *South Africa in Transition. The Misunderstood Miracle*. London and New York: I. B. Tauris.

Gunaratna, R. (2004) 'Defeating Al Qaeda – The pioneering vanguard of the Islamic movements', in R. Howard and R. Sawyer (eds.), *Defeating Terrorism. Shaping the New Security Environment*. Guilford, CT: McGraw-Hill/Dushkin, pp. 1–28.

Günes-Ayata, A. (1994) 'Roots and trends in clientelism in Turkey', in L. Roniger and A. Günes-Ayata (eds.), *Democracy, Clientelism, and Civil Society*. Boulder, CO: Lynne Rienner, pp. 49–64.

Gunther, R. and Diamond, L. (2001) 'Types and function of parties', in L. Diamond and R. Gunther (eds.), *Political Parties and Democracy*. Baltimore and London: Johns Hopkins University Press, pp. 3–39.

Hadjor, K. (1993) *A Dictionary of Third World Terms*. Harmondsworth: Penguin.

Hague, R. and Harrop, M. (2001) *Comparative Government and Politics. An Introduction*, 5th edn. Basingstoke: Palgrave.

Hallencreutz, C. and Westerlund, D. (1996) 'Anti-secularist policies of religion', in D. Westerlund (ed.), *Questioning the Secular State. The Worldwide Resurgence of Religion in Politics*. London: Hurst, pp. 1–23.

Halper, S. and Clarke, J. (2004) *America Alone. The Neo-Conservatives and the Global Order*. Cambridge: Cambridge University Press.

Hammond, P. (2003) 'Review article: Making war and peace', *Contemporary Politics*, 9, 1 (March), pp. 83–90.

Hanf, K. and A. Underdal (1998). 'Domesticating international commitments: Linking national and international decision-making', in A. Underdal (ed.), *The Politics of International Environmental Management*. Dordrecht: Kluwer, pp. 149–70.

Hansen, H. B. and Twaddle, M. (1995), 'Uganda. The advent of no-party democracy', in J. Wiseman (ed.), *Democracy and Political Change in Africa*. London: Routledge, pp. 137–51.

Harding, L. (2001) 'Sex hell of Dalit women exposed', *Guardian*, 9 May.

Harker, L. and Pacey, M. (2003) 'More babies, more votes', *Guardian*, 13 August.

Harris, L. (2002) 'Al Qaeda's fantasy ideology', *Policy Review Online*, August–September, no. 114. Available at <http://www.policyreview.org/AUG02/harris.html>. Accessed 10 March 2004.

Harsch, E. (1996) 'Global coalition debates Africa's future', *Africa Recovery*, 10, 1, pp. 24–31.

Harsch, E. (2002) 'African Union: A dream under construction', *Africa Recovery*, 16, 1, pp. 1, 20–1.

Harsch, E. (2003), 'Africa builds its own peace forces', *Africa Recovery*, 17, 3, pp. 1, 14–16, 18–20.

Havely, J. (2002) 'Afghanistan: Rebuilding a "failed" state', 10 September, CNN.com/world. Available at <http://edition.cnn.com/2002/WORLD/asiapcf/central/09/08/afghan.gov.feat/>. Accessed 10 March 2004.

Hawkins, K. (2003) 'Populism in Venezuela: The rise of Chavismo', *Third World Quarterly*, 24, 6, pp. 1137–60.

Hay, C. (2000) 'Contemporary capitalism, globalization, regionalization and the persistence of national variation', *Review of International Studies*, 26, pp. 505–31.

Hay, C. (2002a) 'Globalization, "EU-isation" and the space for social democratic alternatives: pessimism of the intellect: a reply to Coates', *British Journal of International Relations*, 4, 3 (October), pp. 452–64.

Hay, C. (2002b) *Political Analysis. A Critical Introduction*. Basingstoke: Palgrave.

Hay, C. and Rosamond, B. (2002) 'Globalization, European integration and the discursive construction of economic imperatives', *Journal of European Public Policy*, 9, 2 (April), pp. 147–67.

Hay, C., Rosamond, B. and Schain, M. (2002). Editors' flyer for *Comparative European Politics*, a quarterly journal first published in March 2003. Details at <www.palgrave-journals.com>.

Haynes, J. (1993) *Religion in Third World Politics*. Buckingham: Open University Press.

Haynes, J. (1997) *Democracy and Civil Society in the Third World*. Cambridge: Polity.

Haynes, J. (1998) *Religion in Global Politics*. London: Longman.

Haynes, J. (2001a) *Democracy in the Developing World. Asia, Africa, Latin America and the Middle East*. Cambridge: Polity.

Haynes, J. (2001b) 'Transnational religious actors and international politics', *Third World Quarterly*, 22, 2, pp. 143–58.

Haynes, J. (2002) *Politics in the Developing World*. Oxford: Blackwell.

Haynes, J. (2003a) 'Religion and politics: What is the impact of September 11?', *Contemporary Politics*, 9, 1 (March), pp. 7–16.

Haynes, J. (2003b) 'Democratic consolidation in Africa: the problematic case of Ghana', *The Journal of Commonwealth and Comparative Politics*, 41, 1, pp. 48–76.

Haynes, J. (2003c) 'Tracing connections between comparative politics and globalization', *Third World Quarterly*, 24, 6 (December), pp. 1029–47.

Haynes, J. (ed.) (2005) *Palgrave Advances in Development Studies*. Basingstoke: Palgrave Macmillan.

Hazan, R. (2002) 'Candidate selection', in L. LeDuc, R. Niemi and P. Norris (eds.), *Comparing Democracies 2. New Challenges in the Study of Elections and Voting*. London/Thousand Oaks, CA/New Delhi: Sage, pp. 108–26.

Heine, J. (1999) 'Latin America. Collective responses to new realities', in L. Fawcett and Y. Sayigh (eds.), *The Third World Beyond the Cold War. Continuity and Change*. Oxford: Oxford University Press, pp. 101–17.

Held, D. (1993) 'Democracy from city-states to a cosmopolitan order?' in D. Held (ed.), *Prospects for Democracy*. Cambridge: Polity, pp. 13–52.

Held, D. (1999) 'The transformation of political community: Rethinking democracy in the context of globalization', in I. Shapiro and C. Hacker-Cordón (eds.), *Democracy's Edges*. Cambridge: Cambridge University Press, pp. 84–111.

Held, D. and McGrew, A. (2002) *Globalization/Anti-Globalization*. Cambridge: Polity.

Henderson, C. (1991) 'Conditions affecting the use of political repression', *Journal of Conflict Resolution*, 35, pp. 120–42.

Henley, J. (2004) 'French MPs vote for veil ban in state schools', *Guardian*, 11 February.

Henley, J. and Walker, J. (2003) 'French anti-terror squad arrests key Eta leaders', *Guardian*, 10 December.

Hertsgaard, M. (2000) 'Russia's environmental crisis', *The Nation*, 7 September. Available at <http://www.thenation.com/doc.mhtml?i=20000918&c=1&s=hertsgaard>. Accessed 26 February 2004.

Hettne, B. (2001) 'Europe: Paradigm and paradox', in M. Schulz, F. Söderbaum and J. Öjendal (eds.), *Regionalization in a Globalizing World. A Comparative Perspective on Forms, Actors and Processes*. London: Zed Books, pp. 22–41.

Hewison, K. (1999) 'Political space in Southeast Asia: "Asian-style" and other democracies', in P. Burnell and P. Calvert (eds.), *The Resilience of Democracy: Persistent Practice, Durable Idea*, special issue of *Democratization*, 6, 1, pp. 224–45.

Hilton, I. (2003) 'Just poppycock', *Guardian*, 4 December.

Hirst, P. and Thompson, G. (1999) *Globalization in Question. The International Economy and the Possibilities of Governance*, 2nd edn. Cambridge: Polity.

Hix, S. (2003) *The Political System of the European Union*, 2nd edn. Basingstoke: Macmillan.

Holland, M. (2002) *The European Union and the Third World*. Basingstoke, Palgrave.

Hooghe, L., and Marks, G. (1999). 'Making of a polity: The struggle over European integration', in H. Kitschelt, P. Lange, G. Marks and J. Stephens (eds.), *Continuity and Change in Contemporary Capitalism*. Cambridge: Cambridge University Press, pp. 70–97.

Hopkin, J. (2002) 'Comparative methods', in D. Marsh and G. Stoker (eds.), *Theories and Methods in Political Science*, 2nd edn. Basingstoke: Palgrave, pp. 249–67.

Howard, R. and Sawyer, R. (eds.) (2004) *Defeating Terrorism. Shaping the New Security Environment*. Guilford, Connecticut: McGraw-Hill/Dushkin,

Howell, J. (2003) 'State enterprise reform and gender: One step backwards for women', in R. Benewick, M. Blecher and S. Cook (eds.), *Asian Politics in Development. Essays in Honour of Gordon White*. London: Cass, pp. 83–105.

Huggins, R. (2002) 'Democracy and democratisation', in B. Axford, G. Browning, R. Huggins and B. Rosamond, *An Introduction to Politics*, 2nd edn. London and New York: Routledge, pp. 159–92.

Human Rights Research and Education Center (n/d) 'Asian values and human rights: Letting the tigers free'. Available at <http://www.uottawa.ca/hrrec/publicat/asian_values.html>. Accessed 1 April 2004.

Human Rights Watch (1999) 'Asia'. Available at <http://www.hrw.org/worldreport99/asia/asia2.html>. Accessed 1 April 2004.

Huntington, S. (1968) *Political Order in Changing Societies*. New Haven: Yale University Press.

Huntington, S. (1991) *The Third Wave. Democratization in the Late Twentieth Century*. Norman: University of Oklahoma Press.

Huntington, S. (1993) 'The clash of civilizations?', *Foreign Affairs*, 72, 3, pp. 22–49.

Huntington, S. (1996) *The Clash of Civilizations*. New York: Simon and Schuster.

Huntington, S. (2004) *Who We Are: Challenges to American National Identity*. New York: Simon & Schuster.

Hurrell, A. (2002) ' "There are no rules" (George W. Bush): International order after September 11', *International Relations*, 16, 2, pp. 185–204.

Hutchings, K. (2002) 'Feminism and global citizenship', in N. Dower and O. O'Neill (eds.), *Global Citizenship. A Critical Reader*. Edinburgh: Edinburgh University Press, pp. 53–62.

Imig, D. (2002) 'Contestation in the streets. European protest and the emerging Euro-polity', *Comparative Political Studies*, 35, 8, pp. 914–33.

Imig, D. and Tarrow, S. (eds.) (2001) *Contentious Europeans: Protest and Politics in an Emerging Polity*. Boulder, CO: Rowman & Littlefield.

Inglehart, R. (1990) *Culture Shift in Advanced Industrial Society*. Princeton, NJ: Princeton University Press.

Inglehart, R. (1997) *Modernization and Postmodernization. Cultural, Economic and Social Change in 43 Countries*. Princeton, NJ: Princeton University Press.

International Institute for Democracy and Electoral Assistance [IDEA], 'Women in Politics: Beyond the Numbers' (n/d). Available at <http://www.idea.int/women/parl/studies2a.htm>. Accessed 12 August 2003.

Interparliamentary Union (2003) 'Women in National Parliaments'. IPU home page at <http://www.ipu.org/wmne/world.htm>.

Isaac, J., Filner, M. and Bivins, J. (1999) 'American democracy and the New Christian Right: A critique of apolitical liberalism', in I. Shapiro and C. Hacker-Cordón (eds.), *Democracy's Edges*. Cambridge: Cambridge University Press, pp. 222–64.

Jackson, R. (1990) *Quasi-states: Sovereignty, International Relations and the Third World*. Cambridge: Cambridge University Press.

Jager, de Ricalde, A. (1997) 'Partido Verde Ecologista de México' ('The Green Party of Mexico'), *Synthesis/Regeneration*, 13, Spring. Available at <http://www.greens.org/s-r/13/13-02.html>. Accessed 23 August 2004.

James, P. and Lustzig, M. (2003) 'The US power cycle, expected utility, probable future of the FTAA', *International Political Science Review*, 24, 1, pp. 83–96.

Jaquette, J. (1989) *The Women's Movement in Latin America*. Boston: Unwin Hyman.

Jetschke, F. (2001) First chapter of PhD thesis: 'International human rights norms, transnational networks and domestic political change'. Available at <http://www.asienkunde.de/nachwuchs/noah2001/F-Jetschke.pdf>. Accessed 1 September 2003.

Johnson, P. and Beaulieu, A. (1996) *The Environment and NAFTA: Understanding and Implementing the New Continental Law*. Washington, DC: Island Press.

Johnson, R. (n/d) 'Reconstructing the Balkans: The effects of a global governance approach'. Unpublished manuscript. The Brookings Institution, Washington, DC, USA. Available at <www.cpogg.org/paper%20amerang/Rebecca%20Johnson.pdf>. Accessed 1 October 2003.

Johnston, H. (1992) 'Religious nationalism: Six propositions from Eastern Europe and the former Soviet Union', in B. Misztal and A. Shupe (eds.), *Religion and Politics in Comparative Perspective*. Westport, CT, and London: Praeger, pp. 67–78.

Jowitt, K. (1993) 'A world without Leninism', in R. Slater, B. Schutz and S. Dorr (eds.), *Global Transformations and the Third World*. Boulder and London: Lynne Rienner Publishers and Adamantine Press, pp. 9–27.

Kamrava, M. (1998) 'Non-democratic states and liberalization in the Middle East: A structural analysis', *Third World Quarterly*, 19, 1, pp. 63–85.

Karatnycky, A., Piano, A. and Puddington, A. (eds.) (2003) *Freedom in the World. The Annual Survey of Political Rights and Civil Liberties 2003*. New York, Freedom House.

Karam, A. (1999) *Strengthening the Role of Women Parliamentarians in the Arab Region: Challenges and Options*. New York: United Nations Development Programme.

Karl, T. (1991) 'El Salvador's negotiated revolution', *Foreign Affairs*, 70, 2, pp. 147–64.

Karl, T. (1995) 'The hybrid regimes of Central America', *Journal of Democracy*, 6, 3, pp. 72–86.

Katz, R. and Mair, P. (eds.) (1994) *How Parties Organize: Change and Adaptation in Party Organization in Western Democracies*. London: Sage.

Katz, R. S. and Mair, P. (1995) 'Changing models of party organization and party democracy: The emergence of the cartel party', *Party Politics*, 1, pp. 5–25.

Keck, M. and Sikkink, K. (1998a) *Activists Beyond Borders: Advocacy Networks in International Politics*. Ithaca, NY: Cornell University Press.

Keck, M. and Sikkink, K. (1998b) 'Transnational advocacy networks in the movement society', in D. Meyer and S. Tarrow (eds.), *The Social Movement Society*. Lanham, MD: Rowman & Littlefield, pp. 217–38.

Keegan, W. (2004) 'Trying to cut a dash in the eurozone', *The Observer* (Business section), 22 February, p. 8.

Kellow, A. (2002) 'Comparing business and public interest associability at the international level', *International Political Science Review*, 23, 2, pp. 175–86.

Kent, A. (1999) *China, the United Nations, and Human Rights. The Limits of Compliance*. Philadelphia: University of Pennsylvania Press.

Keohane, R. (2002) 'The globalization of informal violence, theories of world politics, and the "liberalism of fear" ', *Dialog-IO* (spring), pp. 29–43.

Keohane, R. and Nye, J. (1977) *Power and Interdependence: World Politics in Transition*, Boston: Little, Brown (2nd edn. 1987; 3rd edn. New York: Addison-Wesley Longman, 2001).

Kepel, G. (1994) *The Revenge of God*. Cambridge: Polity.

Kesselman, M., Krieger, J. and Joseph, W. (eds.) (2000) *Introducing Comparative Politics*, 2nd edn. Boston, MA: Houghton Mifflin.

Kiloh, M. (1997) 'South Africa: Democracy delayed', in D. Potter et al., *Democratization*. Milton Keynes and Cambridge: Open University Press and Polity, pp. 294–320.

Kitschelt, H. (1986) 'Political opportunity structures and political protest: Anti-nuclear movements in four democracies', *British Journal of Political Science*, 16, pp. 57–85.

Kitschelt, H. (1988) 'Left-libertarian parties: Explaining innovation in competitive party systems', *World Politics*, 40, 2, pp. 194–234.

Klesner, J. (2001a) 'Mexico and Brazil', in M. J. Sodaro, *Comparative Politics: A Global Introduction*. New York: McGraw Hill, pp. 747–808.

Klesner, J. (2001b) 'Divided government in Mexico's presidential regime: The 1997–2000 experience', in R. Elgie (ed.), *Divided Government in Comparative Perspective*. Oxford: Oxford University Press, pp. 63–85.

Knight, D. (2000) 'Environment finance: Groups protest World Bank's loans to Russia', World News Interpress service, September 6. Available at <http://www.oneworld.org/ips2/sept00/02_19_007.html>. Accessed 16 February 2004.

Kohli, A. (1996) 'Symposium: The role of theory in comparative politics', *World Politics*, 48, pp. 1–49.

Krahmann, E. (2002) 'Private actors and the new security governance: Understanding the emergence, problems and options for the privatization of security in North America and Europe'. Paper prepared for presentation at the CPOGG Workshop at Schloss Amerang, 1–3 November.

Krasner, S. (ed.) (1983) *International Regimes*. Ithaca, NY: Cornell University Press.

Kreisi, H., Koopmans, R., Duyvendack, J. W. and Giugni, M. (1992) 'New social movements and opportunity structures in Western Europe', *European Journal of Political Research*, 22, pp. 219–44.

Kumar, C. (2000) 'Transnational networks and campaigns for democracy', in A. Florini (ed.), *The Third Force. The Rise of Transnational Civil Society*. Tokyo and Washington, DC: Japan Center for International Exchange/Carnegie Endowment for International Peace, pp. 115–42.

Kurop, M. Christoff (2001) 'Al Qaeda's Balkan links', *The Wall Street Journal Europe*, 1 November. Available at <http://www.balkanpeace.org/hed/archive/nov01/hed4304.shtml>. Accessed 10 March 2004.

Kurth, J. (1999) 'Religion and globalization'. The Templeton Lecture on Religion and World Affairs, Foreign Policy Research Institute Wire, vol. 7, no. 7. Available at <http://www.fpri.org/fpriwire/0707.199905.kurth.religionglobalization.html>. Accessed 18 March 2004.

Kurtz, M. and Barnes, A. (2002) 'The political foundations of post-communist regimes. Marketization, agrarian legacies, or international influences', *Comparative Political Studies*, 35, 5, pp. 524–53.

Laitin, D. (2001) 'Secessionist rebellion in the former Soviet Union', *Comparative Political Studies*, 34, 8, pp. 839–61.

Lane, J.-E. and Ersson, S. (1994) *Comparative Politics. An Introduction and New Approach.* Cambridge: Polity.

Larose, C. (1999) 'Free trade and social policy'. Available at <http://www.freetradeat10.com/speeches/larose.html>. Accessed 25 February 2004.

Lawson, K. (2002) 'Introduction: Parties and NGOs in the quest for global democracy', *International Political Science Review* (2002), 23, 2, pp. 131–13.

Lawson, L. (1999) 'External democracy promotion in Africa: Another false start?', *Journal of Commonwealth and Comparative Politics*, 37, 1, pp. 1–30.

Lees, C. (2002) 'The political opportunity structure of Euroscepticism: Institutional setting and political agency in European electoral and party systems'. Paper presented at ECPR Joint Workshop on 'Opposing Europe: Euroscepticism and Political Parties', ECPR Joint Sessions, Turin, Italy, 22–27 March.

Leftwich, A. (1993) 'Governance, democracy and development in the Third World', *Third World Quarterly*, 14, 3, pp. 605–24.

Leftwich, A. (1997) 'Conclusion', in D. Potter, D. Goldblatt, M. Kiloh and P. Lewis (eds.), *Democratization*. Cambridge: Polity (in association with the Open University), pp. 517–36.

Leslie, P. (1997) ' "Governing the economy" within economic unions: Canada, the EU, and the Nafta'. Paper presented to the Workshop 'North American Federalism and NAFTA: Three Perspectives', Canadian Studies Program, University of California at Berkeley, 27–29 April. Available at <http://www.ias.berkeley.edu/canada/fedpapers.html>. Accessed 16 February 2004.

Lievesley, G. (1999) *Democracy in Latin America. Mobilization, Power and the Search for a New Politics.* Manchester and New York: Manchester University Press.

Light, M. (2000) 'Democracy, democratization and foreign policy in post-Socialist Russia', in H. Smith (ed.), *Democracy and International Relations*. Basingstoke: Macmillan, pp. 90–107.

Linz, J. and Stepan, A. (1996) *Problems of Democratic Transition and Consolidation. Southern Europe, South America, and Post-Communist Europe.* Baltimore and London: Johns Hopkins University Press.

Lipschutz, R. (1992) 'Reconstructing world politics: The emergence of global civil society', *Millennium*, 21, 3, pp. 389–420.

Lipset, S. M. (1963) 'Economic development and democracy', in S. M. Lipset (ed.), *Political Man*. Garden City, NY: Anchor, pp. 27–63.

Lipset, S. M. and Rokkan, S. (1967) 'Cleavage structures, party systems and voter alignments', in S. Lipset and S. Rokkan (eds.), *Party Systems and Voter Alignments*. New York and London: Free Press, pp. 1–65.

Lowenthal, A. (2001) 'Latin America at the century's turn', in L. Diamond and M. F. Plattner (eds.), *The Global Divergence of Democracies*. Baltimore/London: Johns Hopkins University Press and the National Endowment for Democracy, pp. 312–26.

Lowndes, V. (2002) 'Institutionalism', in D. Marsh and G. Stoker (eds.), *Theory and Methods in Political Science*, 2nd edn. Basingstoke: Palgrave, pp. 90–108.

McCarthy, R. (2001a) ' "I was sold to a man . . . is this Islam?" ', *The Guardian*, 29 January.

McCarthy, R. (2001b) 'Pakistan's women get seats at the bottom table', *Guardian*, 18 May.

Mcdonald, L. (2003) *A Voting Rights Odyssey: Black Enfranchisement in Georgia*. Cambridge: Cambridge University Press.

Macdonald, L. and Schwartz, M. (2002) 'Political parties and NGOs in the creation of new trading blocs in the Americas', *International Political Science Review*, 23, 2, pp. 135–58.

Mcdonnell, H. (2003) 'Environment role for Greens but Socialists unhappy at carve-up', *The Scotsman*, 30 May.

McEwan, D. (1989) 'Germany, Federal Republic of', in S. Mews (ed.), *Religion in Politics. A World Guide*. Harlow: Longman, pp. 83–6.

McGarry, J. (1998) 'Political settlements in Northern Ireland and South Africa', *Political Studies*, 46, 5, pp. 853–70.

McGreal, C. (2000a) 'Clinton's visit shows US fears for Nigeria', *Guardian*, 26 August.

McMahon, P. (2002) 'International actors and women's NGOs in Poland and Hungary', in S. Mendelson and J. Glenn (eds.), *The Power and Limits of NGOs. A Critical Look at Building Democracy in Eastern Europe and Eurasia*. New York: Columbia University Press, pp. 29–53.

Mainwaring, S. (1999) *Rethinking Party Systems in the Third Wave of Democratization. The Case of Brazil*. Stanford, CA: Stanford University Press.

Mainwaring, S. and Scully, T. (eds.) (1995) *Building Democratic Institutions: Party Systems in Latin America*. Stanford, CA: Stanford University Press.

Mainwaring, S., O'Donnell, G. and Valenzuela, J. (1992) 'Introduction', in S. Mainwaring, G. O'Donnell and J. Valenzuela (eds.), *Issues in Democratic Consolidation: The New South American Democracies in Comparative Perspective*. Notre Dame, IN: University of Notre Dame Press, pp. 3–28.

Mair, P. and Zielonka, J. (eds.) (2002) *The Enlarged European Union. Diversity and Adaptation*. London/Portland, OR: Frank Cass.

Mallaby, S. (2002) 'The reluctant imperialist: Terrorism, failed states, and the case for American empire', *Foreign Affairs* (March/April), 81, 2, pp. 2–7.

Malovà, D. and Haughton, T. (2002) 'Making institutions in Central and Eastern Europe, and the impact of Europe', in P. Mair and J. Zielonka (eds.), *The Enlarged European Union. Diversity and Adaptation*. London/Portland, OR: Frank Cass, pp. 101–20.

Mandelson, P. (2003) 'Forget new labour – here comes even newer labour', *Guardian*, 7 July.

Manion, M. (2000) 'Politics in China', in G. Almond and G. B. Powell, *Comparative Politics Today: A World View*, 7th edn. New York: Longman, pp. 419–62.

Marais, H. (1998) *South Africa: Limits to Change: The Political Economy of Transformation*. London and Cape Town: Zed Books and University of Cape Town Press.

Maravall, J. M. (1995) 'The myth of the authoritarian advantage', in L. Diamond and M. Plattner (eds.), *Economic Reform and Democracy*. Baltimore, MD: Johns Hopkins University Press, pp. 13–27.

Marchand, M. (1995) 'Latin American women speak on development', in M. Marchand and J. Parpart, *Feminism/Postmodernism/Development*. London: Routledge, pp. 56–72.

Marks, G. and McAdam, D. (1996) 'Social movements and changing structures of political opportunity in the European Community', *West European Politics*, 19, pp. 249–78.

Marsh, D. (2002) 'Pluralism and the study of British politics: It is always the happy hour for men with money, knowledge and power', in C. Hay (ed.), *British Politics Today*. Cambridge: Polity, pp. 14–37.

Marsh, D. and Furlong, P. (2002) 'A skin, not a sweater: Ontology and epistemology in political science', in D. Marsh and G. Stoker (eds.), *Theory and Methods in Political Science*, 2nd edn. Basingstoke: Palgrave, pp. 17–41.

Marsh, D. and Stoker, G. (2002) 'Conclusion', in D. Marsh and G. Stoker (eds.), *Theory and Methods in Political Science*, 2nd edn. Basingstoke: Palgrave, pp. 311–17.

Martens, K. (2001) 'Applying the concept of "political opportunity structures" in European and International Studies', published in French in *Transnational Associations*, 1, 2001, pp. 2–9.

Martin, D. (1994) 'Religion in contemporary Europe', in J. Fulton and P. Gee (eds.), *Religion in Contemporary Europe*. Lewiston, NY: Edwin Mellen, pp. 1–16.

Mazey, S. and Richardson, J. (1994) 'Interest groups and representation in the European Union'. Paper presented to the workshop, 'Democratic representation and government legitimacy in the European Community', ECPR Joint Sessions of Workshops, Madrid, 17–22 April.

Mendelson, S. (2002) 'Conclusion: The power and limits of transnational democracy networks in postcommunist societies', in S. Mendelson and J. Glenn (eds.), *The Power and Limits of NGOs. A Critical Look at Building Democracy in Eastern Europe and Eurasia*. New York: Columbia University Press, pp. 232–51.

Mendelson, S. and Glenn, J. (2002) 'Introduction: Transnational networks and NGOs in post-communist societies', in S. Mendelson and J. Glenn (eds.), *The Power and Limits of NGOs. A Critical Look at Building Democracy in Eastern Europe and Eurasia*. New York: Columbia University Press, pp. 1–28.

The Mercury (2004) 'Al-Qaeda "targeting Balkans"', 2 February. Available at <http://www.themercury.news.com.au/common/story_page/0,5936,8559943%5E401,00.html>. Accessed 9 March 2004.

Merkel, W. (1998) 'The consolidation of post-autocratic democracies: A multi-level model', *Democratization*, 5, 3, pp. 33–67.

Michel, P. (1994) 'Religion and democracy in Central Eastern Europe', in J. Fulton and P. Gee (eds.), *Religion in Contemporary Europe*. Lewiston, NY: Edwin Mellen, pp. 34–42.

Migdal, J. (1997) 'Studying the state', in M. Irving Lichbach and A. S. Zuckerman (eds.), *Comparative Politics. Rationality, Culture and Structure*. Cambridge: Cambridge University Press, pp. 208–35.

Miller, M. (1995) *The Third World in Global Environmental Politics*. Buckingham: Open University Press.

Miszlivetz, F. and Jensen, J. (1998) 'An emerging paradox: Civil society from above?', in D. Rueschemeyer, M. Rueschemeyer and B. Wittrock (eds.), *Participation and Democracy, East and West: Comparisons and Interpretations*. Armonk, NY: M. E. Sharpe, pp. 83–98.

Mitra, S. and Enskat, M. (1999) 'Parties and the people: India's changing party system and the resilience of democracy', in P. Burnell and P. Calvert (eds.), *The Resilience of Democracy: Persistent Practice, Durable Idea*, special issue of *Democratization*, 6, 1, pp. 123–54.

Mittelman, J. (1994) 'The globalization challenge surviving at the margins', *Third World Quarterly*, 15, 3, pp. 427–41.

Molyneux, M. (1985) 'Mobilization without emancipation? Women's interests, the state, and revolution in Nicaragua', *Feminist Studies*, 11, 2, pp. 227–54.

Moravcsik, A. (1993) 'Introduction: Integrating international and domestic theories of international bargaining', in P. Evans, H. Jacobson and R. Putnam (eds.), *Double-Edged Diplomacy. International Bargaining and Domestic Politics*. Berkeley/Los Angeles/London: University of California Press, pp. 3–43.

Morlino, L. (1998) *Democracy between Consolidation and Crisis. Parties, Groups, and Citizens in Southern Europe*. New York: Oxford University Press.

Morosov, V. (2002) 'Human rights and foreign policy discourse in today's Russia: Romantic realism and securitization of identity'. School of International Relations, St Petersburg State University.

Morris, S. (1995) *Political Reformism in Mexico. An Overview of Contemporary Mexican Politics*. Boulder, CO: Rienner.

Morris, S. (2001) 'Offices, schools, hospitals at end of paper trail from diminishing forests', *Guardain*, 26 June.

Mughni, H. (2000) *Women in Kuwait, the Politics of Gender*. London: Al Saqi.

Mumme, S. (1999) 'NAFTA's environmental side agreement: Almost green?' *Borderlines*, 7, 9, pp. 1–4, 16. Available at <http://www.americaspolicy.org/borderlines/PDFs/bl60.pdf>. Accessed 25 February 2004.

Nagle, J. and Mahr, A. (1999) *Democracy and Democratization. Post-Communist Europe in Comparative Perspective*. London: Sage.

Nardin, T. (2003) 'Epilogue', in F. Petito and P. Hatzopoulos (eds.), *Religion in International Relations*. New York: Palgrave Macmillan, pp. 271–82.

Nayar, Baldev Raj (2003) 'Globalization and India's national autonomy', *Commonwealth & Comparative Politics*, 41, 2, pp. 1–35.

Nelson, J. (2001) 'Globalization of the defense industry', NDIA Conference, 28 March. Available at <http://www.dtic.mil/ndia/2001summit/nelson.pdf>. Accessed 23 February 2004.

Nentwich, M. (1996) 'Opportunity structures for citizens' participation: The case of the European Union'. European Integration online Papers (EioP), vol. 0, no. 1. Available at <http://eiop.or.at/eiop/texte/1996-001.htm>. Accessed 17 April 2004.

Nielsen, J. (1992) 'Muslims, Christians and loyalties in the nation-state', in J. Nielsen (ed.), *Religion and Citizenship in Europe and the Arab World*. London: Grey Seal Books, pp. 1–18.

Nohlen, D. (1992) 'Prasidentialismus versus parlamentarismus in Lateinamerika', *Lateinamerikanisches Jahrbuch*, pp. 86–99.

Norris, P. (2002) 'Gender and contemporary British politics', in C. Hay (ed.), *British Politics Today*. Cambridge: Polity, pp. 38–60.

Norris, P., Kern, M. and Just, M. (2003) 'Framing terrorism' in P. Norris (ed.), *Framing Terrorism: The News Media, the Government and the Public*. New York: Routledge, pp. 3–27.

Nye, J. (2002) 'The new Rome meets the new barbarians: How America should wield its power', *The Economist*, March 23, 2002 Available at <http://www.ksg.harvard.edu/news/opeds/2002/nye_USpower_economist_032302.htm>. Accessed 2 November 2003.

O'Donnell, G. (1973) *Modernization and Bureaucratic Authoritarianism*. Berkeley, CA: Institute of International Studies.

O'Donnell, G. (1994) 'Delegative democracy', *Journal of Democracy*, 5, 1, pp. 55–69.

O'Donnell, G. (1996) 'Illusions about consolidation', *Journal of Democracy*, 7, 1, pp. 34–51.

Ohmae, K. (1990) *The Borderless World. Power and Strategy in the Interlinked Economy*. New York: Harper Business.

Oksenberg, M. (2001) 'Will China democratize?', in L. Diamond and M. F. Plattner (eds.), *The Global Divergence of Democracies*. Baltimore/London: Johns Hopkins University Press and the National Endowment for Democracy, pp. 348–55.

Olson, D. (1994) *Legislative Institutions: A Comparative View*. Aronk, NY: M. E. Sharpe.

Opello, Jr., W. and Rosow, S. (1999) *The Nation-State and Global Order. A Historical Introduction to Contemporary Politics*. Boulder/London: Lynne Rienner.

Organski, A. (1965) *The Stages of Political Development*. New York: Knopf.

Ortíz, R. (2000) 'Comparing types of transitions: Spain and Mexico', *Democratization*, 7, 3, pp. 65–92.

Osborn, A. (2003a) 'EU lifts Turkey's hopes', *Guardian*, 27 March.

Osborn, A. (2003b) 'EU drive to fight global warming', *Guardian*, 13 August.

OSCE (Organization for Security and Cooperation in Europe) (2003) Office for Democratic Institutions and Human Rights, 'United Kingdom elections for the devolved administrations in Scotland, Wales and Northern Ireland', Warsaw: OSCE. Available at <http://www.osce.org/documents/odihr/2003/05/1464_en.pdf>. Accessed 6 April 2004.

Ottaway, M. (2003) *Democracy Challenged. The Rise of Semi-Authoritarianism*. Washington DC: Carnegie Endowment for International Peace.

Owen, R. (1992) *State, Power and Politics in the Making of the Modern Middle East*. London: Routledge.

Ozbudun, E. (1996) 'Turkey: How far from consolidation?', *Journal of Democracy*, 7, 3, pp. 123–38.

Padgett, S. (2000) *Organizing Democracy in Eastern Germany: Interest Groups in Post-Communist Society*. Cambridge: Cambridge University Press.

Parpart, J. 1988. 'Women and the state in Africa', in D. Rothchild and N. Chazan (eds.), *The Precarious Balance. State and Society in Africa*. Boulder, CO: Westview, pp. 208–30.

Pergher, R. (1998/9) 'Globalization and the Welfare State', Paper #4, GSIS, University of Denver, 'Internet seminar: Reforming the Welfare State and Social Security Systems: USA, Germany, Chile – A comparison'. Available at <http://tiss.zdv.uni-tuebingen.de/webroot/sp/spsba01_W98_1/denver12.htm>. Accessed 16 July 2004.

Pesek, W. (2002) 'Vietnam embraces globalization on own terms', *Manila Times*, 21 November. Available at <http://www.globalpolicy.org/globaliz/special/2002/1121vietnam.htm>. Accessed 19 February 2004.

Peterson, D. (1993) *Troubled Lands: The Legacy of Soviet Environmental Destruction*. Boulder, CO: Westview.

Petito, F. and Hatzopolous, P. (eds.) (2003) *Religion in International Relations. The Return from Exile*. New York and Basingstoke: Palgrave Macmillan.

Pettifor, A. (ed.) (2003) *Real World Economic Outlook. The Legacy of Globalization: Debt and Deflation*. Basingstoke: Palgrave.

Pettman, J. (2001) 'Gender issues', in J. Baylis and S. Smith (eds.), *The Globalization of World Politics. An Introduction to International Relations*. Oxford: Oxford University Press, pp. 582–98.

Pharr, S., Putnam, R. and Dalton, R. (2001) 'A quarter-century of declining confidence', in L. Diamond and M. F. Plattner (eds.), *The Global Divergence of Democracies*. Baltimore/London: Johns Hopkins University Press and the National Endowment for Democracy, pp. 291–311.

Philip, G. (1999) 'Institutions and democratic consolidation in Latin America', in J. Buxton and N. Phillips (eds.), *Developments in Latin American Political Economy. States, Markets and Actors*. Manchester: Manchester University Press, pp. 33–48.

Philip, G. (2003) 'Contagious crisis and the end of the Washington Consensus'. Paper prepared for the 2nd ECPR general conference, Marburg, Germany, 18–21 September.

Phillips, K. (2002) *Wealth and Democracy. A Political History of the American Rich*. New York: Broadway Books.

Phillips, N. (1999) 'Global and regional linkages', in J. Buxton and N. Phillips (eds.), *Developments in Latin American Political Economy. States, Markets and Actors*. Manchester: Manchester University Press, pp. 72–90.

Pinkney, R. (1993) *Democracy in the Third World*. Boulder and London: Lynne Rienner.

Pinkney, R. (2003) *Democracy in the Third World*, 2nd edn. Boulder and London: Lynne Rienner.

Poe, S. and Neal Tate, C. (1994) 'Human rights and repression to personal integrity in the 1980s: A global analysis', *American Political Science Review*, 88, pp. 853–72.

Poe, S., Neal Tate, C. and Camp Keith, L. (1999) 'Repression of the human right to personal integrity revisited: A global crossnational study covering the years 1976–1993', *International Studies Quarterly*, 43, pp. 291–315.

Poggi, G. (1990) *The State: Its Nature, Development and Prospects*, Stanford, CA: Stanford University Press.

Portes, A. and Zhou, M. (1992) 'Gaining the upper hand: Economic mobility among immigrant and domestic minorities', *Ethnic and Racial Studies*, 15, 4, pp. 491–521.

Posadskaya-Vanderbeck, A. (1998) 'Redefining democratization: the gender challenge'. Concept Paper for the Soros Foundation. Available at <http://www.soros.org/wp/>. Accessed 7 April 2004.

Postel-Vinay, K. (2001) 'The spatial transformation of international relations', in M.-C. Smouts (ed.), *The New International Relations. Theory and Practice*. London: Hurst and Co., pp. 88–99.

Powell, L. (2002) 'Western and Russian environmental NGOs: A greener Russia?', in S. Mendelson and J. Glenn (eds.), *The Power and Limits of NGOs. A Critical Look at Building Democracy in Eastern Europe and Eurasia*. New York: Columbia University Press, pp. 126–51.

Premdas, R. and Ragoonath, B. (1998) 'Ethnicity, elections and democracy in Trinidad and Tobago: Analysing the 1995 and 1996 elections', *Journal of Commonwealth and Comparative Politics*, 36, 3, pp. 30–53.

Pridham, G. (2000) *The Dynamics of Democratization. A Comparative Approach*. London and New York: Continuum.

Princen, T. and Finger, M. (eds.) (1994) *Environmental NGOs in World Politics: Linking the Local and the Global*. London: Routledge.

Przeworski, A. (1986) 'Some problems in the study of the transition to democracy', in G. O'Donnell, P. Schmitter and L. Whitehead (eds.), *Transitions from Authoritarian Rule: Southern Europe*. Baltimore, MD: Johns Hopkins University Press, pp. 47–63.

Przeworski, A. (1991) *Democracy and the Market Political and Economic Reform in Eastern Europe and Latin America*. Cambridge: Cambridge University Press.

Przeworski, A. (1995) *Sustainable Democracy*. Cambridge: Cambridge University Press.

Przeworski, A., Alvarez, M., Cheibib, J. A. and Limongi, F. (1996) 'What makes democracies endure?', *Journal of Democracy*, 7, 1, pp. 39–55.

Putnam, R. (1988) 'Diplomacy and domestic politics: The logic of two-level games', *International Organization*, 42, 3, pp. 427–60.

Putnam, R. (1993) *Making Democracy Work: Civic Traditions in Modern Italy*. Princeton, NJ: Princeton University Press.

Putnam, R. (1999) *Bowling Alone: The Collapse and Revival of American Community*. New York: Simon & Schuster.

Putzel, J. (1997) 'Why has democratization been a weaker impulse in Indonesia and Malaysia than in the Philippines?', in D. Potter, D. Goldblatt, M. Kiloh and P. Lewis (eds.), *Democratization*. Cambridge and Milton Keynes: Polity Press in association with the Open University, pp. 240–63.

Qvortup, M. (2002) 'The emperor's new clothes: The Danish general election of 20 November, 2001', *European Political Science*, 1, 2 (spring), pp. 17–22.

Radice, H. (1999) 'Taking globalization seriously', in L. Panitch and C. Leys (eds.), *The Socialist Register 1999: Global Capitalism versus Democracy*. London: Merlin Press, pp. 1–28.

Rai, S. (n/d) 'Class, caste and gender – Women in parliament in India', International Institute for Democracy and Electoral Assistance (IDEA), *Women in Politics: Beyond the Numbers*. Available at <http://www.idea.int/women/parl/studies2a.htm>. Accessed 13 August 2003.

Rai, S. (2005) 'Gender and development', in J. Haynes (ed.), *Palgrave Advances in Development Studies*. Basingstoke: Palgrave Macmillan.

Randall V. (1988) 'The Congress Party of India: Dominance and competition', in V. Randall (ed.), *Political Parties in the Third World*. London: Sage, pp. 75–98.

'Religion, Culture, and International Conflict After September 11. A Conversation with Samuel P. Huntington'. Available at <www.eppc.org/publications/xq/ASP/pubsID.1209/ qx/pubs_viewdetail.html>. Accessed 10 October 2003.

Remmer, K. (1989) *Military Rule in Latin America*. Boston: Unwin Hyman.

Report of the Regional Meeting for Asia of the World Conference on Human Rights (1993) Bangkok, 29 March–2 April 1993. United Nations document: A/Conf.157/ASRM. Available at <http://www.unhchr.ch/Huridocda/Huridoca.nsf/0/2c1f4fc6354777f4802568ea00335ffe? Opendocument>. Accessed 1 April 2004.

Reveyrand-Coulon, O. (1993). 'Les énoncés féminins de l'islam', in J.-F. Bayart (ed.), *Religion et Modernité. Politique en Afrique Noire*. Paris: Karthala, pp. 63–100.

Richter, J. (2002) 'Evaluating Western assistance to Russian women's organizations', in S. Mendelson and J. Glenn (eds.), *The Power and Limits of NGOs. A Critical Look at Building Democracy in Eastern Europe and Eurasia*. New York: Columbia University Press, pp. 54–90.

Risse, T. (2000) ' "Let's argue!": Communicative action in world politics', *International Organization*, 54, 1 (winter), pp. 1–39.

Risse, T. and Ropp, S. (1999) 'Conclusions', in T. Risse, S. Ropp and K. Sikkink (eds.), *The Power of Human Rights. International Norms and Domestic Change*. Cambridge: Cambridge University Press, pp. 234–78.

Risse, T. and Sikkink, K. (1999) 'The socialization of international human rights norms into domestic practices: Introduction', in T. Risse, S. Ropp and K. Sikkink (eds.), *The Power of Human Rights. International Norms and Domestic Change*. Cambridge: Cambridge University Press, pp. 1–39.

Risse, T., Ropp, S. and Sikkink, K. (eds.) (1999) *The Power of Human Rights. International Norms and Domestic Change*. Cambridge: Cambridge University Press.

Risse-Kappen, T. (1994) 'Ideas do not float freely: Transnational coalitions, domestic structures and the end of the cold war', *International Organization*, 48, 2 (spring), pp. 185–214.

Risse-Kappen, T. (1995a) 'Bringing transnational relations back in: Introduction', in T. Risse-Kappen (ed.), *Bringing Transnational Relations Back In*. Cambridge: Cambridge University Press, pp. 3–33.

Risse-Kappen, T. (1995b) 'Structures of governance and transnational relations: What have we learned?', in T. Risse-Kappen (ed.), *Bringing Transnational Relations Back In*. Cambridge: Cambridge University Press, pp. 280–313.

Robertson, R. (2003) *The Three Waves of Globalization. A History of a Developing Global Consciousness*. London/New York/Nova Scotia: Zed/Fernwood.

Robinson, N. (2003) 'The politics of Russia's partial democracy', *Political Studies Review*, 1, 2, pp. 149–66.

Robinson, W. (1998) 'Capitalist globalization and the transnationalization of the state.' Paper presented at the Transatlantic Workshop, 'Historical Materialism and Globalization', University of Warwick, UK, 15–17 April.

Rodríguez, V. (2003) *Women in Contemporary Mexican Politics*. Austin, TX: University of Texas Press.

Rosamond, B. (2002a) 'Politics and governance above the territorial state', in B. Axford, G. Browning, R. Huggins and B. Rosamond, *An Introduction to Politics*, 2nd edn. London and New York: Routledge, pp. 481–523.

Rosamond, B. (2002b) 'Political culture', in B. Axford, G. Browning, R. Huggins and B. Rosamond, *An Introduction to Politics*, 2nd edn. London and New York: Routledge, pp. 82–119.

Rose, R. (2000) *The Post-Modern President*, 2nd edn. London: Chatham House.

Rotberg, R. (2003) 'The failure and collapse of nation-states. Breakdown, prevention and fear', in R. Rotberg (ed.), *When States Fail: Causes and Consequences*. Princeton, NJ: Princeton University Press, pp. 1–49.

Roth, B. and Horan, M. (2001) 'What are social movements and what is gendered about women's participation in social movements? A sociological perspective'. Available at <http://womhist.binghamton.edu/socm/intro.htm>. Accessed 6 April 2004.

Rowell, A. (1996) *Green Backlash: Global Subversion of the Environmental Movement*. London: Routledge.

Roy, A. Narain (1999) *The Third World in the Age of Globalization*. London/Delhi: Zed Books/Madhyam Books.

Rüdig, W. (1990) 'Explaining Green Party Development', Strathclyde Papers on Government and Politics, no. 71.

Rüdig, W. (2002) 'Between ecotopia and disillusionment: Green parties in European government', *Environment*, 44, 3, pp. 20–33.

Rudolph, S. and Piscatori, J. (eds.) (1997) *Transnational Religion and Fading States*. Boulder, CO: Westview.

Rueschemeyer, D., Stephens, E. and Stephens, J. (1992) *Capitalist Development and Democracy*. Cambridge: Polity.

Rummel, R. (1997) *Death by Government*. Brunswick, NJ, and London: Transaction Books.

Rupnik, J. (2001) 'The postcommunist divide', in L. Diamond and M. F. Plattner (eds.), *The Global Divergence of Democracies*. Baltimore/London: Johns Hopkins University Press and the National Endowment for Democracy, pp. 327–32.

Sabbagh, R. (1994) 'Jordanian women pay the violent price of traditional male "honour" ', *Guardian*, 28 December.

Sacks, G. (2001) 'Why I miss the Cold War', *Los Angeles Daily Journal* and the *San Francisco Daily Journal*, 2 October. Available at <www.glennsacks.com>.

Sadiki, L. (1997) 'Towards Arab liberal governance: From the democracy of bread to the democracy of the vote', *Third World Quarterly*, 18, 1, pp. 127–48.

Sadowski, C. (1993) 'Autonomous groups as agents of democratic change in communist and post-communist Eastern Europe', in L. Diamond (ed.), *Political Culture and Democracy in Developing Countries*. Boulder, CO: Lynne Rienner, pp. 163–95.

Safa, H. (1990) 'Women and social movements in Latin America', *Gender and Society*, 14, 4, pp. 354–69.

Said, E. (1996) 'War babies', *Observer*, 14 January.

Saif, W. (1994) 'Human rights and Islamic revivalism', *Islam and Christian–Muslim Relations*, 5, 1, pp. 57–65.

Saikal, A. (2003) *Islam and the West. Conflict or Cooperation?* Basingstoke: Palgrave.

Samudavanija, C.-A. (1993) 'The new military and democracy in Thailand', in L. Diamond (ed.), *Political Culture and Democracy in Developing Countries*. Boulder and London: Lynne Rienner, pp. 269–94.

Sapiro, V. and Farah, B. (1980) 'New pride, old prejudice: Political ambition and role orientations among female partisan elites', *Women and Politics*, 1, pp. 13–36.

Sartori, G. (1991) 'Rethinking democracy: Bad policy and bad politics', *International Social Science Journal*, 129, pp. 437–50.

Sassen, S. (2002) 'Global cities and diasporic networks: Microsites in global civil society', in M. Glasius, M. Kaldor and H. Anheier (eds.), *Global Civil Society 2002*. Oxford: Oxford University Press, pp. 217–38.

Scarrow, S. (2001) 'Direct democracy and institutional change. A comparative investigation', *Comparative Political Studies*, 34, 6, pp. 651–65.

Schedler, A. (2002) 'The menu of manipulation. Elections without democracy', *Journal of Democracy*, 13, 2 (April), pp. 36–51.

Scherer, R. (2003) 'US–China trade tensions rise', *Christian Science Monitor*, 2 December. Available at <http://www.csmonitor.com/2003/1202/p01s01-woap.html>. Accessed 23 February 2004.

Schirm, S. (2002) *Globalization and the New Regionalism*. Cambridge: Polity.

Schmitz, H. P. (2002a) 'Diffusion of democratic governance norms: Transnational activism and domestic responses'. Paper presented at the annual meeting of the American Political Science Association, Boston, 29 August–1 September 2002.

Schmitz, H. P. (2002b) 'When networks blind: Human rights and politics in Kenya', in T. Callaghy, R. Kassimir and R. Latham (eds.), *Intervention and Transnationalism in Africa: Global-Local Networks of Power*. Cambridge: Cambridge University Press, pp. 149–72.

Schmitz, H. P. and Sikkink, K. (2001) 'International relations theory and human rights'. Available at <http://www.polisci.umn.edu/courses/spring2001/4485/ir2.pdf>. Accessed 12 December 2003.

Scholte, J. A. (2001) 'The globalization of world politics', in J. Baylis and S. Smith (eds.), *The Globalization of World Politics. An Introduction to International Relations*. Oxford: Oxford University Press, pp. 13–32.

Schraeder, P. (2003) 'The state of the art in international democracy promotion: Results of a joint European-North American Research Network', *Democratization*, 10, 2, pp. 21–44.

Schulz, M., Söderbaum, F. and Öjendal, J. (eds.) (2001) *Regionalization in a Globalizing World. A Comparative Perspective on Forms, Actors and Processes*. London: Zed Books.

Schulze, G. and Urprung, H. (1999) 'Globalization of the economy and the nation state', *The World Economy*, 22, 3, pp. 295–352.

Seenan, G. (2003) 'In-crowd', *Guardian* ('Guardian Society' supplement), 14 May.

Sen, A. (2001) 'Estimates of consumer expenditure and its distribution: Statistical priorities after the NSS 55th Round', *Economic and Political Weekly*, 35 (16 December), pp. 4499–518.

Sen, G. (1999) 'Developing states and the end of the cold war', in L. Fawcett and Y. Sayigh (eds.), *The Third World Beyond the Cold War. Continuity and Change.* Oxford: Oxford University Press, pp. 56–77.

Shaw, E. (2003) 'The Blair Government and the non-problem of globalization', *European Political Science*, 2, 2 (spring), pp. 51–61.

Shin, D. C. (1999) *Mass Politics and Culture in Democratizing Korea.* Cambridge: Cambridge University Press.

Shorrocks, A. and Kolenikov, S. (2001) 'Poverty trends in Russia during the transition'. Available at <http://www.wider.unu.edu/conference/conference-2001-1/Shorrocks_Kolenikov.pdf>. Accessed 8 March 2004.

Shvedova, N. (1998) 'The challenge of transition – Women in parliament in Russia', in International Institute for Democracy and Electoral Assistance (IDEA), *Women in Politics: Beyond the Numbers.* Available at <http://www.idea.int/women/parl/studies2a.htm>. Accessed 13 August 2003.

Skjeie, H. (1991) 'The rhetoric of difference: On women's inclusion into political elites, *Politics and Society*, 19, 2, pp. 233–63.

Skjeie, H. (1998) 'Credo on difference – Women in parliament in Norway', in International Institute for Democracy and Electoral Assistance (IDEA), *Women in Politics: Beyond the Numbers.* Available at <http://www.idea.int/women/parl/studies2a.htm>. Accessed 13 August 2003.

Sklair, L. (2002) 'The transnational capitalist class and global politics: Deconstructing the corporate-state connection', *International Political Science Review*, 23, 2, pp. 159–74.

Skocpol, T. (1985) *States and Social Revolutions. A Comparative Analysis of France, Russia and China.* Cambridge: Cambridge University Press.

Smith, B. C. (2003) *Understanding Third World Politics. Theories of Political Change and Development*, 2nd edn. Basingstoke: Palgrave Macmillan.

Smith, D. E. (1990) 'Limits of religious resurgence', in E. Sahliyeh (ed.), *Religious Resurgence and Politics in the Contemporary World.* Albany, NY: State University of New York Press, pp. 33–44.

Smith, H. (2000) 'Why is there no international democratic theory?', in H. Smith (ed.), *Democracy and International Relations.* Basingstoke: Macmillan, pp. 1–30.

Smith, J. (n/d) 'Globalizing resistance: The battle of Seattle and the future of social movements'. Unpublished manuscript. Department of Sociology, State University of New York at Stony Brook.

Smith, J., Pagnucco, R. and Chatfield, C. (1997) 'Social movements and world politics: A theoretical framework', in J. Smith, R. Pagnucco and C. Chatfield (eds.), *Transnational Social Movements and Global Politics. Solidarity Beyond the State.* Syracuse, NY: Syracuse University Publications, pp. 59–80.

Smith, M. P. (1999) 'EU legitimacy and the "defensive reaction" to the Single European Market', in T. Banchoff and M. P. Smith (eds.), *Legitimacy and the European Union*, London: Routledge, pp. 27–45.

Smith, S. (2002) 'The end of the unipolar moment? September 11 and the future of world order', *International Relations*, 16, 2, pp. 171–83.

Smouts, M.-C. (ed.) (2001) *The New International Relations. Theory and Practice.* London: Hurst and Co.

Snyder, J. (2000) *From Voting to Violence: Democratization and Nationalist Conflict.* New York: W. W. Norton.

Sodaro, M. J. (2001) *Comparative Politics: A Global Introduction.* New York: McGraw Hill.

Standing, G. (1994) 'The changing position of women in Russian industry: Prospects of margin-alisation', *World Development*, 22, 2, pp. 271–83.

Stepan, A. (1988) *Rethinking Military Politics Brazil and the Southern Cone*. Princeton, NJ: Princeton University Press.

Stepan, A. and Skatch, C. (1993) 'Constitutional frameworks and democratic consolidation: Parliamentarianism versus presidentialism', *World Politics*, 46 (October), pp. 1–22.

Stockton, H. (2001) 'Political parties, party systems, and democracy in East Asia. Lessons from Latin America', *Comparative Political Studies*, 34, 1, pp. 94–119.

Strange, G. (2003) 'Beyond "Third Wave" globalization analysis', *European Political Science*, 2, 2, pp. 41–50.

Studlar, D. and McAllister, I. (2003) 'Does a critical mass exist? A comparative analysis of women's legislative representation since 1950', *European Journal of Political Research*, 41, 2, pp. 233–53.

Sullivan, M. (2002) *Theories of International Relations. Transition vs. Persistence*. New York and Basingstoke UK: Palgrave Macmillan.

Swank, D. (2002) *Global Capital, Political Institutions, and Policy Change in Developed Welfare States*. Cambridge: Cambridge University Press.

Tarumoto, H. (2003) 'State sovereignty vs. international human rights?: In the case of expansion in immigrant rights', International Conference: 'Policy and Politics in a Globalizing World', The School for Policy Studies, University of Bristol, UK, 24–26 July.

Tarrow, S. (1995) 'The Europeanization of conflict: Reflections from social movements research', *West European Politics*, 18, 2, pp. 223–55.

Tarrow, S. (1998) *Power in Movement. Social Movements and Contentious Politics*, 2nd edn. Cambridge: Cambridge University Press.

Taylor, I. (n/d) 'South Africa's "democratic transition" in a globalised world: The "change indus-try" and the promotion of polyarchy', Department of Political Science, University of Stellen-bosch, South Africa, unpublished manuscript.

Teather, D. (2003) 'Buffalo moves closer to extinction', *Guardian*, November 20.

'The role of theory in comparative politics: A symposium' (1996) *World Politics*, 48, 1, pp. 1–49.

Thomas, D. (1999) 'The Helsinki accords and political change in Eastern Europe', in T. Risse, S. Ropp and K. Sikkink (eds.), *The Power of Human Rights. International Norms and Domestic Change*. Cambridge: Cambridge University Press, pp. 205–33.

Thomas, S. (1995) 'Religion and International Society'. Paper prepared for the workshop 'Politi-cal Culture and Religion in the Third World', European Consortium for Political Research Joint Sessions of Workshops, Bordeaux, April.

Thomas, S. (2003) 'Taking religion and cultural pluralism seriously: The global resurgence of reli-gion and the transformation of international society', in F. Petito and P. Hatzopolous (eds.), *Religion in International Relations. The Return from Exile*. New York and Basingstoke: Palgrave Macmillan, pp. 21–54.

Thürer, D. (1999) 'The "failed state" and international law', *International Review of the Red Cross*, 836, pp. 731–61.

Todaro, M. (1989) *Economic Development*, 7th edn. New York: Longman.

Tornquist, O. (1999) 'On the dynamics of the Indonesian democratization'. Paper presented at the workshop: 'Democratic consolidation in the Third World: What should be done?', ECPR Joint Sessions of Workshops, University of Mannheim, March.

Törnquist, O. (2001) 'Indonesia's democratization', in J. Haynes (ed.), *Democracy and Political Change in the 'Third World'*, London: Routledge/ECPR Studies in European Political Science, pp. 171–97.

Travis, A. (2004) 'Desire to integrate on the wane as Muslims resent "war on Islam"', *Guardian*, 16 March.

Traynor, I. (2003) 'The privatisation of war', *Guardian*, December 10.

Tremlett, G., MacAskill, E. and Norton-Taylor, R. (2004) 'Who's to blame? The long search for clues to blasts begins', *Guardian*, 13 March.

True, J. and Mintrom, M. (2001) 'Transnational networks and policy diffusion: The case of gender mainstreaming', *International Studies Quarterly*, 45, 1, pp. 27–57.

Tsebelis, G. (2002) *Veto Players. How Political Institutions Work*. New York/Princeton, NJ: Russell Sage Foundation/Princeton University Press.

Turan, I. (2003) 'The Justice and Development Party: The first year in power', Istanbul Bilgi University. Available at <http://www.tusiad.us/Content/uploaded/ILTER%20TURAN-AKP.PDF>. Accessed 15 March 2004.

Turner, F. and Martz, J. (1997) 'Institutional confidence and democratic consolidation in Latin America', *Studies in Comparative International Development*, 32, 3, pp. 65–84.

van der Heijden, H.-A. (2002) 'Political parties and NGOs in global environmental politics', *International Political Science Review*, 23, 2, pp. 187–202.

van der Ros, J. (1994) 'The state and women: A troubled relationship in Norway', in B. J. Nelson and N. Chowdhhury (eds.), *Women and Politics Worldwide*. New Haven and London: Yale University Press, pp. 527–43.

Verdier, D. and Breen, R. (2001) 'Europeanization and globalization: Politics against markets in the European Union', *Comparative Political Studies*, 34, 3 (April), pp. 227–62.

Vidal, J. (1996) 'Harmed and dangerous', *Guardian*, 8 May.

Vidal, J. (2003a) 'Lorra lorry love', *Guardian Society*, 14 May, p. 8.

Vidal, J. (2003b) 'Making waves', *Guardian Society*, 25 June, pp. 12–13.

Villalón, L. (1995) *Islamic Society and State Power in Senegal. Disciples and Citizens in Fatick*. Cambridge: Cambridge University Press.

Vincent, R. J. (1986). *Human Rights and International Relations*. Cambridge: Cambridge University Press.

Vogler, J. (2001) 'Environment', in B. White, R. Little and M. Smith (eds.), *Issues in World Politics*, 2nd edn. Basingstoke: Palgrave, pp. 191–211.

Volpi, F. (2003) *Islam and Democracy. The Failure of Dialogue in Algeria*. London: Pluto Press.

Waldron, A. (1998) 'Religious revivals in Communist China', *Orbis*, 42, 2 (spring), pp. 325–34.

Wallis, D. (2001) 'Democratic transition and consolidation in Mexico', in J. Haynes (ed.), *Democracy and Political Change in the 'Third World'*. London: Routledge, pp. 115–31.

Walsh, N. Paton (2004) 'A triumph of hope over experience: Why Russia's poor still believe the Putin fairytale', *Guardian*, 8 March. Available at <http://www.guardian.co.uk/russia/article/0,2763,1164233,00.html>. Accessed 8 March 2004.

Waltz, K. (1993) 'The emerging structure of international politics', *International Security*, 18, 2, pp. 44–79.

Ward, L. (2003) 'Feminism: Outmoded and unpopular', *Guardian*, 2 July.

Watson, M. and Hay, C. (2003) 'The discourse of globalization and the logic of no alternative: Rendering the contingent necessary in the political economy of New Labour', *Policy and Politics*, 31, 3, pp. 289–305.

Watts, J. (2004) 'China tightens net around online dissenters', *Guardian*, 7 February.

Waylen, G. (1993) 'Women's movements and democratization in Latin America', *Third World Quarterly*, 14, 3, pp. 573–87.

Waylen, G. (2003) 'Gender and transitions: What do we know?', *Democratization*, 10, 1, pp. 157–78.

Webber, M. and Smith, M. (eds.) (2002) *Foreign Policy in a Transformed World*. Harlow: Pearson Education.

Welch, S. (1993) 'Comparability of political culture. Selections from *The Concept of Political Culture*'. Available at <http://db.uwaterloo.ca/~alopez-o/politics/compar.html>. Accessed 3 March 2004.

White, G. and Xiaoyuan Shang (2003) 'State entrepreneurship and community welfare services in urban China', in R. Benewick, M. Blecher and S. Cook (eds.), *Asian Politics in Development. Essays in Honour of Gordon White*. London: Cass, pp. 173–94.

White, M. (2003) 'Blair looks for new third way', *Guardian*, 7 July.

Whitehead, L. (1993) 'The alternatives to "liberal democracy". A Latin American perspective', in D. Held (ed.), *Prospects for Democracy*. Cambridge: Polity, pp. 312–29.

Wiarda, H. and Kline, F. (eds.) (1996) *Latin American Politics and Development*, 4th edn. Boulder, CO: Westview Press.

Wide, J. (2002) 'Women's political representation around the globe'. Paper prepared for the Commonwealth Conference on Educational Administration and Management (CCEAM), 23–25 September, Umeà6, Sweden. Symposium: 'Gender, Democratization, and Leadership around the Globe'.

Willetts, P. (ed.) (1996) *'The Conscience of the World': The Influence of Non-Governmental Organizations in the UN System*. London: Hurst and Co.

Willetts, P. (2001) 'Transnational actors and international organizations in global politics', in J. Baylis and S. Smith (eds.), *The Globalization of World Politics. An Introduction to International Relations*. Oxford: Oxford University Press, pp. 356–83.

Witte, J., Jr. (1993) 'Introduction', in J. Witte, Jr. (ed.), *Christianity and Democracy in Global Context*. Boulder, CO: Westview, pp. 1–21.

Wolf, M. (2002) 'Countries still rule the world', *Financial Times*, 6 February.

Woods, N. (2001) *The Political Economy of Globalization*. Basingstoke: Palgrave.

World Bank (1995) *World Development Report 1995*. New York: Oxford University Press.

World Bank (1997) *World Development Report 1997. The State in a Changing World*. New York: Oxford University Press.

World Bank (2000) *World Development Report. Entering the 21st Century 1999/2000*. New York: Oxford University Press.

World Bank (2001) *World Development Report 2000/2001. Attacking Poverty*. New York: Oxford University Press.

World Bank (2003) *Breaking the Conflict Trap: Civil War and Development Policy*. New York: World Bank.

Worsley, P. (1999) 'Culture and development theory', in T. Skelton and T. Allen (eds.), *Culture and Global Change*. London: Routledge, pp. 30–42.

Wu Chenguang (2002) 'South Weekend', translated by Wang Qian for China.org.cn, 13 July. Available at <www.china.org.cn/english/2002/Jul/36833.htm>. Accessed 26 February 2004.

Yilmaz, H. (2002) 'External-internal linkages in democratization: Developing an open model of democratic change', *Democratization*, 9, 2, pp. 67–84.

Zakaria, F. (1997) 'The rise of illiberal democracy', *Foreign Affairs*, November/December, pp. 22–42.

Index